Communes
and Cults

Communes

AND

cults

• kathlyn gay •

TWENTY-FIRST CENTURY BOOKS
A Division of Henry Holt and Company · New York

Twenty-First Century Books
A Division of Henry Holt and Company, Inc.
115 West 18th Street
New York, NY 10011

Henry Holt® and colophon are trademarks of
Henry Holt and Company, Inc.
Publishers since 1866

Published in Canada by Fitzhenry & Whiteside Ltd.
195 Allstate Parkway, Markham, Ontario, L3R 4T8

Library of Congress Cataloging-in-Publication Data
Gay, Kathlyn.
Communes and cults / Kathlyn Gay.
p.   cm.
Includes bibliographical references and index.
1. Christian communities—United States—Juvenile literature. 2. Utopias—
United States—Juvenile literature. 3. Cults—Juvenile literature. 4. Christian
Catholic Apostolic Church in Zion—History—Juvenile literature. I. Title.
BV4406.U6G38 1997
280'.0973—dc21   96-47842
                                                            CIP
                                                            AC

ISBN 0-8050-3803-5
First Edition—1997

Designed by Kelly Soong

Printed in the United States of America
All first editions are printed on acid-free paper ∞.

1 3 5 7 9 10 8 6 4 2

ACKNOWLEDGMENT

A special thank-you to Pat Culleton for her long-time editorial help, particularly for this book.

CONTENTS

· I ·

". . . Marching as to War"

"Peace to thee. Peace to thee." It was a common greeting, one that many of the adults used as the faithful gathered. Several dozen men in dark blue uniforms with gold braid and military-type caps—part of the Zion Guard—spread out along the drive that circled the site where a tabernacle had once been.

The guards were charged with getting everyone in order for this annual summer event commemorating the biblical Feast of Tabernacles and the opening of Zion City (the kingdom of God on earth) in Illinois, and consecration of a ten-acre plot known as the Temple Site. On this site, the Christian Catholic Apostolic Church of Zion (no relation to the Roman Catholic church) had been built, but it had burned to the ground. Nevertheless, the church had continued, and, in the all-inclusive sense of the term catholic, purported to welcome everyone. In the apostolic sense it was patterned somewhat after the practices described in the biblical New Testament, in which people gave up their land and houses and the apostles of Jesus distributed these possessions among people in need.

I'm sure I wondered on that hot July day in 1940 why we,

our family, joined the parade and marched around a plot of barren land. At ten years old I didn't ask "why" out loud, however. I knew I had no choice, for our family was part of the faithful. I was a member of the junior guard, dressed in the standard uniform for girls: a gold-trimmed, navy blue cape over our "Sunday best" and a blue pillbox hat perched squarely atop the head. The uniform, I recall, was "smart" and highly coveted because it distinctly marked a person as part of the "in" group.

The general overseer, as the church leader was known, and his twelve elders led the procession, each garbed in a long ministerial robe. After them came the deacons and deaconesses. All had draped across the right shoulder white satin banners with the symbol of the church—a shield with a gold cross, a dove of peace, a crown and a sword—which for most of my life I've considered a gross inconsistency: onward for peace with a sword in hand!

As the brass band—in uniform of course—set the pace, the white-robed choir began to sing while marching in solemn, metronome fashion:

Onward Christian soldiers
Marching as to war
With the cross of Jesus
Going on before!

The junior choir members followed, hymn books held high, marching out of step, skipping here and there to catch the beat, marching with scrubbed faces beaming. The junior guard filled in behind. Hundreds of parishioners completed the parade. Off we marched. It seemed a holiday for most of us children, a mission for some of the teenagers and the older followers.

While marching, we sang at the tops of our voices. Even I, doubter that I was at a young age, began to feel a surge of power and glory as the leaders stepped up the pace, swishing their black ankle-length robes, ash-gray with dust at the hems. Around and around the drive we went, circling the high ground and hub of Zion City where Shiloh Tabernacle had once stood.

The tabernacle had been planned as a temporary structure, to be replaced by a great temple patterned after the Mosque of Omar in Jerusalem. At least that was the vision of the founder of Zion City, John Alexander Dowie, who called himself "Elijah the Restorer"—the First Apostle. The three-story wooden building seated nearly seven thousand people and contained a gallery for a three-hundred-member choir, later remodeled and expanded to hold five hundred people plus one of the largest pipe organs in the world. Its walls were covered with hundreds of "trophies"—crutches, braces, high-heeled boots, casts, pill bottles, guns, and numerous other items said to have been surrendered by those "saved, healed, cleansed, and blessed in Zion." But the building was completely destroyed by fire in 1937, apparently the work of an arsonist.

Jutting out from the now barren plot of land and its circular drive were four boulevards, laid out like spokes of a wheel, with all other streets crossing them in a perfect grid. It was a well-designed city, planners from around the world declared, and it would accommodate a population of up to fifty thousand. However, that has never materialized. The plan included business, industrial, and residential zones, wooded parks and tree-lined avenues and boulevards with biblical names such as Bethel, Ezekiel, Galilee, and Horeb. Just across a park from the Temple Site was a four-story church school built of Indiana limestone. Called Zion Preparatory College, it included all the grades and a two-year college. Nearby was a separate gymnasium. Those buildings, too, burned to the ground some years later. So did an entire downtown section that included a church-controlled department store and offices. And a huge 350-room hotel also burned, leaving finally what appeared to me to be a kingdom of ashes.

Zion and the views of its leaders have in many ways been a catalyst for this book. Long ago I left this community where I was born and reared, and I have frequently criticized its restrictive nature and lack of tolerance for "outsiders." But my experiences in Zion sparked a lifelong interest in religions, religious sects, and secular communal groups and cults. This book includes descriptions and stories about a great many of them. It is *not*, however, a how-to book for dealing with controlling groups. Rather, it is meant to show that communal living has a long history in the United States, and that group solidarity can sometimes be beneficial, sometimes repressive, and sometimes destructive—even deadly—for individual members.

As a young child, I often wondered why people chose to be part of an exclusive group in which "outsiders" were said to have a corrupting influence or were simply "evil." This contradicted everything I had ever been taught about Christianity and its inclusiveness. How do self-styled prophets or gurus (spiritual leaders) gain power over thousands of followers, dictating not only their religious life but almost every other aspect of living as well? What causes the rise and fall of the communities they form?

These were the kinds of questions I asked during most of my adolescent and young adult years, although not necessarily phrased in that way. The answers were never simple and seemed to differ with every established group. Yet I also found that many communal societies set up both before and after Zion City were managed in ways similar to that of Zion. And there were people who seemed to share frustrations, concerns, and fears similar to my own.

Most communes, cooperatives, or whatever they were called shared a common purpose: to establish a utopia, a near-paradise on earth, where all were supposed to live in love and harmony. That was certainly the goal of John Alexander Dowie, the founder of Zion.

· 2 ·

BUILDING A "HOLY CITY"

John Alexander Dowie was a Congregational minister who became an evangelist. He emigrated from Scotland in 1893 during the time of the World Columbian Exposition (a world's fair) in Chicago. A portly man with a long white beard that made him look like a biblical prophet, Dowie set up a tabernacle outside the fairgrounds, where he declared his power of healing and became known as Dr. Dowie.

After the fair, Dowie continued as a hellfire warrior against the evil power of Satan. He raged against denominational churches, calling them "apostasies" and proclaiming his hope that his Zion movement, a community of saints, would destroy them. His goal was to establish an "ideal state" for an "ideal people." He began with a communal home in a seven-story building at Twelfth Street and Michigan Avenue in Chicago. This Christian temperance hotel housing numerous families was also the church headquarters.

In his sermons, Dowie often denounced doctors, drugs, and devils, condemning hospitals, pharmacies, the liquor and tobacco industries, and the secular press. Because he attacked so much of the establishment as well as medical quacks, who indeed were common at the time, the authorities retaliated. They frequently accused Dowie of libel or practicing medicine without a license and jailed him hundreds of times. Controversies surrounding him created the kind of stories that newspaper reporters loved, and Dowie was one of the most widely publicized evangelists of the time.

In late 1899 Dowie waged a three-month "Holy War Against the Hosts of Hell in Chicago," which became the title for a compilation of his sermons published in 1900 in book form. He also made plans for a theocracy—a place ruled by God rather than governed by elected officials. His Zion City for Christians was to be built on the shores of Lake Michigan.

Dowie and some of his followers formed an investment association, selling shares for $100 apiece. The association, under his full control, bought up 6,600 acres of prime land forty-two miles north of Chicago. By 1901 he had formed the basis for a theocratic city to be ruled by God with orders delivered through an overseer—Dowie—and his elders. Dowie urged his followers to sell all their possessions and invest in the "holy city" of Zion, where

> the education of all classes should be with reference to making them Christian, as essential to promote not only their own welfare, but also the peace, dignity and best interests of the body politic;
> That business of all kinds—transportation, manufacturing, mercantile—should be conducted on the cooperative plan in such a way that each employee could feel and know that he was sharing in and benefiting by the fruits of his industry.[1]

Thousands heeded the call. There was no need for residents of the town to own their land, businesses, or factories, so said the leader. Rather, they should lease their land for 1,100 years and work for the businesses and factories owned by the Christian Catholic Apostolic Church. In short order, the investment association built several industries, including an entire lace factory imported from England; a lumber company; candy, handkerchief, and canning factories; a commercial baking industry; plus a radio station and publishing company that produced two weeklies: *The Theocrat* and *Leaves of Healing*.

Private ownership of business was considered unnecessary because at the end of the lease period Jehovah was supposed to appear to claim the faithful. But while they were waiting for the Second Coming, those who flocked to the new theocratic Zion City were expected to live by numerous thou-shalt-not rules. Certain foods, such as shellfish and meat of swine, as described in biblical injunctions, were forbidden. There were dozens of restrictions on land use. No one could build a

> distillery, tannery, soap factory, glue factory, gun-powder factory, or bone-boiling factory, saloon or beer garden, cigarette, cigar, or tobacco store; opium joint; or theater or opera house or gambling establishment; or dance hall; or circus; or house of ill-fame; or pharmacy or office of drug or practicing physician; or place for the sale of pork or anything forbidden by God to be eaten as stated in the seventh to the nineteenth verses of the fourteenth chapter of Deuteronomy; or a place for holding meetings or assemblies of any oath-bound secret societies; or any immoral, noxious or dangerous purpose whatsoever . . .[2]

On and on the rules and regulations went. But no matter what the restrictions, new church members, many of them seeking "divine healing," appeared regularly in Zion City, traveling from Australia, Scotland, and many parts of Europe and from across the United States and Canada. Families had to live in tents or rooms in a block-long, three-story Elijah Hospice (later known as the Zion Home) until they could build homes or find rental housing.

All through the first year of development, from sunrise to sunset, a familiar chorus rang out. Hammers, sometimes in unison, sometimes echoing each other, pounded nails into rafters, into siding, into roofs, into place all over Zion City. The hammers were joined by grating saws, picks striking rock, and shovels mixing stones and sand for cement. Shouts from road-grading crews and the testy instructions of landscapers who eventually planted twenty thousand shade trees along streets were occasionally added to the concert. And meantime, more and more people arrived by horse-drawn wagon or by Chicago and North Western Railroad cars.

Within a year Zion was well established as "A Clean City for A Clean People," according to one advertisement. By 1903 it boasted a population of more than ten thousand, and Dowie had realized part of his dream for a theocracy. However, he also created great controversy throughout the state of Illinois and across the United States with his demands that church members reject any medical treatment and drugs for whatever ailment or illness they might suffer. Elders "laid on the hands" and prayed to bring about healing.

Yet, in spite of hundreds of testimonies attesting to divine intervention, Dowie's own daughter, Esther, did not survive terrible burns she suffered when her nightgown accidentally caught fire from a burning alcohol lamp. She was burned over three fourths of her body and was in a semicoma for days. Because of his belief in faith healing, Dowie refused to allow any treatment for Esther's burns except Vaseline applications and saltwater washes. His critically burned daughter suffered for weeks before succumbing at the age of twenty-one to infection caused by the burns.

The death of Dowie's daughter in 1902 tested the faith of some of his followers. His ideas of communal property and grandiose plans to establish other church communities across the United States and particularly a Paradise Plantation in Mexico also caused conflicts. He staged expensive revivals, once ordering nine trainloads of church people to follow him to New York City, where in 1903 he held a series of meetings in Madison Square Garden, laying hands on thousands who came to be healed of ailments ranging from broken bones to cancer. But New York City was not impressed with Dowie and his cause, and the church lost hundreds of thousands of dollars in the venture.

Dowie's exploits eventually led the church and its many business holdings to near-bankruptcy. He suffered a paralyzing stroke in 1905, leaving others to restore solvency and save the church.

The newly elected general overseer, Wilbur Glen Voliva, quickly created more conflict when he took charge in 1906. The church leadership split between those who were faithful to Dowie and those who were ready to follow a new overseer. Then there was the major question of who owned Zion City and its industries, which a Chicago court placed in receivership, appointing a company to take custody of the property until the issue could be decided. Voliva began raising funds to buy back some of the Zion properties from the receivers and soon regained control over most of the industries.

Meanwhile, Dowie remained in his home, a mansion called Shiloh House, that he and his wife shared with their grown son, Gladstone. It was a twenty-five-room brick building with a colorful tiled roof, porticos, etched glass windows, and ornate woodwork, and was filled with expensive furniture. Compared to the average Zion residence, Shiloh House was a veritable palace. Only a few faithful actually visited Dowie at his home and remained loyal to the "prophet" during his last days, although he was widely honored after his death on March 9, 1907.

• REIGN OF THE NEW OVERSEER •

Voliva went on to make a name for himself with his autocratic pronouncements from the pulpit and at other public forums. He supported the ideas of a theocracy and holy living, and was determined to keep Zion the home and headquarters of the church rather than allow it to become a "common" American town. He encouraged passage of an ordinance that stated in part, "no person shall pollute the atmosphere by smoking tobacco in any depot, store, post office, or other public building or upon any public place within the City; nor shall any person be in a state of intoxication in any public place; nor shall any person use profane, blasphemous, or obscene language in any public place, or upon any street."

The laws were strictly enforced. Anyone who tried to test the ordinances was arrested and jailed. Even those traveling through Zion by train could be arrested for smoking while within the city limits. City elections were usually held in buildings controlled by Voliva, and judges were strong supporters of the general overseer. When some minority factions organized an Independent Party and tried to oppose Voliva and his Theocratic Party, they had little success. "Zion men" held most official positions. But that did not stop a war of words on a battlefield of billboards placed strategically around town. Voliva placed one billboard at the edge of the city warning:

This city was established by Zion people and for Zion people only. It is the exclusive headquarters of the Christian Catholic Church in Zion and the private home of its officers and members. No gentleman would break into a church settlement and attempt to hold meetings or to establish a counter organization. Those who do are nothing more nor less than religious bums, tramps and vagabonds with less honor than a gang of highway robbers and thugs. Get out of this community if you have a drop of honest blood and go establish a settlement of your own.[3]

Then an opposing billboard attacked the general overseer:

Voliva does not own us—we are not his sheep. Who is he to tell us what we can say on the street, how to vote, how to live? He is a vicious man lusting for power. Let him talk to his sheep not to us. We live in a free country. We are law-abiding citizens. Someone should stop this man who runs over at the mouth and pen.

Across the street from this billboard another sign countered:

That wretched looking old dilapidated thing across the street (look at it) was put there by a little bunch of idiots and lunatics. They have pimples where they ought to have heads. They vainly imagine they can destroy Zion. God and all the Zion people are laughing at them. . . . pay no attention to this bunch of traitors. . . . they are exactly like their board—badly cracked.

As the word attacks increased in ardor and nastiness, billboards were splattered with paint or black tar. On several occasions, Shiloh Tabernacle was pelted with rocks and windows were broken. The church school was vandalized. And the city was suddenly overrun with reporters from Chicago who were eager to cover the war of words and the eccentricities of Zion's church leader.

• Carrying the Torch? •

Voliva tried to carry on the healing practices that had brought Dowie so much fame, even when there were major scourges such as a smallpox epidemic that raged through the state in 1914. Illinois officials required massive vaccinations against the contagious disease. But Voliva said the state had no right to tell Zion people what to do. Only God could do that.

From the pulpit Voliva condemned "all of you to hell who attempt to vaccinate your children for smallpox. I tell doctors to take their vaccine and go to hell where they belong. Mothers, watch your children. Do not let them be snatched by medical men or you will suffer and your children will waste away before your eyes."

To prove his point, the overseer brought forth a victim, a young boy whose mouth was twisted in anguish. He was a mass of open, oozing sores. His nose was nothing but an ugly gaping red cavity. No bone structure was left. One ear was partially eaten away. His hands were covered with running sores.

"All of this because a mother allowed her son to be vaccinated at the age of nine," he roared. "How can you inject smallpox into your own flesh and blood?"

But Voliva was not victorious in this battle. The state militia came in to enforce a quarantine. Some Zionites, in spite of their belief in the healing power of prayer, were ambivalent about the state action. Whether or not they dared admit it, the quarantine might help reduce the spread of the deadly disease.

Perhaps Voliva's most controversial sermons were based on the evils of the public schools and their "heathen teachings," which included scientific theories. In one sermon I recall, the overseer delivered a long tirade about those who taught the law of gravity. "Bunk! Garbage!" he thundered, and threw a book into the air, letting it crash to the platform, startling not only the congregation but also the elders, who sat so stiffly and solemnly on the platform, six on each side of the pulpit. "You see?" shouted the overseer. "You see? I threw that book up and it went as far as the force behind it would allow. It fell because it was heavier than the air that it displaced. That is the only reason. The law of gravity is all bunk! It's garbage!"

Voliva saved most of his venom, though, for "those teachers who tell their students that the world is round!" The overseer often preached on that subject. He began with a low growl and his voice climbed to a near screech. "In our Zion school we teach children what the Bible says: 'I saw four angels standing on the four corners of the earth, holding the corners of the earth . . .' Now, I say, how can a round world have four corners?"

Once Voliva ordered two of the elders to hold up a map of the world. Slapping the paper front and back, he bellowed: "There you can see it. The world is as flat as this paper. Anyone who cares to refute this statement should study Revelations. The proof is there."

To bolster his arguments in the early 1930s, Voliva distributed a special edition of *One Hundred Proofs that the Earth Is Not a Globe*, a booklet by William Carpenter that apparently was first published in Baltimore, Maryland, in 1885. Those "one hundred proofs" included nonsensical and convoluted statements such as "proof" number twenty:

The common sense of man tells him—if nothing else told him—that there is an "up" and a "down" in nature, even as regards the heavens and the earth; but the theory of modern astronomers necessitates the conclusion that there is not: therefore, the theory of the astronomers is opposed to common sense—yes, and to inspiration—and this is a common sense proof that the Earth is not a globe.[4]

In another example, proof number forty noted that

The Suez Canal, which joins the Red Sea with the Mediterranean, is about one hundred miles long; it forms a straight and level surface of water from one end to the other; and no "allowance" for any supposed "curvature" was made in its construction. It is clear proof that the Earth is not a globe.[5]

Whatever the "proofs" given for a flat earth, the theory just added to all the many questions raised in my mind about the truthfulness as well as the repressiveness of the church's teachings. The food taboos were consistently enforced. The overseer would pound the pulpit when berating those who dared to eat "swine's flesh." He preached that the hog was the greatest disease-producing animal used for food and that it had been "foisted upon humanity by Satan himself." And there were restrictions against such simple pleasures as dancing, card playing, going to movies, and plays (unless it was the Passion Play depicting the life and death of Christ, for which the Christian Catholic Church became famous over the years).

Then in 1937 the church building burned down. In my childish logic, I began to wonder if that was some kind of divine retribution. I was in second grade at the time and remember climbing onto a desk top to look out the classroom window when we children heard that the tabernacle was ablaze. The building was just a block or so away, across a wooded park, and we could see the flames dancing through the trees. At first I was scared. I thought this might be the hellfire and damnation that the overseer preached about. Some of the kids were getting hysterical. But as a great billow of smoke spiraled up and formed a dark cloud that nearly cut off the sunlight, I had an odd sensation. I actually was a bit pleased that the tabernacle was being consumed—something more powerful than the Zion City leaders was at work!

Within ninety minutes the building had burned to the ground, and days later our family, like others in the town, visited the circular plot to stare at the heap of ashes and grotesquely twisted steel and glass. A metal tower that once carried signals from the church radio station stood like a guard over the debris. As we all walked slowly around the Temple Site, I saw a piece of melted glass, a dull blue-gray in color and molded like a smooth stone. I picked up the glass and held it in my palm, thinking it was like a miniature crystal ball. I could look into the future and see myself preserving the glass as a reminder of things past. I carried the memento in my hand while I continued to circle the site, shuffling through the thick ashes, and letting them fall silently over my feet.

Zion City still exists, but it is no longer under the control of the Christian Catholic Church, which in late 1996 changed its name to Christ Community Church. In fact, by the time the Great Depression hit the United States in the 1930s, the theocracy was being undermined by financial problems and once more was faced with bankruptcy, the loss of businesses, and declining support for the church's school system. The city slowly became a "common" American community. Over the years its economic base has deteriorated and little has been done to this day to attract investors. It is now primarily a bedroom community, with a large portion of the older homes turned into rental units housing military families and workers commuting to Chicago, Milwaukee, and other nearby cities.

Zion's fate has been similar to that of other alternative religious comunities and communal societies founded in the United States. Even though communal groups have been part of the American culture since colonial days, few have survived in their original form. As new communal groups have organized, many have repeated the failures of the past, although some have been successful for a time.

· 3 ·

ESTABLISHING CHRISTIAN
COMMUNISTIC SOCIETIES

In North America there has traditionally been a glorification of the individual and individual struggles to overcome nature and human obstacles. However, many Americans have rejected that ideal and adopted another: the concept of living and working together for their own and society's benefit. They have shared property and lived in a communal or communistic way.

For the most part, communistic, or communitarian, groups in the United States were not founded on the principles articulated in the Communist Manifesto of 1848 and practiced in Eastern Europe and China. Rather than being politically subversive, U.S. communistic communities were opposed to revolution as a method for reform. Membership in any community was voluntary, never forced.

Religious communistic communities were common from the late 1700s through the 1800s. The communism practiced was an attempt in some cases to establish societies similar to first-century Christian communities made up of people who followed the teachings of Jesus Christ, considered the Savior of humankind. Early Christians tried to live by the principles of communion, sharing, and caring for one another. They held their property in common, and whatever was produced was divided equally among members of the community.

• TYPES OF COMMUNES •

Roman Catholic religious orders were among the early groups to transport their communal life to the United States. These included Trappists—priests, brothers, and sisters of the Order of Cistercians of the Strict Observance, as it is formally known. Founded in 1098 in Cîteaux, France, the order focuses on meditation, prayer, study, and labor while living a secluded life in monasteries, also called abbeys or cloisters. Trappists attempt to use their prayers to alleviate suffering and to connect with all humanity.

Other types of communities or communes became more prominent and grew in number during the 1800s, particularly with the huge influx of immigrants, some of whom were fleeing religious persecution and were searching for an ideal lifestyle—a utopia, a heaven on earth, a promised land, a Zion (or sacred homeland). They established communistic groups such as the Shakers, the Amana Colonies, and the Perfectionists.

Some communities were set up as models for reform. People believed that individualism could not effectively deal with the growing problems of society brought on by industrialization and deep divisions between property owners and workers. So they based their communities on ideals that could be applied on a small scale, usually with groups ranging from a little more than one hundred to perhaps several thousand people. The founders and followers of such communities often attempted to isolate themselves from the rest of the world, but they hoped the larger society would emulate their way of life.

Throughout U.S. history, communal or communistic settlements have differed in their basic beliefs and customs, but most have shared similar characteristics. They have

- been motivated or led by a person of religious or idealistic zeal;

- required members to live by group rules and regulations;

- attempted to isolate themselves from the rest of the world;

- rejected private property and competition as a basis for the economy;

- stressed collective, or cooperative, production and consumption of goods, from food to manufactured items;

- attempted to eliminate bureaucracy, or a political structure with high and low status, and create a classless society, with each person having equal position;

- tried to create a society based on justice;

- believed a paradise on earth could be achieved.

Today communities with such characteristics would probably be labeled cults because their members conform to group life and, like cultists, appear to lose their individuality and live by the rules of an authority figure. However, there is no universal definition for the term *cult*, and it has been applied to numerous groups with nontraditional lifestyles, particularly alternative religious groups. More detailed descriptions of some cults, especially damaging or destructive cults of modern times, are included in later chapters.

• "SEPARATISTS" FROM GERMANY •

Some of the earliest communal groups in North America were religious sects from Europe, people who left established churches. Their ancestors had lived in a communal way, sharing their beliefs and property since the 1500s. Many were known as "Separatists," because they separated from the established Lutheran church. They were also known as pietists, part of a religious movement that opposed the Lutheran church's formal sacraments and dogmatic theology. Pietists believed in an evangelical religion of the heart rather than a religion of intellect. Their religion was an emotional experience often described as a personal connection with God.

A number of pietists left Germany during the 1700s and 1800s to live in comparative freedom in America. The Anabaptists (rebaptizers), who were unrelated to Baptist sects, were considered the most extreme of pietist groups. They opposed infant baptism and believed that devout Christians should be baptized voluntarily as adults, a radical concept at the time. Anabaptists immigrated from Germany and nearby Moravia (now part of the Czech Republic), Switzerland, and the Netherlands.

Among the Anabaptist groups were those who formed the Moravian church, the Amish (sometimes known as the Plain People because of their plain dress, separation from the rest of the world, and nontechnological way of life), Mennonites, and Hutterites. These German-speaking people opposed government restrictions on individuals, refused to pay taxes, and would not fight in wars. They believed that God directly guided their behavior and religious practices and would not submit to any religious authority. As a result, established churches, along with government officials, tried to crush them. They were often imprisoned, publicly flogged, and tortured.

In the mid-1800s the Hutterian Brethren, or Hutterites, established several communes in what became the states of North and South Dakota, Minnesota, and Montana. But during World War I, they were severely mistreated in the United States, and some were imprisoned and brutalized because of their pacifist stance. Consequently, many moved to Canada, where Hutterite colonies still survive.

In the Hutterite tradition a colony is comprised of about 120 people. When that number is surpassed, the colony divides into another "daughter" group. Hutterites live by a fairly rigid structure that has been passed on for generations. The men work in the fields and workshops, and the women garden and cook. Like many Plain People, Hutterites believe all members of the colony should submit to the will of the community, and that God is the head, with men submitting to God and women subservient to men. Men assume the leadership roles and vote on community matters such as the budget and selection of farm bosses—the men who will oversee hog, poultry, and dairy production and the women who will be head gardener, head cook, and head seamstress.

According to Hutterite basic tenets, "living in community" is the best way to express Christian love. And food preparation and mealtime reflect that community spirit. All members of a colony or community, with the exception of children fourteen years old and under, gather in a communal building for meals. The youngest children, up to age two and a half, eat in their family apartments. Those from two and a half to five years old are served meals in the kindergarten building. Children between five and fourteen take meals in a separate room in the communal kitchen building. According to author Joanita Kant,

> The communal kitchen, dining hall and church facilities are centrally located within the colony, usually along with the school. The centrality of these buildings is symbolic of the importance of what goes on within them. A community, based upon sharing the most basic of resources and providing counsel, support and discipline for each other, must have frequent gathered times. Meeting regularly for meals is a natural way to strengthen the bond of community, as it is in any family.[1]

• RAPPITES •

One group of German religious dissenters began an experiment in southern Indiana. Known as Harmonie, it was founded by George Rapp and his adopted son, Frederick, who emigrated from Würtemberg (or Württemburg), Germany, in 1803.

In Germany Rapp was an avid biblical scholar. He differed with the Lutheran church and began to preach his own doctrines based on New Testament concepts. Revered as a prophet and saint, Rapp brought together a congregation of three hundred families.

About nine hundred people followed Rapp to the United States, although after arriving, some Würtemberg immigrants broke away from the Rappite congregation and followed another leader. At least six hundred people joined Rapp in setting up a colony in Pennsylvania. Members of the community agreed that all their cash and property would be used for the benefit of the community. Further, they promised "to submit to the laws of the community, to show a ready obedience to the superintendents, to give the labor of their hands for the good of the community, and to hold their children to do the same." In turn George Rapp and his associates promised all members a "secular and religious education" and to provide them "all the necessaries of life, to support them and their widows and children alike in sickness, health, and old age." If a member left the community, his money was "refunded to him without interest." If he had made no capital investment, the money awarded to him was determined by his conduct.[2]

The original community quickly prospered, with its sawmill, tannery, and a storehouse filled with surplus grain, which was used to produce whisky. Although members drank very little, the Rappites became famous for their distillery and were known for their cellars of fine wine.

Father Rapp, as he was called, banned marriages except for those married before joining the group. People were required to practice celibacy, just one of the many sacrifices they were expected to make to prepare for what Rapp believed would be the Second Coming of Christ within their lifetime. Married couples lived in homes, but single men and women lived in separate dormitories.

Within a few years, the community was producing so much surplus grain and other products, such as cloth from their woolen mill, that they had to find markets for their goods. But the colony was twelve miles from a navigable river, which was a distinct disadvantage. In 1813 the Rappites decided to search for another site. They chose a tract of government land and several adjacent farms, a total of about thirty thousand acres, located near the mouth of the Wabash River on the Indiana-Illinois border. By 1815 they had sold their Pennsylvania property and improvements for only $100,000 and had founded the village of Harmonie.

If it were not for accounts of travelers, little would be known about the Rappite community, later called New Harmony. None of the one thousand original members left written records. But visitors often wrote about the thriving community and its leader.

Father Rapp maintained tight control of Harmonie. He was said to be a commanding presence at six feet tall with "a patriarchal beard and stately walk." He played on the superstitions of many members, frequently saying he had received heavenly visions regarding the affairs of the community.

It was rumored for years (and the story still persists) that Father Rapp built a tunnel from his cellar to the grain storage area and went through this passage to "appear as from the ground, mystifying the simple workmen, and perhaps leading them to believe that their labors were constantly within the range of his observation." Another story claimed that he "entered his pulpit through a tunnel leading to the church porch from his house just across the road." Father Rapp presided over all religious services, and preached "humility, simplicity, self-sacrifice, neighborly love, regular and persevering industry, prayer, and self-examination. In addition, he demanded that each evening any one who had sinned during the day should come to him and confess his transgression."[3]

The thrift and industry of the Rappites not only brought prosperity but also created jealousy among people in neighboring communities, according to reports from visitors. At the same time, Rapp feared prosperity would affect his followers, forcing them to lose sight of their initial goals. These may have been factors in Rapp's decision within ten years after founding Harmonie to sell the village and move back to Pennsylvania, where the Rappites settled a third town called Economy. The Rappites continued to prosper there but apparently sought no new members, and the communal way of life vanished soon after the death of Rapp at the age of ninety.

Harmonie was sold in 1824 to Robert Owen, a successful industrialist and social reformer in Great Britain. Owen had no plans for a religious utopia. Instead, he envisioned an experimental community where there would be universal happiness achieved through education and communal living, as described in chapter five.

• THE COMMUNITY OF TRUE INSPIRATION •

One more group of pietists from Germany followed the teachings of Ludwig Gruber and Johann Friedrich Rock, who believed that God spoke directly to his people through individuals. Divine guidance was provided through a specially endowed person called *Werkzeuge* (instrument), who presented inspired testimonies to the people. The *Werkzeuge* was the ordained leader of the community.

During the early 1700s, Gruber and Rock traveled throughout Germany and Switzerland, forming small congregations of followers and a church known as the Church of the True Inspiration or the Community of True Inspiration. Like many other separatists and pietists, True Inspirationists refused to go along with the doctrine of the Lutheran church and would not perform military service for the government. Although they were persecuted throughout the century, True Inspirationists managed to maintain their community into the 1800s, when they were led by Barbara Heinemann, a young servant girl, and Christian Metz, a carpenter. Both were endowed with what followers called the miraculous gift of Inspiration, but Barbara Heinemann apparently lost her calling when she married in 1823. Although she and her husband stayed within the community, they were under censure for a time, and *Werkzeuge* Christian Metz took over as leader.

By 1842 continued persecution forced Metz to seek another home for Inspirationists. Metz with three of his followers traveled to the United States and bought five thousand acres of land in the Seneca Indian Reservation near Buffalo,

New York. Not long afterward more than eight hundred Inspirationists sailed from Germany to their new home, establishing the Ebenezer Community. The congregation did not originally plan a communal system, but some of the members could not afford to buy land, so a constitution was adopted in which community members shared property and businesses.

As the community grew, more land was needed, and leaders went to the Midwest, choosing eighteen thousand acres in the Iowa River valley, where Metz and the True Inspirationists built a village in 1855. The site was chosen because of the availability of building materials (stone and timber), good farmland, and water supply, and because it was isolated enough to be a peaceful haven from the outside world. Church members believe the name of the village was given to them through an inspired testimony, commanding the people to call their village Amana, which means to remain true and comes from the Song of Solomon (4:8).

After the initial village was built, five others followed: Middle Amana, High Amana, West Amana, South Amana, and East Amana, plus a later village called Homestead. Homestead was purchased because it was the site of a railroad station and a shipping point for the Amana farm produce and manufactured products. Today the seven villages are collectively known as the Amana Colonies and comprise about twenty-six thousand acres.

Each of the Amana villages maintained the communal system, and Christian Metz led the entire Community of True Inspiration until his death in 1867. No *Werkzeuge* appeared after that until Barbara Heinemann regained her standing in the community. She once more "fell into Inspiration" and directed the thirteen trustees who managed internal and business matters of the Amana Church Society. Since *Werkzeuge* Heinemann's death in 1883, however, there have been no further inspirations. Nevertheless, the Amana Church Society still includes readings from a book of inspired testimonies in services.

The seven villages remained under a truly communist system for eighty-seven years. Similar to the Rappites, each member of the Community of True Inspiration was "duty bound to hand over his or her personal and real property to the Trustees for the common fund." A member was then entitled to "free board and dwelling" plus support and care during sickness and old age. Those who left the society, "either by their own choice or by expulsion," were repaid any money put into the common fund plus interest.[4]

Each village kept its own books and managed its own affairs, but sent all accounts to the society's headquarters in Old Amana (or the first Amana) to determine profit and loss. If a village suffered from hard times, there was usually a surplus in other villages to make up losses. Although all houses were part of the communal property, each family lived in a separate home. Every member of the community also received an allowance from the common fund for clothing and other personal needs, thus satisfying "that desire of every human heart to have something of its very own. Indeed, the separatism of the Amana home, though not in accord with the principles of complete communism," was said to have been an important factor in the success of the Community of True Inspiration for so many years.[5]

The Amana communal society lasted longer than most established communistic communities in the United States, but several factors contributed to its decline. One was an open youth rebellion beginning in the late 1920s. According to historian Lawrence Rettig, the rebellion came about because many young people had "learned about the ways of the world from their contact with tourists and from increasing trips to the outside." Young people wanted to live like other Americans. They pressured to play baseball, a forbidden sport, and to reduce the number of religious services—eleven each week—that they were required to attend. They also rebelled against work assignments made by the elders, who offered no choice in jobs. Some revolted against rules banning "worldly," or modern, conveniences, such as electricity.[6]

Style of dress was a major concern to rebellious young women, and one Amana teenager aired her views to a reporter for the *Kansas City Star*:

> We are sick and tired of this 'old fogeyism' that masquerades as religion. It isn't religion, it's darned foolishness. When bobbed hair and short skirts came in, many of us girls in Amana wanted to follow the fashions and dress like all the other young women of the towns around us. But no. We were told that short skirts and short hair were sinful. . . .
>
> The old fogies threatened to expel us if we broke away from those hateful styles, but there were too many of us. . . . They can't tell us younger women that a woman's morality and Christianity depends on the way she wears her hair. We can go barelegged and wear bathing suits and still be Christians. It's not the way you dress, it's what's in your heart that decides whether you are a Christian or not.[7]

The deepening economic depression in the United States had a major effect on the Amana Colonies also, forcing leaders to reorganize and give up the communal system. It was a time that today is still known as the "Great Change." A profit-sharing corporation was set up, ending the church's management of businesses. Members of the community purchased their own homes, maintained their own properties, worked for wages or became business proprietors, and dealt with all other aspects of private ownership.

The transition from communal life to private enterprise was not easy. For example, there were not enough jobs for everyone who needed to work for wages to support themselves. "Under the old system there had simply been too many cobblers, basket makers, tailors, carpet weavers, saw mills, and dairies for the corporation to support profitably. Many had to be abolished," wrote historian Rettig. "Those without jobs were encouraged to go into business for themselves . . . however, few were willing to take the risks involved." Instead, they found jobs in nearby towns.[8]

In spite of the frustrations and numerous problems associated with reorganization, the transition to private enterprise was accomplished by 1932. Today, the Amana Colonies are designated a national historic landmark and are a major tourist attraction. The Amana Church Society still exists, although membership has dwindled over the years to about four hundred. Those who remain part of the congregation also "remain faithful" according to the literal meaning of Amana.

· 4 ·

CELIBACY, COMPLEX
MARRIAGE, AND POLYGAMY

Most of the religious communal societies of the 1700s and
1800s had rules and regulations about relationships between
men and women, boys and girls. Members were often separated by gender. Some, like the Rappites, were required to
practice celibacy; sexual relationships and marriages were
banned. Other communal groups promoted multiple marriage
or numerous sexual partners.

· ANN LEE AND THE SHAKER BEGINNINGS ·

One of the longest-lived American groups to require celibacy
was the United Society of Believers in Christ's Second
Appearing, or the Millennial Church. Commonly known as
Shakers, this group of religious zealots stemmed from England and was first led by Ann Lee of Manchester.

As a child Ann Lee had little education except for what she
gained in the workplace, and she never learned to read or
write. She apparently had visions and came to believe that
humankind was depraved. When she reached marriage age

she began to express her hatred of sexual union and considered it indecent. However, at her friends' urgings she eventually married, and she and her husband, a blacksmith like her father, had four children, all of whom died in infancy.

When Ann's father joined the Shakers, she, too, at the age of twenty-three, became involved in this sect, described by one historian as being

> subject to those frenzied physical manifestations of religious zeal that are characteristic of revivalists in general. At their religious meetings they shook and trembled, whirled like dervishes, danced, sang, and cried out in strange tongues derived from the spirit world. These good people were derisively called the Shaking Quakers, or Shakers.[1]

The Shakers were part of a growing number of Spiritualists who claimed to communicate directly with spirits and trembled when filled with "the spirit." As Ann Lee became more involved with the Shakers, she and others began disrupting various other church congregations during worship, preaching that the Shakers were the only true religion. As a result she was often attacked by mobs and was arrested and jailed numerous times.

According to Shaker history, while Ann Lee was in jail in 1770, she experienced a vision that pointed the way for salvation and eternal life. After her release from prison, she told her followers that they could not be Christ-like—attain the spiritual qualities attributed to Jesus Christ—unless they renounced sexual gratification and became celibate. From then on, she was known as Mother in Christ and called Mother Ann.

Among the doctrines she inspired and her successors preached was that God was both male and female, a dual person; that Christ appeared as a spirit in the form of Jesus, the male, and then in Ann Lee, representing the female element. Neither Jesus nor Mother Ann was worshipped, however.

In 1774 after many conflicts with authorities, Ann Lee again received a vision that told her to go to America and found the Church of Christ's Second Appearing. She along with her husband, several relatives, and a few other followers, sailed from Liverpool and after a three-month journey landed in North America. Not long afterward, Ann Lee's husband decided the celibate life was not for him, and he ran off with another woman.

The Shakers as a group apparently dropped out of sight for a time as they cleared wooded land for a settlement a few miles from what is now Albany, New York. In 1780 while many Americans were fighting a war for independence from Great Britain, the Shakers gained public attention with their outspoken refusal to take up arms in the revolution. A New York commission was set up to track down British sympathizers as well as colonists trying to avoid military service. The commissioners were convinced that the Quakers planned to undermine U.S. freedom and independence. As a result, ten Shaker leaders, including Mother Ann, were imprisoned. After her release, Ann Lee continued to bring converts to the Shaker settlement, but the society did not advocate communal life until after her death in 1784.

• SHAKER COMMUNES •

The Shakers established their first commune at New Lebanon, New York, in 1792, and over the next eighty years established more than fifty communes, or families, as they were called. Why did so many communities form at this time? During the 1800s a revivalist movement, which included camp meetings with evangelistic preaching and testimonies, spread across the United States. Shakers often attended these meetings, speaking about their faith and bringing numerous converts into the Shaker communes. These "gatherings," as they were called, created a number of new Shaker families in Ohio, Kentucky, and Indiana.

Each Shaker family consisted of anywhere from thirty to ninety members, and two or three such families might be part of a Shaker society living in a single village. The society was governed by a hierarchy of leaders: a ministry was at the top, followed by elders, deacons, and trustees.

There was no discrimination on the basis of skin color, and men and women were considered equal in terms of leadership and the administration of a commune. But daily work was divided along traditional lines. Women prepared communal meals, cleaned, did the laundry, sewed, and operated such industries as weaving, basket making, and preserving food, while men did the heavy farm labor and worked in the mills, tanneries, and other industries.

Members came into the society from nearly all walks of life and from nearly all religious groups. One young man, William Byrd, whose ancestors were wealthy Virginia planters with political influence, joined the Shaker community at Pleasant Hill, Kentucky, in 1826, when he was just twenty years old. William was not only attracted by the Shaker religious beliefs but also by the group's emphasis on a healthy diet and lifestyle. Apparently he suffered from an intestinal disorder, which took his life two years later.

As with other new arrivals, William was a novitiate and was required to learn about the group before he could enter the church. He also had to settle into one of the Family Dwelling houses at Pleasant Hill. He had his own room that needed to be furnished and was helped in the process by a Shaker trustee, Francis Voris. William described the process in one of his frequent letters to his father, Charles Willing Byrd, a federal judge:

> Frances [sic] procured for me a buroe [bureau], to keep my cloathes and other things in. It was not quite finished when he bought it, although it had been made some time before. I suppose altogether it will not cost me more than eleven dollars. . . . I found it necessary likewise to get a [new] stove into my room, as I could not read with any satisfaction in the publick part of the house. . . . I do a little manual labour about the house, and stables, and walk, and ride, occasionally, the former every day, and the latter . . . not unfrequently.[2]

Like some other communes of the time, children who came with their parents were separated by gender. They were placed under the supervision of special caretakers, who were responsible for all aspects of the children's lives, from discipline to worship. Although rules were strict in many communes, the Shaker regulations were among the most rigid. One Shaker in New Hampshire described what was expected of young boys within the commune:

> Whenever they leave their house or shop, they are required to go two abreast and keep step with each other. No loud talking was allowable in the court-yards at any time. No talking or whispering when [going] . . . to their work, their school, their meetings, or their meals; a still soft walk on tiptoe, and an indistinct closing of doors in the house; a gentle, yet a more brisk movement in the shops; a free and jovial conversation when by themselves in the fields; but not a word, unless when spoken to, when other brethren than their care-takers were pre-

sent. . . . We allowed them to indulge in the innocent sports practiced elsewhere. But wrestling and scuffling were rarely permitted. No sports were allowed in the court-yards, unless all loud talk was suppressed.[3]

The orderly life was not confined to children. Almost every detail of a Shaker's existence was covered by a rule that had to be followed precisely. There was, for example, an exact time to rise in the morning (4:30 in the summer and 5:30 in the winter) and a strict schedule for the day's activities. Shakers were required to begin the day by getting dressed in a particular way—the right side first. Rules also required "stepping first with the right foot as you ascend a flight of stairs, folding the hands with the right-hand thumb and fingers over the left, kneeling and rising again with the right leg first."[4]

Shakers lived in a communal dwelling house, with parlors, a dining room, kitchen, and baking room on the ground floor. Meeting rooms were on the next floor and sleeping rooms were on the two floors above, men occupying one side and women the other. All "retiring rooms" accommodated four to eight people and were furnished exactly alike—simply, with no decorative items allowed. A wide hall separated the dormitories, and strict rules of chastity kept the brethren and the sisters apart night and day. They were only allowed to visit each other at a set time and in a specified manner.[5]

Like most other communal societies, Shakers held their property in common and depended on agriculture and some industries to maintain their lifestyle. Because of their efficiency, the Shakers produced a surplus of goods and many of their products were sold across the United States. They became known for their laborsaving devices and elegantly simple furniture that is copied by manufacturers today.

After the Civil War, revivalism declined, as did converts to Shaker communities. Because of celibacy, Shakers produced no heirs to carry on their communes. As older members died, membership, which had reached a peak of about six thousand in the early 1840s, began to drop dramatically. In 1991, the Shakers' last religious leader died, but Shaker sites in New England, Ohio, and Kentucky have been or are being restored, preserving much of the Shaker culture.

• PERFECTIONISM •

About the time the Shakers reached their peak in membership, another communistic experiment began under the leadership of John Humphrey Noyes. Noyes preached a way of salvation known as Perfectionism—attaining perfect love with God. However, the community he founded became famous for its nontraditional views about marriage and producing children.

Noyes was from an affluent and well-established political family and was a graduate of Dartmouth College. He intended to study law, but at the age of twenty experienced conversion. He enrolled at the Andover Theological Seminary in Andover, Massachusetts in 1831, intending to study for the ministry. He was disappointed with the restrictive nature of the school and transferred to Yale's Divinity School. During his second year at Yale, he began to preach and write about his belief that an individual could attain perfection on earth and after salvation could not fall from grace. He contended that a person should be guided by inner convictions, not the authority of the church.

Noyes converted several of his family members to his cause, and for several years he traveled throughout the Northeast delivering his message and seeking other converts. In 1838 he married one of them, Harriet A. Holton, who helped him gather an informal association of followers.

As followers increased, Noyes laid the foundation for a

communistic society, using an inheritance from his father. The elder Noyes had divided his Putney, Vermont, estate among his children in 1841, eight months before he died. In 1844 Noyes with his brother and two brothers-in-law formed a legal organization to manage their financial affairs and later to allow others to join their group by investing time and labor rather than money. The group was comprised of about three dozen people, including nine children, and they supported themselves by operating two farms (part of the Noyes inheritance) and a store. Three households were set up, and according to researcher Maren Lockwood Carden, members of the community "voted unanimously for the 'theocratic' government of John Noyes. He allowed no opposition to his doctrines or to his organization of the three households. Even his sisters submitted to his choice of husbands for them."[6]

• COMPLEX MARRIAGE •

The group remained intact for about four more years, during which Noyes developed his ideas about marriage based on his interpretation of the biblical statement "in the resurrection they are neither married nor given in marriage."[7] Although most biblical scholars understand the verse to mean that resurrected people have no sex, Noyes claimed just the opposite. In his view, the biblical verse referred to an ideal system of complex marriage in which everyone is equally loved and all men are married to all women. In the afterlife, monogamous marriage, exclusive attachment to one person, did not exist. According to his doctrine, any man and woman might freely cohabit, providing there was mutual consent.

Along with his system of complex marriage, Noyes advocated "male continence," a practice of self-control during which the male interrupts sexual intercourse to prevent pregnancy. This practice developed because Noyes was opposed to "random procreation." He also believed women should be able to avoid the suffering of childbirth that was so common at the time. However, he favored what he called "scientific propagation," whereby sexual relationships were governed to produce "spiritually superior" people.

The community at Putney began to experiment with Noyes' ideas, which brought a great deal of condemnation and hostility from neighbors and others in the "outside" world. In 1847 Noyes was arrested for the illegal marriage system practiced at Putney. Before his trial, his legal counsel warned that there might be mob action against the community and advised Noyes to leave the state. Noyes immediately left, convinced that the practices he advocated could exist only in a kind of utopia separated from the rest of the world. In 1848 he bought land on the former Oneida Indian Reserve in Madison County, New York, where he established the Oneida Community. There all property was held in common and members paid for necessities from a common fund.

Based on agriculture and small industries such as blacksmith shops and lumber mills, the community was similar to the communistic experiments of the Shakers as well as the New Harmony experiment in Indiana more than a decade earlier. For several years, members suffered severe hardships, but they were saved from financial ruin by Sewell Newhouse, an inventor of steel animal traps. After Newhouse joined the Oneida Community, he helped establish trap manufacturing. This and later industries such as a silk mill improved the community's economy.

As the commune prospered, branches were organized in several New England states, but these were later closed. The Oneida Community and a settlement at Wallingford, Connecticut, became the center of this Perfectionist experiment, with the two communities operating as one. About 250 members lived in Oneida and another 50 in Wallingford.

In the 1860s a large brick Mansion House was built to house most of the Oneida Community members. Children lived in one wing of the mansion from the time they were weaned as infants until they were thirteen or fourteen years old. Parents visited their children often, but nurses and other caretakers were responsible for the upbringing of the children.

• MUTUAL CRITICISM •

During its three decades of communism, the Oneida Community was disciplined and managed by a system of mutual criticism. If a member had a moral problem or felt a sense of guilt about some "sinful" act, he or she could request criticism by a committee of members or by the entire community. Or a member might be selected for criticism. The person being criticized remained silent during a session, and afterward made a public confession and resolved to follow the community's recommendations for improvement.

One applicant for membership who volunteered for criticism described the experience this way:

> Here was I who had been doing my utmost to lead a right kind of life; had been a labourer in churches, in religious meetings . . . had always stood ready to empty my pockets to the needy . . . I, who for months had been shaping my conduct and ideas into form . . . to match the requirements of the Oneida Community, was shaken from centre to circumference. Every trait of my character that I took any pride or comfort in seemed to be cruelly discounted. . . . For weeks after I found myself recalling various passages of my criticism and reviewing them in new light; the more I pondered, the more convinced I became of the justice of what at first my spirit had so violently rebelled against.[8]

Although this particular applicant did not join the Oneida Community, he still remained sympathetic to the group. And apparently for group members, mutual criticism, which is used in a more sadistic form by modern-day cult leaders to control members, was effective. As researcher Maren Lockwood Carden pointed out:

> Members' self-esteem depended almost exclusively upon their fellow Perfectionists' approval. They only left the "home domain" occasionally, and they were frowned on for talking too freely with local outsiders working in the Community businesses. . . . A member had only his private or Community standards by which to judge his actions.[9]

By the 1870s some members of the Oneida Community became dissatisfied with the religious zeal of the founders and the communistic way of life. In addition, the community had been under constant attack from leaders of religious denominations and some academics who labeled the Perfectionists immoral because of their complex marriage system. Eventually, Noyes was forced to leave Oneida once again, seeking refuge in Canada. He also proposed that the complex marriage system be renounced in deference to the growing public criticism of his community.

In 1879 the community gave up its sexual practices and many couples married. Although the community attempted to sustain communism, that system, too, was abandoned shortly after. In 1881 the community reorganized as the Oneida Community Limited, and shares of stock were divided among 226 members.

Some of the members remained at Oneida while others left to join orthodox Christian groups. A few attempted to set up a new communistic society, but it did not materialize. As a legal company, the Oneida Community continued to manufacture a variety of products, and by 1920 Oneida silverware and stainless steel tableware were known for quality worldwide.

The Oneida Community Mansion House still stands today, preserved by descendants of the original community and other supporters who live in the building. Costs for maintenance are financed in part by admission fees for guided tours and profits from communal meals, guest lodging, and special events such as weddings.

• LATTER-DAY SAINTS •

While the Shaker and Oneida Community experiments were under way, the Church of Jesus Christ of Latter-day Saints, also known as the LDS Church or the Mormons, brought together "an astonishing number of people willing to sacrifice for the whole," historian Robert Hine noted.[10]

As is true of other religious groups out of the mainstream, the LDS Church throughout its turbulent history has often been labeled a sect or cult. Yet the Mormons have become so well established that today many Americans consider the church a major denomination in the United States.

The LDS Church was founded in 1830 by Joseph Smith of Palmyra, New York. Although Smith's family followed the teachings of various religious denominations, Joseph became deeply concerned about his spiritual life. In the 1820s he began to search for a "true" Christian religion.

According to LDS history and doctrine, which fills many volumes, Smith experienced his first vision at the age of fourteen. In the vision, both God and Jesus Christ appeared to warn him against joining any particular Christian sect or denomination. Several years later, he is said to have seen the angel Moroni, "a prophet who had lived on the American continent" and came back "to reveal the existence of a record written on gold plates which had lain hidden in the ground for fourteen centuries." The record was said to be the history of an ancient people, descendants of Hebrews who emigrated to the North American continent. Moroni told Joseph he was "to translate the record and publish it" using the Urim and Thummim, stones described in Hebrew scriptures that were like oracles, consulted to determine the will of God. The angel also described a breastplate of the type worn by ancient high priests and gave "the location of the plates . . . buried in a hillside about three miles from his [Smith's] home."

For the next four years, Moroni appeared annually to tutor Joseph about his responsibilities in regard to the plates, or tablets as they are sometimes called. Then in September 1827, Joseph went to the Hill Cumorah, where the plates were located. "Moroni gave him the plates, the Urim and Thummim, and the breastplate," LDS history records.[11]

Joseph Smith began translating the plates in 1828 but was interrupted by family responsibilities and loss of the translation. Joseph and several other scribes, including Emma, his wife, Martin Harris, and Oliver Cowdery eventually completed the translation in 1829, and the Book of Mormon was published for sale the following year. Meanwhile, church history states, John the Baptist appeared to Joseph Smith and Oliver Cowdery, inducting them into the priesthood. It is said they were also visited by Apostles Peter, James, and John, who proclaimed Smith and Cowdery elders of the new church.

After the Mormon church was formally organized in 1830, Prophet Joseph, as he was called, and some of his followers were constantly harassed and persecuted by members of other churches and local authorities. Many non-Mormons (or Gentiles, as they were known by Mormons) opposed some of the basic Mormon beliefs as outlined by Joseph Smith, such as the doctrine that the Book of Mormon was equal to the Hebrew and Christian scriptures revealing God's word.

Like other self-proclaimed prophets before and after him, Joseph Smith and his followers planned to establish a Zion, a holy city or a new Jerusalem, where they hoped to have a safe haven from the tribulations that were expected to descend on the wicked of the world. They gathered first in New York, but because of persecution, some converts moved to Kirtland, Ohio, near Cleveland. There Joseph Smith established an economic system, called the Law of Consecration, to help the poor and immigrants coming to Ohio.

The system was similar to other communal experiments. Members of the church consecrated, or deeded, "all their property, both real and personal, to the bishop of the Church." The Mormon bishop "would then grant an 'inheritance,' or stewardship, to an individual from the properties received. The size of the stewardship depended on the circumstances, wants, and needs of the family, as determined jointly by the bishop and the prospective steward."[12]

Smith and his followers later moved to the land they called Zion in Jackson County, Missouri, where they built a temple, but opponents of the church drove them out in 1837. Smith was jailed, but his captors allowed him to escape within a few months, and he helped found the city of Nauvoo on the Mississippi River in Illinois. But persecution continued, especially after rumors spread that Smith had instituted polygamy, the practice of men marrying multiple wives. In 1844 Smith and his brother Hyrum were arrested, then attacked by a mob, shot, and killed.

After Smith's death, the Mormons were in disarray. Several groups split from the main church, which was led by Brigham Young. Because of increased tyranny against the Mormons, Young and his church members left the Midwest in

1847 and made a long trek through harsh terrain and bitter winter weather to Utah. There Young selected a site in the Great Salt Lake valley for the church headquarters—Salt Lake City.

• CONVERTS •

Word of the Mormon community and the church's gospel spread worldwide, drawing converts from numerous states and other countries. The Stucki family of Switzerland, which included four young children, were among those who emigrated during the 1860s and headed for Salt Lake City.

Mary Ann Stucki was only six years old when she and her family, along with other Swiss, sailed for the United States and landed in New York City. The Swiss traveled by train to Florence, Nebraska, stopping near what is now Omaha. There the men built wooden handcarts to carry their family belongings as they trudged across the plains and mountains to Utah.

Between 1856 and 1860 about three thousand people pulled or pushed these two-wheeled handcarts to the Mormon Zion, following ox-drawn wagons carrying food and other supplies. The Stuckis were with one of the last groups to make the trip in this manner. As Mary Ann Hafen (her married name) recalled years later,

> We set out from Florence on July 6, 1860, for our thousand-mile trip. There were six to our cart. Father and mother pulled it; Rosie (two years old) and Christian (six months old) rode; John (nine) and I (six) walked. Sometimes, when it was down hill, they let me ride too.[13]

At first Mary's father tied the family cow, which was taken along to provide fresh milk, to the back of the cart. Soon, though, he hitched up the cow in front to pull the cart and to carry Mary's mother, who suffered from swollen feet. One day, however,

> a group of Indians came riding up on horses. Their jingling trinkets, dragging poles and strange appearance frightened the cow and sent her chasing off with the cart and children. We were afraid that the children might be killed, but the cow fell into a deep gully and the cart turned upside down. Although the children were under the trunk and bedding, they were unhurt . . . after that father did not hitch the cow to the cart again.[14]

By September the entire group reached their destination and "some yelled and tossed their hats in the air." They were welcomed by earlier settlers, who brought them food. The Stuckis were given "a little house near the river Jordan, three miles from town," and Mary's father began working on the public road for which he "was paid in produce, mostly flour and potatoes."[15]

As the community prospered and grew, Young revived Smith's stewardship plan along with the intended purpose of the church, to establish a kingdom of God on earth. He sent groups of Mormons throughout western territories and states to set up colonies. But "outsiders" often opposed these communities because of the Mormon practice of polygamy, which was outlawed by the federal Edmunds Act in 1882.

The practice of polygamy prevented Utah from becoming a state until after 1890, when the church banned it. Although the ban caused some groups to leave the church, the Mormons have grown to about nine million members worldwide, with churches in more than 150 countries.

· 5 ·

EARLY
SECULAR COMMUNES

Along with the many sectarian (religious) communistic societies established in the 1800s, numerous secular, or nonreligious, communes were founded. In all, more than one hundred communal groups were formed in the nineteenth century, a period known as the "golden age of community experiments" in the United States.[1]

In many ways, the religious communities paved the way for secular communities, and even though there were differences in the two types of communes, members of various communities often exchanged ideas. Frequently they were in the same areas, and some sites were used at different times by both religious and nonreligious groups.

In the view of historian Arthur Bestor, "sectarian communities undoubtedly suggested to many Americans the possibility of social reform by means of communistic or co-operative colonies." Bestor suggests that the religious experiment "contributed greatly to the success of Owenite propaganda"[2]—the ideas of Robert Owen, who took over Harmonie, Indiana, after the religious Rappites failed. Owen used the community as a laboratory for his own economic experiments.

• NEW HARMONY AND OTHER "OWENITES" •

From 1800 to the 1820s, Robert Owen managed the New Lanark textile mills in Scotland, and it was there that he first applied his ideas. In New Lanark, Owen theorized that the deep discontent and misery of the mill town were caused by the general problems of the society in which workers lived. He set out to improve his employees' living and working conditions through educational programs (including nursery school), shorter working hours, and financial assistance for ill workers. He also proposed that communities of five hundred to two thousand people be set up in a scientific manner, replacing the family as the form of social organization.

Owen publicly advocated his ideas in articles and speeches. He also shared some of his concepts in letters and publications that, over a period of several years, he sent to George Rapp in Harmonie. The correspondence prompted Rapp to send a representative to England to see Owen and propose that he buy Harmonie. Owen eventually moved with his family to the United States, and in 1824 he purchased the Rappite community for $150,000.

Renaming the village New Harmony, Owen formed the Preliminary Society of New Harmony with the stated purpose of promoting "the happiness of the world." He hoped to set up an "empire of peace and goodwill," which he thought would lead "in due season, to that state of virtue, intelligence, enjoyment, and happiness which it has been foretold by the sages of the past would at some time become the lot of the human race."[3] He expected that his ideas for community life would spread worldwide.

Owen declared that since he was the proprietor and

founder of the system and had paid for it, he was entitled to appoint a committee to manage the society's affairs. Numerous provisions were outlined for membership in the society. For example, members were expected to willingly provide their services for the good of the society and to be "temperate, regular, and orderly in their whole conduct." However, the constitution for the Preliminary Society was vague and no one could be sure exactly what kind of community Owen planned to establish.

One month after the Preliminary Society was formed in 1825, Owen left for England and did not return until January 1826, six months later. Not long afterward, a group of scientists and teachers arrived on what became known as the "boatload of knowledge." The community was reorganized under a second constitution that awarded equal privileges to all members rather than according to the worth of an individual's services, as provided in the first constitution. For example, a skilled laborer received the same amount as an unskilled worker.

Due to lack of leadership and no binding force such as religion to hold the members together, the society failed to become a true community. In less than two years, New Harmony failed. But Owen's ideas were the basis for other communities, including the Blue Spring Community near Bloomington, Indiana, an experiment called Maxwell in Ontario, Canada, and one in Yellow Springs, Ohio, now the site of Antioch College. But by 1830, all of the Owenite communities had disintegrated.

Yet, the experiment at New Harmony brought about one of the first free coeducational public school systems in the nation and a free public library system. Owen's son, Robert Dale, became a staunch advocate for women's rights and the emancipation of slaves. The village itself was not completely abandoned; some intellectuals stayed to make their homes in the community. And some original structures and sites from the communal living experiment have been preserved and are now historical attractions.

• FOLLOWING A FRENCH MASTER •

Perhaps one of the most elaborate and bizarre schemes for an ideal society on a global scale was developed by Charles Fourier of France, who published numerous books and articles on what became known as Fourierism. Fourier hated the social problems associated with industrialization and believed that all classes of people should work together cooperatively. He claimed he alone understood God's true plan for a harmonious universe, which depended upon "the law of attraction" and the gratification of passions. In Fourier's view, passion not only brought pleasure but also led to "spontaneous association of human beings for the purposes of work," as Mark Holloway explained in his book on utopian communities. According to Fourier, the basic association was a group made up of at least seven people. Those seven would be divided into subgroups:

> two persons in each wing representing the "ascending" and "descending" extremes of tastes and tendencies, and three in the centre to maintain an equilibrium. Thus the two wings will engage with each other, and will also combine to engage with the centre, in friendly rivalry and competition. There will be Groups for every conceivable occupation, from that of growing roses . . . to that of raising poultry or driving elephants in the Burmese jungle.[4]

In Fourier's plan, at least five groups made up a series, "which again had a centre and two wings." Several series comprised an association of between 1,600 and 1,800 people, called a phalanx. Individuals were allowed to choose occupations, and work was supposed to be varied, with each person belonging to thirty or forty groups and working no more than two hours with each group. The idea was to provide complete self-fulfillment.

Each phalanx would be given about three square miles of farmlands and orchards, and a three-story communal building called a phalanstery would house all the residents. The building was supposed to include apartments, dining hall, kitchens, schools, recreational facilities, and even a hotel and ballroom. Members of a phalanx could be stockholders but that was not a requirement. Credit at a fixed rate was to be given for work, and each member would be charged for living expenses.

These are just a few of the vast number of details that appeared in Fourier's plan, which filled volumes. He believed his theories would spread and be applied around the world. Although some historians have called Fourier's view of utopia more like a fairy tale than a practical theory, several attempts were made in France to establish phalanxes. Not long after Fourier died in 1837, one of his disciples, Albert Brisbane, brought Fourierism to the United States.

Brisbane adopted the most workable aspects of Fourierism and described them in a book published in 1840, *Social Destiny of Man*. Brisbane's interpretation of Fourierism impressed Horace Greeley, who at the time was editor of the *New Yorker* magazine and later editor of the *New York Tribune*. Greeley became an enthusiastic supporter of Fourierism and provided space in the *Tribune* for a regular column on Fourieristic Associations and Phalanxes. During the early 1840s, the fanfare about Fourierism was so prolific that the doctrines became very popular in the United States. According to Holloway,

Associations and Conventions of Associationists began to spring up everywhere, but especially in the northeastern states, where a particularly sharp economic crisis had recently caused much unemployment. The anti-slavery movements also helped the growth of Fourierism; for as the former movement gathered momentum it began to include as one of its aims the abolition of wage-slavery as well as chattel-slavery . . . [5]

Phalanxes also began in Ohio, Indiana, Illinois, Iowa, Michigan, Wisconsin, and Texas. Forty to fifty of these communities were established between 1840 and 1860. All failed, usually within a year or two, although a few managed to survive for periods ranging from five to twelve years. Most did not have a unifying force such as religion to hold them together and often there were not enough farmers to provide the food needed for survival.[6]

• Far West Communes •

From about 1885 through the first decade of the 1900s, a number of communal experiments began in the Far West, in northern California, Oregon, and Washington. Some of these experiments were founded by religious groups such as the Mormons and the German Separatists, but others were prompted by socialist and labor movement leaders.

At least six communitarian experiments established in western Washington were based on the ideal of sharing social and economic activities. One of the first was the Puget Sound Co-operative Colony initiated in 1887, partly as a protest against the Chinese, who had been encouraged by business leaders to immigrate to Seattle and work for low wages. Several white labor organizations in Seattle agitated against the Chinese workers, causing riots and eventually bringing about the deportation of hundreds of Chinese. Among the members of these organizations was George Venable Smith, who founded the Puget Sound colony.

Smith was prompted by an anti-Chinese organizer, Judge

Peter Peyto Good, who had drawn up a plan for a utopian community with cooperative homes, hotels, and industries. Good died before his ideas could be put into effect, but Smith helped set up a corporation and select the colony site, a plot of land that was part of the small community of Port Angeles on the Olympic Peninsula, where there was a natural harbor within the Strait of Juan de Fuca and Puget Sound. To become a member of the colony, a person could buy shares of stock or one or more lot interests. The colony plan prohibited private enterprise, competition, and individual taxes, and called for each laborer to "work at his preferred trade," which somehow was supposed to provide all the basic needs of the colonists.[7]

For several months, George Smith toured such U.S. cities as San Francisco, St. Louis, Kansas City, Chicago, and Cleveland to publicize the colony plan and to attract members. The first colonists arrived at the townsite in January 1887, and by midyear there were more than 240. Although a lumber mill, a brick-making kiln, and shops and homes quickly appeared, a system of communal living never truly developed. In the first place, members did not share expenses equally, and the membership never included enough farmers, fishermen, and other laborers to do the work needed for survival.

The colony was governed by a board of trustees, including Smith, who was president. But some of the trustees became disenchanted with the cooperative venture and became determined to develop the land so that it would bring a profit to investors. The members voted Smith off the board, and he left the colony to practice law in Port Angeles. By the end of 1888, most of the colonists had left and the Puget Sound Co-operative became part of Port Angeles, now an important city on the Olympic Peninsula.

A communitarian experiment named Equality was set up in 1897 as a way to socialize the entire state of Washington. According to University of Washington historian Charles

LeWarne, the founders were members of a political party called the Brotherhood of the Co-operative Commonwealth. They hoped to develop a model cooperative to demonstrate

> the advantages of common production, distribution, and consumption of goods and a pure democratic government. Once secure, it could aid the establishment of similar colonies. If all were located in one sparsely populated state, the colonists could inaugurate a socialist government; when one state and its congressional delegation were captured, the Socialists would then convert the nation.[8]

Equality Colony began on a farm in Skagit County, Washington, and remained intact for about ten years. At its peak, there were about three hundred Equality colonists, bonded by their belief in socialism and communal living. But the experiment failed, as had many others before it, because of poor management and low production. Some members went off to establish their own colonies and others simply rejoined the mainstream society.

The most famous colony in the state was Home. It was established in 1896 by anarchists who believed in individualism and distrusted, even despised, authority of any kind. Home stressed tolerance and self-reliance, and for several years existed with little interference from neighboring communities. But when an anarchist unconnected with the community shot President William McKinley in 1901, outside forces became extremely hostile to Home colonists. Anyone with antigovernment views became suspect.

When the president died eight days later, groups of "patriots" and federal officials harassed the colony. Eventually, the threats against Home and its members subsided, and the colony continued to thrive. However, Home never was a communistic society and communal living was not part of daily life. People lived in their own homes and cooperative efforts were voluntary. Although Home continued as a colony until 1921, it, too, was the victim of internal strife, disorganization, and idealism that could not be applied in a practical manner.

Communistic or communal groups reached their peak in the United States during the nineteenth century, and by the first decades of the 1900s their numbers had dramatically declined. Financial problems caused many failures. Sometimes agriculture and simple trades did not provide enough income, and in some cases there was not enough money to expand or to recruit new members. Public, governmental, and media hostility sometimes contributed to the downfall of a community. And some communes failed because members lacked commitment to common goals.

Failures of the past, however, did not prevent later groups from trying to form communities outside the mainstream. Attempts at cooperative or communal living surged again after mid-century.

· 6 ·

MODERN
COMMUNAL LIVING

The late 1960s to the 1970s was a time when many people were disillusioned and disturbed by the Vietnam War and civil rights injustices in the nation. Tens of thousands of Americans sought alternative religions and lifestyles. Rejecting traditional ways, they set up anywhere from two thousand to as many as ten thousand communes. (Some estimates have ranged as high as thirty thousand.)

Those dropping out of mainstream society and demanding freedom of expression and religious liberty were frequently labeled "hippies," "flower children," "'60s people," or simply "people." They were likely to join communities or communes that many in the general public stereotyped as nests of revolutionaries or anarchists, filled with people intent on erotic pleasures.

Even as hippies turned to communal life, so did more traditional folks. From the 1950s on, communes were founded by Quakers, Mennonites, Baptists, Catholics, and other religious groups. The communities were not necessarily established as utopias. Rather, they were called "intentional communities," a term used to distinguish them from other settlements. They were usually set up as models for social change.

Some, for example, were patterned after Dorothy Day's hospitality houses of the 1930s and 1940s. In 1934, to help victims of the Great Depression, Day cofounded a Catholic Worker movement "based on religious principles, Catholic social teaching, personal moral responsibility, a decentralized society, the dignity of labor, nonviolence, works of mercy and voluntary poverty," as one writer put it.[1] Day herself continually spoke out against materialism in whatever form it took and worked to restore dignity and self-respect to the poor, homeless, and unwanted, particularly in New York City.

• COUNTERCULTURE COMMUNES •

Numerous firsthand reports during the 1960s and 1970s indicated that "doing drugs," nudity, group marriage, sexual experimentation, and other radical practices were part of hippie communes. But the main purpose of many counterculture communes was to escape technology and the fast-paced mainstream society. Many wanted to embrace a simple, tribal way of life. Back-to-nature communes were typical.

One example was a commune known as Morning Star (or Morningstar) located north of San Francisco, California, on thirty hilly acres owned by Lou Gottlieb, a folksinger with the Limelighters. Gottlieb and his friend, Ramon Sender, decided in 1966 to open up Gottlieb's retreat and invite the "naked, homeless, and harmless," and anyone who loved the land to share it. More than a hundred hippies from San Francisco took up residence the first year, living in tents, treehouses, shacks, or just out in the open. There were no sanitary or other modern facilities.

Ron Roberts, a sociologist who visited the commune in

1970, noted that only a four-wheel drive vehicle could maneuver the "dirt, clay, and rock road leading to the top of the Morningstar land," which Roberts thought was probably intentional since the commune was often harassed by police intent on arresting drug users. At the time, Morning Star was "not a commune in an absolute sense since everyone 'does his own thing' where and when he pleases," Roberts reported.[2] Another visitor noted that Gottlieb and Sender subscribed to the view that nature should "take its course. Nature knows best. Balance will be restored if only man will stop trying to 'fix things.' It is only man who persists in trying to foul-up nature."[3]

In 1968, a Gottlieb follower, Bill Wheeler, opened up his 320 acres about eight miles from Morning Star for another commune. A Yale graduate and architect, Wheeler had located his studio and home on his land, but allowed anyone who wanted to drop out of the conservative lifestyle of the larger society to settle on his acreage, which became known as Wheeler's Free Ranch.

Both Morning Star and Wheeler's Ranch were affected by problems associated with the transient nature of the populations. Historian Robert Hine reported that at Wheeler's Ranch

> hepatitis occasionally assumed serious proportions. The frontier remedies for it, radishes, ginseng, and special herb teas were prescribed. In the fall of 1968 racial tensions surfaced around the black members. There were drug excesses, as when punch was overdosed with LSD. . . . But most difficult . . . was the absence of unity among the various paths to self-awareness, between the competing teachings of Jesus or Buddha [or various gurus]. . . . Only the land, the place, held them together.[4]

Opposition from local authorities also created major difficulties. Because of health hazards and illegal drug use, the communes were subjected to numerous raids. In 1969 Morning Star was bulldozed by the county sheriff's department; four years later Wheeler's Free Ranch met the same fate.

• THE FARM •

Harassment by authorities was common for a communal group founded by Stephen Gaskin in the early 1970s. Gaskin earned a masters degree from San Francisco State College and taught an experimental course on mysticism and spiritual reawakening. He advocated self-fulfillment and believed that could be accomplished in a "developmentally progressive human habitat." In 1970 he left San Francisco to find such a place, and a year later he and more than three hundred followers settled on three square miles near Summertown, Tennessee, southwest of Nashville.

Described as a "cooperative enterprise of families and friends," the Farm, as it is called, was established as a community from which members could "by action and example, have a positive effect on the world as a whole." The Farm membership includes people from diverse religious backgrounds who consider themselves "free thinkers" and part of a spiritual community. As spokesperson Albert Bates explained: "In keeping with our deep reverence for life, we are pacifists, conscientious objectors, and most of us are vegetarians. On Sunday mornings many of us like to gather for group meditation and church services out in the meadow." [5]

Bates maintains a World Wide Web home page for the Farm with a link to frequently asked questions (FAQs) about the community's purpose, vision, and operations. In response to the question "What is the Farm?" the posted answer is:

Among ourselves we try to use agreement and mutual respect to generate a friendly working environment. We recognize that there are many paths toward realizing personal ideals and that people have a wide range of individual social values, but as a group, we do not accept the use of violence, anger or intimidation for solving problems. The fabric of our community is created by our friendship and respect for one another, and for our land. The institutions we have developed to organize our community have changed over the years and will probably change more. The Farm is not really what we are doing—it is how we are currently doing it. It is a process, rather than an end-result.

Another response to an FAQ explained that when the settlement began, people lived in old school buses and army tents, even in below-zero temperatures, until more permanent homes could be built from "salvaged, recycled and local materials. . . . On a budget of $1 per person per day and no grants, no food stamps, and no welfare, the 320 original settlers bought the land, erected the buildings, and became agriculturally self-sufficient within 4 years."

During those first years, the Farm began producing its own food supply, "established a construction company with more than 80 skilled craftsmen, built schools, greenhouses, dry goods and grocery stores, and automotive, welding, woodworking and machine shops." Members also "established child nutrition and sanitation standards, fire codes, and electrical, heating, lighting, and housing safety standards." By 1978, the Farm included a clinic, laboratory, and infirmary and also a wide range of innovative programs in preventive medicine, to serve members as well as people nearby who had little if any access to medical care.

At first Farm members operated their economy like a traditional communal society with all resources held in common. But in 1983, the commune reorganized. Now, to maintain the Farm, all adult members pay weekly or monthly dues "based on a budget that is drafted and redrafted at town meetings and voted on, line-by-line, once a year." Members earn their income in nearby towns working in local businesses or they work in one of the Farm's industries, which include a book publishing company, a soy dairy, and a dye works.

Summing up the present-day situation on the Farm, Bates noted:

> After more than two decades on this land, we appreciate even more the security of a tight-knit, compassionate, community environment. Our children have the freedom to explore the woods or go anywhere in our town in safety. The adults they interact with are honest and caring. We have very nurturing and healthful surroundings. No one has to carry the burden of his or her problems alone, or to bear the entire brunt of some catastrophe.
>
> We hold as a common belief that our outward works and goals should be seamless with how we choose to live—and we choose to live in community with one another. [6]

• INTENTIONAL COMMUNITIES •

The Farm is just one of hundreds of communities that are part of the intentional community (IC) movement, which actually began long before the 1960s. In 1948 Community Services Incorporated of Yellow Springs, Ohio, was formed to study small communities, but it later became a kind of networking organization for communal groups. Nearly four decades later, the association was incorporated as the Fellowship for Intentional Community (FIC), a nonprofit educational organization.

According to the Fellowship, its "work is based on four common values: cooperation, nonviolence, inclusivity, and unrestricted freedom to leave a group at any time." FIC promotes these values by acting as a clearinghouse for information about intentional communities, encouraging communication and trust between communities, and exchanging technical information and ideas for forming and maintaining communities. The organization also tries to broaden awareness in the larger society about intentional communities and their goals.[7]

Although an intentional community may appear to be the same as a commune or communal society, it was defined by one longtime communitarian, Dan Questenberry, as

> a group of people living cooperatively, dedicated by intent and commitment to specific communal values and goals. Life inside each community is managed using established decision-making processes. Generally, intentional communities place high value on the shared ownership or lease of common facilities—housing, land, commercial buildings—which often serves to demonstrate communal values and goals to the wider society.[8]

According to FIC, "more than 8,000 people, including over 2,000 children, live in 186 of the more established North American intentional communities and extended family groups," but they represent only a small portion of the total number of intentional communities throughout the continent. Millions of Americans share cooperative living arrangements but are not listed with the FIC. Most of the groups that FIC lists are located on rural sites and 80 percent of the rural communes hold their property in common. In addition, there are more than forty listed urban communities with common holdings.[9]

U.S. intentional communities and communal families are located in most of the states from Alaska to Florida and from Hawaii to Maine and in the District of Columbia. They are known by such names as Common Ground Community, Valley of Light, Cooper Street Household, Consciousness Village, the Family, Zen Bones Intentional Spirit, Catholic Worker House, Sojourners Community, Tolstoy Farm, and Koinonia Partners.

• COOPERATIVES AND COHOUSING COMMUNITIES •

Since the late 1980s, numerous intentional communities have been set up on a cooperative basis or designed as cohousing living arrangements in both rural and urban areas. Cooperatives include student cooperative housing on college campuses, houses in major cities that are maintained in common by residents, senior cooperative housing, or single houses with small intergenerational groups. The Hawk Circle Cooperative in Tipton, Iowa, is an example of the latter type.

Hawk Circle members live in a six-bedroom house on six acres, sharing costs and paying a monthly fee to cover their mortgage, utilities, food, and other expenses. Consensus is an important part of the cooperative, and members try to balance ideas and perspectives, believing that the best decisions come when the process is shared. Members describe their cooperative on their World Wide Web page:

> Our most basic belief is that all people are of value and all deserve respect. Members are expected to listen carefully to each other and work hard to find areas of agreement and understanding rather than contention. At all times, the Cooperative is intended to be a safe place, physically

and emotionally. We strictly forbid aggressive behavior, including physical and emotional abuse. We encourage diversity; it enriches our lives and strengthens the basic values and goals of the group.

While the Cooperative has specified values and policies concerning a number of issues, the open consideration of differing values and opinions strengthens the group by adding new perspectives and information. By pooling our differences we can make better decisions. Rather than dismissing ideas or people because they appear to be conservative, liberal or otherwise, we work to combine the best ideas available to us when making decisions. No one has a monopoly on the truth, but everyone holds a piece of it. We have all been raised in a competitive culture, and learning to live cooperatively is an ongoing and sometimes frustrating process. We do our best to encourage each other and improve our abilities to live cooperatively through discussions, workshops, and in day-to-day living.[10]

Cohousing is somewhat different from a cooperative living arrangement in that members usually live in their own homes and share land in common, which is developed as open space, gardens, and recreation areas. Usually there is a common house where residents can meet to share meals and to socialize. Typically, a neighborhood is designed and built by the people who live there. Working together cooperatively to make decisions creates a close community.

The basic concepts for this type of communal living were developed in Denmark. The movement in the United States was spurred by two architects, Katey McCamant and Chuck Durrett, who visited Danish communities and then toured the United States and Canada to present slides of the cohousing approach to living. In 1988 the two also published *Cohousing:*

A Contemporary Approach to Housing Ourselves. Since then dozens of cohousing communities have formed across the United States. Most maintain World Wide Web pages to describe who and what they are and their progress.

In Port Townsend, Washington, for example, the RoseWind Cohousing community is still in the process of developing. The RoseWind plan, like many cohousing communities, is set up to assure privacy and personal freedom but at the same time create a sense of community with "common areas and facilities which invite frequent use, as well as many opportunities for shared practical and social activities. From start to finish, the development and management of the community is in the hands of the people who live there."[11]

Whatever the type of intentional community established, most include members who strive to live in a cooperative, peaceful manner, respecting the environment and the diversity of people, and committed to helping each other. But these communities are seldom in the public spotlight. Instead, attention usually focuses on bizarre or dangerous cults that have also been part of the communal scene. Some of these groups have been or are so destructive that they are called "killer cults."

· 7 ·

CULTS

According to some estimates, about twenty million people have been involved in cults at one time or another since the 1970s, although that total varies with the way a cult is defined. Some would insist, for example, that one person's cult is another's religion and vice versa. But not all cults are based on shared religious beliefs. Some cultlike groups may be founded on strong political views. Others may form around environmental causes, health fads, self-improvement goals, or other shared interests.

Cults attract individuals from almost every walk of life and age group. People between the ages of eighteen and twenty-five are said to comprise the largest groups of cult members, perhaps because when some young people leave home for college or a job, they are lonely and want to be part of what appears to be a caring group. Thus they are vulnerable to cult recruiting.

In an article for *Redbook* magazine, Michael D'Antonio described how eighteen-year-old Diane Savill became involved in a cultlike group while a student at Rutgers University in New Brunswick, New Jersey. Savill joined a Bible study group called Campus Advance, which is affiliated with the International Churches of Christ, a sect that split off from the established Church of Christ. "Within days, she was immersed in round-the-clock study sessions. Deprived of sleep and food, Diane was convinced the group's leaders spoke for God when they said she must reject her parents, dump her boyfriend, and abandon any friends she couldn't convert to the faith."[1] Diane believed her new friends really cared about her because, as she said: "They 'love-bombed' me all the time, telling me how wonderful I was, how I was going to be such a good recruiter for their church."[2]

Group members used more than "love-bomb" tactics. They also used fear and guilt, backed by Bible verses taken out of context and distorted, to persuade Diane that she was destined for hell if she did not obey the biblical directives. "Her doubts were interpreted as blasphemous," D'Antonio reported. "After one all-night session, the leaders insisted that she stay to be baptized rather than go home for scheduled medical tests."

When Diane talked to her parents on the phone, her folks realized something was wrong and rushed to the campus. With the help of her parents and a campus minister, Diane was able to see that the self-proclaimed church group was trying to control her thoughts and actions. She was able to leave the group without any damaging effects.[3]

• TYPES OF CULTS •

Not all groups described as cults are harmful. Some, in fact, may be beneficial to members. However, the term *cult* is most often used to label a group considered radical by mainstream society. In the popular media and among critics of cults, the term almost always has a negative, even evil, connotation.

Certainly some cults are damaging—they may even destroy individual members. These cults are led by people who lust for power and believe they and their followers are chosen to bring their visions—often corruptions of established religious doctrines—to the world. Leaders claim to be god or godlike, and have both physical and spiritual control over their followers.

• IDENTIFYING DANGEROUS CULTS •

According to experts, a number of characteristics when taken all together distinguish a dangerous cult from a benign one. While these characteristics vary in degree and the way they are described, an individual who belongs to a damaging cult or cultlike group usually is

- deprived of basic freedoms;
- subjected to indoctrination and manipulation by a charismatic leader who is considered godlike or claims to be a god and controls member behavior through guilt, humiliation, and fear;
- required to obey all cult doctrine;
- pressured by other members to conform to group codes and behaviors;
- restricted or prevented from contact with people outside the cult;
- encouraged to violate personal ethics or deceive "outsiders" to prove group loyalty;
- restricted or prevented from leaving the cult.

Some of these characteristics would apply as well to members of communes and communistic groups discussed in previous chapters. Lifestyles of various communal groups can appear cultlike and abusive to many whose lives follow traditional patterns. But most people who join upright communities accept the group's principles and believe they are beneficial, and members who disagree with the standards are usually free to leave. In other words, in a benevolent community, free will is respected and members are encouraged to make their own choices.

Sometimes dangerous cults can be identified by the high-pressure sales pitches they use to attract new members. They are also likely to demand that members try to recruit friends and relatives to the group.

Some destructive cults encourage sexual relationships with group leaders or demand that members take part in violent acts on behalf of the leader or leaders. And a number of cults stockpile weapons, believing they need to protect themselves from outsiders, particularly government authorities. Perhaps the most destructive cults are those that preach an apocalyptic, doomsday message—the world is about to end and all will be destroyed if members do not follow the "right way" of the cult leader. Preparing for the end was the main purpose of a cult led by Reverend Jim Jones in the 1970s. Jones shocked the world when he forced more than nine hundred of his followers to commit suicide or ordered their murder, because he was convinced Armageddon was at hand.

• JIM JONES AND THE PEOPLE'S TEMPLE •

"The babies were the first to die. The cyanide was squirted into their little mouths with syringes," reported Marshall Kilduff, a correspondent with the *San Francisco Chronicle* who investigated the Reverend Jim Jones for more than two years and reported the horrific massacre of his followers in Jonestown, Guyana, in November 1978. After the babies were destroyed,

> then came the older children. They lined up in the central pavilion, where Jim Jones had addressed them so many times. This time they did his bidding again. They lined up to accept cups of Kool-Aid laced with poison.
>
> Next came their parents and the old folks. They, too, waited their turn to obey the orders to die, while armed guards stood by ready to shoot down any who tried to escape.

What kind of person would order the mass suicide of his followers? What prompts someone who claims to be a church leader to destroy his own congregation? Such questions have never been fully answered, but since the tragedy in the Guyana jungle, some facts about Jones have been recorded.

From early childhood, Jones was often on his own. His father was an invalid, and his mother worked in a factory and at odd jobs to support the family. Although a loner, Jones tended to be religious and would attend Sunday school at various churches in the small town of Lynn, Indiana, along the Ohio River. At times he pretended to be a preacher and gave sermons to any youngsters who would join his "congregation."

Jones left Lynn to attend high school in Richmond, Indiana, a larger town, and began to talk seriously about becoming a minister. He advocated racial equality, which was not well accepted in his part of Indiana or by his father, a member of the white supremacist Ku Klux Klan (KKK).

He attended Indiana University at Bloomington for a time and also Butler University in Indianapolis. Jones married during his college years, and he and his wife, Marceline, established a home in Indianapolis, where in 1956, at the age of 25, he started his own church, the People's Temple. The church was in a changing neighborhood and attracted a racially mixed congregation. In an attempt to apply his views on integration, Jones adopted seven children of African, Asian, and European ancestry and encouraged his followers to do likewise. He was a strong advocate for the poor, and he and his congregation raised funds to serve meals to the needy and for a jobs program.

Jones's activism, particularly his stand on civil rights for people of color, brought him and his family public criticism, harassment, and threats on their lives. Apparently Jones was sincere in his civil rights and social justice views, but he became increasingly dictatorial, demanding absolute loyalty and subjecting members to hours of interrogation if they criticized him or the church. He began to call himself a prophet of God and demanded that his followers call him "Father." He also claimed to be a divine healer, faking many "cures" by ordering a follower to pretend to be seriously ill and then experience a "miraculous" recovery. In addition, he predicted a nuclear holocaust, and he set out to find a refuge for his flock that would be safe from nuclear disaster and free of racists. He chose the town of Ukiah in northern California.

By the mid-1960s, Jones and the disciples who followed him from the Midwest had established themselves in Ukiah. Then in late 1972 the church and congregation moved to San Francisco. For several years, little was known about the secretive church, except for humanitarian activities that Jones and his aides publicized. However, a few members dropped out of the group and began to talk to reporters. These former members, who feared for their lives, told stories almost too bizarre to be believed.

According to ex-member reports, Jones controlled his followers through a variety of manipulative means. One was sex, which was often the subject of his sermons. To demean them, Jones would force members of his congregation to say they were homosexual or to strip in public. He often claimed that he was the only one allowed to have sexual intercourse, and even though he was still married, he demanded relations with selected women and men and sometimes minor children in his congregation. He ordered divorces and arranged new marriages. In some cases, he demanded that married couples abstain from sex and separated children from their parents, cutting family ties and making himself the central figure in their lives.

To maintain discipline, members were required to spy on one another and were subjected to intense, hostile interrogations about their activities and loyalties. Any infractions of the rules resulted in beatings, a form of abuse common in destructive cults. The beatings took place on the Temple stage with Jones calling out the number of each stroke. One teenager was beaten so badly that her behind looked like raw hamburger. The victims were required to go to the microphone and thank Jones for their punishment.

Young children who misbehaved were taken to the Temple infirmary, where nurses used an electric cattle prod or a heart defibrilator "to send an electric shock through the child's body," according to investigative reporter Marshall Kilduff. One member told him "there was never any sound but the screams of the children... When the sobbing, sniffling youngsters returned they were usually repeating 'Thank you, father. Thank you, father.'"[4]

• JONESTOWN •

News stories about Jones's activities and brutalities began to emerge about 1977, with a few negative accounts appearing in the San Francisco newspapers and in Associated Press reports.

Quietly, San Francisco officials looked into charges against Jones that included "homicide, child abduction, extortion, arson, battery, illegal drug use, diversion of welfare funds, and kidnapping. But the investigators . . . could not confirm a single charge, or develop enough evidence to sustain a single prosecution," according to Kilduff.[5]

The investigations convinced Jones that the FBI, CIA, and the U.S. media were conspiring to destroy his church. He decided to set in motion a plan he had harbored for years: to move his flock to an isolated jungle compound in Guyana (formerly a British colony) in South America, where about fifteen People's Temple members had been clearing land over a period of two years since the beginning of 1975. By late 1977 most members of the Temple had left San Francisco and were in Guyana. Some of the more than nine hundred congregants who eventually joined the compound were writing letters to friends and family describing a "paradise" on earth.

However, the few who were able to leave the church painted a vastly different picture, one of brutality, and some relatives of members called on the U.S. government to investigate. An eleven-page affidavit signed by an ex-member described the sunup-to-sundown workday, the punishments that had become evermore barbarous (ranging from dropping children by a rope into a well and dunking them under water to putting adults in three-by-three-by-six-foot sweatboxes) and the rehearsals for a mass suicide.

But no action was taken until U.S. Representative Leo Ryan of San Mateo, California, began to listen carefully to anxious relatives and ex-cult members and escorted fourteen relatives of cult members to Guyana in November 1978. For days, Ryan and his entourage were detained by Guyana officials in the capital city of Georgetown. Finally, Ryan, several news reporters, and a few of the relatives were permitted to fly to Port Kaituma, 150 miles from the capital, the only way except by boat and on foot to get to Jonestown.

Through reports from cult members in San Francisco, Jones had heard about Ryan and his entourage and ordered guards to stop them at Port Kaituma. He later sent a truck for the group and granted an interview, then allowed Ryan to stay overnight in the compound. The next day, Ryan, several reporters, and about twenty members who wanted to escape the compound were at the airstrip in Port Kaituma ready to fly out, when they were ambushed by Jones's guards. Representative Ryan, two news reporters and a news photographer, and a young woman who hoped to escape were shot to death. Ron Javers, a reporter, survived a gunshot wound in the shoulder. He learned days later about the hundreds in the cult who had committed suicide. Jones, too, was dead, leaving behind a still unsolved mystery about the people who followed a madman to live and die in a hell they themselves had helped create.

· 8 ·

MORE DAMAGING AND DESTRUCTIVE CULTS

The Jonestown suicides and murders prompted numerous investigations into cults, communal groups, and alternative religions that were considered bizarre, damaging, or destructive. Among the groups receiving the most attention since the 1980s have been the Unification church (Moonies), the Church of Scientology, the International Society for Krishna Consciousness (Hare Krishnas), and groups involved in satanism and witchcraft. None, however, gained as much media coverage as a religious sect, later labeled a cult, known as the Branch Davidians, many of whose members perished by fire after a standoff with federal agents in 1993.

Dozens of books on cults have been published in recent years, some of which are listed in the Further Reading section at the back of this book. Information about them is also available on the Internet. Some cultlike groups, cult critics, and ex-cult members have established World Wide Web home pages.

Only a few destructive cults are described here, but they are representative of how they operate. In addition, the stories from ex-cultists in the next chapter point up the dangers of some groups.

• THE MOVE CULT •

One cult that formed in the 1970s and gained widespread attention was the American Christian Movement for Life, or Move, for short. Vincent Leaphart, an unschooled black man in his fifties, and Donald Glassey, a white man in his twenties, founded Move to promote a back-to-nature philosophy. However, the commune was not in a rural or natural setting—it was in a large home owned by Glassey in a racially mixed urban neighborhood of West Philadelphia. Eventually thirty-five members crowded into the home—men, women, and children, among them "ex-cons and drug addicts," according to author James Boyle in his book *Killer Cults*.

Leaphart became leader of the commune, changing his name to John Africa, and all members except Glassey took the same last name. Glassey meantime began a yearlong writing project to record John Africa's teachings. The work eventually was used as the group's bible and was full of instructions on how to live a healthy life by returning to nature. It was also

> laced with conspiracy theories—among them that street drugs were a government plot to subjugate blacks—as well as detailed lessons on disparate subjects such as veterinary care, the tyranny of science, breast feeding, and the inevitablity of confrontation with the System [established authorities and institutions].[1]

Confrontations became common from 1973 to 1985, and increasing violence prompted Glassey to leave the cult. John Africa deliberately sought media attention. He and his followers appeared at numerous public events, screaming obscenities and their opposition to "the system." Yet they seemed to have no special political goal, and they became a public nuisance. According to Boyle,

> Neighbors regularly called the cops about the Move dogs, cats, and other animals roaming freely; the junk, garbage, and human waste tossed out of windows; the naked toddlers wandering around unsupervised; the racket and the threats.[2]

Police kept a constant watch on the group, and members often tried to provoke a confrontation by bellowing at officers through loudspeakers set up outside their headquarters, daring them to attack. Move members were arrested hundreds of times, usually for health and zoning violations. In August of 1978 a shootout with police resulted in the death of a police officer. Three other officers and four firefighters who had blasted the house with water hoses were wounded. Nine Move cultists were convicted of the crimes and sentenced to life in prison. The remaining cultists left town, and the mayor of Philadelphia ordered the Move house torn down.

However, that was not the end of the cult. A few years later, members established themselves in another West Philadelphia house and once more began deliberate confrontations with police. Neighbors again began complaining about the filth, noise, and stench from Move headquarters. In May 1985 police ordered cultists out of the house, but they replied with the taunt "Come and get us."[3] After that, the scene was like a virtual hell, with police firing into the house and firefighters pouring water into it. Then police dropped a canvas bag with a bomb on the house, blowing a hole in the roof and setting that building and other homes on the block afire.

In the Move house, eleven people died, including John Africa. Sixty-two homes in the neighborhood were destroyed.

"Never before in U.S. history had civil authorities dropped a bomb on an American city, and the reaction to the debacle was fierce," Boyle wrote.[4] Although many Americans were opposed to Move, they were highly critical of the police attack and Mayor W. Wilson Goode who ordered it. Few believed it was necessary to bomb a house and burn down an entire neighborhood just to get rid of a cult.

• THE ECCLESIA ATHLETIC ASSOCIATION •

In 1980 Eldridge Broussard Jr. founded another urban cult, the Ecclesia Athletic Association. Broussard, along with several followers who believed he was anointed by God, sold their possessions and opened a group home in an abandoned bakery in the predominantly black neighborhood of Watts in Los Angeles. There they began their efforts to work with inner-city children, using discipline and athletics as part of a program to get kids out of the ghetto through Olympic competition. A few years later, they moved part of their operations to a rural area near Portland, Oregon, where they housed and "trained" fifty-six children.

In 1988 after Broussard's eight-year-old daughter Dayna died from a brutal beating, federal authorities began an investigation of Ecclesia. To discipline his daughter for some unknown misbehavior, Broussard ordered that food be withheld from her. When Dayna stole something to eat, she was punished by one of Broussard's followers, who struck the girl 250 times with a garden hose, plastic pipe, and a leather barber strop. The defendant charged with killing the girl testified that Dayna was splashed with water to revive her during the beating. She died that evening of what the coroner declared was blunt-force head injuries. According to court testimony, children routinely received similar beatings as punishment, particularly when they would not or could not perform athletic drills.

The federal indictment against the group charged that Ecclesia and its leader planned to train the children for the Olympics and obtain corporate sponsorship for their performances. Broussard died of natural causes in September 1988 before his trial began, but seven Ecclesia followers were sentenced to prison terms for their part in Dayna's death and for violating the civil rights of the other children.

• HOLY ALAMO CHRISTIAN CHURCH •

Another more repressive and violent cult leader, Tony Alamo, whose real name is Bernie Lazar Hoffman, and his wife, Susan, established the Holy Alamo Christian church and commune in Saugus, California. The Alamos began their operations in Los Angeles in the 1960s, taking teenage drug users off the streets and providing them with food and shelter. The two gained attention during the 1970s and 1980s because of reports that they controlled their followers through intimidation and beatings. They also exploited their disciples, forcing them into slave labor to produce goods for a multimillion-dollar clothing chain owned by the Alamos. The businesses, located in California, Arkansas, and Tennessee communes, manufactured rhinestone-studded denim jackets that were very popular and sold for up to $600 apiece. Only Alamo and his wife profited from the sales.

In 1988 Alamo ordered his followers to punish an eleven-year-old member, Jeremiah Miller, by beating him with a three-foot wooden paddle more than 140 times, according to a lawsuit alleging child abuse filed on the victim's behalf. Jeremiah's beating was punishment for what was called misbehavior, such as asking a science question in a history class and wearing an Alamo-designed scarf without permission. After authorities began investigating the case in 1989, Alamo disappeared. He was captured in 1991 in Tampa Bay, Florida, where he lived in a $300,000 house and continued to operate his lucrative business ventures. He was arrested on a number of charges, including child abuse, threats on the life of a federal judge, and tax evasion.

Alamo was convicted in 1994 of filing a false tax return and evading an income tax debt of more than $2 million. After he received a prison sentence, the child abuse charge was dropped because a further conviction would not add more than a few months to the federal sentence. Jeremiah Miller, however, had previously won $550,000 in damages in a civil lawsuit in 1990.

• THE GURU RAJNEESH •

Still another infamous cult leader of the 1980s was Bhagwan (meaning god) Shree Rajneesh, who left Poona, India, because of tax and other legal disputes, and came to the United States in 1981. Rajneesh preached a blend of Eastern religion, pop psychology, and free love, and with his followers, known as Rajneeshees, set up a commune called Rajneeshpuram on sixty-four thousand acres in a mountainous area near Portland, Oregon. A fifteen-mile winding road led to the community. According to a *Washington Post* report in 1985, "In less than four years, the Rajneeshees—working 12 hours a day, seven days a week . . . paved roads, created a man-made lake, [and] built housing."

Among the three hundred buildings were "cafeterias; a disco with a bar and gambling tables; a modern 147-room hotel; a small shopping mall with boutiques, jewelry store, hair salon, pizzeria and bookstore; and a 4,000-foot runway for the Air Rajneesh fleet of DC3s. Followers [made] their way around the huge commune on a fleet of yellow school buses labeled Rajneesh Buddhafield Transport." The community also included "a vineyard, intensive farming projects, [and] a sophisticated recycling project."[5]

Eventually the commune became home for about four thousand Rajneeshees, wearing red robes and pendants with Rajneesh's photo. In addition, two thousand others visited for weeks or months at a time to study with Bhagwan. Followers bought their guru a fleet of Rolls Royce cars, one for each day of the month, and when Rajneesh drove into the commune he was greeted by members lining the roadway chanting, playing instruments, and jumping and weeping with joy.

Although the Rajneeshees considered their incorporated city a utopia, they were often compared to cultists in Jonestown. They believed they would be attacked by federal authorities, and their compound was heavily armed. Guards traveled with Rajneesh wherever he went.

Over a period of four or five years, numerous complaints were filed against the cult, and people living in the nearby town of Antelope were incensed when the guru's followers took over all the elected positions in the town and changed its name to City of Rajneesh.

In 1985 Oregon law officials issued criminal indictments against some cult members and their leader. Among those indicted was Ma Anand Sheela, Rajneesh's tough-talking, gun-toting personal secretary. She controlled the commune like a dictator and was convicted of numerous crimes: "attacking the guru's doctor with a poison-filled syringe, setting fire to the county planning office, giving glasses of poisoned water to two county officials, creating the largest electronic eavesdropping system in state history, arranging 400 sham marriages so foreign disciples could stay in the United States, and masterminding a food poisoning outbreak that sickened 750 diners at restaurants in The Dalles, 80 miles away."[6]

Sheela served twenty-nine months of a four-and-a-half-year sentence in a federal prison. Other commune members also were convicted of various crimes, including a plot by four leaders to murder former U.S. Attorney Charles Turner of Portland in an attempt to derail a grand jury investigation.

In 1985 when Rajneesh tried to fly out of Oregon one night, he was arrested on a charge of immigration fraud. He was eventually deported to India, where he died five years later of heart failure.

However, that was not the end of his cult, and there were still other destructive groups in the United States. In the 1990s Americans were shocked once more by news of the Branch Davidians. Living in a compound called Mt. Carmel near Waco, Texas, the Davidians were of little public interest until they came under siege by federal agents—officials of the FBI and the Alcohol, Tobacco, and Firearms (ATF) agency.

• FOUNDING THE BRANCH DAVIDIANS •

When the federal agents surrounded the Davidian compound, it was under the leadership of a self-proclaimed messiah who began life in 1959 as Vernon Howell. He was given his father's family name, although his father never married his mother. Vernon lived for a time with his grandparents, who recalled that at four or five years old, he loved to go to church. He became an avid student of the Bible, especially the New Testament.

Like Jim Jones before him, Howell began preaching to anyone who would listen to him. He became a religious fanatic, condemning to hell everyone who would not accept his brand of salvation and holy living. He also loved rock-and-roll and taught himself to play guitar, sometimes setting up to perform in an open-air pavilion near a community pool.

Howell joined the Seventh-Day Adventist (SDA) church in Tyler, Texas, when he was in his twenties. The SDA church is basically a Protestant evangelical denomination that refers to the Bible for basic doctrine but also to the teachings of Ellen Gould Harmon White, who organized the church in the mid-1800s and established a Saturday sabbath. Adventists believe intensely in end-of-times prophesies that predict a great battle between the Antichrist and his evil forces, who will persecute the righteous, God's true believers.

After joining the church, Howell attended a series of revival meetings called Revelation Seminars that, according to one news report, "featured dramatic, even frightening images in a multimedia portrayal of Armageddon," where the struggle between good and evil is expected to take place. The video featured "earthquakes, pestilence, and religious persecutions . . . combined with . . . current events that seemed to point toward the imminent millennium," the thousand year reign of Christ on earth. Howell was deeply affected by the portrayal but was convinced that there was something missing in the video. There was no mention of the seven seals, as described in Revelation, the final book of the biblical New Testament that includes prophecy about the end of the world. The seals bind a scroll that predicts the afflictions to come before the Apocalypse. Only a new prophet would be able to open the seventh seal, and Howell believed he was that person.[7]

During one Saturday service in Tyler, Howell brazenly and without an invitation took over the pulpit, preaching and haranguing about his biblical interpretations for forty-five minutes. After that, he was no longer welcome. He began attending a church in Mt. Carmel, near Waco, Texas. The church was founded in the early 1900s by Victor Houteff, a Bulgarian immigrant who once had enthusiastically embraced the Seventh-Day Adventist doctrines. Houteff had broken away from the Adventists to preach what he called a divinely inspired truth regarding the correct understanding of "the remnant," a term for the 144,000 people who would be saved at the Second Coming of Christ while the rest of the world was destroyed.

Like many other self-proclaimed "prophets" before him, Houteff searched for a place to establish a community of his followers, and after investigating sites in various parts of Texas, settled on a 189-acre tract of land near Waco. Houteff named his colony Mt. Carmel Center, which eventually included a total of 377 acres. By the late 1930s, about 125 people had joined the group. They became known as Davidians, deriving their name from Houteff's belief that the colony would establish a City of David, a New Jerusalem, a Zion—in short, a "holy city"—in Palestine.

After Houteff's death in 1955, there were numerous squabbles among the Davidians about who would lead them. The group, which had by then taken the name Branch Davidians, disbanded for a time, selling much of the Mt. Carmel land. But in the 1960s they began again under the leadership of Ben and Lois Roden, who claimed to own the rights to Mt. Carmel property because they were Houteff's spiritual heirs.

By the time Vernon Howell joined the Branch Davidians in the early 1980s, he had spent a couple of years in California, hoping to become a rock star. When he failed, Howell returned to Texas and quickly became not only a rock band leader, but also the disputed head of the Davidians. Mt. Carmel leader Ben Roden had died, and the church was under the control of Lois Roden. However, her leadership was constantly questioned and threatened by her son, George, who "believed he had been groomed from infancy to become the great leader of the Branch Davidians," according to Brad Bailey and Bob Darden, authors of a book on the Davidian cult.

But in 1983, George's mother anointed "Vernon as the next prophet, bypassing George completely."[8]

The next year Howell married a fourteen-year-old girl, Rachel Jones, whose parents were Davidians. Vernon and Rachel eventually had two children. As the years went on, Howell created a harem of women and girls, one of them Rachel's twelve-year-old sister, who had three daughters fathered by Howell. Howell also reportedly became sexually involved with Lois Roden, who was by then in her late sixties.

Throughout 1984 George Roden challenged Howell's leadership with numerous legal proceedings, and in 1985 forced Vernon Howell and his followers out of Mt. Carmel. The group set up a primitive camp of unheated shacks and rusty buses, with no toilet facilities, in a woods near Palestine, Texas. At the same time, Howell arranged performances for his Messiah rock band at bars and saloons in and around Waco.

In 1987, while Roden continued his legal battles to maintain control of the compound, Howell with seven of his men returned to Mt. Carmel. They invaded the place, prompting a shootout with Roden and a maintenance man, who was the only other person around at the time.

Howell and the followers with him were charged with attempted murder. The seven were eventually acquitted, and in Howell's case, a mistrial was declared. Later on, charges were dismissed.

Roden became increasingly deranged, and in 1989 was charged with murder in a case unrelated to Howell. Roden was found innocent by reason of insanity and was sentenced to the state mental hospital for an indefinite period of time.

With Roden no longer on the scene, Howell was in complete control of Mt. Carmel and its members, who turned over most if not all of their resources to him. Howell had been preaching, gathering converts, and soliciting funds from groups of Seventh-Day Adventists across the United States and in Australia and Great Britain. In 1990 he legally changed his name to David Koresh, stemming from his belief that he was head of the biblical House of David. Koresh in Greek means Cyrus, the name of a Persian king who freed the Jews from captivity and allowed them to return to Israel.

• DAVID KORESH AND RANCH APOCALYPSE •

Few outside the compound were aware of David Koresh's teachings or the kinds of activities that went on at Ranch Apocalypse, as Koresh began to call it. But beginning in 1991, stories slowly emerged as some followers left the cult and related their experiences. Apparently Koresh surrounded himself with a guard of about twenty "lieutenants" known as the Mighty Men. These guards helped him stockpile weapons, including assault rifles, taught cult members how to shoot to kill, and kept strangers at bay by greeting them with drawn rifles.

Koresh also ordered women and girls—but not men—to take part in military maneuvers, forcing them to drill in temperatures over 100 degrees. He enforced strict vegetarian dietary rules, some of which had little meaning, such as forbidding the combination of oranges and grapes at a meal, but at the same time he indulged in hamburgers and any other foods he enjoyed, without regard to a dietary code.

Marc Breault, a member of the Messiah band, was one of the first defectors to speak out against Koresh. After about three years with the cult, Breault left the Branch Davidians in 1989, returned to his home in Australia, and immediately began a campaign to free other cultists from Koresh's influence. He wrote a book about his experiences and also contributed manuscripts for posting on the Internet's World

Wide Web pages. In 1992, for example, he explained Koresh's basic theology of the seven seals.

According to Breault, who has consistently referred to Koresh as Howell, Koresh convinced his followers that they could go to heaven if they learned the secrets of a scroll protected by the seven seals that no one could open except the Lamb of God. Koresh spent hours convincing his listeners that he could reveal the secrets of the seven seals, thus in his logic, he was "the Lamb." His group followed him blindly and centered their lives around him because they were fully convinced he was the only one capable of interpreting the seals.[9] They believed David Koresh was Jesus Christ and they were prepared to make the ultimate sacrifice for him. As one ex-Davidian who was sent home because he was "going in and out of reality" stated: "I would have killed for him [Koresh]. I would have died for him. I didn't want to leave."[10]

Breault also expressed concern about Koresh's obsession with sex and his pronouncement during a Bible study that "as the Lamb of God, [Koresh] was entitled to have all the women and girls sexually. Only he had the right to procreate. [Koresh] stated that he would give married couples time to adjust to this new 'revelation,' as he called it."[11]

Breault was especially worried about what Koresh "was doing to young girls." He cited as an example an eleven-year-old girl, Kiri Jewell, who was being primed to become one of Koresh's "wives," joining her divorced mother, Sherri, as part of Koresh's harem. After leaving the cult and searching for months, Breault was able to locate Kiri's father, David, who was a disc jockey at radio station WNDU in South Bend, Indiana. After Breault told David Jewell what was going on with his daughter, Jewell was able to gain custody of Kiri. He was at her side when she was called to testify at a 1995 congressional hearing on the events that transpired at Mt.

Carmel. During that hearing, Kiri, who was then fourteen years old, read a statement that included what one reporter called "chilling" details of

> the day she found herself alone with Koresh in a Waco, Tex., motel room. He kissed her and rubbed his private parts against hers, she recalled, saying she "had known this would happen sometime, so I just laid there and stared at the ceiling. I didn't know how to kiss him back."
>
> "I was all freaked out," said Kiri, who also recounted Koresh's graphic description of sex acts with other women and children.

In addition, Kiri described the cult's suicide plan and Koresh's instructions on how to shoot oneself "if necessary in this battle with Babylon."[12] That battle, Koresh preached, would be with infidels—unbelievers—and to him, his "prophecy" was fulfilled when federal authorities surrounded his compound in February 1993.

After reports from Koresh's neighbors and others that the cult was amassing an arsenal in preparation for the Apocalypse, ATF agents planned to raid Mt. Carmel and administer a search warrant for weapons. But Koresh and his followers received a warning about the raid and ambushed the government agents when they arrived. According to news reports, gunfire continued for forty-five minutes. Four ATF agents and six Branch Davidians were killed.

As news of the shootout spread across the nation, TV crews and reporters arrived by the dozens to witness what became a fifty-one-day standoff in which FBI and ATF officials tried to force Koresh and his followers out of their compound. Only a few Davidians left the building before it was consumed by fire on April 19, killing eighty people, including Koresh and twenty-two children.

Ever since the terrible fire, which many Americans watched with horror on TV, there has been controversy over who was responsible for the blaze. Some insist to this day that federal officials were responsible, because they did not heed warnings that Davidians would fight to the end or commit suicide rather than surrender to the ATF and FBI. Others claim that Koresh had planned and ordered his followers to set the compound afire. In either case, Davidians believed that Mt. Carmel was a sanctuary where the faithful could safely await destruction of the world. Even when this proved to be untrue, some followers simply decided not to escape the blaze because they expected eternal life. Others were unable to get out safely.

Numerous articles and books have been written about David Koresh and his Apocalypse Ranch, some critical of the Branch Davidians and some in support of the cult. Whatever the view, and despite information revealed about Koresh and his followers or other destructive cults, such groups continue to form and some people continue to live by the dictates of a charismatic, fanatical leader rather than thinking critically for themselves.

• 9 •

BEING WARY AND
MAKING DISTINCTIONS

Just eighteen months after the Waco disaster, a Swiss-based apocalyptic cult called the Order of the Solar Temple, with branches in the United States and Canada, made headlines worldwide. In October 1994, fifty-three members of the cult died in ritual murders and suicides. The dead included the cult's leader, Canadian Luc Jouet, who preached that death was "pure illusion" and that the world would soon end in a terrible conflagration brought about by the immoral acts of humankind.

A little more than a year later, in December 1995, French authorities investigated a scene in a remote Alpine forest, where they found the burned bodies of sixteen more members of the Solar Temple. "Authorities believe that the dead were shot, drugged, or asphyxiated before they were burned," and "suspect that the killers are among the dead," according to a report from the Associated Press.[1]

Fears about destructive cults escalated worldwide during the 1990s. Experts on alternative religions and cults believe there will be more terrorist attacks or collective murders/suicides. The Third Millennium, the thousand-year period beginning with the year 2000, has special significance to groups of religious zealots. Cults based on millennialism, a belief in Christ's reign of one thousand years after a catastrophic war or natural disaster, may be particularly prone to violence because the cult members believe God has given them the right to rid the world of "evil." As the righteous, they will then go to paradise. In short, religious doctrine justifies potential violence.

• DOOMSDAY CULTS ON THE RISE? •

Whether or not cults commit terrorist acts, apocalyptic groups are expected to grow in number during the years ahead. In addition, existing groups based on doomsday beliefs continue to preach their end-times doctrine. One group called the Church Universal and Triumphant (CUT), which began in Southern California but is now based in Montana, requires members to build bomb shelters in preparation for the nuclear war and economic collapse that they predict for the future. CUT's leader, Elizabeth Prophet, based her predictions on what she claimed were direct messages from "ascended masters," who include Jesus, Buddha, and King Arthur.

Jehovah's Witnesses have long warned that Armageddon is approaching. Their *Watch Tower* and *Awake* publications, which members distribute door-to-door as they bear witness to their beliefs, carry graphic descriptions along with illustrations predicting what the end of the world will be like. In a story posted on the Internet, one former member of the Witnesses recalled how she felt as a young girl when she sat

for what seemed like hours, looking and studying every detail in these pictures. The little babies being destroyed, old men and women sucked into the earth, people screaming with their arms outstretched, as if pleading for help. I did not see these as being wicked people . . . . I felt sorry for them. It broke my heart. I had nightmares all the time for several years.[2]

Being indoctrinated with doomsday predictions or other ideas that instill fear, guilt, and dependency makes it very difficult for a person to leave a group. When members of alternative religious groups and cults do break away, it may be because they are disillusioned with a leader and the philosophy or religious doctrine. Or perhaps family members or friends hire a counselor to intervene or families intervene on their own, convincing their loved ones to cut their ties with a controlling group.

After leaving a group, some ex-cultists continue to suffer from fear and guilt. Some go through periods of deep depression and need counseling or the help of support groups. Since the 1970s, various organizations have formed to provide counseling for ex-cultists and to distribute information about the possible dangers of today's cults or cultlike groups.

To support and help cult survivors, some ex-cultists and former members of alternative religious groups have posted their stories (and warnings) on Internet bulletin boards and World Wide Web pages. Why? Because cults use the Internet to reach millions of potential converts, according to Janja Lalich, a former cult member who now manages a support group for ex-cultists and has coauthored two books on the subject.

Cult members are part of numerous Internet forums and newsgroups that focus on meditation, self-help, and so-called New Age thinking. Lalich explained that cultists engage in "love-bombing," repeatedly praising potential members, "then slowly they reveal their path to a solution" for a particular problem or issue. But when members of a group tell you "they've got the one answer, the one path, there's something suspect there." Lilich warned, "They'll try to get you to spend money, sign up for something."[3]

Among those who have posted their stories on the Internet are former members of

- the Church of Jesus Christ of Latter-day Saints (Mormons);

- the Unification church (Moonies);

- the Church of Scientology, founded in 1955 by L. Ron Hubbard, a former science-fiction author;

- the International Society of Krishna Consciousness (Hare Krishnas), based on Hindu teachings and initiated in the United States during the 1960s by the late A.C. Bhaktivedanta Swami Prabhupada of Bengal;

- the Local Church and the Living Stream, based in Anaheim, California, and founded by a Chinese immigrant known as Witness Lee, who claims to have established the "only true church."

• AN EX-MOONIE TURNED COUNSELOR •

One individual posting his views about cults on the Internet is Steven Hassan, a former Moonie. Hassan is now a licensed counselor and "has been involved in educating the public about mind control and destructive cults for nearly twenty years," his home page states.[4] When Hassan was a student at Queens College, New York, he was recruited into the Unification church, which became popular in the United States during the 1970s.

The church was founded in Seoul, Korea, in 1954 by Sun

Myung Moon, who claimed to be God's messenger, the successor to Jesus Christ. Like many other self-styled prophets before him, Moon preached that he would create a kingdom of God on earth. Moon brought his church to the United States in 1959, but he gained little attention until the 1970s and 1980s, when he set up numerous private businesses to support his plan for a worldwide theocracy. Through dozens of these "front organizations," Moon acquired great wealth, which was tax-exempt because he claimed these organizations were part of his church structure. However, in the early 1980s he was convicted and served a jail term for income tax evasion. He was released in 1985.

While in the United States, even when in prison, Moon sent out an army of young people, known as Moonies, to solicit funds for his church by selling flowers, peanuts, and other items to passersby on street corners and in other public places. Steven Hassan was part of that army in the 1970s, and he eventually became a high-ranking official of the church. Then, while recuperating after a serious car accident, his parents took the opportunity to bring in several former Moonies to "deprogram" him.

Deprogramming is a controversial tactic to get cult members to realize that they were "programmed"—conditioned to think and behave in a way determined by the cult or alternative religious group. In some early instances of deprogramming, cult members were kidnapped and forced, sometimes by brutal means, to remain in a secured place. Then a deprogrammer in marathon sessions of talk and more talk tried to destroy the cult member's belief system. Some deprogramming still goes on, but it is more common today for those who leave a cult to go through what is called exit counseling.

Hassan renounced the Moonies for their dishonesty and gave police a set of documents describing Moon's secret plan to "take over the world." Hassan became an exit counselor and also wrote a critically acclaimed book, *Combating Cult Mind Control*, published in 1988. In his book, Hassan explains how he trains family and friends to use nonthreatening techniques to help a person who has been under the control of a group to think critically.[5]

• SAVING YOUNG CHILDREN OF CULTS •

A well-known clinical psychologist, Margaret Singer of the University of California at Berkeley, has lectured widely on techniques to help former cultists, particularly young children and teenagers who come out of destructive cults. Usually these young people are in "great need of support, for they face extraordinary adjustment problems," Professor Singer writes.

Singer and other counselors point out that children growing up in cults may emerge from them with deep emotional scars. Frequently, youngsters have been terrorized by physical brutality and constant warnings about the evils of the world. They have no self-esteem, no understanding of positive family relationships, usually cannot make independent decisions, and may exhibit inappropriate sexual behavior because of sexual abuse. It is common for cult children to be undernourished and in poor health.

Yet, as Singer shows in her book *Cults in Our Midst*, children born and raised in a cult can be taught to reconnect with the outside world. The task is sometimes enormous, but Singer provides examples of young people who have survived and now lead productive lives. However, she stresses that "many children reared in cults are truly victims who are especially alone and without advocates." In her view, family members, friends, counselors, teachers, and others have the responsibility of providing a support network of loving and understanding people to help ex-cultists carry on.[6]

• DESTRUCTIVE CULTS VS. •
SUPPORTIVE COMMUNITIES

In spite of all the publicity given to negative, dangerous, and sometimes evil aspects of some cults, it is important to remember that destructive cults and communes attract only a small percentage of Americans. These groups are not the same as those in which members strive to maintain a cooperative, supportive, peaceful way of life. Nor are they comparable to the long-lived communal groups of the past that were held together by a common mission: bettering humankind.

What about communal groups today? What are their prospects for survival? Obviously, there is no perfect community. Utopia exists only in fiction or in our imagination.

If communes of today thrive, it will be due in part to members having the freedom to think for themselves and being able to cooperate with one another. Survival will also depend on whether members are able to overcome envy, greed, intolerance, and other characteristics that cause friction and dissent.

Despite social and economic problems that threaten the stability of communal living, there will probably continue to be religious people who search for a Zion or a paradise, and others who will seek to set up secular communes. They may do so because they want to live in an environment that promotes equality, cooperation, fellowship, peace, protection of natural resources, and other qualities considered beneficial to members and the larger society. However, for those who search for community—indeed, for all who seek a better world—whether motivated by religious beliefs or social/economic concerns, the challenge in the years ahead, is to apply some of the humanitarian ideals of communal living to the real, pluralistic world that we all share.

SOURCE NOTES

CHAPTER 2

1. *Souvenir of Zion City*, booklet, no publishing date.
2. Lease agreement in author's collection.
3. From a photograph of this billboard called "A Perfectly Plain Notice" in the author's collection.
4. William Carpenter, *One Hundred Proofs that the Earth is Not a Globe*. Special Ed. (Zion, Ill.: Wilbur Glenn Voliva publisher, 1929), 12.
5. Ibid., 17.

CHAPTER 3

1. Joanita Kant, *The Hutterite Community Cookbook*. (Intercourse, Penn.: Good Books, 1990), 18.
2. George B. Lockwood, *The New Harmony Movement*. (New York: D. Appleton and Co., 1905), 12.
3. Ibid., 20–22.
4. Bertha M. H. Shambaugh, *Amana: The Community of True Inspiration*. (Reproduction of the original 1908 book, State Historical Society of Iowa, 1988), 384–386.

5. Ibid., 139.

6. Lawrence L. Rettig, *Amana Today: A History of the Amana Colonies from 1932 to the Present* (South Amana, Iowa: apparently self-published, 1975), 7–8.

7. Ibid., 9.

8. Ibid., 23.

CHAPTER 4

1. Mark Holloway, *Heavens on Earth: Utopian Communities in America 1680-1880.* 2nd Ed. (New York: Dover Publications, 1966), 56.

2. Stephen J. Stein, ed., *Letters from a Young Shaker: William S. Byrd at Pleasant Hill* (Lexington, Ky.: University Press of Kentucky, 1985), 57.

3. Quoted in Charles Nordhoff, *The Communistic Societies of the United States: From Personal Observations.* (Originally published by Harper & Brothers, 1875. New York: Dover Publications, 1966), 178.

4. Ibid.

5. Ibid., 166.

6. Maren Lockwood Carden, *Oneida: Utopian Community to Modern Corporation.* (Originally published by John Hopkins Press, 1969. New York: Harper & Row, 1971), 19.

7. New Testament, Matthew 22:30.

8. Quoted in Carden, *Oneida*, 73.

9. Ibid., 74.

10. Robert V. Hine, *Community on the American Frontier: Separate But Not Alone.* (Norman, Okla.: University of Oklahoma Press, 1980), 210.

11. Church Educational System, *Church History in the Fulness of Times.* (Salt Lake City, Utah: The Church of Jesus Christ of Latter-day Saints, 1993), 44.

12. Ibid., 96–97.

13. Mary Ann Hafen, *Recollections of a Handcart Pioneer of 1860.* (Lincoln, Neb: University of Nebraska Press, 1983), 22.

14. Ibid., 23.

15. Ibid., 26.

CHAPTER 5

1. Mark Holloway, *Heavens on Earth: Utiopian Communities in America 1680–1880.* 2nd ed. (New York: Dover Publications, 1966), 16.

2. Arthur Bestor, *Backwoods Utopias: The Sectarian Origins and the Owenite Phase of Communitarian Socialism in America, 1663–1829. 2nd enlarged ed.* (Philadelphia: University of Pennsylvania Press, 1970), 58.

3. *Holloway,* Heavens, 105.

4. Ibid., 135.

5. Ibid., 142.

6. Robert V. Hine, *Community on the American Frontier: Separate But Not Alone.* (Norman, Okla.: University of Oklahoma Press, 1980), 209–210.

7. Charles Pierce LeWarne, *Utopias on Puget Sound.* (Seattle: University of Washington Press), 18.

8. Ibid., 56.

CHAPTER 6

1. Tim McCarthy, "Light of Day Shines Yet at Catholic Worker." *National Catholic Reporter,* 21 May 1993, 9–12.

2. Ron E. Roberts, *The New Communes: Coming Together in America.* (Englewood Cliffs, N.J.: Prentice Hall, 1971), 48.

3. Richard Fairfield, *Communes USA: A Personal Tour.* (Baltimore, Md.: Penguin Books, 1972), 249.

4. Robert V. Hine, *Community on the American Frontier: Separate But Not Alone.* (Norman, Okla.: University of Oklahoma Press, 1980), 236.

5. Albert Bates, "The Farm FAQ." Internet World Wide Web page: <http://www.gaia.org/farm/general/farmfaq.html>

6. Ibid.

7. FIC Editorial Board, "Fellowship in the Nineties: A Continental Network Open to All." Internet World Wide Web page: <http://www.well.com/user/cmty/index.htm>

8. Dan Questenberry, "Who We Are: An Exploration of What 'Intentional Community' Means." Internet World Wide Web page: <http://www.well.com/user/cmty/fic/cdir/art/05quest.htm>

9. Ibid.

10. Rollie at Hawk Circle, "Hawk Circle Cooperative." Internet World Wide Web page: <http://www.well.com/user/cmty/hawkcircle.html>

11. "RoseWind Cohousing, Pt. Townsend, WA." Internet World Wide Web page: <http://www.eskimo.com/~stoitt/rosewind.htm>

CHAPTER 7

1. Michael D'Antonio, "The New 'Hidden' Cults Want You." *Redbook*, April 1995, 93.

2. Quoted in ibid., 96.

3. Ibid., 97.

4. Marshall Kilduff and Ron Javers, *The Suicide Cult: The Inside Story of the Peoples Temple Sect and the Massacre in Guyana.* (New York: Bantam Books, 1978), 64–65.

5. Ibid., 89

CHAPTER 8

1. James J. Boyle, *Killer Cults.* (New York: St. Martin's Press, 1995), 115.

2. Ibid., 117–118.

3. Quoted in Associated Press, "Ten Years After MOVE Inferno," 6 May 1995, electronic version, no page number.

4. Boyle, *Killer Cults*, 137.

5. Mary Thornton, "Guru's Followers Keep the Faith—Rajneesh Commune in Oregon Transcending Local Opposition." *Washington Post*, 28 April 1985, A4.

6. Sally Carpenter Hale, "Guru's Commune Now Abandoned." Associated Press, 10 December 1995.

7. Jim McGee and William Claiborne, "The Transformation of the Waco 'Messiah'–Koresh Sought God, Sex, and Rock-and-Roll." *Washington Post*, 9 May 1993, A1.

8. Brad Bailey and Bob Darden, *Mad Man in Waco*. (Waco, Texas: WRS Publishing, 1993), 68, 72.

9. Marc A. Breault, "Vernon Howell and the Seven Seals." <http://www.mainelink.net/~mswett/seals.html>, May 13, 1992.

10. Quoted in Alice Scott, *The Incredible Power of Cults* (Colorado Springs, Col.: Blue River Publishing, 1994), 51.

11. Quoted in Tim Madigan, *See No Evil: Blind Devotion and Bloodshed in David Koresh's Holy War*. (Fort Worth, Texas: Summit Group, 1993), 117.

12. Sue Anne Pressley, "Teenager Tells Waco Panel of Koresh's Lust." *Washington Post*, 20 July 1995, A1.

CHAPTER 9

1. Associated Press, "Murder Inquiry Opens into the Solar Temple." *Philadelphia Inquirer*, 25 December 1995, 3.

2. Anonymous, "Freedom from Fear." Internet World Wide Web page: <http://caladan.chattanooga.net/~erickett/>

3. Marlene Gyudal, "Internet Provides Recruiting Fodder for Cults." *Hayward Daily Review*, Haward, Calif.: Cal-State University, Hayward, 13 November 1995, electronic posting, no page numer.

4. Biography Steven Hassan, Internet World Wide Web page: <http://www.tiac.net/users/shassan/bio.html> no date.

5. Ibid.

6. Margaret Thaler Singer, with Janja Lalich, *Cults in Our Midst: The Hidden Menace in Our Everyday Lives* (San Francisco: Jossey-Bass Publishers, 1995), 269.

FURTHER READING

Andres, Rachel and James R. Lane, eds. *Cults and Consequences: The Definitive Handbook*. Los Angeles: Commission on Cults and Missionaries, Jewish Federation Council of Greater Los Angeles, 1988.

Batz, Jeannette. "'I Got Caught Up in a Cult,'" *Seventeen*, September 1995, 178–185.

Boyle, James J. *Killer Cults*. New York: St. Martin's Paperbacks, 1995.

Bromley, D.G., and A.D. Shupe, Jr. *Strange Gods: The Great American Cult Scare*. Boston: Beacon Press, 1981.

D'Antonio, Michael. "The New 'Hidden' Cults Want You," *Redbook*, April 1995, 93–97.

Fairfield, Richard. *Communes USA: A Personal Tour*. Baltimore: Penguin Books, 1972.

Harrary, Keith. "The Truth About Jonestown," *Psychology Today*, March/April 1992, 62–88.

Hine, Robert V. *Community on the American Frontier: Separate But Not Alone*. Norman, Okla.: University of Oklahoma Press, 1980.

Holloway, Mark. *Heavens on Earth: Utopian Communities in America 1680–1880*. New York: Dover Publications, 1966.

Kaihla, Paul. "A Deadly Tradition; Apocalyptic Cults Have Flourished in the West for 2,000 Years," *Maclean's*, 17 October 1994, 20–21.

Kilduff, Marshall, and Ron Javers. *The Suicide Cult: The Inside Story of the Peoples Temple Sect and the Massacre in Guyana*. New York: Bantam Books, 1978.

Lewis, J.R., and J.G. Melton, eds. *Church Universal and Triumphant in Scholarly Perspective*. Stanford, Calif.: Center for Academic Publication, 1994.

Long, Robert Emmet, ed. *Religious Cults in America*. New York: H. W. Wilson Company, 1994.

Madsen, Carol Cornwall. *In Their Own Words: Women and the Story of Nauvoo*. Salt Lake City, Utah: Desert Book Co., 1994.

Melton, J. Gordon. *Encyclopedic Handbook of Cults in America*. New York & London: Garland Publishing, 1986.

Melton, J. Gordon, and Robert L. Moore. *The Cult Experience: Responding to the New Religious Pluralism*. New York: Pilgrim Press, 1982.

Miller, Maryann. *Coping with Cults*. New York: Rosen Publishing Group, 1990.

Miller, T., ed. *America's Alternative Religions*. Albany, N.Y.: SUNY Press, 1995.

Nordhoff, Charles. *The Communistic Societies of the United States: From Personal Observations*. New York: Dover Publications, 1966.

Pickford, Kaylan, as told to Claire Safran. "I Lost My Daughters to a Cult," *Redbook*, March 1995, 54–60.

Porterfield, Kay Marie. *Straight Talk About Cults*. New York: Facts on File, 1995.

Roberts, Ron E. *The New Communes: Coming Together in America*. Englewood Cliffs, N.J.: Prentice Hall, 1971.

Rudin, James and Marcia. *Prison or Paradise: The New Religious Cults*. Philadelphia: Fortress Press, 1980.

Scott, Alice. *The Incredible Power of Cults*. Colorado Springs: Blue River Publishing, 1994.

Singer, Margaret Thaler, with Janja Lalich. *Cults in Our Midst: The Hidden Menace in Our Everyday Lives*. San Francisco: Jossey-Bass Publishing, 1995.

Stein, Stephen J., ed. *Letters from a Young Shaker: William S. Byrd at Pleasant Hill*. Lexington, Ky.: University Press of Kentucky, 1985.

Streiker, Lowell D. *Mind-Bending: Brainwashing, Cults, and Deprogramming in the '80s*. Garden City, N.Y.: Doubleday, 1984.

INDEX

About the Author

Kathlyn Gay is the author of numerous informational books for young people on a wide range of topics. She and her son, Martin, joined forces to write *Voices From the Past*, a series dealing with major U.S. wars, and *The Information Superhighway* for Twenty-First Century Books.

Kathlyn Gay and her husband, Arthur, reside in Illinois.

Sweet and Sour

Asian Voices
Series Editor: Mark Selden

Sweet and Sour

Life-Worlds of
Taipei Women Entrepreneurs

Scott Simon

ROWMAN & LITTLEFIELD PUBLISHERS, INC.
Lanham • Boulder • New York • Toronto • Oxford

ROWMAN & LITTLEFIELD PUBLISHERS, INC.

Published in the United States of America
by Rowman & Littlefield Publishers, Inc.
A wholly owned subsidiary of The Rowman & Littlefield Publishing Group, Inc.
4501 Forbes Boulevard, Suite 200, Lanham, Maryland 20706
www.rowmanlittlefield.com

PO Box 317
Oxford
OX2 9RU, UK

British Library Cataloguing in Publication Information Available

Library of Congress Cataloging-in-Publication Data

Simon, Scott, 1965–
    Sweet and sour : life-worlds of Taipei women entrepreneurs / Scott Simon.
    p.   cm. — (Asian voices)
    ISBN 0-7425-1608-3 (cloth : alk. paper) — ISBN 0-7425-1609-1 (pbk. : alk. paper)
        1. Businesswomen—Taiwan—Taipei—Case studies. 2. Entrepreneurship—Taiwan—
Taipei—Case studies. I. Title. II. Series: Asian voices (Rowman and Littlefield, Inc.)
    HD6072.6.T282T357 2003
    338'.04'0820951249—dc21
                                                                                                2002154990

Printed in the United States of America

∞™ The paper used in this publication meets the minimum requirements of American
National Standard for Information Sciences—Permanence of Paper for Printed Library
Materials, ANSI/NISO Z39.48-1992.

To my parents,
Angela and Dan

Life consists of controlling one's own fate within a limited career. The meaning of life is being one's own master.

—Taiwanese sociologist Michael Hsiao Hsin-huang, quotation found printed on the back of a disposable chopstick wrapper in Formosa Chang's Restaurant, Neihu District, Taipei.

Contents

Preface

Sweet and sour pork, hot and sour soup . . . some of the most popular dishes in Chinese cuisine excite the palate with contradictory tastes. In Taiwan, the small mango fruit that comes to market at the beginning of the season is called "lover's fruit." Like love, people say, it is simultaneously sweet and sour. Life in Taiwan is similarly an exercise in contradictions. Taiwan is a land where some scholars (mostly men) celebrate Confucian "traditions" that keep women in the home; yet feminists (mostly women) march through the streets to "take back the night." It is a land where many people consider themselves to be sexually "conservative," but where prostitution is one of the most visible "entertainment" industries. This book is about such contradictions in the lives of Taipei's women entrepreneurs. A study of women entrepreneurs reveals their lives as a precarious balance of contradictions: between global capital and local interests, between capital and labor, between Taiwanese workers and foreign *Gastarbeiter,* between older and younger generations, between "Native Taiwanese" and "Mainlanders," between Han Chinese and ethnic minorities, and most of all, between men and women. These contradictions and tensions, which arise from conflicts over power, are at the core of human life.

This study gives voice to a group of women at the forefront of social change in Taiwan: the women entrepreneurs who serve coffee, sell furniture, and even fix automobiles or manufacture computer parts in Taipei. This book addresses questions of entrepreneurship and empowerment, interrogating the very concept of empowerment and asking what women actually gain individually and collectively from entrepreneurship. It looks both at and beyond the roles of women as wives, mothers, lovers, and daughters. Most of all, it draws attention to the dimension of women as individuals and agents—as individuals engaged in processes of self-realization in concrete social situations. This research project is important in the study of Chinese and Taiwanese cultures, as traditional approaches in the West have unduly emphasized family and clan to the exclusion of understanding individual agency and other dynamic forces at play (Dissanayake 1996: xi). This is especially true in the study of Chinese entrepreneurship, where much of the literature focuses heavily on Confucianism and family dynamics. Feminist anthropologists such as Hill Gates and Susan Greenhalgh are notable exceptions, and have strongly influenced this present work.

This study of women entrepreneurs addresses the following questions. In what circumstances do women become bosses, instead of taking public roles of merely "helping" their husbands? What about divorced women, lesbians, or other women who may not have husbands or male lovers and patrons? What about women of lower social classes, who lack the means to start manufacturing firms with their husbands but might do petty entrepreneurship on their own? What about women abandoned by their husbands or in situations where husbands are incapable of adequately caring for the family? Most important of all, to what extent does entrepreneurship empower women and what are its limitations? These questions are discussed in this book in dialogue with the women entrepreneurs themselves.

This ethnography is self-consciously a collaborative research project. The women in this book generously shared their life histories with me in the full knowledge that those narratives would be translated into English and published for a global audience of readers. Some of them even accepted my invitation to read their chapters and comment on them before publication. Some women participated in this project because it gave them a chance for creative and public self-expression. Some even specifically asked that I use their real names—or in one case, the pseudonym she uses in "real" life—in the book. Others requested that I omit several things, include specific sections of interviews, and/or use pseudonyms to protect their anonymity. I have followed their instructions to the best of my ability.

These women entrepreneurs would surely be frustrated if I transformed their stories into abstract scholarly discourse for only a few initiates of academic jargon. Most of them participated in this project because they have something to say, and all of them did so because they believe constructive dialogue is possible. The narratives in this book represent the ways in which we worked together to mutually understand our common world. Together we have learned more about how power is distributed between men and women in contemporary Taiwan, and how individuals struggle for specific forms of power in specific situations. Although our point of departure is Taipei, it is hoped that the lessons to be learned in that cosmopolitan city are relevant to other localities in our globalizing, but still patriarchal, world. Concerned as it is with the gendered struggles of real people in real situations, this book is inspired more by feminism than by any other body of theory.

To a very limited extent, this book is a dialogue with Simone de Beauvoir and Jean-Paul Sartre. That is partly a result of the research methodology, as both were interested in learning social facts from life narratives. This book has been strongly influenced by the conversations I had in its *naissance* with my neighbor and friend Roan Ching-yueh, who not only is an architect, novelist, and scholar, but has also translated Jean Genet's *Our Lady of the Flowers* (with its introduction by Sartre) into Chinese. More importantly yet, I myself first read de Beauvoir's *The Second*

Sex only because I saw it in Chinese translation in the homes and stores of several of the women in this book. I subsequently read it and discussed it with some of them, which led me to see many similarities between the situations of women in Taiwan, North America, and France. Since that book is an important part of the life-world of some of the women I encountered, I made it part of my own world and make frequent reference to it throughout this text.

Acknowledgments

This book would have been impossible if not for the moral support, encouragement, and intellectual stimulation of many people. It is impossible to thank everyone, and I apologize for any omissions. First of all, I thank Academia Sinica in Taipei for its generous support in the form of a two-year postdoctoral fellowship that allowed me to complete field research in Taipei and work at the Institute of Sociology. I benefited greatly from seminars, social events, and conversations with the entire team of scholars both in that institute and in the Institute of Ethnology. In particular, I am strongly indebted to the circle of feminist scholars there, which includes Lu Yu-hsia, Yi Chin-chun, Chang Chin-fen, Yu Wei-hsin, and Fan Yun. My thinking on ethnicity and identity was strongly influenced by Chang Mao-kui, Wang Fu-chang, and Wu Nai-teh. Wang Fu-chang was especially generous in permitting me to retabulate data as needed from his Ethnic Relations Survey. I also learned about small businesses in general from Shieh Gwo-shyong and Ka Chih-ming. For their intellectual stimulation during fieldwork and initial writing, I am grateful to Paul Festa, Huang Shu-ling, Yang Fang-chih, Bi Heng-da, Roan Ching-yueh, and Linda Arrigo. Thanks especially to Mark Selden, series editor of *Asian Voices* for Rowman & Littlefield, and Laurel Bossen of McGill University, who provided generous comments and helped me whip the manuscript into a book. Most of all, I thank the women entrepreneurs who so generously participated in the creation of this book by filling out surveys, providing life histories, and even looking over chapter drafts. I am thankful for the support of Wang Li-ling, Sophie Hong, Sharon (who uses that English name as her public identity), and the many others who are represented here only by pseudonyms.

For teaching me to listen to women's voices, I should thank as well the women who taught me the importance of doing so, including my mother, Angela Simon, my Canadian grandmother, Kay Thompson, who convinced me to come to Canada, and my never-married aunt Marion Thompson, who first gave me an outsider's perspective on marriage. I am especially grateful to my paternal

grandmother, Mary Simon, who was herself a woman entrepreneur of sorts because she sold pies to local restaurants in Rockford, Ohio, and took care of children in her home. Having taught me the power of a working woman's agency
from a very young age, she made it possible for me to see women entrepreneurs
where many other scholars have not. I met women like her all over Taipei. Not to
leave out the men, I also thank my father, Dan Simon. Ma Ti-khai also supported
me emotionally throughout the project. They all put up with my long absences
from home and for that I am grateful.

Notes on Language and Romanization

Reflecting the global nature of Taiwan, the dialogues presented in this book actually happened in Mandarin, Taiwanese, Japanese, English, and even French, all of which I speak at varying levels of proficiency. Since some of the people I interviewed do not have strong identities as "Chinese" and even reject such an identity, I was faced with a difficult decision about how to represent the names of individuals and the words they speak for a primarily anglophone readership. In general agreement with Murray and Hong (1994) that it is a form of symbolic violence to represent Taiwan as merely a part of Chinese culture, I have tried my best to represent as fully as possible the ethnic diversity of Taiwan. More importantly, I think that the women in this book have a right to represent themselves as they themselves see fit. I thus adopt Taiwanese usage for personal names and spoken terms in many places to respect and follow their preferences.

From the perspective of sinologists, that means that I have had recourse to a very idiosyncratic form of romanization. I romanize personal names of informants in the language they use at home: whether that be Mandarin, Taiwanese, Hakka, Tayal, or Ta'u. I also romanize the words they use according to the language spoken. For the convenience of foreign scholars, I have written Mandarin common nouns in the Hanyu Pinyin current in China and North American academia, although some of my Taiwanese colleagues and informants encouraged the use of Taiwanese Tong-yong Pinyin. Some words, such as the Taiwanese *thau-ke-niu* ("boss-lady"), are completely different in Taiwanese and Mandarin (*laobanniang*); whereas others, such as *nuqiangren* ("strong woman") are used only in Mandarin. I have preserved them in their original forms and placed a glossary of Mandarin and Taiwanese terms at the back of the book. This policy is not an ideological gesture on my part. It is rather an act of respect towards the women who so generously shared their lives with me, and it accurately reflects the messy social reality of Taiwan.

For most proper nouns, including Taiwanese place names, I use the modified Wade-Giles system common in Taiwan and used officially by the post office, as this best reflects local usage. For the benefit of scholars who may wish to consult the Chinese works cited here, however, I have used *Hanyu Pinyin* and Chinese characters for book and article titles in the bibliography. Since Hanyu Pinyin is the most common form of romanization used in Western libraries, this usage should enable readers to consult the original works. In respect for individual authors, however, I have rendered author names in the Latin spelling that they have chosen to use on their own publications. Even this policy, however, does not eliminate all symbolic violence. Wang Hao-wei, for example, used the Taiwanese word for "men" (*chabolang*) as his book title, which then sounds ridiculous when pronounced in Mandarin. Since Tayal anthropologist Masaw Mowna is not even Han Chinese, it is as absurd to insist on using Hanyu Pinyin in rendering his name in English as it would be to use Ma Kesi (Karl Marx).

Chapter One

Introduction

It was a cold, winter day in Taipei. I had come to a rather desolate area just off Civic Boulevard in Chung-shan District in order to do survey research with women entrepreneurs. An elevated limited-access road runs above Civic Boulevard, letting most Taipei drivers pass over the neighborhood rather than driving through it. Taking advantage of the absence of cars and busses, motorcyclists race down the tunnel-like Civic Boulevard at breakneck speed, as if competing in the Grand Prix. Apart from a few betel-nut stands and a car wash, there are few signs of business activity on that stretch of road.

As soon as I arrived in that neighborhood, I knew it would be a difficult afternoon. I parked my motorbike next to a dilapidated house. The first floor was clearly occupied, but the second floor was boarded up. I scanned the immediate neighborhood: most of the storefronts were vacant. Tattered red posters pasted on closed-up steel doors announced "store for rent." There were a few noodle shops, a simple hair salon, and a general store. But the shops were empty and there were no pedestrians on the street.

I had come with the hope of studying women entrepreneurs. But the people I met seemed mean and defensive. Even just asking if the owner was male or female elicited brusque responses of "the owner's not here," "I'm not interested," or "I don't want to buy anything." I came across one man asleep at the cash box in his general store, and merely left him at peace. I stood in front of a rice store, wondering if I should continue my quest or move on to friendlier turf and come back later. A young man came out of the store and asked if I was lost. I explained to him that I was doing research on women entrepreneurs and looking for people to interview. "This rice store is owned by a man," he said, "but go interview her. She is a female entrepreneur." He indicated a woman selling fruit from the back of a truck near a small park.

I walked over and bought some oranges. I said I was doing research, and asked if she could help me fill out a small survey on female entrepreneurship. She looked suspicious. "Does this have anything to do with taxes?" she asked, eyeing the survey form. I assured her that my research had nothing to do with the tax bureau or any other government institution, and I handed her a pen. She started to fill out the survey, indicating that she was a forty-one-year-old migrant from Pingtung and had only a middle school education.

Suddenly, an older woman, another fruit vendor who had already refused me, came running down the street yelling, "They're coming!" The woman from Pingtung thrust the survey back into my hands, slammed shut the back of her truck, and started frantically hiding boxes of fruit among the shrubs at the edge of the park. I helped. Once the boxes were well hidden, I sat on a metal railing. "Come sit with me," I said. "They won't be suspicious if you're sitting here talking to a foreigner."

She sat next to me and asked, "Are you '*Amen*'?" indicating the common assumption that I—as a foreigner—am actually selling Watchtower tracts or Books of Mormon. I said no, repeating that I was writing a book on women in business. As we spoke, a yellow truck passed by, loaded with assorted furniture and potted plants. A sign on the truck indicated it was the Department of Sanitation. "There they are," she said. "If they see my boxes of fruit, they'll take them away." I sympathized with her, saying she is just a common person trying to make a living. "This happens at least once a day," she said. "The sanitation department won't let us put fruit on the street. And the police check to see if we have permits. In Taipei, they are always arresting people. In Pingtung, they leave us alone, but in Taipei they control things too strictly."

Such petty entrepreneurs are found in all but the most exclusive neighborhoods of Taipei. They are quite often migrants from rural, southern Taiwan. They are poorly educated, and some cannot even read. They lack the skills that would land them better jobs. They lack the capital needed to enter the formal sector and sell from much more comfortable and stable storefronts. State attempts to control their activities raise the transaction costs they face working in the informal sector. They live on the edge of urban society, struggling to raise families and get by from day to day. Their lives stand in stark contrast to the software companies, glittering department stores, and comfortable coffee shops of other districts in Taipei. On the streets, they are the most visible of Taipei's women entrepreneurs, but they represent only one part of the women's economy in Taiwan's national capital.

Women entrepreneurs run businesses all over Taipei. They not only own fruit stands and food stalls, but also software and construction companies, exclusive boutiques, and luxurious restaurants. Even as I chatted with this fruit seller from Pingtung, other women entrepreneurs were driving on the freeway above us on the way to appointments with business partners, family members, or lovers. The diversity of these women and the richness of their lives deserve anthropological study, yet their voices are rarely heard in academic discourse. A study of such women's lives promises to reveal new perspectives on the development story once known as the "Taiwan miracle."

WOMEN AND THE FAMILY IN TAIWAN

Although Taiwan is known for its large number of small family firms, the contributions of women to the Taiwanese economy and family life have only gradually captured the attention of researchers. The first generation of scholarship on Taiwanese family businesses, written without reference to feminist anthropology, focused mainly on the family as a unit. With the exception of Hill Gates (1987), they paid scant, if any, attention to the different roles played by men and women in such businesses (de Glopper 1978, Harrell 1985, Ka 1993, Niehoff 1987, Stites 1982, 1985).[1] Writing largely from the perspective of the male entrepreneur and head of household, researchers often overlooked female agency and adopted the perspective of male household heads. Justin Niehoff, for example, interviewed male entrepreneurs and concluded that Taiwanese manufacturers "structure the organization of production in such a way as to further the household's genealogical goals" (1987: 308).

Such studies rendered the family unproblematic. Individuals apparently were subordinate to the need to produce genealogies in the patriarchal family and lineage. Individuals with needs and desires, loves and hates, and struggles and compromises were neatly situated within a picture of apparent Confucian harmony. When women were mentioned at all in these studies, it was primarily as wives and daughters trapped in a rigid kinship structure, rather than as individuals with hopes and aspirations of their own. Few scholars even bothered to interview women, assuming that they really were subordinate to the needs of men.

The limits in these early studies have since been made obvious by nearly two decades of feminist scholarship. Most importantly, early studies obscured gender inequalities and conflicts within Taiwanese families and manufacturing enterprises, virtually ignoring the different roles played by women and men, male control of labor power and finances, as well as the common use of unremunerated female labor in family enterprises. Such shortcomings were addressed by a second generation of scholars who put women at the center of their analyses (e.g., Gates 1989, Greenhalgh 1994, Hsiung 1996, Oxfeld 1993, Skoggard 1996). The main theme in this second generation of scholarship is the extent to which women in family enterprises are exploited and subordinated to the needs of a patriarchal family system and capitalist economy. Greenhalgh (1994), for example, argued that an unequal gender-based division of labor in Taiwanese firms is a political construction of family/firm heads pressed by the national and global political economies to build factories out of meager family resources.

Further studies of women in Chinese and Taiwanese family enterprises, however, showed that subordination is only part of the picture. Feminist scholars have shown that women can gain status and power as *thau-ke-niu* ("boss-wives"), whether they do so in Taiwan (Gates 1996, Kao 1999, Y.-H. Lu 2001), the People's Republic of China (PRC) (Gates 1996), or even Chinese-owned firms in the diaspora (Oxfeld 1993). Hill Gates (1996, 1999) notes that successful businesswomen can be found everywhere in China and Taiwan, creating new female identities of substantial power and esteem. Petty capitalism, she argues, is one of the few routes whereby women can gain individual wealth, autonomy, and social power. Women sometimes dominate family enterprises, and their entrepreneurial abilities often overcome gender as a factor in decision making in such firms.

This study picks up the next thread in the discourse by focusing on women who run their own businesses. A study of Taipei women entrepreneurs is important at the turn of the twenty-first century, as women have made important contributions to the construction of civil society in Taiwan since martial law was lifted in 1987 (Weller 1999). A study of Taipei women entrepreneurs is also relevant as a lesson in social development in other countries, especially in an era when microenterprise is widely proclaimed by the Grameen Bank and other nongovernmental organizations (NGOs) as a solution to poverty and as a form of gender empowerment. This women-focused ethnography, with lessons to be drawn on gender and agency, will also have implications for a wider academic literature on "Confucian" culture and entrepreneurship in East Asia (e.g., Chung-hua Institute for Economic Research 1989, Brook and Luong 1997, Hefner 1998, Redding 1990, Silin 1976, Wou 1992).

ENTREPRENEURSHIP

For the purpose of this study, I use entrepreneur as a gloss for the Taiwanese concept of *thau-ke*, often translated as "boss." In my survey research, I have followed the rule of self-definition, allowing the people interviewed to determine themselves who is a boss and who is not. The concept is clearly unproblematic in cases where the individual involved has invested significant amounts of capital, has a fixed business location separate from her residence, and hires paid labor. Yet even the smallest of petty entrepreneurs sometimes perceive themselves as thau-ke based on the fact that they work on their own account and have invested their own capital. I accept those self-definitions, as they reveal a sense of purpose and intention, the main markers of entrepreneurship. The concept of entrepreneur here thus refers to people who start their own business with capital that they control themselves, regardless of scale.

The gendered distinction between thau-ke and "boss-wife" (thau-ke-niu) is crucial to the discussion, especially in cases where a woman and husband work together. Frequently, it is assumed that the man is the "boss" and that the wife merely "helps out." In cases of women entrepreneurs, however, husband and wife reverse the conventional roles, making women into bosses in the business sphere. In cases where women work with their husbands, I thus refer to the boss or entrepreneur as the partner who is most active in the enterprise, who first initiated the business idea, who organized capital and controls it, and/or who makes most day-to-day business decisions. Another important dimension of the boss is that he or she is the public face of the business, the one who deals with the public. In some cases, therefore, I conducted surveys with women who fit very closely into the portrait of the thau-ke-niu, but only to the extent that they work with their husbands. They do not, however, fill the stereotypical role whereby "men manage outside affairs, women manage inside affairs" as mentioned by Oxfeld (1993) and Greenhalgh (1994), because they insisted that they themselves are the bosses and that their husbands are the ones who take a subordinate role in their firms. Studying these women as entrepreneurs follows their own practice of referring to themselves as thau-ke.

Even in the United States and Great Britain, the share of small entrepreneurs has remained roughly stable over the past fifty years. In some countries, including Taiwan, Spain, and Italy, the self-employment rate exceeds 20 percent and has for decades. In Taiwan, petty entrepreneurship continues to draw individuals out of the labor market. One major reason is that while self-employment involves high risk, it often provides higher income than work in the formal sector, especially since the Taiwanese economy is dominated by small, family firms that pay low wages and offer few benefits (Yu 2001b). The majority of Taiwanese street peddlers, not to mention entrepreneurs at larger scales of activity, report that they have intentionally left the labor market in order to take advantage of the greater flexibility and higher income of self-employment (P.-F. Tai 1994: 135).

There is no evidence to suggest that petty entrepreneurs would prefer formal sector employment or that there is a strong tendency for them to leave the sector. On the contrary, entrepreneurship has remained the job many Taiwanese men and women desire most and one whose values "permeate the rest of the working class" (Gates 1987: 77). Entrepreneurship makes it possible for people to combine desires for independence and social mobility with traditional Chinese values of frugality and hard work. Starting a small business is thus a claim on empowerment.

EMPOWERMENT

In this book, I use empowerment, or the enhancement of human freedom, as an indicator of and motivating force behind social development (Sen 1999). This idea has long been central to political economy, as Adam Smith and Karl Marx were both concerned with human freedom, albeit in different ways. Following Giddens, I define empowerment as "the power of human beings to alter the material world and transform the conditions of their own actions" (1991: 138). Such an approach makes it clear that empowerment has been distributed unevenly in every society. Women, for example, have gained less empowerment than men during the process of development in most countries due to distributional rules followed within families and other social institutions (see Tinker 1990). In recent decades, feminist groups around the world have thus begun emphasizing women's empowerment (e.g., Bulbeck 1998), recognizing that no nation is free as long as half of its population is oppressed.

Female entrepreneurship has been widely promoted as a means of empowering women in developing countries by giving them autonomous sources of income, as well as promoting other social benefits including lower mortality and fertility rates (Sen 1999: 201). Microcredit programs targeting micro- and small enterprises in places as varied as Iowa and Bangladesh are usually based on the assumption that self-employment empowers individuals, primarily women. Microenterprise programs, including the Grameen Bank and similar programs inspired by it elsewhere, have thus financed women entrepreneurs and advised them on how to run small businesses. Ethnographic studies of women entrepreneurs are needed to explore how the women themselves perceive their lives and to present their entrepreneurial strategies in different cultural contexts. Since empowerment usually begins with self-realization and consciousness raising, it is important to understand how entrepreneurial women perceive their own identities.

THE POWER OF SELF-IDENTITY

Personal development, identity, and consciousness are important topics in contemporary Taiwanese society. Best-sellers in Taipei bookstores include a wide range of self-help books, guides to negotiating everything from love and romance to starting small businesses, and pop psychology. Talk shows on the radio and over 100 cable TV stations often interview people and focus on their narratives of self-development. Bookstores, publishing houses, community colleges, churches, NGOs, and the Taipei municipal government all offer seminars and retreats dealing with self-development of all kinds from gender awareness classes to "coming out" workshops for gays and lesbians. Such events are well attended.

Religious groups also fill their own market niche, offering classes on Ch'an philosophy, meditation, chanting, and other lessons that explicitly promise self-fulfillment and individual freedom. Syncretic religions like I-Kuan-Tao attract adherents with promises to reveal the secrets of the believer's "true self." In addition to Chinese versions of predicting fate, most Taiwanese people also know their Western horoscopes. Perceived along with blood types to be accurate indicators of personality, they are a frequent topic of conversation among friends as well as new acquaintances meeting for the first time. Pisces and Cancer have become forms of identity as important to some individuals as gender or nationality. It is important to note that most of these self-reflexive endeavors, or at least those groups in which I have participated, are attended far more by women than by men.

Sartre's existentialist philosophy is surprisingly relevant to this modern project of self-realization and, thus, contains concepts useful to understanding the lives of Taipei women entrepreneurs. Sartre's philosophy is based on a distinction between *l'être-en-soi* ("being-in-itself") and *l'être-pour-soi* ("being-for-itself"). L'être-en-soi is the realm of pure existence and immediate consciousness. L'être-pour-soi is the self-reflexive self that seeks personal development through freely chosen fundamental projects of existence. All people embark on their projects of self-realization through personal narratives, holds Sartre, yet they usually become aware of personal liberty only through moments of anguish and suffering. A personal crisis can create rupture in a person's life, as pain awakens her and encourages her to change her life in new, even revolutionary ways (Sartre 1943: 480). In existentialism, the self is created through negation, through self-reflection and discovery of what-one-is-not, the *néant*. Individuals who refuse to wake up to their human potential, instead subscribing to dogmas and other prescribed ways of being, are said to live in bad faith.

These ideas are not unfamiliar to Taiwanese people. Zen master Dr. Daisetsu Suzuki (1960), whose books are widely available in Taiwan, found Buddhism compatible with existentialism. He was especially taken by the similarities between Buddhist sudden enlightenment and existentialist rupture or epiphany. In Taiwan, Master Shengyan's interpretation of the Heart Sutra (Shengyan 1997) similarly covers many themes found in Sartre's existentialism. Both describe the human consciousness as a mirror for self-reflection, and both find meaning in nothingness. In both cases, individuals become aware of their true existence through suffering, and learn through similar paths of sudden enlightenment or existentialist rupture. The main difference is that Master Shengyan encourages his disciples to focus on the immediate consciousness of being (being-in-itself), whereas Sartre emphasizes the freedom found in pursuit of being for itself. In both existentialism and modern Buddhism, individuals deal with similar self-reflexive projects, yet in vocabularies derived from different times and places. In contexts ranging from feminist discussion groups to Zen training seminars, those projects emerge and are constantly refined through life narratives.

Even in the West, people construct their narratives through themes of chance, luck, destiny, and fate (Langness and Frank 1981: 116). In Taiwan (Harrell 1987), Buddhism provides the vocabulary women use to discover design in their personal narratives. Primary among these terms is *en-hun* (*yuanfen* in Mandarin), roughly glossed as "destiny" or "fate." En-hun is the product of karma, the cause-and-effect relations that bring individuals together in different kinds of relations, or individuals to certain places and jobs. I was often told that I must have been Chinese in a past life; that is what gave me a fated relationship with Taiwan. Although Buddhist texts present far more complex descriptions of what happens at the moment of death, popular conceptions of the self in Taiwan perceive a unified self that persists beyond death in an endless series of reincarnations. Relations between individuals are central to human life, and the relationships that form are determined by en-hun. It is often believed that individuals meet again in life-after-life existence.

Feminism empowers women to take control of their own destinies, a project that requires conscious, gender-oriented being-for-itself. Perhaps the most widely read feminist is Simone de Beauvoir (1989 [1952]), who attempted with difficulty to put Sartre's existentialism into practice *as a woman*. Her book *The Second Sex* has been translated into Chinese and published in Taiwan. I have seen well-worn pocket versions on the bookshelves of many Taipei women entrepreneurs as well as in coffee shops frequented by women. Her self-reflexive feminism promises enlightenment and liberation for women. At the same time, de Beauvoir also criticizes Sartre's naïve optimism about human liberty and underestimation of forces of oppression. The definition of empowerment used in this book underscores the fact that different people have different abilities to fulfill Sartre's promise of self-realization. As long as people are oppressed along axes of gender, ethnicity, and class, Sartre's promises of freedom are mere fantasy for many people. Taiwan provides just one example of how gender identities are constructed within specific webs of power.

WOMEN'S POWER IN THE FAMILY

For women, the family of marriage is one of the main sources of identity. Taiwanese (e.g., Ho 1994, Hsu 1998, Hu 1995) and Western (e.g., Gates 1989, Greenhalgh 1994) feminists thus generally agree that Taiwanese and Chinese women have been subordinated within the family. By "marrying out" of her natal family and becoming a member of her husband's family, a woman begins married life as a virtual stranger in a new household. She starts her quest for power in the family from nearly zero, having to negotiate a life path between two families, whereas a man is firmly established as a member of one single family from birth to death. Even if she enters marriage with a substantial dowry, a young bride has little symbolic capital to use in power strategies with her new family. This movement between families makes women more self-conscious than men of power relations within families. As oppressive as this system may seem, women have long developed strategies to cope with it, as Margery Wolf illustrated in her ethnography of rural Taiwan in the 1960s (1972).

The emergence of women entrepreneurs should be seen as part of the rapid social change that has transformed Taiwan (Marsh 1996) over the past forty years, not the least being changes in family structure (Hu 1995, Thornton and Lin 1994). Even in rural Taiwan, there has been a growing tendency for women to maintain and cultivate good relations with their natal families after marriage (Gallin and Gallin 1982), which has surely made the transition to new families of marriage less disempowering. This has been especially necessary for entrepreneurial families because affinal relatives can provide useful contacts and capital in a network-oriented business culture (Greenhalgh 1988).

For young women's marital lives, the most important change has been a shift from the extended family to conjugality. Rapid urbanization has meant that most families now live in urban apartments designed for nuclear families rather than in rural, extended family compounds. Throughout Taiwan, stem families have become the norm, as elderly parents now tend to live with one son and his wife, rather than with several sons and their wives. From the perspective of younger sons and their wives, this structural change has led to a dramatic increase in nuclear families.

The burden of these changes has been heavy on older women (Hu 1995). Mothers-in-law once held substantial power over the labor of young wives who married into rural families. Now, however, it is often the mothers-in-law who have to move—from their rural towns to urban areas where their sons have found jobs—and find that household labor is now dictated by younger, better educated women who may very well have careers of their own. The older generation of Taiwanese women once looked forward to greater power and respite from childcare responsibilities in old age. With the social transformation that has occurred, however, the younger generation has gained power. Mothers-in-law often are saddled with childcare duties in old age, a chore that many older women describe as onerous (Hu 1995). Hu and Chou (1997) thus argue that older women are the main victims of Taiwan's rapid industrialization and social change. Young brides, however, have been empowered by this change, since it is now easier for them to keep working after marriage. Relatively easy access to grandmothers as childcare providers, even in urban Taiwan, is one of the variables contributing to married women's higher labor-force participation compared to Japan and South Korea (Yu 2001a).

WOMEN'S POWER IN THE WORKPLACE

Although Taiwan has come a long way towards gender empowerment, women still face problems in the workplace. In 2000, the Directorate General of Budget, Accounting and Statistics (DGBAS 2000) released a comparative study of Taiwan's gender relations based on statistics from the United Nations Development Program's Human Development Index and Gender Empowerment Measure. The gender empowerment measure includes indices of the proportion of women lawmakers, percentages of women among managers, professionals, and technical workers, and women's earned income share. Internationally, while Taiwan ranked 17th, it placed far ahead of all other Asian countries, including Japan (35th), China (36th), and South Korea (69th). The study indicated that women in Taiwan do comparatively well in terms of educational level and economic power. The rise in educational levels is particularly impressive. In 1979, fully 70 percent of women ages 20 to 69 had only a primary school education or less. By 1995, that number was only 39 percent, because most women gained further education. The percentage of working-age women with junior college– or university-level training jumped from 16 percent to 37 percent.

In spite of such rapid changes, women still have less power than men in public affairs and business decision making, as in most other countries. Women, for example, only occupy 14.1 percent of Taiwan's administrative and managerial positions. Although Taiwan is in 62nd place in that regard, it is still ranked ahead of

Japan, South Korea, and China. The low percentage of women in managerial positions suggests the existence of a strong glass ceiling limiting women's advancement in all of those countries. As Taiwanese sociologists Chang Chin-fen and Yi Chin-chun (2000) observe, married women are disadvantaged in employment stability and promotion, especially in the private sector. Whereas married men can expect their wives to take care of family duties for them, married women have to bear a disproportionate share of childcare and other home duties. As they have to find replacements for caring duties in the household, women are less flexible than men in regard to working overtime, going out of town on business, or relocation. Since such restrictions make women less flexible in meeting the demands of business, they are disadvantaged vis-à-vis men in terms of promotion and job stability. Considering the problems that women face both at home and in the workplace, private entrepreneurship seems like an attractive alternative to many individuals. Gender, however, is not the only axis of identity that Taiwanese women have to negotiate. Ethnic identity is also salient in contemporary Taiwan.

ETHNIC IDENTITY IN TAIWAN

There is great ethnic diversity in Taiwan. The two main groups are the "Mainlanders," who came to Formosa with the Kuomintang (KMT) after 1945, and the "Native Taiwanese," who arrived from China between the seventeenth century and the beginning of Japanese rule in 1895 and who were already living on the island for generations before the KMT takeover.[2] Mainlanders now comprise approximately 13 percent of the country's population, but have long controlled the reins of power. Native Taiwanese comprise more than 85 percent of the population, including 73 percent of the population who are Minnan and 12 percent who are Hakka. An additional 2 percent of the populace consists of Austronesian aborigines, who are related to the Polynesians, Maori, and other Pacific Islanders. Although intermarriages do occur and Native Taiwanese have taken more power since the 1980s, the Mainlanders monopolized the best positions in government, education, state industry, and culture for the first few decades after KMT takeover (Gates 1987). They still have power and influence in society well beyond their numerical representation in the population. Due to political tensions and economic inequalities, ethnic identity is important in Taiwan and is a component of many life narratives in this book.

LIFE HISTORIES

The bulk of this ethnography consists of life-history interviews, which I have transcribed, translated into English, and then transformed into the chapters of this book. Since life histories give voice to the women who tell them, each one presents one side of an incredibly complex series of human stories. As entrepreneurs, most of these women express a strong sense of agency in the business sphere. When they talk about men, however, many of them portray themselves as victims of their husbands or lovers. As members of different ethnic groups, they also try to present their own groups as possessing higher morality than others. The stories are thus inevitably self-serving, as each one presents the protagonist in what she herself perceives as the best possible light. Yet this dynamic is of interest in itself, not only because these are voices that most of us have never heard, but also because it provides insight into the changing nature of Taiwanese society. Details on methodology are included in the appendix for interested readers.

In a very real sense, the women entrepreneurs in this book play at being women and entrepreneurs, just as the waiter in Sartre's *Being and Nothingness* plays at being a waiter. "He is playing, he is amusing himself," wrote Sartre (1956 [1943]: 59). "But what is he playing? . . . he is playing at *being* a waiter in a café. . . . [He] plays with his condition in order to *realize* it." Knowing that they are being watched and that their stories will be told to the world, the women entrepreneurs in this book play at being eel exporters or ex-beauty queens or café owners. They play at being wives or lesbian lovers, mothers or daughters-in-law, bosses or confidants for other would-be women entrepreneurs. They also play at being Mainlanders, Native Taiwanese, aborigines, or global personalities. The fact that they (we) perform and construct identities in creative ways is not just a product of the research methodology. As interactional sociologists have long known (Goffman 1959), human life is an interactive performance. This book is as much a performance in itself as it is an attempt to render those social processes visible.[3]

ENTERING THE FIELD

Such research was not without its challenges. Life-history interviews were relatively easy to arrange, primarily through networks of social contacts. Cold calls on strangers found through my random sample of neighborhoods were difficult. I had already lived in Taiwan for three years, spoke fluent Mandarin and some Taiwanese, and had research experience in both urban and rural areas of southern Taiwan. But the small storekeepers and entrepreneurs of Taipei proved to be very different from the manufacturers I had studied in Tainan and Kaohsiung Counties. In that project, I was only refused by three of the seventy-two factories I approached for research. In Taipei, however, the pace of life was faster and the entrepreneurs I sought out were busier. They were also already accustomed to brushing off foreigners, whom they often suspect of being Mormon missionaries.

For most of the first year I did research, moreover, part of the problem seemed to be my institutional affiliation with Academia Sinica, which was written on my name card and survey materials. Translated literally, the Chinese name of the institution means "Central Research Institution." Well-educated, middle-class entrepreneurs in good neighborhoods were easy to approach, as they were familiar with my institutional affiliation. In rougher neighborhoods, I had to deal with lower-class, less-educated entrepreneurs. Many are in the informal sector and operate in a gray zone where survival requires such practices as avoiding taxes or operating businesses without the proper licenses. They thus deal frequently with policemen and other government officials in stressful situations. They reacted with the same lack of enthusiasm that urban petty entrepreneurs in America would exhibit if I approached them and said I was coming to research them as an employee of the Federal Bureau of Investigation.

One hot and sunny afternoon, I had already walked up and down En-ping Bak Road for nearly four hours in search of women entrepreneurs to fill out my survey form. The faded colonial architecture in one of the older city neighborhoods recalls the imperial pretensions of Meiji Japan. The stretch of road that I had selected consisted of jewelry shops, textile and sewing goods wholesalers, and the usual mix of betel-nut stands, noodle shops, and coffee houses. The density of women to men entrepreneurs was lower than in many other neighborhoods, and in several stores I encountered hostility even when just inquiring if the "boss" is a man or a woman. One woman looked at my papers, said, "Taxes, taxes, taxes. It's all taxes," turned her back, and ignored me completely. I was already covered with sweat and starting to feel grumpy.

Three older men were drinking beer at a table set up on the sidewalk. One of them called out to me in Japanese. When I responded in Japanese, he smiled broadly and invited me to have a beer with them, an invitation I gladly accepted. He asked what I was doing. I explained my project, as well as the frustrations I felt at so much rejection.

"You can't blame them," he said. "People here don't want to have anything to do with the government. Do you know what happened here when the KMT came to Taiwan? It happened on this very street. I was here, and saw it with my own eyes. Their military was very corrupt, and they took advantage of us Taiwanese. Some soldiers tried to stop a woman from selling cigarettes, and they hit her on the head with their gun. When people tried to defend her, more soldiers came. They killed a lot of people. I saw it myself down there at the traffic round." He pointed to the dilapidated market in the traffic circle down the street. "When you write your book," he said, "write about that. Let people know what happened."

He was referring to the incident of February 28, 1947, which happened shortly after the KMT took control of Taiwan. A conflict between a defiant woman cigarette seller and a soldier enforcing the state tobacco monopoly sparked a riot and inspired islandwide calls for democratization. In the brutal suppression of the subsequent democracy movement, Kuomintang forces killed more than 20,000 civilians.[4] The women I met were as strong and defiant as that woman peddler fifty years ago. Many of them identified themselves as "Taiwanese" in contrast to the "Mainlanders," who came to Taiwan with the KMT. And some of them even associated me with the very same American-supported KMT state that oppressed them.

In March 2000, however, political winds turned in my favor. When Nobel Prize–winner and Academia Sinica President Lee Yuan-tze publicly supported presidential candidate Chen Shui-bian, he brought media attention to Academia Sinica. After that, my research proceeded more smoothly. People generally asked, "Is that Lee Yuan-tze's Academia Sinica?" and responded helpfully to my survey research when I answered in the affirmative. This experience reinforces one of the basic arguments of this book. All human relations, whether between bosses and workers, between men and women, or even between anthropologists and their informants, are profoundly shaped by shifts in the politics and economies of their times. At the same time, however, the political economy is shaped by individuals: by defiant women entrepreneurs, by violent police officers, and by a Nobel Prize winner willing to publicly support his favorite candidate. I now turn to a descriptive portrait of some of those characters: the often defiant, feisty, hardworking and ambitious women entrepreneurs of Taipei.

NOTES

1. Most feminist-inspired research at the time was focused instead on women workers in large factories (i.e., Arrigo 1980, Diamond 1979, Kung 1994 [1983]).

2. Immigration from China was nearly impossible during the Japanese occupation, 1895–1945, especially during the war years.

3. For Sartre's approach to life history, see his analysis of Jean Genet (Sartre 1963 [1952]).

4. For more detailed accounts, see Gates (1987), Kerr (1965), Lee, Myers and Wou (1991), and Phillips (1999).

Chapter Two

Social Contexts of Female Entrepreneurship

Women entrepreneurs have become increasingly visible in Taiwan since the 1990s. Many popular books have been published on the subject (e.g., Chou 1999, T.-W. Chang 1991, Chieh 1993, Hsieh 1999), and women entrepreneurs are brought up in other contexts as well. Psychiatrist Wang Hao-wei, best known for his argument that men are oppressed by social expectations that they provide for housewives and children, attributes the emergence of women entrepreneurs to men's failure to be the sole breadwinners of their families (1998: 200). When men get laid off or fail in business endeavors, he says, their wives often have to pick up their families' economic responsibilities by opening small businesses such as roadside food stalls. This argument fails the litmus test of feminism, however, as it assumes that women react primarily to the success or failure of men in their lives and that they would (and should) remain in the home as housewives if only their husbands were sufficiently successful.

Among the books published on women entrepreneurs, those that advise women on how to go into business are of particular interest. The metanarrative of these texts is usually based on a dichotomy between tradition and modernity, Chinese and Western, male and female. They are thus still embedded in the Republic of China (ROC) national imagination of Taiwan as the carrier of Confucian culture. Chieh Ma (1993), for example, assumes that Taiwanese women have only recently begun leaving the home sphere, and attributes the presence of women entrepreneurs to the growth of Taiwan's service sector after 1986. Chang Tien-wan, as well, contrasts the housewife of "tradition" to the "modern" entrepreneur:

> In past generations, people thought, "an untalented woman is the most virtuous." Without economic ability, without the baptism of knowledge and education, she only had to marry a good husband as a lifetime source of clothes and food. But now women are better educated. After the second world war, women were more courageous in seeking economic independence, and have thrown off subordinate roles in

14

life. . . . Women have broken through the binds of tradition. They can sit down equally with men, compete with them in the workplace, and encourage one another. In the past, women were more likely to be boss-wives, the woman behind every successful man. Now more and more women are coming out of the closet, becoming bosses, industrialists and entrepreneurs on their own. (T.-W. Chang 1991: 1)

Chang Tien-wan's book is by no means an exercise in radical feminism. Her narrative assumes that the housewife (or boss-wife) is the norm; that women entrepreneurs must come out of the household to work; that the road to entrepreneurship will be lonely; and that it could potentially entail conflict with in-laws and husbands. She thus encourages would-be women entrepreneurs to think first of their husband's families: "Marriage is more important than work. There will be times of power, and times of loneliness. Every woman entrepreneur should consider whether or not they are supported by their parents-in-law, their children, and their families" (T.-W. Chang 1991: 15).

It is interesting to note the order of relations that should concern the would-be woman entrepreneur: the parents-in-law come first, followed by children and then other family members (presumably including the husband). Chang ignores completely the existence of unmarried, separated, or divorced women, and she also overlooks their natal families. It is also worth noting the class position implicit in Chang's analysis. She neglects entirely women who have to find work outside the home because their husbands' salaries are too low to support the family, as well as farming women, who have been involved with both agricultural labor and marketing for centuries. The social norm for Chang is the postwar, middle-class, urban housewife.

These manuals for would-be women entrepreneurs are filled with useful tips for entering into specific occupations, and even list success rates and profit margins for different kinds of businesses. It is of anthropological interest as well to note the occupations considered appropriate for women. Chang Tien-wan (1991), for example, specifies food and beverages, beauty, clothing, trade, consulting, and franchise operation as "suitable" for women. Chieh Ma, who says women are "the liveliest of economic animals" (1993: 11), provides a similar but longer list of enterprises which she finds appropriate for women: flower shops, coffee shops, teahouses, cosmetics shops, rental clothing shops, fashion boutiques, modeling agencies, lingerie stores, beauty salons, marriage services, direct sales, maid services, in-home nursing, elder care, health foods, insurance, ice cream stands, bakeries, and noodle stands. Almost all of these are either extensions of women's traditional role in the family as caregiver and food provider, or related to the "feminine" concerns of health, beauty and fashion.

By the end of the decade, however, some feminists had discovered women entrepreneurs and begun depicting them as gender radicals and role models. Feminist journalist Chou Chien-I, who has a master's degree in sociology, depicts women entrepreneurs as very different from women of previous generations. In her introduction, she depicts women of today as "running out into the space under Heaven, among the men" (1999: 2). The first life story in her book is that of twenty-six-year-old Peng Yu-ching, a radical feminist and graduate of National Taiwan University. Peng opened up the women's coffee shop "Witch's Store" directly under FemBooks, Taiwan's premier women's bookstore. Chou introduces her by detailing how she scared off male customers by decorating her store with women's underwear, thus signaling her interest in attracting a female clientele. This example of a radical feminist makes entrepreneurship appear to place women in the feminist avant-garde.

Especially since successful women entrepreneurs are often described in the media as "strong women" or as pioneers in a new, pro-feminist Taiwan, many Taiwanese still consider it unusual for women to go into business for themselves or with others rather than to work for their husbands. When I first began my research, fellow scholars and women friends alike cautioned me of the difficulties I would encounter, as there could not possibly be many women entrepreneurs. One female friend, a design teacher, said, "You won't find many women entrepreneurs in Taiwan. Entrepreneurship contradicts the three obediences and four virtues [of Confucianism]."

Many Taiwanese expect women entrepreneurs to be unusually strong. One woman, an artist, told me that women entrepreneurs are most likely women who have encountered problems with men and thus no longer wish to be housewives. She anticipated that I would find many divorced women, as well as single women intent on avoiding marriage. A well-known male fiction writer said, "Many of them are the little wives (mistresses) of wealthy men. Those men set them up in business so that they will have something to do." I soon discovered that these stereotypes are far removed from reality.

This public discourse deals primarily with some kinds of women entrepreneurs, and carries a strong middle-class bias. Most women entrepreneurs in these books and other forms of public discourse are middle-class entrepreneurs: the women one meets at FemBooks, at the Women's Awakening Foundation, at the Rotary Club section for women entrepreneurs, or in the Chinese Women Entrepreneurs Association. There is much to learn from these women, and stories of such middle-class women have contributed much to my understanding of Taiwan. But not all women can afford to make a choice between the existence of an urban housewife and the career of an entrepreneur. Some women entrepreneurs more closely resemble an elderly night-market vendor who answered my question about expectations for women to stay at home with an impatient, "Impossible!" "After the war," she said, "everybody was very poor. The only way to survive was for both men and women to go out and work." Since their stories remain untold, even in Taiwan, a combination of ethnography and survey research remains the best way to understand the diversity of women entrepreneurs.

DEMOGRAPHIC PROFILES
OF TAIPEI WOMEN ENTREPRENEURS

A gendered portrait of entrepreneurship in Taipei was gained from the survey of Taipei enterprises I took in a random sample of urban neighborhoods (*lin*) from

August 1999 to November 2000. Of the 762 enterprises surveyed, 28 percent self-identified as women-owned businesses, 60.5 percent as men-owned businesses, and 6.8 percent as businesses owned jointly by men and women. The remaining businesses were thirty-four corporations, such as banks and fast-food chains, one state-run enterprise, and one nonprofit NGO. Of the 213 women-owned businesses identified through the survey, 122 women entrepreneurs agreed to participate in the study by filling out a four-page survey. The study, by revealing the following demographic characteristics of Taipei women entrepreneurs, provides a wider social context for the life narratives in subsequent chapters.

Ethnicity

The ethnic composition of Taipei women entrepreneurs reflects the historical conditions of Taiwan. The main axes of ethnic identity are Native Taiwanese, Mainlander, Hakka, and aboriginal. Under the Chiang regime, Mainlanders tended to hold the reins of power as government officials, managers in state-run firms and major industries; as well as in the spheres of the arts, the media, the military, and education. Most Native Taiwanese, virtually excluded from the higher echelons of power, were thus forced by circumstances to focus their energies on agriculture, small-scale entrepreneurship, and labor-intensive manufacturing (Gates 1987: 56). In this sense, Taiwanese entrepreneurs long resembled Bonacich's "middleman minorities" (1973), who seek out niches in private enterprise because they are excluded from other avenues of social mobility. This is even more true of women entrepreneurs, who also face gender discrimination in the job market.

Surprisingly, these ethnically based occupational patterns are still visible in the population of women who become entrepreneurs. At 77 percent, the percentage of Native Taiwanese in my sample is higher than their representation of 65.6 percent in the general population of Taipei, suggesting that Taiwanese women are more likely to start their own business than are other women. On the other hand, the 13.1 percent of Mainlander women in business is lower than their proportion of 25.9 percent in the general population. The ethnic distribution of women entrepreneurs compared to the general Taipei population is indicated in table 2.1.

Table 2.1. Ethnicity of Women Entrepreneurs

Ethnic Group	Women Entrepreneurs	Taipei Population
Native Taiwanese	77.0	65.6
Mainlanders	13.1	25.9
Hakka	4.9	7.7
Aboriginal	0.8	0.2
Other	4.1	0.6

Sources: Fieldwork; Academia Sinica Institute of Sociology 1992

Educational Attainment

Taipei women entrepreneurs seem to be better educated than their counterparts in Taipei's population of women over the age of fifteen: 45.1 percent and 35.3 percent of women entrepreneurs have completed senior high school and postsecondary education, respectively, as compared to 30 percent and 30.9 percent in the general population (see table 2.2). There is a possibility of a sampling error here, as more educated women are likely to be more comfortable with both foreign researchers and survey instruments than less educated women. I think, however, that the larger percentage of senior-high and postsecondary educated women among women entrepreneurs reflects well the social reality of women in the workplace. Women with more education are more likely than lower-educated women to feel the effects of a "glass ceiling" in the workplace, simply because they are competing with men for managerial and administrative positions. Lower-educated women and men, however, tend to remain in manual-labor positions. With lower expectations in the first place, they do not feel the same frustrations of gender-based discrimination in promotion. In light of my field research and the relevant sociological research, especially by Baraka (1999) and Chang and Yi (1999), I think that the high percentage of educated women among women entrepreneurs is partly a reaction against gender discrimination in the workplace. Women with higher education levels are also more likely to succeed in entrepreneurship because they are better skilled and have better social networks.

Age Distribution

Of the 116 women who agreed to tell me their age, the median age was forty-one years old. Only 8.6 percent of the women entrepreneurs interviewed were less than thirty years old (see table 2.3). At 66.4 percent, a large percentage of women entrepreneurs is middle-aged (35–54). Several factors may contribute to this age distribution. For most entrepreneurs, it is important to gain work experience and save sufficient funds before going into business. They also need time to develop the social networks essential to financing and running a business. Some women go into entrepreneurship only after they have become aware of gender-based discrimination in the workplace or, in the case of women who left the job market to

Table 2.2. Educational Attainment of Women Entrepreneurs

Educational Level	Women Entrepreneurs	Taipei Women over Age Fifteen	Taipei Men over Age Fifteen
Illiterate	0.8	3.7	0.8
Elementary school	9.8	20.0	15.4
Junior high	9.0	15.0	16.5
Senior high	45.1	30.0	28.8
Postsecondary education	35.3	30.9	37.9

Sources: Fieldwork; Taipei City Government 2001

Table 2.3. Age Distribution of Women Entrepreneurs

Age Bracket	Women Entrepreneurs	Taipei Women over Age Fifteen
15–19	0	11.0
20–24	0.8	12.3
25–29	7.8	13.8
30–34	14.7	14.2
35–39	18.1	13.4
40–44	20.7	8.9
45–49	11.2	6.0
50–54	16.4	5.3
55–59	1.7	4.2
60–64	6.9	3.6
65–69	0.8	2.9
70–74	0.8	1.9
75–79	0	1.3
80 and above	0	0.7

Sources: Fieldwork; Executive Yuan Census Bureau 1992

give birth to children, have had trouble reentering the job market. At any rate, entrepreneurship tends to be a middle-age occupation.

Marital Status

In terms of marital status, there is little difference between women entrepreneurs and the general Taipei women population, an observation that refutes the hypothesis that "for a woman, family and business do not mix" (Skoggard 1996: 151). Since very few women marry under the age of twenty, and I have only interviewed one women entrepreneur under the age of twenty-five, who happened to be married, I have compared only the marital status data on women over the age of twenty-five in my sample and the 1990 census. I found that the percentages of single, married, and divorced women do not vary significantly between women entrepreneurs and women in general: 12.4 percent of women entrepreneurs are single and 79.3 percent are married or cohabiting, compared to 15.3 percent and 73.7 percent in the general population (see table 2.4). The divorce rate for women

Table 2.4. Marital Status of Women Entrepreneurs

Marital Status	Women Entrepreneurs	Taipei Women over 25	Taipei Men over 25
Single	12.4	15.3	21.4
Married (or cohabiting)	79.3	73.7	73.1
Divorced (or separated)	5.8	3.8	3.1
Widowed	2.5	7.3	2.4

Sources: Fieldwork; Executive Yuan Census Bureau 1992

entrepreneurs, at 5.8 percent, is slightly higher than that of the 3.8 percent of women in the general population. The percentage of widows in my sample, at 2.5 percent, is lower than for that of the widows in the women's population at large, at 7.3 percent, probably because many retire from business activities with old age.

GOING INTO BUSINESS: THE FIRST STEPS

When asked about their motivations for going into business, the entrepreneurs themselves dispelled many popular stereotypes. In response to my survey, only one woman said her boyfriend helped her set up a business (see table 2.5). Three of them said they went into business because of a divorce, and three of them said they did it because they wish to avoid marriage. The most common response, made by 63 women surveyed (51.6%), was "personal interest." The next common responses were "to supplement an inadequate family income" (20.5%), "husband's suggestion" (12.8%), and "don't like to have a boss" (9%). The latter response is also a common justification given by men for why they go into business for themselves (Bosco 1995, Shieh 1992).

The "other" responses provided valuable insights into female entrepreneurship. Some were idiosyncratic, such as the florist who said she went into business due to the "will of God" and the fifty-nine-year-old woman who opened up a noodle shop in the first floor of her house "to pay property taxes." Two women were drawn to particular occupations as social missions, such as the woman who opened a restaurant "to promote organic food" and the childcare-center owner who reported going into business because she likes children and "wants to give them ideals." In those two cases, entrepreneurship is clearly a "fundamental project" in the existential sense.

Many women were motivated to go into business because of relations to other people in their kin and friendship networks. Two women went into business at the suggestion of their fathers, and one sixty-three-year-old woman took over the noodle stand of a younger sister who emigrated to the United States. Another

Table 2.5.   Motivations for Female Entrepreneurship

Personal interest	51.6%
To supplement an inadequate family income	20.5%
Other	13.9%
Husband's suggestion	12.3%
To avoid marriage	2.5%
Divorced, need to support myself	2.5%
Widowed, need to support myself	0.8%
Boyfriend set me up in business	0.8%

Source: Fieldwork.
Note: N = 122, multiple responses possible.

went into business after a female friend approached her and asked her to become a business partner. Some of their motivations are related to specific problems and interests of women. Three said they went into business for themselves because it is easier to manage childcare responsibilities as an entrepreneur than as an employee. Three older women said they went into business because they were bored after their children grew up.

Many women are motivated to go into business by economic exigencies, as is reflected in the 20.5 percent who said they did it because their families needed extra income. Other women offered their "other" responses as reactions to poor employment prospects. One said she is unemployed and needed to go into business because "Taiwan doesn't have a good enough welfare system." One fifty-year-old woman opened up a beverage stand on the first floor of her home to provide waged jobs for her two unemployed sons, saying that they would otherwise have trouble finding work. One florist said, "Everyone needs a job. This is my job." For these women, entrepreneurship is just an alternative to formal employment. These women, with their small food stands and temporary stalls, are present in large numbers in night markets and on street corners all over Taipei. They often perceive themselves as victims of unemployment rather than as entrepreneurs and creative agents.

Role of Husbands in Women's Firms

There is some overlap between women as thau-ke ("bosses") and women as thau-ke-niu ("boss-wives"), or women who run businesses with their husbands (Kao 1999, Y.-H. Lu 1998), as husbands are not entirely absent from women's companies. Boss-wives, the more common role for women in Taiwanese firms, work for their husbands' companies and do not self-identify as "boss." This does not mean that boss-wives are not equal partners in firms identified as male-owned. Taiwanese sociologist Lu Yu-hsia (1998, 2001), in fact, has found that women do often achieve positions of power and equality in such firms. There is also a small intermediate category of women who identity themselves as equal partners with their husbands. Much of the difference between these three categories lies in self-identification rather than in the degree of power wielded by women in the businesses. In this study, "women entrepreneur" refers to women who self-identify as the main owner of the business, even if their husbands participate in the business. If the husbands are strongly involved in the businesses, most women identify the men as bosses and themselves as boss-wives.

A majority of the self-identified women entrepreneurs responded either that their husbands play no role at all in the business (45.1%), or that they have no husband or significant other (10.7%) (see table 2.6). Their companies are thus purely women-owned and -operated firms. When men do participate in their wives' companies at all, it is primarily as providers of capital: 28.7 percent of women entrepreneurs report that their husbands have provided them with capital. Only 11.5 percent reported that their husbands work as employees in their

Table 2.6. What Husbands Do in the Business

Have no role	45.1%
Provide capital	28.7%
Work as employees	11.5%
No husband	10.7%
Other	5.7%

Source: Fieldwork
Note: N = 122, multiple responses possible.

companies, doing jobs such as TV or car repair, cooking in a restaurant, or taking care of other tasks. Another 5.7 percent responded "other," saying that their husbands "help out" occasionally (two people), "give advice" (two people), or "clean the store" (one person). In two cases, husband and wife run separately registered stores in the same occupation, but in different locations. In the case of an electronic appliance store in the formal sector, that strategy was probably chosen primarily to dilute the officially reported profits and thus to lower the collective tax burden of the two individual stores. In the other case, where both husband and wife sell fruit from the back of different trucks, tax considerations were probably less important than widening their markets.

In most cases, the husbands are also entrepreneurs and/or have more lucrative jobs than working for their wives. In answer to the question about the occupation of their husband or significant other, 54.9 percent said business or commerce. The second most common response at 14.8 percent was "service job," followed by "worker" at 12.3 percent. It thus seems very common for women to marry into families of the same social class, with both husband and wife in business, albeit in different locations and in different fields. Although the businesses may have developed after the marriages, this shows that women tend to marry people with the same inclination to go into business. Women in such families are also more likely to succeed in business because their families of marriage can provide them with the beginnings of necessary social networks. Table 2.7 shows the occupational distribution of their husbands.

Table 2.7. Occupation of Husbands or Significant Others

Commerce/business	54.9%
Service industry	14.8%
Worker	12.3%
No husband	7.4%
Government	2.5%
Military	2.5%
Other	2.5%
Teaching	1.6%
Farming	0.8%
No answer	0.8%

Source: Fieldwork
Note: N = 122

Getting Capital

Getting capital is one of the most important obstacles to entrepreneurship and the first burden that each woman entrepreneur must overcome. Many women business owners complain about the difficulty of getting bank loans and other institutional forms of credit, especially if land and housing are registered in their husbands' names and cannot be used as collateral for their business loans. Survey responses indeed show that only 12 percent of women entrepreneurs got initial startup capital from bank loans. This supports the common belief that women face gender discrimination in the credit markets, although further knowledge about men entrepreneurs—studied as men rather than as universal human subjects—would be necessary to test the hypothesis statistically.

Women rely mostly on their own efforts when starting up their businesses: 63.2 percent of women responding said they got startup capital by working elsewhere and saving up the money themselves.[1] Revolving credit societies are also a common way of raising startup capital: 18.8 percent of the respondents said they got their startup capital on this type of informal credit market. Many women, including those who do not open their own businesses, invest in revolving credit societies to earn the high interest rates.[2] It is also common for women to get capital from relatives and friends: 12 percent reported getting startup capital as gifts from parents and 10.3 percent from husbands; 5.1 percent took loans from relatives; 6.8 percent sought out friends to invest in their firms as shareholders; and 3.4 percent of the women said that they started their business with their dowry money. Table 2.8 illustrates the sources of startup capital for Taipei women entrepreneurs.

Scale of Women-Owned Businesses

The scale of women-owned businesses, measured both by capital invested and number of workers, tends to be very small. Of all the businesses surveyed, the median amount of capital invested was NT$1,000,000.[3] In terms of capital invested,

Table 2.8. Sources of Startup Capital

Private savings	63.2%
Revolving credit associations	18.8%
Bank loans	12.0%
Provided by parents	12.0%
Provided by husband	10.3%
Shareholders	6.8%
Loans from relatives	5.1%
Dowry	3.4%
Provided by boyfriend	0.8%
Other	0.8%

Source: Fieldwork
Note: N = 117, multiple responses possible

the smallest entrepreneur was a woman who set up a breakfast stand in front of her house. Since she bought the stand and other materials second-hand from another neighbor, she invested only NT$5,000 to go into business. The largest business in the survey was a wine and gourmet foods import company, which also had a large retail store in the exclusive neighborhood of Tianmu. They started with an initial capital of NT$70,000,000.

The median number of workers in this sample of women-owned enterprises was only two people. Over a third of the women interviewed (33.6%) do not hire employees and tend to work alone, with only occasional help from family members (see table 2.9). Those with only one to four employees composed another 45.9 percent of the sample. Those who hired only one person tended to rely on family members, especially sisters and children, for assistance in running the business, but beyond that scale they tended to hire on the labor market. Of the women interviewed, 16.4 percent hire five to ten workers, and only 4 percent hire more than ten employees. The largest employer was a medical equipment manufacturer and exporter with forty employees. Taipei women entrepreneurs thus are predominantly microentrepreneurs, whom Hill Gates (1987) classified as part of the working class.

Common Occupations for Women

Most women entrepreneurs work in occupations traditionally considered to be "women's work," including food preparation, weaving and clothing production, as well as care provision for children, elders, and men. Of the 213 women entrepreneurs surveyed, 40 percent are in businesses related to food production and sales, the largest category in that group being coffee shops. A further 21.6 percent are in clothing-related businesses. Care provision is also a major area for women entrepreneurs, with 8 percent engaged in care for children, elders, and men. Another 5.7 percent are engaged in beauty professions.

Further analysis shows that women consistently choose occupations regarded as feminine. Even in the "other retail" category, for example, women are concentrated in the sales of flowers, gifts, and crafts. In the service professions, women are concentrated in food preparation, laundry and clothing repair, care professions, and beauty professions. In the "other services" category, pet care has the largest number of women entrepreneurs. Women, however, are rarely seen in professions such as car and motorcycle repair, manufacturing, and trading. The distribution of women entrepreneurs according to occupation is listed in table 2.10.

Table 2.9. Number of Employees Hired by Women Entrepreneurs

Self-employed, no workers	33.6%
1–4 workers	45.9%
5–10 workers	16.4%
More than 10 workers	4.0%

Source: Fieldwork
Note: N = 122

Table 2.10. Common Occupations for Women Entrepreneurs

Occupation	Number	Occupation	Number
Food- and Drink-Related		Other Retail	
Restaurant	13	Flowers	8
Coffee shop	18	Gifts and crafts	10
Snack shop/noodles	13	Eyeglasses	1
Roadside food stand	3	Bookstore	2
Bakery	4	Toy shop	1
Beverages/shaved ice	6	Telecommunications	4
Pub	2	Hardware store	2
Convenience/food store	8	Art gallery	3
Rice store	1	Pharmacy	1
Fruit stand	8	Exercise equipment	1
Tea leaves	1	Video store	1
Betel nuts	5	Antiques	1
Candy shop	1	Jewelry	2
Alcohol store	2	Electronics	2
Total	85 (40.0%)	Furniture	1
Clothing-Related		Household goods	1
Clothing boutique	31	Total	41 (19.2%)
Cloth/curtains	3	Other services	
Women's lingerie	1	Pet salon	3
Leather goods	2	Photo processing	2
Shoes	3	Kitchen/bathroom installation	1
Laundry	2	Gas-appliance installation	1
Clothing repair/tailor	4	TV repair	1
Total	46 (21.6%)	Motorcycle repair	1
Care-Related Services		Car repair	2
(children, elders, men)		Delivery service	1
Afterbirth maternity care	1	Total	12 (5.7%)
Day care	8	Miscellaneous	
Schools for children	6	Trading company	1
Nursing home	1	Manufacturing	1
Brothel	1	Publishing house	1
Total	17 (8.0%)	Total	3 (1.4%)
Beauty-Related			
Hair salon	5		
Facial care/consulting	4		
Beauty goods/cosmetics	3		
Total	12 (5.7%)		

Source: Fieldwork
Note: N = 213, multiple responses possible

Women entrepreneurs nevertheless frequently insist that women are capable of any occupation they wish to pursue. Many either refused to answer my question concerning what occupations are most suitable for women, or insisted that it depends entirely on the woman's own wishes. One TV-repair-shop owner, to give just one example of such a response, went so far as to say that:

> Women are much better than men at everything. Women are better at all kinds of business. They are even better at repairing motorcycles, because they are more meticulous. They are better at dealing with customers, handling money, everything. On the surface, men appear to be the bosses and women seem to stand behind them in second place. But actually, it is often the woman who is in charge. . . . Give a woman an unfamiliar task and she will do it. A man will be afraid, and his thoughts will scatter from east to west. Women are stronger than men, better at enduring hardship and pain. It's in-bred. Men are stronger and more muscular, but that's all. They lack ability.

Whether they sell flowers or repair motorcycles, women entrepreneurs make greater contact with the outside world through entrepreneurship than they would as housewives. Since entrepreneurship gives women new forms of identity beyond marriage and the family, it can empower women both at home and in the wider society. Women entrepreneurs themselves perceive their jobs as empowering, with 77.9 percent agreeing with the statement "entrepreneurship gives women more free space." Yet it is in the life histories of individual entrepreneurs that empowerment is most visible. It is also in life histories that strategies to gain that power are most easily observed. Those life histories thus make up the heart of this book.

NOTES

1. Men are far more likely to inherit family firms from their parents. In spite of legal changes protecting women, most families still follow the custom of passing their businesses and other forms of immovable property to sons as inheritance. Daughters receive a dowry in movable property at marriage, which is justified as the equivalent to an inheritance. For women with entrepreneurial inclinations, a dowry is certainly less useful than inheriting the whole family firm.

2. In summer 2002, the interest rate on revolving credit societies was approximately 15 percent *a month*. High interest rates reflect high risk.

3. For the period 1999 to 2001, US$1 equaled approximately NT$32.

Chapter Three

Two Street Vendors

Fifty-five-year-old Tan So-hoa was one of the first women to participate in my survey research. Since she lived and worked on the street a few houses away from my home, moreover, I continued to visit her on a nearly daily basis afterwards. So-hoa's business was vital to the neighborhood, yet miniscule. It consisted merely of a pushcart, a table, and two chairs set up outside the front door of her apartment building. Most mornings between six and ten o'clock, she sold homemade soy milk, egg tortillas, and rice balls to commuters rushing to work and school. Most of them just stopped their cars and yelled orders out the window. Even bus drivers pulled up to buy rice balls and soy milk, much to the irritation of passengers and drivers stuck in traffic behind them. In the two years that I ate there, I only once had to share the small table with another customer, who was in fact seeking converts to a Buddhist sect instead of just coming to eat.

Perhaps because of the micro scale of her business, So-hoa told her story in a different way than most of the women entrepreneurs in this book. She has never been interviewed by the media or by graduate students writing theses, nor has she ever been approached by young women seeking advice on business and careers. Unlike more successful women entrepreneurs, she has no highly developed life narrative to relate. Instead her story is told in snippets of conversation, minimalist poems recited over months and years. Yet she is as keenly aware of social and economic changes in Taiwan as other women and comments on them frequently. When I noted that many of the more traditional breakfast places in the neighborhood, where soy milk is sold with pastries like *shaobing* and *youtiao*, had gone out of business, she said:

> Only old people eat this now. Children all want to eat hamburgers and milk-tea. That's why you see so many fat children now. In fact, soy milk is much better for you, but they see the other children eating hamburgers so they want to eat them too. They eat all that stuff, and they drink cola.

She is acutely aware of the competition from businesses perceived as more modern. Hamburgers and sandwiches, although not considered by adults to be appropriate for "real" meals of lunch or dinner, are common breakfast fare in Taipei. Her main competitors are thus not similar food stands, but local chains of small hamburger stores that, like McDonald's, offer a standard menu with relatively standard quality. One day, she pointed at Mei-er-mei, the franchised breakfast-hamburger store visible down the street:

> It's not easy to do this now, because of chain stores like that. They make a lot of money. Their overhead is low, so they make more profit on each item. Some people tell me to sell sandwiches and milk-tea, but it would be a bother. You have to buy so many things like bread, ham, and eggs, and find a space to put it down somewhere. I would have to lug all that down from my apartment every day, set it up, and then I wouldn't make any more money than I make now. This is easier.

Making soy milk is nothing new to So-hoa. When she was growing up in a family of eight children in Chiayi, her parents ran a tofu shop and she helped out. She pointed out the change in technology she has witnessed: "I learned how to make soy milk from my mother. Back then, we did it all by hand with a mortar and pestle."

So-hoa has never thought of herself as an entrepreneur. Having moved to Taipei as a woman worker in the 1960s, she married a factory worker and moved in with his family. After her first pregnancy, she retired from the workforce and concentrated on taking care of her children until they got older and she grew restless. She said she went into business only because "I was bored. My children grew up and I didn't just want to sit around the house doing nothing."

When I asked what "grown up" means to her, she said:

> When they go to school. When they are babies, I had to feed them, bathe them, and do everything for them. But then they got old enough to do those things for themselves. They could feed themselves, bathe themselves, and go to school themselves. Since I didn't have to do anything for them, I became bored. I opened a seafood place.

She stressed, however, that just opening up a business by no means defined her as an entrepreneur. "It wasn't a *restaurant*," she said. "It wasn't anything so formal. I just rented a small storefront and cooked seafood to sell. I only had one or two employees." She sold seafood for ten years, closing only when the building she rented was torn down to make way for road construction. After a few months at home, which she described as boring, she decided to go back into business and bought a second-hand food stand for NT$2,000. Consistent with her repeated assertions that she is not an entrepreneur, she contrasted her choice of work activity to the choice of other older people to stay at home and play mahjong. In contrast to her earlier business, her current stand is largely a choice of retirement activity:

> I'm old. This isn't a store. I don't hire people. I just got tired of sitting at home and watching TV. I was afraid I would get senile. I thought I should get some exercise and

use my brain. So I talked to a friend who was doing this, and decided to do it myself. That's all there is to it. Some people tell me I should start playing mahjong. Then I'll use my head and won't go senile. But I don't want to gamble. I tell my children not to gamble, too. They should earn money from a regular job, even if it's not much money, but they shouldn't try gambling to earn money.

So-hoa described herself as part of the working class:

I don't earn much. But I don't want to just sit at home. People will say I'm not earning my own money. My son gives me money, and my husband earns money. But this way I can contribute too. Nobody can say I'm not earning money. I can't go out and work (*siong-pan*) because nobody wants an old woman. But this way I can earn my own "work money" (*kang-chi*, money earned from manual labor). It's just like going to work for someone else, and then I get *kang-chi*. The only difference is that I do it myself.

Always comparing her situation to that of factory workers, So-hoa said:

Actually, it is better to go to work. You get a regular salary, and you have regular hours. You get to relax on weekends. Doing this, I don't get weekends off. And I don't know how much money I will make. But if I didn't do this, I don't know what I would do. Watch TV? Sleep? I don't know what I should do, so I do this. That's all there is to it. There is no reason to research that.

To a certain extent, her humility seems well placed. Her story is scarcely one of a successful entrepreneur. After she closes her soy milk stand at ten o'clock in the morning, she goes to market and buys food for their noon and evening meals. She spends the rest of the day cooking, cleaning, and taking care of her elderly parents-in-law. Her husband and unmarried adult son live at home, but she barely mentions them except to say that they have working lives of their own in nearby factories. Her life seems ordinary, but fortunate when contrasted with that of some other women, a fact that she knows well from seeing the experience of neighbors such as betel-nut seller Lim Koat-ho.

A BETEL-NUT SELLER

The ubiquitous betel-nut stands constitute one of the most visibly gendered segments of the Taiwanese street economy. The betel nut, fruit of the Areca catechu palm, has mild stimulative properties. Of neither Chinese nor Japanese origin, it is chewed throughout South Asia, Southeast Asia, and the Austronesian-dominated areas of the South Pacific. It thus remains as a visible reminder of aboriginal influences on Taiwanese culture. Sold as the young fruit, cut in half and plastered with lime, it is known as *chhi-a*. Served as *pau-hiu-a*, it is wrapped with the lime condiment in leaves that gives it a strong mint-like flavor. No matter how it is prepared, it is enjoyed primarily by factory workers, taxi drivers, and other male members of the working class who need to maintain physical stamina while working. Women, with the exception of aboriginal women, rarely chew it. It colors the saliva and stains the mouth of those who chew it a bright red. As a visible class marker (Wu 1996b), moreover, it is deplored by the middle class. The government frowns upon its widespread use, because betel nuts cause oral cancer and because hillside betel-nut plantations are prone to dangerous mudslides.

Betel-nut stands line the streets and highways of Taiwan. Any place south of Taipei City, betel-nut stands are likely to be brightly lit glass booths occupied by scantily clad young women dressed to attract the business of working-class men. Many of them are teenagers, sent to work by their parents to earn NT$20,000 to NT$30,000 a month in wages plus additional "tips" if they allow themselves to be kissed or fondled by clients. In the more closely regulated streets of Taipei, however, betel-nut stands are likely to be modest stands staffed as well by older women or even men. According to a survey taken by the Taipei Municipal Government in 2000, more than 600,000 betel nuts are sold daily in 1,300 betel-nut stands in the city. Only 258 of those stands are legally licensed. Most of them also sell other products, chiefly cigarettes and beverages.

For one hot summer in Taipei, I got into the habit of frequently stopping at Lim Koat-ho's betel-nut stand in an alley near my home, a place I had initially visited while doing survey research. The attraction that brought me back again and again was not betel nuts but her other product, shaven ice (*chhoa-bing*) served with a sugary fruit and candy sauce. I was intrigued by the fact that she divided up the store with her brother, she specializing in chhoa-bing and he in the sale of betel nuts. When she filled out the survey, she said that the betel-nut stand was also hers, but she had given it to her brother after his chicken farm in Nantou County was destroyed in the major earthquake of September 21, 1999. I was intrigued by this case of unusually close cooperation between a woman and a member of her natal family, as it seemed to fit into what Bernard and Rita Gallin (1982) described as an increasing use of affinal ties in entrepreneurial families. When I asked if I could do a life-history interview with this forty-one-year-old Native Taiwanese woman, I did not know what I was asking. I helped her and her brother at the labor-intensive task of rolling betel nuts in leaves as I conducted the interview, anticipating just an ordinary work history.

Koat-ho was born in Taipei and grew up in the central historical district of Hsimen Ting. Her parents ran a plywood factory together and were able to support her through junior college. She got her first work experiences while in junior college, taking temporary jobs at a pharmacy, a bureau of the national customs agency, a bank, and an accounting firm. She even worked for two months on the assembly line in a factory producing inflatable plastic dolls for export. After graduation, she worked in a bank until marriage.

At this point in her narrative, her brother interrupted to say, "After she got married, she wasn't allowed to work anymore." Visibly agitated by his statement, she protested, "That's not the way it was!" I asked if her bank had the once-common practice of requiring women to leave their jobs at marriage. He said, "Yes." She exclaimed, "That's not it!" After heated debate with her brother, she decided to relate to me the story of her failed marriage. It turned out that she had quit that job at the bank because her boss liked her, but she wanted to marry another man. She married the owner of an ironworks factory and worked as the thau-ke-niu, or boss-wife:

> I did everything from accounting to production. I even went out and did sales, then came back and gave the orders for production. I worked on the assembly line, and I even swept the floors when we closed up at night. Of course, I was the one who had to sweep the floors. The craftsmen refused to sweep the floors and told us to do it ourselves. In the beginning, we had a lot of workers, but in the end it was just my husband and I.

Like many other labor-intensive Taiwanese companies in the 1990s, they could eventually no longer compete with the lower labor costs of China. She stopped working for the company in 1992 and looked around for an alternative income source. The solution was just across the street:

> Do you see that place selling sausages across the street? He used to sell betel nuts there, but business was bad. He asked me if I wanted to take over and see what I could do with it. I decided to try it out. As I did it, my self-confidence increased, and my business got better and better, so I kept doing it.

By this time, her brother and parents had already moved to Nantou County in central Taiwan. Her brother, who had worked at the Kentucky Fried Chicken headquarters in Taipei, noticed the need for chickens. He started his own company as chicken supplier, and relocated with his parents to Nantou to raise chickens together. Since Nantou is known for its betel nuts, visits to her parents also gave Koat-ho a chance to study new techniques. When I asked her where she learned the techniques of selecting fresh betel nuts and properly mixing the lime, she replied:

> At first, the neighbor taught me a bit. But after he saw that my business was so good, he regretted selling it to me. He wanted the betel-nut stand back, but how could I give it back when I was earning so much money? Instead, I went to Nantou and stayed with my brother. That is where I learned how to prepare the best-tasting lime. Since I was serving better betel nuts than most betel-nut stands in Taipei, I got a lot of customers. And, since I was earning more money from betel nuts than he was from ironworks, [my husband] closed down the factory.

Koat-ho needed the extra labor in her successful betel-nut stand, but her husband was unwilling to work for her. Instead, he invested in a Taoist temple with his landlord:

> We were getting by with that [betel-nut stand] until it happened. My husband was possessed by a spirit and forced to become a tang-ki ("spirit medium"). When he was possessed, there was nothing I could do about it. He just suddenly got very sick and couldn't get better. He went around asking Taoists what was wrong. Some very profound people

said that he was possessed by a spirit and needed to become a tang-ki. We had to open a temple, so we opened up a temple right here where this shop is. A temple is very complicated, with lots of strangers coming in and out, and a lot of things happened. But he needed to do it, and he helped a lot of people. Being a tang-ki is kind of like being a priest, except he would go into trances. You can't say he was injuring himself, because nobody would do that to himself. But he would go into a trance and flail about until blood ran from his wounds.

When I asked if he is still a tang-ki, she said she didn't know. That temple, she said, had brought about the end of her marriage: "I don't even know where that person is anymore. That person just ran away. All I know is that people who are possessed should be tang-ki for all their lives. Can you change? How should I know?" She blamed events on the moral failings of her landlord, who had helped her husband set up the temple:

At the time, we said we were doing good deeds, so we helped him as much as we could. My husband and I did almost all the work. I didn't suspect that it might be demonic. We were cheated by him. Since he had already submitted to those evil ways, it was normal that we would separate. But there were also external reasons. He ran off with another woman. I don't know where he is. He just abandoned me and our daughter to run away with another woman. We got divorced.

A few months after their divorce, on September 21, 1999, an earthquake of magnitude 7.6 on the Richter scale hit central Taiwan. Nantou County was especially badly hurt. Koat-ho's brother and parents survived the earthquake, but their chicken coops were destroyed entirely. With roads and bridges destroyed as well, they saw no hope of reconstructing their lives in the near future and returned to Taipei. She said, "I asked my brother to come and sell betel nuts, since business was so good that I couldn't handle it alone anymore. I simply decided to ask him to come and do it. That is when I started to sell shaved ice, and that is how I got to know you!"

She began by explaining the economics of betel nuts and shaved ice. She said that the population of betel-nut chewers remains relatively stable, yet the number of betel-nut sellers is expanding rapidly, creating intense competition. In our neighborhood, she said, there were once only five betel-nut stands, but they rapidly increased to about fifteen. Faced with new entrants in the field, betel-nut sellers compete by either lowering their prices or improving their quality, which can justify a slightly higher price. That strategy, however, leaves them with higher costs and lower profits. Betel nuts, she said, gives them a gross profit of 40 percent. Due to the lower costs of the raw ingredients, shaved ice is more profitable and grosses 70 percent earnings. "The problem with shaved ice," she said, " is that it is seasonal."

Like ice-cream-stand owners in North America, she closed up shop when summer ended. She found a new job as a waitress in a restaurant. When I asked if she planned on selling shaved ice again the following summer, she said, "I will if I have to. Anyway, it seems as if a lot of people like it." Noting the change in occupation, I asked whether she prefers working for others or running a small business. She said:

> With shaved ice, you rely on the weather to eat. When the weather is hot, you get a lot of business. When it rains or turns cold, nobody wants to eat ice. In winter, absolutely nobody eats it. As for the money, of course it is better to go into business, because the money is more flexible. If you work, you always get the same wages for the same amount of work. You don't get a lot of money, but at least it is stable. If you want to earn more money, you have no way to do so, but if you run your own business, business is sometimes good and you can earn a lot more money with the same amount of work.

Since she was leaving her own business for a waitress job, her brother jokingly called her a member of the "floating proletariat." On the topic of women entrepreneurs, she stated her opinion bluntly:

> Only women who are forced to rely on themselves open up businesses. If your husband is good, why would you open up a business as a sole proprietorship? That would be impossible! Maybe some women have exceptional talents, or maybe their husbands can forgive them for doing that, but I think that very few women own their own businesses. It is poverty that makes people change, and when people are poor they will do anything.

DISCUSSION

The life narratives of So-hoa and Koat-ho open up the discussion of female entrepreneurship from the perspective of working-class women. Their stories already provide access to a set of cultural norms about marriage to which all Taiwanese women refer, although there is great individual variance in the extent to which they accept, reject, or passively resist such norms. In spite of some alternatives such as uxorilocal marriage, the cultural norm in Taiwan is the patrilineal Chinese family. From the viewpoint of men, the patrilineage is a stable continuity running through the male descent line for generations. Women are like streams of water flowing between families identified by male surnames, and are socially identified primarily with families of marriage rather than with families of blood descent. When women marry into new families, they thus find themselves faced with certain social expectations and initially with very little social capital. The Taiwanese proverb sums up the expectations succinctly: marry a chicken and follow a chicken; marry a dog and follow a dog (*ke ke sui ke, ke kau sui kau*).

In a life-history analysis of thirty-five widows, Hsu Min-tao (1998) found six cultural themes through which most Taiwanese women perceive marriage: marriage as a "no-return-trip," "fitting-in," continuity of the family line, "one man in a lifetime," dependence, and subordination. The overall impression is one of subordination. By "fitting-in," women are expected to change their social roles and even personalities in order to adapt to a new family. By "one man in a lifetime," women are expected to be faithful to one man over a lifetime, yet they are also expected to tolerate their husbands' marital affairs (Hsu 1998: 531).

So-hoa has followed these expectations well. She has "fit in" to his family well, as can be seen in the way she identifies so closely with her husband, his family, and his social class. Married to a working-class husband, she adopts that class identity as her own, even though her soy milk stand draws upon skills she learned growing up in a petty entrepreneurial household. She accepts willingly her fate of running a business in the morning and taking care of her husband's family for the rest of the day. So-hoa is an example of a good Taiwanese wife and mother, and she seems happy to assume that role.

Koat-ho, however, is an example of a woman for whom the system has been a failure, since her husband was unable to sustain the family. Her life history reveals the strength of the ideology that women must follow men, as well as the problems it can cause in a marriage. Although understood as spirit possession, her husband apparently had a major emotional crisis after his company failed and he became dependent upon his wife's betel-nut stand for a livelihood. His refusal to appear dependent on and subordinate to his wife made him unwilling to work in her betel-nut stand, and he looked for an alternative source of income by investing in a temple. Koat-ho also suffered from the ideology that a woman should tolerate her husband's affairs, but largely because he failed to uphold his side of the bargain to support her and eventually left with the other woman. For Koat-ho, therefore, entrepreneurship was not an occupational choice, but rather was tied to her husband's inability to stay in business himself, a failed marriage, and painful divorce. It is not, however, what she would have chosen for herself. Since her fate and class standing are tied to her marriage, the shifts in her life depended largely on her husband.

The stories of these two women are important because they reveal that class identity is different for women than for men. Within a society like Taiwan where social mobility is rather fluid, a man's social class depends to a larger extent on his own efforts and abilities. An ideology that women should follow their husbands, however, means that women are more likely to rise or fall in the class system according to the abilities or destinies of their husbands. For women, class is more often than not a question of marrying the right husband, a dynamic that reinforces the importance of the family of marriage as a central axis of identity for women. The rest of the narratives in this book thus illustrate how women use entrepreneurship to express agency within the family system and/or to challenge its limitations in creative ways.

Chapter Four

A Stone Cutter

Forty-six-year-old Fan Fut-moi, who owns an export company specializing in jewelry and prayer beads, is in many ways a typical Taiwanese wife and mother. Fut-moi was born to a Hakka family in Miaoli, the fourth in a family of five children: the oldest and youngest were boys, and in the middle were three girls. She thinks such a mix of genders is "the most ideal family." Her father worked at Taipower, the state electric company, and was transferred to Hualien in 1959 when Fut-moi was only five years old. Shortly after moving to Hualien, however, he left Taipower, bought some land, and went into sugar-cane farming. Fut-moi subsequently helped out on the farm until graduation from middle school:

> When it was time to go to college, we moved to Taipei. By 1971, we were all in Taipei. Only my parents were left in Hualien. The two of them were left there alone tending the fields and we only went home to visit them on holidays. Eventually, they didn't want to live like that anymore and the whole family moved to Taipei. We bought a house and moved in permanently.

They moved into public housing in the Minsheng Community of eastern Taipei. Like many of their neighbors, they started accepting subcontracting orders for export processing:

> At that time, our government was promoting "Living Rooms As Factories." We did clothing. We fastened buttons to shirts, which I understand were exported to America. I had just graduated from high school, and helped out. That counted as household work. Our provincial governor Hsieh Tung-min said that everyone should do household production. It became very fashionable for people to make small things, like shirts or caps, at home. He asked families to do a lot of work, because overhead is low and you don't have to hire a lot of workers. You just worked at home. If you had the time, you worked. The most important reason was that small companies didn't have much capital, but they wanted to do export trade. So that's what we did; we

helped people cut holes and sew buttons. Later, they had simple machines to do it, and we could work even faster. There were also electrical appliances, small parts that could be manufactured at home. That's what it was like at the time. Now nobody wants to do such work, since the pay is too low. Some people also say that the smell is bad, and the work is bad for their health, so they don't do it. Modern people have that consciousness. Back then, we made clothes, even though it produced a lot of dust and injured our lungs. In those days, people didn't think so much.

In Taipei, she added, people have made so much money on real-estate investment that they no longer need to accept subcontracting jobs. In the Minsheng Community, for example, her family had purchased a house for about NT$1,000,000 in 1971. By 2000, it was worth more than ten times that amount, and the house had given them adequate collateral to take loans for other investment projects. Since all of her neighbors had the same experience, moreover, few families were willing to subcontract industrial production in the now prosperous neighborhood. Her marriage, moreover, took her away from subcontracting into management.

MARRY A CUTTER, FOLLOW A CUTTER

At the age of twenty-six, Fut-moi got married, moving from clothing production with her parents to stone cutting and jewelry production with her husband. She recalled how they started out in the early 1980s:

> His father was a stone cutter, and he sold for export. When his father got old, his older brother took over the company. He concentrated on exports, doing only a small portion of the production himself. He had two or three employees, and the rest he bought from subcontractors. After a while, he decided to stop production entirely and only do trade. So we bought his factory in Hualien. At first, it was very difficult for us, but after a while we found our own way to produce and make a profit. We did quite well after that.

Fut-moi and her husband were originally subcontractors for his brother, stringing bracelets in their Taipei apartment. In 1985, her husband moved to Hualien to take over production in his brother's factory, returning home only on weekends. She remained in Taipei to take care of sales. They developed a very clear-cut division of labor in the company, with him in charge of production and her in charge of sales and finances. She attributed her business skills to the training she received by following her husband into business:

> None of my brothers and sisters are in business. I am in business because of my marriage. My husband says I have learned a lot from him, that at first I was very dependent on him, and responsible for nothing. I didn't do anything, and always wanted him to help. He said, "Think of a solution for yourself." And eventually I began to grow. Now I don't have to ask him anything. I can do it myself.

Like many other women, she describes her marriage as "fitting in," as she had to adapt to the lifestyle of a new family:

After I got married, I hardly ever met with my friends. Everything I did was for my children and for our company. I just lived in that small circle. I didn't think it was difficult, because I was inside. People said I worked all the time, and it is true that I was always busy with children and work. Moreover, I lived with my parents-in-law. My life was very simple. But afterwards we moved out.

She bore two children, a boy and a girl who are now fourteen and nineteen years old. In addition to her work, she takes pride in her two children, whom she has raised largely by herself. Yet work has shaped their family life in ways that she regrets:

Since he [her husband] was in Hualien, he only came home once a week. The children also got used to that. On Saturday, when their father came home, they would be afraid because he was a stranger to them. By the time they got acquainted with him, it was the third day and time to leave again. That's how they grew up. Maybe father and children lost something because of that. They lost intimacy and a kind of mutual interaction between parents and children.

Knowing that many women report troubles with their mothers-in-law, I asked about her husband's family. She replied:

My father-in-law has already passed away. My mother-in-law is still here. She lives with his younger brother. They live in Taipei. She is almost eighty, but in good health. After we got married, we lived with them for five or six years. I had a good relationship with them. My mother-in-law spoils me, but she doesn't get along with my brother-in-law's wife so well. She likes me better. Sometimes she comes back to visit or calls, but we don't live together.

Like many Taiwanese women, she has maintained close and meaningful relations with her family of birth: "I am on even better terms with my own family, because my mother lives nearby. Both of my parents are seventy-five and in good health. My sisters also live in Taipei. My brother lives with my father nearby. We visit each other often."

FROM THAU-KE-NIU TO THAU-KE

By the 1990s, rising wages had made production in Taiwan unprofitable. Factories operating in China could tap a nearly unlimited source of cheap rural labor and produce much more cheaply than companies using subcontracting networks or factory production in Taiwan. Taiwanese manufacturers, moreover, have been challenged by rising environmental standards and new environmental protection regulations that add to the cost of production at home. Faced with these challenges, Fut-moi's company finally moved production to the Guangdong Province of China in 1993. They registered the factory in China under her husband's name, but placed the trading company and its property under her name in Taipei. They were unwilling to move the entire company to China since they feel the mainland is still too unstable and they want to keep open the option of returning to Taiwan if need be. Fut-moi thus moved into the gray area between boss-wife and woman boss. She explained how the two companies work together to lower the transaction costs faced by Taiwanese investors in China:

> A lot of it is now "triangular trade." I take the orders in Taiwan. We produce on the mainland, and we export directly from the mainland. But we settle accounts in Taiwan. Since we settle accounts in Taiwan, it is called triangular trade. If we shipped the goods to Taiwan first [rather than exporting directly to foreign markets], we would have to pay more for shipping and we would have to pay import tariffs. That would raise the costs too much.

In Taipei, she runs a trade office and warehouse with four employees. The warehouse is for storing goods and sorting them before shipping them to customers in Taiwan and abroad. She remains in charge of taking orders and accounting, just like she had done when production was done in Hualien. She does about half of her husband's export trade herself, the remainder being done by professional trading companies:

> We make a lot of stones. We make Buddhist prayer beads for sale to Japan. We make stone necklaces for the European market, and also Muslim prayer beads for the Middle East. Our most expensive products are sold to Japan. The European necklaces are of medium quality, and the Middle Eastern quality is poor to medium. We do everything from stone and crystal to plastic. For Japan, we also sell name chops.

Fut-moi's company is legally a separate corporation from her husband's factory in China. A closer look at actual company practices, however, reveals a strong overlap between their two companies and individual private accounts. Actual practices are calculated carefully to spread risk and lower transaction costs, including higher costs that arise from taxes:

> Taiwan is like this. You have to incorporate. A corporation has a person in charge. When we need a formal check, we use the company check with the company seal. But if they don't need that seal, I write a personal check. I can either use my checks or my husband's checks. My husband has company checks. He also has private checking in Hong Kong. I have my own account in Taiwan. We don't use company checks unless we absolutely have to. I use my own personal checks.

The use of personal rather than company checks is obviously a way of making business transactions look like personal transactions and thus minimizing taxes.

Women have learned the legal dangers of creative accounting practices, however, because some men have registered companies in their wives' names solely to avoid personal responsibility. Many women thus insist on personal control of their own checking accounts and greater power in the companies. Fut-moi could quickly think of examples of how other women have gotten into legal trouble by trusting their husbands too much:

> The checks are all single-person accounts. Before, there were joint accounts for husband and wife. As a result, the husband would intentionally bounce checks, and the wife would get put in prison for it. The husband would be outside drinking beer. Now everyone has separate accounts; there are no more joint accounts. Everyone is responsible only for the checks they write themselves.

Fut-moi was surprised when I told her that many American couples only have joint accounts, a fact that she interpreted as a lack of autonomy on the part of American women. She explained the practical benefits to the family of maintaining separate accounts:

> Taiwan isn't like that. If you only have a joint account, and your credit rating becomes bad, you can't use either name to open new accounts. If you have separate accounts, and one person gets a bad credit rating, you can still use the other person's name to open accounts. If you both have a bad credit rating, they won't let you open checking accounts and write checks. In that case, you can do nothing.

Fut-moi's trading company was established in order to lower transaction costs, including taxes, and spread the risk of triangular trade between Taiwan, China, and Hong Kong. She is thus not an independent woman entrepreneur in the same sense as those who start businesses with their own capital and on their own initiative. She has, however, become a boss in the sense of representing her business to the outside world and making independent business decisions. Most importantly, she is recognized socially by her family and friends as an autonomous women entrepreneur. The arrangement has given her a strongly independent lifestyle and a job she enjoys.

CUTTING STONE IN TAIWAN

Fut-moi, who had married a stone cutter, served as the thau-ke-niu in her husband's factory until 1993, when he moved production to China. As thau-ke-niu, she was in charge of finances and labor relations in the company. After the company moved production to China, she took charge of the trading company in Taiwan that sells those stones to foreign markets. Her own position, itself determined by changes in the wider regional and global political economy, allowed her to observe how structural changes affected labor relations. She described the labor process in their Hualien plant:

We were in Hualien, where a lot of people do stone work, but our work was different from other factories. In marble cutting, the workers cut off big slices for construction materials. But we did very small items, very delicate pieces of jewelry, and each piece had to have a small hole drilled precisely in the center. Quality was of the essence. We did the entire labor process, from cutting large pieces of stones to making small pieces of jewelry, all in one factory. Some entrepreneurs just do one part in a division of labor. The way they do it, one person just cuts big stones, then sells it to the next factory, which does the next step. And then there are subcontractors. But we did the whole thing.

The difficult, dirty, and dangerous labor process was one of the biggest challenges to the company, as few Taiwanese people were willing to work in stone cutting during a period of rapid economic expansion and low unemployment. Futmoi thus relied on a labor practice common throughout Taiwan. She hired aboriginal workers, who face discrimination in other sectors of the labor market, to do the manual work:

We hired aborigines since it was such heavy labor. Some people don't like that kind of work, because the diesel oil used when cutting stones pollutes the air. And the oil makes you feel dirty. A lot of people don't like it, but the labor process in this industry is like that. A worker is responsible for a lot: cutting stones down in size, slicing them into thin sheets, etc. Now, there is a machine that cuts stone automatically, but you have to measure the stones very precisely and then it will do the cutting for you. That doesn't take much skill. Then there is another machine that cuts the pieces into even smaller pieces, and another one for polishing. Then another machine is used to cut the holes. The whole process is well regulated. But many people don't follow instructions well.

In a trope frequently used to justify unequal positions in an ethnic division of labor, she described aboriginal workers as morally inferior to her own ethnic group of Han Taiwanese. In particular, she described them as lazy, indolent, and prone to drinking:

Aboriginal workers think that if you have a little bit of money, you can just go out and spend it all. At first, we were outsiders and didn't know what they were like. My husband rented a house and made it into a dormitory. Then, after we gave them their monthly wages, they would ask for time off from work and eat it all up. With even the smallest excuse, they would go out to eat and drink. When they got drunk, they wouldn't show up for work. In the end, we took the dormitory away.

In the 1980s, rising wages began to cut into their profits. She credited the crisis not only to the rising NT dollar, but also to state policies of minimum monthly wages and stipulated annual wage increases, which she perceived as too pro-labor:

Wages are always rising in Taiwan. Every year they raise the wages, but productivity has not risen accordingly. The government sets a basic wage. When state workers get an increase, manufacturers have to follow along. Wages increase every year, and prices also go up. But over the years, there is no way for your production to keep up with the rise in costs.

Low unemployment and growth in the service sector, which contributed to a labor shortage in manufacturing, made it difficult for her to find workers even in aboriginal communities. In a moral discourse common among employers at the time (Lee 1997), she complained about increasing laziness in Taiwan:

A lot of people, moreover, are unwilling to work. Ten years previously, a lot of people needed work, and would come to me. Since they needed work, they worked very hard. But by 1990, they didn't need wages since their land and houses had increased so much in value. Some of them have even more money than their bosses. If people came to work, it was only so that people won't say they are unemployed. If you asked them to do overtime, they would refuse. They wanted leisure time to spend with their wives. But sometimes you need people to do overtime, since you have to fill orders. That's one reason why we had to move. The biggest problem was labor. Workers are hard to control and don't like to work. They like to leave and take easier jobs. They like service jobs, like in KTV parlors. They aren't willing to do this kind of job.

The end of martial law in 1987 also had negative effects on the manufacturing sector, as neighbors of small industrialists started to organize environmental groups and protest against industrial pollution. In the leather industry in Kaohsiung, for example, tanneries have been shut down due to successful lobbying by environmentalists (Simon 1998b). In Hualien, complaining neighbors posed a relatively minor challenge:

Our neighbors also complained about the pollution and the noise. It used to be an industrial zone, but it evolved into a residential zone. We were the noisiest and the most polluting factory around, so the neighbors complained. Since we had to keep good relations with them, we were always the ones cleaning out the sewers. After all, we were emitting the most oil.

Summarizing these problems, she said:

That is why manufacturing has no future in Taiwan. We have done our research. We went [to China] rather late. A lot of people in our industry went even before the Tiananmen Square incident [June 4, 1989]. Of course, there were others who went even later, but we were among the biggest ones. We were the last big factory to go.

MOVING TO CHINA

In 1993, they closed down the factory in Hualien and moved most of the production to China. Only a small amount of subcontracting, stringing finished stones onto bracelets, is still done in Taiwan and then only by older rural women. She says that subcontracting to older, poorly educated women is the only way she can find workers in Taiwan at a competitive price. The rest of the production had to move:

> Originally, we thought we would keep producing in Taiwan until it became completely impossible, and then sell off our machines to someone who wanted to do production in China. We found an interested buyer, but he wasn't in this profession. He suggested that we manage production in China ourselves. He said that he would rent us land in China, and that it would cost almost nothing to ship machines over and start production. So my husband went over to investigate. At first we were hesitant to take that step, thinking we could just retire from that and concentrate on trade. But finally we decided to go.

Initially lured by China's low wages, tax incentives, and other benefits, they soon discovered that investing in China entails unexpected expenses due to weaker infrastructure and less efficient business institutions than in Taiwan:

> In the beginning we weren't planning on investing so much, but once we got there things were completely different. For example, the electricity went out almost every day, so we had to buy a power generator. At first we would have liked to buy a used one, but we ended up buying new—and two of them. We also have a problem with supplies. In Taiwan, we can just buy the stones when we need them, for just-in-time production. But in China, it might be a long time before the materials arrive. Since purchasing is inconvenient, we have to buy and store more raw material.

Instead of using stone quarried in Hualien, they began tapping into a global network of markets, importing stones from South Africa. They had to adjust to a different work ethic in China, setting up a strict factory regimen to maintain order. Chinese workers, rather than Formosan aborigines, thus came to occupy the position of subordinate other in her heart. She described the difficulties they had as they set up a factory with dormitories for over 200 migrant workers from the countryside:

> At first it was difficult because Taiwan and China are so different. We had to train the people not to work so carelessly. My husband has to stay there to supervise the workers. If you tell them to do the work one way, they might still do it another way if you don't supervise them closely. At first we even had to help them change some of their daily habits, like teaching them to throw rubbish in the rubbish bin. Nowadays, Taiwanese children don't litter; they throw rubbish in the bin, or carry it in their hands until they find one. But in China, they just throw rubbish on the ground. We had to fine them, and give rewards to people who report on other workers littering. Taiwanese factories are almost all very orderly.

Fut-moi attributed the different work ethics of Taiwanese and Chinese workers to differences in education:

> There are big differences in levels of education. Their high-school graduates are not as good as our middle-school graduates. Some of them graduate from primary

school, and they can't even write Chinese. My husband teaches them to read and do math. Since daily habits and thinking are so different, it is important to manage them well. Many investors in the mainland fail. There are many reasons for that, and one of them is labor management. You have to put a lot of heart into it.

In spite of the fact that they offer education to workers, labor mobility has proven to be as much of a problem in China as it is in Taiwan:

There aren't enough workers. We can't retain workers. They come from the interior provinces of the mainland, and live in the factory. They go home for the New Year, and don't necessarily come back.

When I asked how they find the workers, she said that it is part of her job to re- cruit young women from the countryside:

Sometimes they come looking for work on their own. Sometimes I go out to the countryside and look for workers myself. But some of them say that the working con- ditions aren't good enough, or the pay is too low. They just leave their jobs and go home. I don't know why. Maybe it is because they are too young. They are all teenagers, since they have to have good eyesight for the job. After they pass the age of twenty-five, they can only work as kitchen *obaasan* ("old women").

Although the high labor mobility would suggest her workers think otherwise, Fut-moi asserted that her company is a model of effective factory management and humane labor relations:

Our management is very good. Hong Kong bosses don't care about their daily lives. But we have a lifestyle contract with many regulations, like what time they have to sleep. We don't allow them to gamble, and we're very strict about that. We also don't permit them to drink alcohol in the dormitory or get in fights.

In spite of the protracted difficulties encountered while trying to find and train good workers in China, Fut-moi has been impressed with her workers:

They can use human labor to unload the rocks from the trucks. In Taiwan, we use a machine for that, but in China we don't need to. I've seen them construct roads and bridges by hand, and they do it all very orderly. They do the same when they unload our rocks, lining them up neatly in rows.

THE PAINS AND PLEASURES
OF RUNNING A BUSINESS

When I asked her if she finds it painful to live separately from her husband for so long, she said:

Sometimes. But there are many ways to live. A lot of people ask me why I don't move to China. You think about that a lot, but then there is the problem of the children's education. You have to take care of that. Another problem is that you shouldn't move the center of your business. We still have our original customers here. Also, the mainland is not stable, so we don't dare to put everything there. Just in case things go bad there, we can always come back. Maybe someday we won't have to continue with "triangular trade," in which case we can move to Hong Kong.

Many of her friends wonder how she can tolerate a long-distance relationship. Even her cousin, through whose introduction I was able to meet her, has speculated idly about whether or not her husband has a mistress in China. She, however, focuses on her work and says she has come to enjoy the freedom she gains from his absence:

> When you gain something, you also lose something. The important thing is how you think about the gains. Some people say, "Husband and wife are a family. They should live together all the time." Of course, that is the best way. Since I can't do that, I think to myself, "When my husband isn't here, I am freer and have more time." I can do what I want, when I want. Now I sometimes even think, "Oh, he's come back, so now I have to accommodate his schedule." When he wants to do something, I have to accompany him, even if I don't want to. I've started to think like that, as have many of my friends [whose husbands are also in China]. When he first went, he cried every day, and we always called each other on the phone. But then, he eventually started coming back only once every three months.

Fut-moi describes herself as equal, rather than subordinate, in the relationship she has with her husband. When friends ask if her husband has a mistress in China, she plays the role of patient wife and said she tries not to worry about that since she has no control over the situation anyway. When people ask if she has affairs, she brushes it off as a joke. Referring to sexual advances from male customers, she said, "Sometimes I have a lot of pressure, because he's not here. When there are problems at work, I have to take care of them myself. Some customers also cause problems. They give me pressure [for sex], but you have to reject them." She also reports that she encounters sexism in her business dealings with men:

> Our society puts men first. When a woman does business, people look down on her. But when they need you, they still look for you. Some people think it is different doing business with a woman. They even think there is a "woman's price" and will try to bargain more than they would with a man. Those are disadvantages, but I think they are not so important. Sometimes, women can do things more carefully than men, paying attention to things that men overlook.

In general, she focuses on the pleasurable aspects of her work:

> You suffer a lot, but it has a result like the blossoming of flowers, because you put your heart into it. Then, you feel like you reap the fruits of your harvest. You can't use money to assess the value of bringing a project to completion. There are challenges. You have a project to do, and nobody can tell you how to do it. When you encounter

problems, you have to fix them by yourself. Maybe it is because my husband isn't here. When nobody is here to help you, you have to think for yourself. That is rewarding, and it brings about personal growth.

DISCUSSION

This chapter and other research on thau-ke-niu (Y.-H. Lu 1998, 2001) suggest that there is ample room for women's agency and empowerment *within* Taiwanese family firms. Fut-moi's life has changed dramatically from the 1970s and 1980s, when Taiwanese families were encouraged to make living rooms into factories (Hsiung 1996, Skoggard 1996). During that period, tens of thousands of Taiwanese families participated in subcontracting networks, taking orders from larger factories or trading companies that produced sport shoes, plastic goods, stuffed toys, and other commodities for the export market. Wives were expected to stay at home and focus their labor power on production, a practice later condemned by feminists as patriarchal subordination (Greenhalgh 1994, Hsiung 1996).

In time, however, some of those subcontracting families expanded to the point where they needed to hire outside labor and could be considered as family firms rather than merely home workers. Men who became bosses (thau-ke), a word composed of the characters for "head" and "family," represented their families to the outside world by taking orders from larger companies (Shieh 1992). Wives gained status by taking over control of other workers, and became known as boss-wives, or thau-ke-niu. In the usual cases in which they managed the company finances, they rose to important positions of trust and power (Kao 1999, Y.-H. Lu 1998). As these thau-ke-niu learned important business skills, new tendencies in the 1990s and 2000s have allowed some of them to emerge as bosses in their own right.

One such tendency is the marked shift of industrial production from Taiwan to China. Statistics published by the Investment Commission of the ROC Ministry of Economic Affairs show the extent of this "mainland fever" among investors. From 1991 to the end of 2000, 22,974 major Taiwanese investments in China were approved by Taiwanese authorities and accounted for a total of $17.10 billion U.S. dollars. China, attracting 38.82 percent of Taiwanese total foreign investment, is the favored destination for Taiwanese capital (Chinabiz 2001). This investment has occurred in spite of the fact that the Taiwanese government has placed limits on the size of permitted investments in China, has only permitted certain industries to legally relocate there, and has tried to encourage investment in Southeast Asia as an alternative.

As Taiwanese bosses retake the mainland economically, their wives are often left behind in Taiwan. Many entrepreneurial families have thus become divided across the Taiwan Straits, with the husband taking care of the company in China and the wife remaining with the children in Taiwan. Taiwanese entrepreneurs are widely known for taking mistresses or even establishing second families in China, causing some Taiwanese wives to demand that their husbands get vasectomies before leaving Taiwan (*Taipei Times* 2001), a strategy unlikely to stem the number of second wives.[1] Like women left at home during wartime, however, these boss-wives have gained considerable freedom for themselves. Some women have taken advantage of their husbands' absences to start their own businesses or to take on new leadership roles in their family business in Taiwan. This is one economic change that has opened up new room for female entrepreneurship, and Fan Fut-moi is just one example.

Fut-moi, however, has not rejected "patriarchy" in the sense encouraged by some members of the Taiwanese feminist movement. Instead, her narratives reveal a sincere commitment to the ideals of "fitting in," "one man in a lifetime," and other feminine virtues. Although she has followed the gendered expectations of "marry a chicken, follow a chicken," she has not suffered as much as feminist metanarratives would suggest. By going into business with her husband, she managed successfully to both raise their children and stake out important claims to power in their business. Structural changes in the Taiwanese economy, and the opening of lucrative opportunities, led the family to shift their production to China. They split the company into two legal entities, his factory in China and her trading company in Taipei, and she has adopted the social identity of woman entrepreneur. Her success in business has enhanced her social capital within the family and contributed to the good relations that she has with her in-laws. Her ideological claims to fidelity and chastity are also ways to augment and conserve this social capital.

Since she had the high-trust position of managing the company finances, their relationship became based on mutual interdependence rather than on male power and female subordination. This form of empowerment is quite common in the life trajectories of wife bosses (Y.-H. Lu 1998). Fut-moi's life might have remained that of such a thau-ke-niu if it were not for changes in the political economy of production. It was only with her husband's departure for China that she became recognized as a boss in her own right.

A comparison of Fut-moi's experience with that of the two women in the previous chapter is also quite interesting as it reveals the class differences that divide women entrepreneurs. What is remarkable is the way in which Fut-moi adopts the identity of entrepreneur and leader in the labor process so readily and naturally. Whereas Tan So-hoa and Lim Koat-ho view themselves as only workers, Fut-moi readily identifies herself as an entrepreneur and even a capitalist. Since they identify strongly with their own classes, naturally expressing subject positions as worker or capitalist, their narratives illustrate well the conclusion made by Taiwanese sociologist Wu Nai-teh (1996a) that there is a strong sense of class identity in Taiwan.

These class differences are reflected in their lifestyles and consumer choices (Wu 1996b). Fut-moi travels abroad frequently, and mixes comfortably at bourgeois dinner parties where she can demonstrate her knowledge of French red wines in the company of other entrepreneurs, architects, authors, and even a foreign anthropologist. Tan So-hoa has a limited social life, is unfamiliar even with downtown Taipei, and once spent nearly an hour with me describing the novelty of her first visit to a coffee shop in 2000. Fut-moi is more empowered than the other two women. The way in which she has empowered herself and achieved social mobility, moreover, reveals the differences in what class means for women and men. For women, class is largely a question of marrying into the right family and playing their cards right within that social field. It may be too strong to refer to thau-ke-niu as "vassals" of their husbands, as Simone de Beauvoir did of women who follow their husbands' careers (1989 [1952]: 429). Nonetheless, their lives have historically been shaped by the careers of their husbands more often than men's careers have been shaped by those of their wives. As the next chapter demonstrates, entrepreneurship can help women resist those cultural forms of power in the family.

NOTE

1. I know one man who turned down a lucrative job in China because his wife made that demand.

Chapter Five

A Ritual Goods Seller

One would never guess that forty-five-year-old Ong Siok-ting once spent her days sweating away as a production worker in her husband's subcontracting firm. Her Buddhist paraphernalia shop near the Taipei train station suggests an entirely different plane of existence from that experience. The air is thick with incense and sandalwood, and the sound of Buddhist chants reverberates from the stereo system. Siok-ting and her husband, who both exhibit a seriousness of purpose by wearing buttoned-up Sun Yatsen suits to work, sit behind the counter and encourage guests to sit down on a wooden chair and relax with a cup of *pu-er* tea. They sell a variety of Buddhist items: books on esoteric Buddhism, Buddhist rosaries, textiles, and even exotic Tibetan relics crafted from the skull bones of renowned lamas. They demonstrate the antiquity and value of their most exotic and expensive items by showing customers pictures of similar items in English-language catalogs from the British Museum and other foreign museums.

Siok-ting herself makes frequent trips to Tibet, purchasing stones to make rosaries and consulting with lamas for her own spiritual practice. Each time she returns, she decorates the altar in her store ever more elaborately with new Buddhist figures, drapes of cloth, and painted mandalas. Several times she has even succeeded in arranging visitor visas for lamas from Tibet to spend six months at a time in Taiwan. They live in her home, and spend hours in her shop every day dispensing tips on Buddhist practices to her friends and clients.

Siok-ting's story of becoming an entrepreneur, which draws on Buddhist narratives of fate and the benevolent mercy of a living bodhisattva, shows that she made the transition to woman boss through a combination of her own perseverance and sheer luck. In the common trope of Taiwanese entrepreneurs, Siok-ting starts out her narrative with reference to a poor childhood, as one of seven children born in the family of a bus driver:

We just lived one day at a time. My parents moved around a lot, so I was always adapting to a new life. I always had to go to new schools, and explain that I had moved from such-and-such a place. Since our family background was very bitter, I also had to do a lot of manual labor. From that kind of life I learned to have independent roots. I learned that you need independent thinking to get what you want. An individual needs to open up her own road. Like me, since I can't write articles so well, the best I can do is do business! I think that if I do business, I can do a lot of things.

She was not able to go into business as early as she would have liked, however:

In fact, I only started doing business six years ago, when I was thirty-nine years old. Before then, I was a housewife. The only opportunity I had was to go into business with my husband. We did steel fixtures, the kind of fixtures they use in industry. But I always thought I should start my own business. Of course, there has to be the right karmic relation of cause and effect (*yinyuan*). Every day, I lived like that. I didn't think I could live like that for an entire life, every day just cooking and taking care of children. I thought my life goal shouldn't be just living like that. So I always hoped that I would get a chance.

Siok-ting describes her earlier life of marriage and following her husband into Taipei County's then-booming small- and medium-enterprise sector as a period of trials and bitterness:

When I got married to my husband, he bought himself a piece of machinery and started making cylinders. Maybe women were relatively *stupid* [emphasis hers] back then. In choosing their husbands, they didn't think too much, just "he's not so bad. I'll marry him." Not like the strong-willed women of today. So, after marriage I just went into business with him doing iron working.

She described that process in a vocabulary of alienation:

I was in charge of drilling holes. Now, when that iron part came to me, I had to drill four holes. There were two iron bars, and you had to drill four holes in them. I drilled those holes every day. Now, my eyes weren't so good, so when I drilled, sometimes the holes would be off center. But I couldn't refuse to do the work, because we didn't have the means to hire workers. I had to help my husband do that work. But since my eyes weren't good, the holes I drilled would be off center. Then, he would scold me. He would take it and say I was just playing around, not concentrating on drilling the holes correctly. I found it really boring ... I thought how could a woman do that kind of man's work ... iron works ... but I didn't intentionally do a poor job.

That alienation, however, eventually led to a change in her life goals:

Doing that kind of work didn't make me very happy. Because of that, I decided I definitely did not want to depend on men for my livelihood. I definitely wanted to start my own business. It was precisely that experience that made me think that I should depend on myself. That was my experience. I worked with him for about thirteen years, drilling holes for thirteen years, husband and wife working together. We did it until he was able to hire workers, and then I retired. About five years after retirement, I started doing volunteer work because I like worshipping the Buddha very much.

Doing volunteer work with Buddhist charities, Siok-ting traveled to Buddhist countries throughout South and Southeast Asia. After seeing poverty in several countries, she made it her goal to earn money through entrepreneurship and contribute a portion of the profits to economic development projects:

> I was already old when I started doing business. I saw many poor people, both here in Taiwan and abroad. For example, I went to Tibet, Thailand, and the South Pacific. I saw many Chinese people who had come into the Golden Triangle region from China, who had fled from the civil war between the KMT and the communists, but who had no way to return to their own country. I found them really pitiful. Seeing that made my heart sour. Maybe it is because I also grew up in poverty, and I am also a mother, but I understand. I thus vowed that I would go into business. And when I made enough money, I wanted to help those people. That's the most important thing of all.

Tears filled her eyes as she continued:

> Now, if you want to help people, you have to have economic resources of your own. I figure that money isn't very important to me personally. It isn't something that I need a lot of. But, if I have the ability, I think that the best way I can help is to go into business and earn money. That was my goal at the time, my plan, and my hope. I just thought that if I earn ten dollars, I would be able to use five dollars to help people and five dollars to keep doing business.

She discussed her plans with a Tibetan lama, eventually using Buddhist concepts to build up the social capital needed to support her desired new lifestyle:

> Because I was doing volunteer work, I asked that living bodhisattva to help me, to give me the karmic relationship needed to start a business. The master said to me, "you will go into business." You could say that I was just "playing" at first. I went into a friend's store [who was selling cloth imported from Tibet] and said, "This store is very special. I like it very much." I wanted to do that kind of business. Suddenly that friend helped me rent a room, sent me some clothes, and told me to sell them. That's how I started. I went into business by accident. So I think it was the bodhisattva who helped me. Afterwards, that person who helped me immigrated to Canada.

It took some negotiation before her husband agreed to help her purchase that store:

> When I decided to open a store, I told my husband. He said, "No way!" He had no faith in me. He thought I was kidding. How could one go into business at an age of nearly forty? He didn't have any faith in me, but I told him, "If you invest you will have a 50

percent share, but if you don't invest in it, there is no hope at all." In Taiwan, you can succeed only if you work hard. Since I talked like that, my husband invested in me. I opened up a small shop selling clothes and food goods. I had no experience, but I was very industrious. After I started, I thought, "How should I sell things?" When people came in, I said, "Take a look around." If they saw something they liked, I said, "I'll give you 10 percent off." I just learned from experience, learning from feeling around in the dark. I started to make plans, splitting my money three ways: one-third is capital, one-third is for cash flow, and one-third is money for donations.

Ong Siok-ting then opened a small shop on Nanking East Road, selling Tibetan clothes and crafts. When the lease ended after two years, she moved to her present location near the Taipei train station. As she grew in her own practice of Tibetan Buddhism, she began to specialize in ritual items. Hers is now the only store in Taipei that sells the skulls of deceased lamas, as well as other rare Tibetan ritual goods. She is notorious among other proprietors of Buddhist goods stores, some of whom gossip jealously that she must have illicitly used supernatural powers to build up a successful enterprise so quickly. Siok-ting explains the Buddhist meaning of her store:

The things that I sell are different from what other more ordinary stores are selling. First of all, people have to understand what kind of things these are. Second, only people who are interested in these things will come in. And they will bring their friends. Our customers aren't people who go out window-shopping and then drift in and buy. It's not like that. It is a very extraordinary store. And it has a religious meaning. In addition to earning money, I hope that I can encourage people to study Buddhism. Because a bodhisattva is just like Jesus. He can encourage people to be good. He is loving and is virtuous. So, when I do this work, if someone comes with a question I will tell him to practice Buddhism well. That is also part of my job.

Appropriately, Siok-ting's philanthropic works have been primarily focused on Tibet. She raised funds in Taiwan to finance the reconstruction of one well-known lamasery in Lhasa that was destroyed during the Cultural Revolution.[1] She has also contributed to highway construction in Tibet, and housing construction for people displaced by hydroelectric dam construction. She spends six months a year in Tibet, and has personally supervised the construction of a housing project she helped fund. It is only through business and the social networks she gained through her store that she was able to raise so much money for Tibet:

The only reason I have that ability is because I have gone into business. If I hadn't gone into business, I would even have trouble taking care of myself. I stick to my own ideas, my own way of looking at things, and my own thoughts. Because I have been so persistent, I have been able to earn money and help people who need help. In fact, my motivation for going into business wasn't seeing my children grow up and then thinking I want a really high standard of living, or I want something for myself. I just thought that human life is very short, so we should do some beneficial things. But I didn't grow up in a good environment. I wasn't, for example, the descendant of an industrialist, so I had to depend on my own efforts. Also, being from that generation, I had no way to receive a very good education. I couldn't study abroad or emigrate or go to a very good school. But I know how to love. I wasn't thinking of how much money I wanted to earn in how many years. I didn't think that way, because I didn't study economics.

A CHINESE HEART

Noting that the person who initially helped her start a business immigrated to Canada, she contrasted her own decision to stay in Taiwan with other Taiwanese entrepreneurs:

Lots of Taiwanese people eventually emigrate. I love my country very much, but now people with a lot of money often think of emigrating. But I think, I have yellow skin. No matter where I go, I am still a Chinese. I love my country, even though my country is a very small country. Lots of countries oppress us for political reasons.[2] But, I still love my country and think I can learn from our former president Chiang Kai-shek, the way he avoided that shortcoming [lack of ethnic pride]. When he went to Japan to study and people cheated him, he would say "I am proud to be a Chinese even though my country is very small. I should have very solid roots." So, even though I have traveled to many countries, I can't envy those people or emigrate. I think it is only those emigrants who are laughable, because in the end they all come back to Taiwan to earn money. I like living in this, my country of Taiwan.

BALANCING PHILANTHROPY AND A FAMILY

Siok-ting was initially able to embark on ambitious projects of entrepreneurship and philanthropy because her husband was already making sufficient income to support the family and was willing to support her in her projects. Nonetheless, her projects often take her away from her family, as she frequently travels alone to China and Southeast Asia:

Actually, at the time when I went into business I didn't give any thought at all to waiting for my children to grow up. At the time, my [youngest] child was in the third year of elementary school, about eight years old. And the other one, he was already involved in the monastery, studying for periods of three months at a time with a Buddhist monk from Thailand. He became a monk at the age of thirteen.

Siok-ting sees her family life and business as entwined and mutually reinforcing rather than problematic. She boasts proudly that her only son is a Buddhist monk and that she has also contributed to his monastery:

His monastery is in Chungli. Actually, if you have time, you can help that school write some articles. Let lots of people know about that school. They have students from India, Sri Lanka, Thailand, the Philippines, Tibet, and Nepal. Lots of people study there for free. That money comes from the dharma heart (*faxin,* generosity) of some Taiwanese people. Now, my own son became a monk at that academy. We give money to such places. The only reason why I have that ability is because I have gone into business.

Siok-ting proudly added that her daughter, a student in Kaohsiung's Wen Tzao University of Foreign Languages, is also a very independent woman and has dreams of her own:

Every since she was in junior high, she has been interested in foreign languages. Her goal is to live in France or somewhere. That is her goal. I'm very proud of her. She's only a teenager, but she is very brave. She tells me exactly what she wants. She's not like the people in my generation. The girls in my generation didn't dare to demand anything from their parents. The children of today are very intelligent. In junior high, my daughter would tell me how she could reach her goals. And my youngest child is in the first year of junior high. We are a small family, but I have managed it well.

When I asked if she has any advice for other women interested in going into business, she said:

Without the support of a family or without a husband, setting up a business would be difficult because of the problem of raising capital. You don't want to look at this store. This store, all the way it is decorated and furnished, that took a lot of money. But that money is the product of doing business and slowly accumulating money. If a woman wants to do business, when she first starts out, if she is a small person, she shouldn't try to do it too big. If it's not too big, she can have an attitude of testing the waters. You can have a goal. For example, if you can survive for one or two years, you can keep doing business and improve slowly. You don't want to immediately jump in completely. I have seen people who immediately invest millions of dollars, and then they close up after doing it for only two or three months. So I think, at first you should determine where is your goal, what is your motivation, and if you are suitable for this kind of life. At first there will be a period . . . for me it was about three years . . . three years is rather quick. You have to wait it out. But your goal is the most important. You can't say "I'm losing money" and then suddenly give up.

About gender and entrepreneurship, she said:

I encourage women to be economically independent. Modern women aren't dependent on men like in the past. All women should want to have their own lives, and their own businesses. That benefits this society, this country, in fact all of humanity, because once a woman has the ability, she will naturally help others.

She summed up her life and entrepreneurial career by saying:

If I hadn't gone into business, I would have trouble even taking care of myself. I would not be able to help people do the things they want to do. Even though I started business at the relatively old age of forty, I still think that I have done well. I know that I am a person with ideas, because I made the right decision. I stick to my own ideas, my own way of looking at things, my own thoughts. Because I have been so persistent, I have been able to succeed at earning money to help those people who need help. It doesn't matter if you do it through a religious group or a social group, but it is a very good thing to help others.

Taiwan's economic development and the rise of a consumer-oriented service sector gave Siok-ting the chance to create a job for herself that she finds meaningful. Whereas she was once frustrated by dependence on her husband, her husband eventually became dependent on her. Due to increasing wage levels in Taiwan, her husband's factory eventually became less profitable than her store. He was thus drawn into her business, and helps out daily in the store. He tells a story of how the Taiwanese economy took a downturn, industry moved to the mainland in search of lower wages, and his factory could no longer compete. "It was no longer profitable," he said when I visited him once for tea, "so I gave it to my brother."

Siok-ting's experience is also interesting because she has used her store as a base for social activism. Buddhist faith is at the center of Siok-ting's business plans, as well as the center of her identity. Entrepreneurship can thus do more than empower women within the family context. The influence of women entrepreneurs can expand to the wider society and even beyond Taiwan. Due to her activities elsewhere in Asia, Siok-ting has become a philanthropist and a model for women in the developing countries she visits. Looking back at her accomplishments, she says, "Life after forty has been the most beautiful time in my life."

DISCUSSION

Siok-ting's story is illustrative of how women entrepreneurs have benefited from the growth of the Taiwanese service sector. The same rise in wages that made labor-intensive production unprofitable also led to the formation of a large middle class with disposable income to spend on domestic retail and service industries. In 1978, Taiwan's service sector was 43 percent of GDP; by 2001, it had increased to 67.2 percent (DGBAS 2002). This has given women considerable opportunity to open up new businesses providing services and goods. These new businesses can sometimes be as profitable—or even more so—than the labor-intensive workshops that once dominated the economy. Siok-ting's small retail store in Buddhist ritual goods is only one example among many.

Several themes arise from Siok-ting's narrative. One of the most notable themes is a common perception that women have been empowered through the economic development of the past generation. According to her, the women of twenty-five years ago, when she was embarking on marriage, were "stupid" and "not like the strong-willed women of today." The contrast between the women of 1970 and those of 2000 runs throughout her narratives, and she evaluates the changes positively. She speaks proudly of her daughter, who studies French at a prestigious language academy and would like to live in France. She also argues that women should go into business if they so desire.

Her memories of "following" her husband into manufacturing are strongly reminiscent of the analyses of feminist anthropologists (especially Greenhalgh 1994) who have worked on family firms in Taiwan. She describes that work as boring and alienating, and said she did it only to obey her husband. Unlike feminist anthropologists, however, she emphasizes her own agency. Like the moment of Buddhist enlightenment or existentialist rupture, she realized that following her husband into manufacturing made her unhappy and she decided to change her life. The main moment of change was when she first viewed poverty in Southeast Asia and decided to go into business herself to help others. The alienation she first felt in her husband's company eventually precipitated an "entrepreneurial event" (Shapero and Sokol 1982: 77) and led her to open up her own company.

Siok-ting, however, did not directly attack the Confucian ideology that Greenhalgh (1994) argues subordinates women in Taiwanese family firms. Instead, she strongly affirms Chinese cultural themes and incorporates them into her public identity. With her Sun Yatsen jacket and frequent trips to China, in fact, she embraces a Chinese identity more than most people I have met in Taiwan. A supporter of the KMT and often quite nationalistic, she associates goodness with Chinese culture. Since I am interested in issues of economic development and have contributed financially to her projects, for example, she has frequently praised me, saying, "Scott, on the outside you look like a foreigner, but on the inside you are like a Chinese person. You are generous and compassionate like a Chinese person." It is worth emphasizing, however, that her version of Chinese goodness is primarily that of the compassionate Buddhist bodhisattva helping others, rather than that of the Confucian scholar focused on continuation of his family line. In her narrative, moreover, she argues that women achieve goodness better than men, since women will "naturally help others." Chinese Buddhism—as part of Chinese culture—has thus become an important source of social capital for her. As we will see in later chapters, that religion is an important part of many women entrepreneurs' lives.

Going into business for herself, however, was a major change in her life and was initially opposed by her husband. Involvement with Buddhist groups and her desire to help Buddhists gave her the social capital that she needed to convince him. It also helped her build up a strong social network of supporters willing to finance her projects in Tibet and Southeast Asia. Her skill in managing social networks was clearly visible in the way she actively kept contact with me, introduced me to others, and also met other women entrepreneurs through the networks I established in my research. Her extroverted personality makes her highly skilled at networking.

These examples in the previous two chapters illustrate some of the weaknesses of structural feminism as a tool for understanding the position of women relative to men. Women are not necessarily everywhere subordinate to men, and do not necessarily become vassals to their men as "economic head of the joint enterprise." There is ample room for women's agency. Fut-moi and Siok-ting have both negotiated well in their marital and economic relationships with men. Fut-moi's joint enterprise is two-headed, yet Siok-ting has clearly taken over the reins of power. They both have done so through reference to capitalist ideologies of success and hard work; yet Siok-ting also manipulates well social capital accumulated from Buddhism. Taiwan's free-market economy has given them the opportunity to convert social capital into financial capital and back again, consistently reaping a profit from the exchange. They are both examples of women who have gained greater personal space by successfully combining business and family. They strongly believe that women should be autonomous from men and control their own economic lives. I encountered many women like them during fieldwork, even as some of them are much more modest about their achievements.

NOTES

1. At her request, I have agreed not to name the monastery in any publication in the event of potential political changes in China that could endanger them for having close contacts with Taiwan.

2. In the convoluted logic that KMT ideological training has produced, she is actually referring to Taiwan when she says "Chinese people" live in a "small country." China, of course, is the oppressive country she avoids naming.

Chapter Six

A Hairdresser

I was initially able to interview Tiu Bi-hoa, and establish long-term rapport with her, due to the special nature of her occupation. Bi-hoa, a Taiwanese woman of nearly fifty, is a professional hairstylist. This occupation has traditionally been considered a low-class occupation in Taiwan, Japan, and other parts of Asia. Women who cut hair have customarily been looked down upon in Taiwanese society because they have frequent contact with strange men and touch their bodies. The potentially sexual undertones of the occupation are clearly understood in Taiwan, which is why brothels often masquerade as "barbershops," with barber poles, smoky windows, and service twenty-four hours a day (Skoggard 1996: 143–44). Women in this field gain little social capital from their occupations.

I first met Bi-hoa in September 1999, when she was running a simple barbershop and photo-finishing service in Taipei's Hsin-yi District. At the time, I was new to Taipei and just starting my research project. I first encountered her while doing surveys, and subsequently started to visit her as a regular customer to have my hair cut. After several visits, during which I discussed at length the nature of anthropological research, she agreed to a taped life-history interview on the condition that I conduct the interview while having a facial treatment done in her basement studio. I continued to visit her as a regular customer until I left Taipei in July 2001, following her each time she moved to a new location. I visited her again in the summer of 2002.

FROM A SMALL TOWN TO THE BIG CITY

Bi-hoa presents herself as a dutiful wife who identifies primarily with her family of marriage, even to the exclusion of her family of birth. When I first asked about her family life as a child, in fact, she was surprised and asked, "By family, do you mean my childhood family?" When I answered in the affirmative, she then continued to describe her humble family background in Tainan County, a narrative that illustrates well the Chinese family system as lived in rural Taiwan:

I grew up in a small town: Hsinying, Tainan County. My family wasn't considered a large family, and it wasn't a small family either. All together we were six children. I was the third child. Above me were an elder brother and elder sister. I was in the middle. Below were two younger sisters and one younger brother. We grew up in an agricultural society, since Taiwan was just beginning industrialization. Back then, our life wasn't very good. My father had been an adopted son, because my paternal grandfather didn't have a son of his own. He only had a daughter. He adopted my father to continue their lineage.

Her grandfather treated his biological daughter more favorably than he did his adopted son:

My grandfather was in the construction industry. For Hsinying at the time, his construction company was considered quite successful. But my father was an adopted son, and there is a difference between an adopted son and a [biological] daughter. He wasn't so good to his adopted son, since he wanted to provide more for his own daughter. Back then, in the 1950s, to tell the truth, nobody's life was very good. Back then, getting even an apple to eat was already quite something . . . but they were eating very well. We had no way to live as well as my aunt and her two daughters and one son. They were able to attend Normal University in Kaohsiung.

In her family, however, the girls were expected to forgo their own education in order that their brothers could go to school:

My sister always liked to study. She even got scholarships, but back then it wasn't like today when you can just keep going on in school. You had to take tests, and if you were successful, you could continue in school. She tested into the Tainan Girls Academy. Back then, getting into the Tainan Girls Academy was quite an accomplishment, but you still needed to pay tuition and have money for living expenses. Our life, especially since my father was an adopted son, wasn't that good under my grandfather's control. People back then thought women don't need to have a good education. Only boys needed to go to school. So my sister couldn't go to school. My sister was quite upset, but there was no other way. There was just no way.

Bi-hoa and her sister were encouraged to learn the trade of cutting hair, training which could be accomplished in a relatively short period of time at less cost to the family. Bi-hoa described the decision-making process in her family:

Since we were not so wealthy, it would have been a burden for the family to put the girls through school. After I finished primary school, my mother said that the boys should continue in school and the girls would learn a trade. My elder sister also studied cutting hair. Since my sister liked school, she was more interested in studying. But I was not so interested in school. It didn't mean much to me if I could study or not.

In the end, my brother wasn't good school material; he didn't study so well. Since he wasn't so good in school, they sent him off to learn a trade in paints and oils. My brother was like that.

She immersed herself willingly in a new life:

I was capable of learning whatever people taught me. And I was very ambitious. I always ensured that my skills were better than everyone else. In that salon, there were lots of "elder sisters." They did very well, but they were much older than me. I had just graduated from primary school. I was only about fourteen or fifteen years old. They were all seventeen or eighteen years old. But even as a little girl without much education, I had my own agenda. I knew how much I wanted to learn by the end of this month, and how much by the end of next month. If I didn't make progress, I wasn't happy. I studied like that in Hsinying for one year and learned all the basics. I could pretty much do it all. Back then, all girls wanted to move to Taipei. We had a relative in Taipei. Like me, she had graduated from primary school. When she returned to our home, I always looked at her with the envious eyes of a country person. I just said to my mother, "I want to go up to Taipei." So I came up to Taipei.

Bi-hoa recalled the lively urban atmosphere of Taipei in the 1960s, when she moved to Hsimen Ting:

It was far more exciting than it is today! Now it has really gone downhill. The hot spots were Hsimen Ting and En-ping Bak Road back then. That was the most exciting time of all! Back then, eastern Taipei was all just rice fields.

Like many other rural-urban migrants (cf. Ka 1993), she constructed her new life with the help of relatives who had already moved to the city and were involved in the same occupation:

My mother had her cousin's husband take me to Taipei. After I came to Taipei, I started out by working in a salon in Hsimen Ting. When they closed, I moved to another shop. As far as I was concerned, that shop wasn't very good. I wanted a job with a future, so I moved over to Chungshan North Road, Chinghuang Market. Back then, it just happened that we also had a relative who was doing the trade over there, and I got in with her introduction. Once there, I got to know a very good friend named Lim Su-ran. She was a famous stylist, and her technique was very good. She also knew how to take very good care of people.

For the first ten years of her career, she was primarily concerned with taking care of her natal family in Hsinying:

That was the happiest time of my life. I was seventeen years old, young, and ambitious in my work. My personal development was very good, and the money was not bad. I could help my family. My family needed a lot of help. By then, my grandfather had died, so my father was on his own with an independent life. My father continued to follow my grandfather's trade in construction. But construction requires a lot of capital. I was earning so much money that I could send money home and help my father with his expenditures. Our life had already changed. I was the one earning money, so I made sure that my family was economically stable. My younger brothers and sisters could all continue to go to school. One younger brother and a younger sister graduated from high school. And my youngest sister graduated from Taiwan Normal University. Even my older sister, the one who liked to study, could finally go to school.

MARRIAGE:
NEW PRIORITIES AND NEW PROBLEMS

Bi-hoa postponed her marriage until the age of twenty-six. She described it as a turning point in her life:

> I was happy. But then, I started to hang out with the boss's son. I had already been working for them about six years. He said, "Your personality is not bad and you are also kind of pretty." So, we decided to get married.[1] I married the oldest son. My husband was a college graduate. He worked for a state-run company, and I worked in their shop. That was my work back then.

After marriage, she was no longer expected to contribute to her natal family, but rather to work for her family of marriage. Since her husband was the oldest son, he had a responsibility to his family to earn as much money as possible, and she committed herself to that project:

> My second son was born at that time. Now since the oldest son [her husband] has to make a lot of money to carry on the family line sufficiently, I decided to help out and start a business. We started a dimsum restaurant. The whole family worked together: my husband, his father, and his younger brothers. Now when you are young and go into business too early, you can't avoid problems like insufficient experience. Also, when family members do business together, you can't fire anyone. If you fire someone, you end up not doing it.

Disagreement among brothers soon led to them closing down the restaurant. Bi-hoa's husband went back to his job in the state sector, and she took over management of her father-in-law's barbershop. She described her main goal as taking care of her immediate family:

> I didn't want to be too ambitious. All I wanted was a large living space. I'm easily satisfied. My husband went to work. I think that's really good. And I managed a very small beauty salon. We lived like that, and our children slowly grew up. I think the most important thing is that the children are well cared for. So, I rented a place near where we lived. That's where the children went to primary school and middle school. I could keep an eye on them after school. Because in middle school and primary

school, if both parents are too busy doing business, it is easy for the children to turn bad. I definitely wanted to pay attention to them.

The problems began when her husband was fired from his job. Bi-hoa initially responded with a strategy of acting as job broker and sending him to her own family network in the South:

> After a while, my husband wasn't doing so well at work. I introduced him to a relative in Hsinying so he could work for him. That work was in the south, at a pharmaceutical company in Hsinying. But my husband missed his family. He couldn't get used to living in the south and wanted to come home. Now when he came back home, there were some incidents, like he would go and drink with classmates.

Her husband then had his first experience with depression:

> At that time, my oldest son wanted to test into technical high school. That year, my husband was relatively nervous. One day he went to eat and drink with classmates, the next day his spirits were not good, he had kind of a precarious feeling; he just stayed home and got sick. Now while he was sick, we used the collective powers of the whole family to comfort and help him. The most important thing in our lives was to help him recover back to normal.

With both sons attending cram school and taking tests for admission into school, the financial pressure on the family was very heavy. Her husband slowly recovered from the first incidence of depression and initially planned to return to the pharmaceutical company in Hsinying. Using the Buddhist term for a chance or opportunity (*jiyuan*), she described what was yet another fateful moment in their marriage:

> He had the chance to go to China with a company that was investing in the mainland. But when he actually went, he didn't say anything. Then he came back shortly afterwards and didn't do any work. With no work at all, he was nervous again when he came back. He was unemployed and stayed at home.

Repeated failures in his career led to further depression and an even more onerous burden for Bi-hoa:

> When he came back from the mainland five years ago, he didn't work at all at first. Then he found another job in a Tainan machinery factory after an introduction from a friend. But when he was working there, he wasn't as successful as we would have liked. Maybe because he missed his family, or maybe he couldn't get used to living away from Taipei. I don't know why, but he came back. When he was sick, his mood would change. Sometimes it would get bad. Now he needed encouragement, he needed comfort. And his health wasn't so good. I asked if he wasn't suffering from too much stress, too many kinds of stress. It became my role to take care of the shop and make all the money for the family.

Failure contributed further to her husband's depression. Bi-hoa alluded sadly to the violence as she described their difficulties at the time. Throughout it all, she tried to hold to the feminine virtues of tolerance, forbearance, and patience:

> Back then, his mood . . . well . . . even if I don't describe it . . . you generally know . . . sometimes he had a bad temper at home . . . between husband and wife, things didn't go so well . . . because he has a good heart, but . . . how can I explain this . . . a man, he doesn't like to say he is at home every day, he was nervous. . . . He loved his family, he loved me, but sometimes, he would say that he wants to get a divorce or something. . . . I know his desire to get divorced was because he didn't want me to have a bitter life with him. I was very patient with him. So we just kept on going. Even if he is not very successful at work, I said, we could open a shop together. Back then, my own business wasn't doing very well either. I thought maybe we could try something together. I could help him by giving him a change in his environment.

She drew upon her own resources, a storefront she had purchased in 1985 and initially rented out to a childcare center, and drew up a business plan for her husband:

> I noticed that one of my husband's friends was doing photo developing. I thought that was a rather laidback job. Since my husband had already been sick, it wouldn't be right to ask him to do more stressful work again. Instead, I encouraged him to start a small business developing film. Film developing isn't very easy to do these days. When outsiders start up, first of all, they don't understand it. Investing in a film development store also requires millions of dollars. It is a high capital business. So for outsiders, it is very hard.

Since her husband was also educated in an ideology that says men must be financially independent and support their families, rather than being supported by their wives, that decision was also difficult for him. Unfortunately, the enterprise also turned out to be a business failure:

> People say, "opening a store is easy, closing a store is hard." It wasn't that customers weren't good, but we didn't earn any money, so two years ago I moved here to my present place. To tell the truth, our business was ruined, and we had lost money. Having lost money, I thought starting all over again would surely be difficult. People are not afraid of bitterness, but I was afraid of getting sick. Because if one gets sick, one can do nothing. Isn't that right? The most important thing is peace in the family, just a little peace, and good health. I believe that with that you can keep going. Things will get better. So, I kept that heart. I lost money, but God loved me very much. When I sold the store, I got a good price.

She moved the photo developing equipment into a section of her own barbershop, and tried to run the two businesses together, him developing film and her cutting hair in the same place. That, however, put her husband under even greater pressure and he started thinking about other career options:

Once again, I helped my husband start up in business. When you start a business, you have to walk one step at a time. Starting to walk that road again will surely be diffi-cult. But I wasn't afraid. I comforted myself by saying that God was good to me. He let me do it quite well, but it still wasn't as good as I would have liked. And in those circumstances, my husband was very unhappy. He kept thinking about the mainland, thinking things must be quite good in the mainland. He kept thinking about going there and doing something.

Bi-hoa described his ambitions as unrealistic and doomed to failure, yet she had little say in the matter:

He went to Nanjing. But it wasn't as good as he thought it would be. He went and came back. Then he went again and came back again. He went several times, always going and coming back, going and coming back. But he didn't make any money. He just spent money! And he left the store alone. I thought surely he would fail, but all I could do was say, "Don't worry. As long as you like it, that's OK."

When I asked what kind of business he was doing, her harsh tone of voice re-vealed the impatience and anger she felt about his activities at the time, as well as her low appraisal of his abilities:

He wasn't doing business! He just went over to see if there was any business he could do. But you need capital to do business. If you don't have capital, you can't do anything! But . . . how should we say it . . . maybe his life space wasn't big enough or something. . . . He was running away. It was running away. The way I see it, he was running away.

It was even more painful when he failed again in China, only to return to Tai-wan angry, bitter, and violent. When he returned to Taipei, the stress on their mar-riage worsened. She struggled to hold back tears as she continued:

His temper started to get bad again. It was like that again, and I could see that he was quite pitiful like that. I didn't know what to do. At the shop, business wasn't so good. We were losing money. Our marital relationship wasn't so good. We would fight. . . . To tell the truth . . . that kind of business . . . I was just getting by.

This time he was able to find a job himself on the job market in Taipei:

There were lots of opportunities and chances (*jiyuan*). At that time I saw a newspa-per ad, and strongly encouraged him to apply for the job. He was lucky to get the job, and went to that company to work. At work, that company also respects him very much. And his salary and rank are not bad. So he was lucky.

Having described the work histories of her husband and herself in great detail, Bi-hoa contrasted her own ability to patiently endure hardship with her husband's emotional reactions. Drawing upon the common idea that women are stronger than men, she attributed that difference to essential gender traits:

Both men and women can manage a business. Men have their businesses. But women are relatively flexible. Men love face more. When women have a job to do, they won't be afraid. It doesn't matter if they do well or not. If you ask a woman to do something, she will just stand up and do it. Men aren't like that. They love face and they are easily hurt.

His new job, which was found independently of her efforts and family networks, gave him the face he needed. Since he was able to support their family financially, moreover, she was suddenly able to dedicate more time to her own business. She alluded to a real-estate purchase she was contemplating:

> I am still running my business here. I have run the beauty shop here for two years, but I am in the middle of some big changes. That's to say that I was dependent on luck (*un-khi*). Most of the time, my luck wasn't as good as I would have liked. When it wasn't as good as I would have liked, it wasn't that customers weren't good enough to me. Since business isn't so great, I have found another space.

LOOKING FORWARD TO A NEW MILLENNIUM

With 2000 approaching and career changes in mind—yet to be revealed to me—she summarized her life so far:

> For nearly thirty years, I have taken good care of my family, I have taken good care of my children, and I have also taken care of my husband. Now as to those problems we have had along the way, and our personal development, I still think that he has a very gentle character. In our thirty years of marriage, for twenty-two years—when he was independent enough in his career—he was a good husband. He is basically a good person. When business wasn't good and our income wasn't good, stress made him angry and he was like that. But up to now, he has been working in that same company.

Looking into the future with measured optimism, she said:

> I believe that the year 2000 will be a new beginning in my life. Marriage will be successful. My life (*jin-seng*) is like that. My father-in-law and mother-in-law are still alive. Their health is quite good. I also have an uncle and an aunt. They are also doing well. That's the way my life is. In my way of looking at human life, I think that I am doing fine. That is because I am a person who is easily satisfied. I don't make problems. If my life is composed of three minutes of misery for every seven minutes of happiness, then I am happy. So, I can't complain.

In the nearly two years that followed, I saw Bi-hoa make a number of important changes in her own career. In early 2000, she sold the photo developing equipment, gave up the management of her barbershop, and rented the storefront to an upscale beauty-salon chain. The neighborhood barbershop with concrete floors, plaster walls, and simple chairs gave way to an interior design of steel and glass, mahogany tables stacked with French fashion magazines, and professional hairstylists who charged ten times more for a haircut than what she herself had been charging previously. She earned a rental income from that shop.

For several months, Bi-hoa continued to do facial treatments and beauty consulting from a room in the basement. By summer, however, she and her family moved to a new apartment she had bought in a high-rise beyond Sogo Department Store in trendy eastern Taipei. She transformed the living room into a small beauty salon with two chairs and one sink, and continued working from home. The advantages of working alone from home, she explained, were twofold. First, she no longer had to hire employees in an industry characterized by high labor mobility. Second, she could go underground, relying on her former clients and word-of-mouth advertising, rather than a visible storefront, for business. That strategy enabled her to avoid formal registration and the need to pay taxes. She augmented her income further by selling beauty supplies, and later by selling long-distance telephone service through a direct-marketing scheme. She has succeeded in creating a comfortable life for herself and her family in Taipei.

DISCUSSION

Bi-hoa is part of the generation of young women studied by the feminist anthropologists in Taiwan during the 1970s, and is quite typical of that generation. It was quite common at that time, for example, for girls from poor families to give up their education so that their brothers could go to school (Greenhalgh 1985: 276). At the time, even apprentice training such as Bi-hoa received was rare for daughters, which suggests that her family was relatively wealthier than her modesty allows her to reveal. In Susan Greenhalgh's study of Taiwanese families from 1960 to 1978, 25 percent of the sons and only 4 percent of the daughters received apprentice training (1985: 282). Bi-hoa's delayed marriage was also part of the normal pattern. As Anru Lee (forthcoming) points out, this kind of delayed marriage among women workers permitted them to continue giving financial support to their natal families longer than had been possible in agricultural Taiwan. Once those workers had finished paying for their siblings' education, they were then expected to marry and transfer their loyalties from one family to another.

Bi-hoa is extremely hardworking and industrious. She reports that she works eleven hours a day. Yet it is clear that her identity does not revolve around her work as a "fundamental project," nor is it a calling in the Weberian sense. When I asked her what she gains from her business ventures, she simply said, "It doesn't matter how much money you earn in a day, an occupation is still a person's work. Everyone has to work, right?" For her, entrepreneurship is neither an identity nor a lifestyle choice. It is simply the best way she knows of taking care of her family. Bi-hoa's social identity is that of wife and mother, and revolves around her family of marriage.

Although she is humble about her business accomplishments, Bi-hoa is by no means poor. She has long been able to make independent investments in real estate, and most recently has been able to buy an apartment in one of the most expensive neighborhoods in Taiwan. She is thus wealthier than many North American academics. She has also been willing to spend part of her wealth by, for example, taking her two sons on trips to the United States and Europe. Her occupation may lack social prestige, but it has brought her a not insignificant income.

Attention to issues of power in the family shows that both men and women are constrained by ideological rules, even as they bring varying degrees of social capital to the family. As feminist scholars working in Chinese communities have clearly shown, women are disempowered by patrilocal norms in marriage that trade women like commodities (Gates 1989). The patrilocal practice of moving out of their natal families and into their husbands' households, where they have to start from a low entry position and prove their value through labor, is the main problem for young married women. Bi-hoa takes visible pride in the fact that her own labor has made her the breadwinner in the family.

It would be an exaggeration, therefore, to argue that women are completely subordinate to men in this marriage system. They are aware that marriage is a power game, and they often play it as well as they can. First of all, women have long been aware of positional power in families, for example, and taken sibling order into consideration as they make choices of marriage partners. As Margery Wolf noted in the late 1960s, "Many mothers are reluctant to marry their daughters to an eldest son because it means more work . . . and because the eldest son is more likely to have his mother in his home for as long as she lives" (1972: 143). Mothers understand well the power games into which they are sending their daughters, and they know how to look out for their daughters' welfare.

The eldest brother in a family occupies a structurally important position with greater responsibilities than his younger siblings, a pattern which holds true throughout Chinese cultural areas. In my M.A. thesis research on Taoist monasticism, for example, I found that elder brothers are far less likely to become monks in China than are younger brothers—unless they have previously married and fulfilled their duties of providing sons for the patrilineage (Simon 1994: 48). Gay men in Taiwan, who might otherwise prefer not to marry women, also feel the pressures of structural position when they make decisions about whether to accept a gay identity or marry and fulfill the needs of their families to continue the lineage. Considering that young men are also restrained by structural positions in the family, Susan Greenhalgh (1994) thus discusses sons as among the subordinate members of the patriarchal family.

Bi-hoa refers to these structural restraints on eldest sons as she explains her husband's behavior and her place in his family. When they opened up a restaurant, for example, she explained it as something he was obliged to do, rather than as a decision that they made purely out of their own interests. Sons in general, but especially the eldest sons, are expected to make a relatively large income and support their parents. Their wives are expected to help them achieve this goal, a responsibility in entrepreneurial families that leads them to become thau-ke-niu, or boss-wives. This social pressure surely made it all the more difficult for him to accept working for his wife's relatives, and to live far away from his parents.

Although neither men nor women are entirely free of personal pressure in this family system, one still cannot make the case that men and women are equally restrained. These structures of power and the ideologies that reinforce them generally work to the advantage of men and to the disadvantage of women. When men work for their families, they are perceived as filial sons and morally correct. Women, however, are discouraged from having too much contact with their natal families. Women may even be censured by their in-laws if they spend too much time with their biological parents (Hu 1995: 11). These structures, by distancing women from the financial and emotional support of their natal families, tend to disempower women, and explain why some women opt out of marriage entirely in an age of rising feminist consciousness. It is for this reason that some Taiwanese feminists, like Hu (1995), criticize the Confucian ideal of "three generations under one roof" and advocate instead close conjugal relations in nuclear families.

One aspect of marriage in Taiwan, which ensures that virtually all women start out their marriages in a position of relative power weaker than their husband, is hypergamy. Men are expected to choose wives who are beneath them in all aspects: younger, physically shorter, less educated, and from families of lower income or social status—and the women are expected to stay that way. These social norms of who should enter a marriage ensure male superiority much more thoroughly than gender alone. When these norms are violated, as in cases where a woman earns a greater income on her own or when her family has an unexpected rise in social status, the power of the husband is threatened and new stresses are placed on the marriage. Taiwanese psychiatrist Wang Hao-wei (1998) has illustrated well how such situations can easily lead to masculine crises and domestic violence.

The cases presented so far illustrate the diversity of ways in which women can deal with these problems and empower themselves more in their families. In some cases, entrepreneurship can be a successful part of these strategies. Fan Fut-moi, for example, was able to gain a great deal of power vis-à-vis her family of marriage by running a trade company successfully and in connection with the firm already established by her husband. Ong Siok-ting used a different strategy by leaving her husband's business, starting out on her own, and then incorporating him into her enterprise. This was partly due to conjunctural circumstances, as his company was no longer profitable and he had few other choices. The fact that she ran her business within a Buddhist ideology of compassion, moreover, made it an acceptable option for him. He can thus claim that he and his wife are both dedicated to Buddhist practice and charity. Men derive social identity primarily from their performance in the public world, and her company gives him a new, socially accepted way of doing that well.

Bi-hoa had a more difficult career. When she married, she apparently followed the informal rule of hypergamy by marrying her boss's son. Yet later in the marriage, her family's contacts in the pharmaceutical and machine-tool industries in Tainan meant that she would eventually be able to broker her husband's entry into the labor market, a definite shift in the power balance of the marriage. Her initial attempt to find her husband a job in Tainan failed, but largely because of his shortcomings rather than because of hers. If that strategy had succeeded, it would have elevated her position and increased her power in his family. Most importantly, it would have inverted the usual power structure of patrilineal logic by making him dependent on her family rather than leaving her dependent on his. As I have seen in both this study and among leather tanners in a prior period of field research (Simon 1998b), such strategies are rarely acceptable to men in the long term. First, men perceive it to be a loss of face if they have to seek employment with their wives' relatives. Second, they rarely have access to positions of power, which are usually reserved for the sons of the owners, and are perceived as outsiders. Bi-hoa's plan of sending her husband to work in Tainan had little chance of success.

Her husband continually resisted her strategies to find him a job, especially when they violated normative standards of masculinity. It was certainly a loss of face for him to accept a job from his wife's relatives; and an even greater loss of face to accept a manual job developing film in his wife's hair salon. These factors, more than homesickness, contributed to his dissatisfaction and eventual decision to "run away" to China. The gender ideologies of marriage made it difficult for them to find creative solutions acceptable to both partners.

Emma Goldman stressed the material reasons why women stay in unequal marital relations (Connell 1987: 113). Yet there are cultural reasons as well. In Taiwan, women are indoctrinated from childhood to believe that feminine virtue means "one man in a lifetime" (Hsu 1998). Women like Bi-hoa, who identify with these virtues, simply do not consider the possibility of divorce and remarriage, even if they have the financial means to do so. Bi-hoa, who commands property and a good income, and whose husband is more dependent on her than she is on him, has the economic power needed to demand a divorce. And since she is already in an occupation tainted with sexual conations, she would have little to lose in social prestige as a result of divorce. Yet even when her husband suggested divorce, she was unwilling to entertain the possibility.

Desire and cathexis, or the emotionally and erotically charged dimension of human relationships (Connell 1987: 112), are often ignored in studies of gender and power. I would argue, however, that they are important in Bi-hoa's case. What emerges from her narrative, but even more from visits to her shop and home, is that she and her husband love each other very much. In spite of the difficulties they have gone through and even in spite of the fact that he once suggested they divorce, she chose to stay with him. Entrepreneurship enabled Bi-hoa to support her marriage and make the best of even the most difficult situations. It allowed her to stay with the man she loved and help him fight through depression. One cannot but admire her strength and persistence in the face of enormous emotional challenges.

Bi-hoa, like many other married women entrepreneurs, is a successful Taiwanese woman in the sense meant by Margery Wolf: "a rugged individualist who has learned to depend largely on herself while appearing to lean on her father, her husband, and her son" (1972: 41). The following two chapters look at even more rugged individualists who have opted out of heterosexual marriage entirely.

NOTE

1. They married at the suggestion of his father. Bi-hoa's husband told me, "She started working in our shop when I was in my second year of high school. She was still there when I was in third year, in fourth year, and even all the way through college. All the other girls kept changing jobs, but she was always there and working hard. My father knew she would take good care of my family and suggested we get married. Since I had no objections, we got married."

Chapter Seven

A Café Owner

Old Orchard Café is one of Taipei's best-known cafés. At NT$200 for a cup of coffee, it is also one of the most expensive. But its special atmosphere, with plush leather chairs and coffee stirred by hand in old-fashioned coffee siphons, has permitted it to withstand strong competition from Starbucks and other coffee chains. There are two branches in Taipei, one in Taichung, and more recently, one in Shanghai. Ma Ya-hung, the fifty-two-year-old owner of the enterprise, still enjoys sitting in the café and chatting with the taxi drivers and businessmen who make up the majority of her clientele. In conversations with customers, she identifies herself boldly and proudly as a second-generation Shanghainese. Her family background, however, is as complex as Taiwanese society. Based on early memories, she distinguishes herself from other Mainlanders:

> My father is Shanghainese. My mother is Native Taiwanese. My parents spoke to each other in Japanese while I was growing up, since my mother had received a Japanese education and my father had lived in the Japanese sector of Shanghai. So we are very complex: I grew up speaking Taiwanese. I understand Japanese and Shanghainese, but I had to use Mandarin at school. That's the environment that I grew up in.

Like many Taiwanese people, Ya-hung begins her life narrative with reference to her family background. She uses the narrative to create an identity distinct from the Mainlanders who came to Taiwan with Chiang Kai-shek and took high-ranking posts in the government or military. Her father, she recounted, came from a wealthy family, landed gentry in the countryside near Shanghai. At the age of eighteen, her father moved to Shanghai and found a job selling Western clothes with a Japanese trading company. With the conclusion of World War II, Taiwan was taken over by the Chinese KMT and it became possible for Chinese citizens to visit the island. Ya-hung emphasizes that her father came to Taiwan *as a tourist* and met his wife in the port city of Keelung. She crafts her narrative carefully to distance herself from Chiang Kai-shek and negate a KMT/Mainlander identity:

> In 1946, some of his friends said that Taiwan is the treasure island of Formosa. The climate is like spring year-round. So my father came to Taiwan with some friends as a tourist. After he arrived in Taiwan, he met my mother. That's how my younger brother and I were born.

Ya-hung's mother had recently returned to Taiwan from a job serving as volunteer nurse on the Japanese front lines in Southeast Asia. They courted for three years, during which time her father lived on remittances sent from his family in Shanghai. In 1948, they married, and bore Ya-hung as their first child. Ya-hung's father originally hoped to eventually return to Shanghai with his wife and children. With the founding of the People's Republic of China in 1949 and Chiang Kai-shek's retreat to Taiwan, however, he was suddenly separated from China and forced to start a new life in Taiwan:

> He was different from other Mainlanders, since his circumstances were different from those that came over with the government. Most people can say that their fathers were in government or in business. But my father did neither. He simply came here as a tourist, and then had to stay behind. After that, his life was a tragedy. Why is that? Those Mainlanders who came with the government had salaries, ranks in the government, and free housing. The business people who came over had a lot of money. But my father had none of that. I grew up in a family without roots.

Her mother's family worked in management at the state-owned Taiwan Fertilizer Company during the Japanese occupation. The transition to ROC rule was difficult for the KMT administrators of such state firms due to language barriers between incoming carpetbaggers and the local population. Companies such as this were originally managed in Japanese; employees were Native Taiwanese who spoke Japanese and Taiwanese, but no Mandarin. The new Chinese administrators who came with Chiang Kai-shek spoke Mandarin, but neither Japanese nor Taiwanese. In this situation, Ya-hung's father was able to find work as a translator during the handover to Chinese Mainlander management.

By 1953, the handover was complete, and Ya-hung's father no longer was needed as a translator. Not wanting to live in the shadow of his in-laws, he decided to move his family to Taipei. As Ya-hung said, "A man can't live with his in-laws forever. He has to start his own family, and provide for them on his own." It proved difficult, however, to live up to those gendered expectations. Although his wife found a stable job as a midwife in a state-run hospital:

> He would lose face if he relied on my mother's salary. There wasn't much he could do, since he couldn't speak Taiwanese. But he had a lot of nice clothes that he brought over from Shanghai. He had cashmere suits imported from England. He also had

leather shoes; I still remember that thick cow leather. My father started to sell his clothes. He also sold his Rolex watch.

She recalled how selling clothes eventually turned into a small business:

> There were also other Mainlanders there, soldiers who had deserted the ROC army. They hung out around the Ban-ka train station. They set up a market there, selling raincoats, army surplus goods from the Americans, hats, whatever. My father set up a team of Mainlanders, about eight or nine people. They rode bicycles through the suburbs of Taipei, buying old clothes and housewares like fans and woks from relatively wealthy people. Then they sold them from a stand in the market.

In 1956, moreover, his wife left him "since their personalities didn't match" and returned home to Keelung. Subsequently, Ya-hung's father had to earn a living and raise children alone in even more difficult circumstances. Ya-hung's childhood memories are thus stories of poverty. She recalls vividly attending the Catholic Church with her brother in order that they could collect the milk powder, rice, candy, and clothing distributed by USAID and the American NGO World Vision. By the time she reached the second year of high school, she had to quit school and start earning money for her brother's education. She eventually supported him all the way through junior college.

A YOUNG WOMAN ENTERING SOCIETY

By 1964, Taiwan was already beginning the labor-intensive production of textiles, electronic goods, and bicycles for the American market. Young women streamed into the factories as a new labor force (see Arrigo 1980, Diamond 1979, Kung 1994 [1983]), amidst fierce competition in an economy where laborers far outnumbered jobs. Sixteen-year-old Ya-hung tried to get one of the lucrative jobs as a spinner in a textile factory. It was good work at the time, she said, "NT$500/month, three meals a day, and bus transportation to and from work." Without family connections, however, she was unable to get such a job. She turned instead to the dance halls for work, a job that brings disrepute to young women because it gives them many opportunities to meet men:

> Since I couldn't get a job in a textile factory, I went to a dance hall and worked at the cash counter. After all, I studied business in high school and had a good grasp of basic accounting principles. I went to the Venice Dance Hall on En-ping North Road. The big disadvantage of that job is that people will think that you are a bad girl. And it was commercial work. But there was nothing else I could do. At least the salary was high. A factory worker could earn NT$500 a month; I could earn NT$1,000 in a dance hall. One disadvantage was that I had to ride a bicycle to and from work, in the middle of the night, through the cold and rain. There were advantages and disadvantages. One advantage was that I learned how to manage personal relations. A disad-

vantage was that I often had to be with disgusting people. In that kind of pleasure industry, one grows up quickly.

Ya-hung recalled how she started work in a dance hall:

I didn't apply for that job. I had a friend who worked there. Once she had to take care of some family problems, so I substituted for her. The boss liked me. He liked my attitude at work, since I am very lively and like telling jokes. My heart was very carefree. At first there were only four people working there, but then it became five because the boss liked me for my attitude towards work. I worked at the cash counter, calculating the patrons' accounts. We didn't call those girls "accountants"; we called each other "sisters." I liked to finish today's tasks today. I wouldn't just look at the clock and then leave. We worked from 12:30 P.M. to 12:30 A.M. But I sometimes stayed later to finish the accounting. So the boss didn't want to see me leave.

"At the time," said Ya-hung, "I didn't give any thought at all to the possibility that taking that job would influence my future. I just thought: it's twice the pay and you get paid for having a good time!" It was just a matter of time, however, before that job changed her life. It led her to meet her future husband.

PUSHED TO THE BRINK

At the age of 25, Ya-hung married a Mainlander from Zhejiang Province whom she met at work:

All of my colleagues had boyfriends. We would go out together in groups of men and women to do things like view the flowers on Yangming Mountain. That's how I met a man. We were pretty conservative. I had some traditional Chinese attitudes. First, "Marry a chicken and follow a chicken; marry a dog and follow a dog." Second, women should do household chores. But I was raised by my father. Since he is a man, he couldn't do those things. And I didn't live with my mother, so I learned all of those things from his friends' wives.

After marriage, Ya-hung became a rather traditional thau-ke-niu, following her husband into business. They attempted one kind of small business after another: real estate, wood-working, and a trading company. She lived very much like Fan Fut-moi and Ong Siok-ting, although the companies her husband started were apparently less successful:

He was ten years older than me. I thought an older man would be more stable. But he was so proud of himself that he was always getting into fights in public places. And he was always embarking on some business project. Some were successes; some were failures. He was immature. Suddenly one day, he bought a chemical factory. His friend just said, "Let's open up a chemical factory," and he did it. But you know what men like. He would earn a dime, and then find some excuse to go spend it on alcohol and card playing. My father had always taught me "Marry a chicken and follow a chicken." So I thought I should tolerate his behavior. But I found that to be a kind of compromise; I was always giving in.

She wiped back tears from her eyes as she continued to relate the story of her marriage, in a narrative tinged with ethnic tension:

It's very sad when you discover that the person you are with isn't the person you would like him to be. My husband is a Mainlander, but he was always doing business with that Taiwanese ethnic group. He started to learn those Taiwanese attitudes of male chauvinism.[1] He started to say, "She doesn't matter. Anyway, it's just 'flower drinking.' If a man doesn't drink, how can he do business?"

Two years later, Ya-hung gave birth to her son. It was then that she discovered how far her husband had drifted away from her:

When I gave birth to my child, I couldn't find my husband. I spent one day and one night in the hospital, but couldn't find my husband. My mother was far away, and I couldn't find my husband, so I gave birth to that child alone. I was in labor for thirty-six hours. It was so hard I wanted a caesarian delivery, but the doctor insisted that a natural childbirth would be better. I vomited several times, and eventually passed out. When I came to, they were giving me oxygen. My father was waiting at the door. Back then, men weren't allowed in to see women giving birth, even if it was a relative. The nurse told me that I had given birth to a boy. I don't know what happened, because I passed out and then only came to when they gave me oxygen. But I later found out that they had given me a caesarian delivery. At my most critical moment, my husband was gambling and he had a mistress at his side.

After returning home with her son, she continued to perform the roles that she believed to be proper for a wife and mother: childcare, cooking, washing clothes, and making breads and cakes. She took great pride in the Shanghai dishes that she cooked for her family. She also managed the family finances well, and had the foresight to register two Taipei apartments in her own name. Yet her marriage failed to improve:

I was so naïve. My husband's lifestyle was just gambling, dancing, drinking. I said, "What are you doing? You are ruining our family." But he wouldn't listen. Finally, I walked out of that marriage. I just walked right out. Mr. Simon, I'll tell you why I went into business in Shihlin [district of Taipei]. This is where I got married. This is where I gave birth. This is where I fell down, and this is where I will stand up again.

Initially indecisive about how to handle her unhappy marriage, she turned to her natal family for support:

My husband kept finding mistresses, one after another. I was tired, and my health deteriorated. I just wanted to leave those painful days. I told my father, "The times have changed. I would really like to listen to your 'Marry a chicken and follow a chicken,' but if I continue like this, my heart will break." I started to cough, and then I developed a terrible disease—depression. I spent a lot of time in hospital emergency rooms. I just couldn't take it any longer. I told my father, "If I listen to you, it will be the end of me. You and my brother will be left alone. And my child is even more pitiful. Who will take care of him? With that kind of a father, who will teach the child?" At first I thought I should stay in our marriage for the child, but that is not something that can be decided by one person. It takes two people. If I am willing, my husband should be willing too. If he is not willing, there is nothing I can do. My father talked to my husband and he said he would change, but he couldn't. Already seduced by those material goods, his life goals had changed. His heart was no longer in our marriage, and it became a family crisis. When I decided to leave that family, it was the only way to really save the family and my child.

Her decision to divorce her husband came as a painful moment of existential anguish, a fateful moment when she literally stood on the abyss and contemplated suicide:

At my saddest moment, I took my child, when he was still an infant, to the Chung Shan Bridge. That's where I grew up. I don't know how it happened, but I just walked to the top of the bridge with my child and prepared to jump from the bridge with him. At that time, my mental health had already collapsed. I don't know how I got home, since there is a blank in my memory. I just remember that I came to, and my mother was there. She said the police had come to her. A woman on the road had seen me, a lone woman standing on the bridge in the night with a crying child in her arms, and called the police. I ignored everyone who spoke to me. The police took me in, and called my mother. That's what my mother told me. After that, I started to see psychiatrists. One of them told me I needed a change in environment.

No longer trapped in indecision, she boldly chose to divorce her husband and go into business for herself.

BEGINNING A NEW LIFE FROM KAOHSIUNG

When newly divorced Ya-hung moved to Kaohsiung in 1976 with a two-year-old child, a number of factors made it possible for her to go into the café business. The first was an introduction to the business from an acquaintance. She said, "The first thing I did in Kaohsiung was look for a friend of mine. She was running a café at the time. I went to her café to chat. As it happened, one of the waitresses couldn't come to work that day. So I just stepped in to help out."

She also had the advantage of coming from a family that drank coffee at home every day. She explained how her mother had brought that habit, unusual in Taiwan at the time, with her from Vietnam:

My mother worked as a nurse for the Japanese. She was sent to Southeast Asia—you know, Vietnamese coffee is very good—and brought back coffee beans. When she made coffee at home back then, when I was four years old, the neighbors would smell it and ask what she was cooking. Coffee wasn't served in coffee houses like today. That only became popular in the 1970s. My mother always made coffee at home, so I grew up drinking it.

She also had the advantage of a good relationship with her younger brother, whom she had supported all the way through a junior college degree in restaurant management. Maintaining good relations with her natal family gave her the support she needed upon getting a divorce:

> I called up my brother and asked if he wanted to come down to Kaohsiung and open up a café with me. Twenty years ago, that was a new field. I said we should try it out. Back then our café was very small. We only had four or five tables, and each table was only large enough for two or three people.

Most importantly of all, she had access to capital. While following her husband as boss-wife, she had already been wise enough to purchase two apartments in her own name. That helped her gain access to capital:

> I went back to Taipei, and tried to borrow money from friends. I already had two apartments in Taipei, and was prepared to sell one so that I could buy a café. My friend suggested that I don't do that. He said that he would loan me the money. He said that if I failed, I could sell the apartment and return the money to him. If I succeed in business, I can pay him back without having to sell my apartment. After all, there are transaction costs in selling a house, and it also takes time. That friend was my brother's classmate. He was concerned about me, and encouraged me to leave that life of darkness. That's how I opened up the first Old Orchard Café. My brother and I opened it in 1976.

Her first café was successful, and allowed her to grow in business:

> We were lucky. Within a year, we could return all the money we had borrowed. Of course, the work was very hard. Most people work for eight hours a day. I worked for seventeen hours. I did everything. It was like having two jobs, but I was able to return the money I had borrowed more quickly that way. My brother said, "It would be even better to run two cafés." He said that would be a better investment than earning interest on savings; by investing in another café, we could make one plus one become three. Taiwan still didn't have chain stores or franchises at the time. We were among the first. With a chain store, you can make one plus one equal three, four, or even five. We opened the second shop in Taichung. We made it our goal to have one store each in Kaohsiung, Taichung, and Taipei.

The main emotional challenge was opening up in Taipei. Returning to her hometown, however, was a way of achieving emotional closure:

> Why did I come to Taipei last of all? This is where I fell. I was afraid to come back until I had succeeded on my own. When I came back to this place, I was nervous, afraid.

Maybe it was a lack of self-confidence. Or maybe it was because of the way people gossip in Chinese society. In this kind of environment, people saw me as a bad woman. They said that I didn't love my husband, that I didn't want my family, and that I had taken away their property. They said I didn't forgive and support my husband. They said I left him because he fell into bad circumstances. It was all that kind of talk. I just ignored them. I figured, I should be silent and then act. When the act was accomplished, then I could speak.

In 1984, she opened up her first café in downtown Taipei:

When I opened that Taipei shop ten years later, I arrived in the city with a heart full of joy, fear, and worry. I was afraid to encounter that evil again. I hate the way people talk and gossip. But the joy was there because I could say, "I have already come this far. The past no longer exists for me." Everything I had planned to accomplish by the age of fifty had already been done, and ten years ahead of my plan.

Ya-hung has been so successful in Taiwan that one of her clients even copied the name and opened over eighty Old Orchard Cafés in China. She pursued him in the Chinese courts, won her case, and now hopes to retake the mainland herself with cafés in Guangzhou, Shenzhen, Shanghai, and other coastal cities. In 2002, she opened up her first café in Shanghai.

NOT JUST BUSINESS

In addition to her successful business, of which Ya-hung is justifiably proud, she also takes pride in having accomplished several other personal goals. The first is having raised her son in difficult circumstances as a single mother:

We were a single-mother family, and he had to follow me all over the province. But I remained faithful to one principle. Since I myself didn't have a mother, the first thing I always kept in mind was keeping him at my side. I definitely wanted to be by his side as he grew up. When I went to Kaohsiung, I took him to Kaohsiung. When I went to Taichung, I took him to Taichung. And when I came to Taipei, I helped him transfer to a school in Taipei. Since he has lived in all three cities, he has had to adapt to new classmates, new schools, new environments, and different living standards. Why did we leave Kaohsiung? I couldn't get used to Kaohsiung: they run red lights, wear slippers when they ride motorcycles, and wear undershirts to go shopping. I didn't want my child to grow up in that kind of environment.

Although she taught her son to make coffee, he had no plans to take over his mother's business at the time of this research.[2] Ya-hung was planning instead to cultivate some of her employees to eventually take over management of the cafés in Taiwan. Some of her employees, including two young members of the Amis tribe from rural Hualien County of eastern Taiwan, live with her in Taipei. She describes that choice of workers as a way of helping aboriginal people, who often face discrimination on the job market. She says she would like to see them open up their own cafés, perhaps as part of tourism development in their home community.

Ya-hung and her brother also own two villas in Taichung. In 1985, she was able to convince both her parents to live with her, albeit in emotionally charged circumstances. By doing so, she fulfilled her lifetime dream of reuniting her family:

> I found my mother and brought her home to live with me in my house. Of course, my mother and father didn't get along, but my house had four stories and a big garden. My father lived on the first floor, my mother on the second, I lived on the third, and my son had a play area and study room on the fourth floor. I used all of my heart to bring my family back together. My brother lived next door with his wife. We ate together almost every day, and I cooked for them.

After the death of her father in 1992 and the graduation of her son from high school, she has been able to dedicate more time to charitable work. She has done volunteer work visiting handicapped people in their homes. She also enjoys taking care of injured and stray animals. Until she finally gave in to her mother's objections, she even ran an informal dog shelter from her own home:

> The first floor was for newly arrived dogs. I would observe them to make sure that they were healthy. The second floor was for those dogs that had already been vaccinated. The third floor was where I lived with my favorite dogs. And my mother lived on the fourth floor. My mother said I was crazy! But I have always done such naïve things. Those things are normal in foreign countries, but here people just laugh at me.

By the time I met Ya-hung, she had already given away all but one Siberian Husky, which she kept as a treasured pet. At my introduction, she became a good friend of Ong Siok-ting and a supporter of her charitable work in Tibet. Her involvement with charity has become part of her personal identity, especially as this allows her to gain respectability and augment social capital.

REACHING TOWARDS THE GOOD

Ya-hung has lived her life on the margins of respectability. As a young woman, she worked in a dance hall, with its erotic implications of uncontrolled contacts between men and women. Even moving into the coffee business was only slightly more reputable, as cafés in Taiwan have often carried an aura of the erotic:

> In the Japanese period, coffee was served in *te-diam-a* ("teahouses"), along with alcohol or tea, by young women. I think you know what I mean. Men went to that kind of place to see women. If you smelled coffee, you knew it was that kind of place.

Social relations between the sexes have freed up considerably in the past twenty years in Taiwan. The social meaning of cafés has also changed with the introduction of Japanese café chains in the 1980s and Starbucks in the 2000s. Opening a café, however, still remains a favored option for divorced women. Late hours and frequent contact with unknown men continue to make it a somewhat marginal occupation, and the moral connotations are only slowly fading away from the business. Due to her occupational history as well as her decision to divorce her husband, Ya-hung has long been forced to endure the gossip of neighbors and acquaintances.

Reflecting on her past, however, she stressed how even her work in a dance hall contributed to her family, something she only understood completely after the death of her father:

> When I took that job [in the dance hall] I was only thinking about how to ease my father's burden and support my family. After my father died, I found out that he probably would have committed suicide if I hadn't found that job, because after his death, I opened a box of his personal effects and found several suicide letters. His wife had left him, he had two small children to raise, and he had no way to return to the mainland. His life was a failure and he became mentally ill. It was a pressure to raise two children, and we had to be educated. There were several times when he wanted to leave this world; he wrote many suicide letters. Even though I didn't know about that at the time, I didn't want my father to suffer so much and went out to earn money. Even if I sacrificed a lot, it didn't matter. The important thing was not to let all three of us die of starvation. I gave up school, and let my brother get an education instead. If I hadn't done that, my father would have committed suicide a long time ago.

Having led such a difficult life herself, she takes a critical view of Taiwan's economic development and argues that Taiwan has overlooked what she calls "moral development":

> In the past fifteen years, the Taiwanese economy has developed very rapidly. It has gone from a very poor country to one of the wealthiest in the world. But in addition to over-abundance, there is also a dark side to the story that nearly everyone overlooks. We Taiwanese people had to pay a heavy price for our wealth, especially in terms of morality. People only respect fame, power, and money. Even teachers and parents think like that. After I reached the age of forty, I started to think about those hidden dimensions of economic development. That's why I work with the handicapped. The social welfare system is inadequate and they have poor emotional lives as well, so they enjoy talking to me. Even their own parents, siblings, classmates, and friends don't have time for them. The biggest problem they have is emotional relations. Even if they find a partner who is willing to love them, their parents and friends won't support such a relationship and they get abandoned. After enduring that again and again, they become hurt and impatient.

In her discourses on economic development, Ya-hung notes that rapid economic growth has given Taiwanese people ample opportunity to work hard and earn higher material standards of living. In the process, however, many people have forgotten other values of appreciating nature or taking care of others less fortunate than themselves:

I have been very fortunate to participate in the economic miracle, because I have been able to fulfill my life dreams. I am also fortunate *that I have not lost myself.* Many of my friends are lost. Now what do I mean by lost. I still keep in touch with those friends, but they live in another life-world.[3] They boast of their good relations with certain politicians, saying that they just have to talk to the right person and they can do whatever kind of business they want [with the government]. They say that going through the back door gets things done more quickly. They say I am stupid for not getting involved in such things. But if there is a problem, aren't they the ones who have to go to jail?

She contrasts her own ethics to those of her husband, his business acquaintances, and the male customers that frequent her shop. In reference to certain corrupt business practices, like exchanging bribes to politicians in exchange for construction contracts, she asserted that women are morally superior to men:

My way of thinking is different from that of men. If I got in trouble, what would happen to my father, my mother, my child? They have more chutzpah, and say that I am just stupid. A project that takes them one year to accomplish, takes me three. They have entered another life-world. Those men can afford to buy a new Mercedes-Benz every year. They live very luxurious lives. But I don't envy them. I don't think that it is necessary to have a Mercedes-Benz or a BMW to be happy. I am happy raising my puppies and kittens. I don't demand much from life, and I think I am happy that way.

She argued, however, that Chinese women have long been unable to so freely determine their own lives:

Chinese women have many no's, many limitations, many things that they can't do, many responsibilities. They are expected to always give, to provide for the family, children, husband, and old people. They are heavily burdened and un-free. Only now are young Taiwanese women coming out of that. I'm not willing to live like a bird in a cage. Going into business and getting a divorce enable me to leave that all behind. I am very happy now.

DISCUSSION

If marriage is indeed the "perverted" institution that de Beauvoir claimed it to be (1989 [1952]: 479), then divorce seems to be the most reasonable alternative for married women who feel oppressed by the men in their lives. Previous chapters, highlighting the life narratives of women who managed to successfully integrate work and family, show that marriage is not necessarily unrewarding, even for women in a patriarchal society. Not all women, however, are happy in their marriages or able to make changes they find acceptable. In this chapter, I show how entrepreneurship, as a form of economic empowerment, can become a strategy for women to gain economic independence and leave unhappy marriages. As de Beauvoir pointed out, "Divorce is only a theoretical possibility for the woman who cannot earn her own living" (1989 [1952]: 480). For some women, entrepreneur-ship is the most realistic way to translate that theory into practice.

Taiwan, with rapidly rising wages over the past thirty years and ample oppor-tunities for female entrepreneurship, has given women increasingly greater chances to opt out of unhappy marriages. These changes are reflected in higher di-vorce rates. Taiwan now has the highest divorce rate in Asia. In 2000, one couple got divorced for every 3.5 couples that got married (Central News Agency 2001). From 1971 to 2001, the percentage of divorced people in the population rose from 0.75 percent of the population to 4.5 percent (DGBAS 2002: 9). Of the women en-trepreneurs in this study, 5.8 percent are divorced. The experience of Ya-hung il-lustrates well how these changing expectations have changed the lives of Taipei women, and how entrepreneurship can empower women.

Many Taiwanese women report that the biggest problems in their lives are caused by unfaithful husbands. In many Taiwanese male business circles, it is even considered prestigious for a man to take a mistress. In the past, women were en-couraged to tolerate their husbands' affairs and many still do. Patience and toler-ance are considered to be feminine virtues, and male sexuality is considered to be almost uncontrollable. Cultural ideologies reinforce the institution of marriage, primarily by rewarding individuals who conform to it with increased social capi-tal and punishing those who deviate from its expectations. By adhering to those ideals, many women gain the symbolic profit of social recognition and/or the ma-terial profit of financial support from the husband and his family.

Forty years ago, Taiwanese women apparently expected little emotional fulfill-ment from marital relations with their husbands. When Margery Wolf did re-search in rural Taipei County in the late 1950s and 1960s, she found that women gained emotional satisfaction primarily from their "uterine families," or ties to their children, rather than from relations with their husbands (1972: 36). The emotional fulfillment and sexual exclusivity that modern, urban women desire from their husbands is more similar to what Giddens calls the "pure relation" of late modernity (1992). Those desires are reflected in rising divorce rates, rising ages of first marriage, as well as in cases of women taking legal action against their unfaithful husbands. They can also be heard in the discourses of television and radio talk shows, and seen in the near universality of love, rather than arranged, marriages. When I read and discussed Giddens's *Transformation of Intimacy* as the only male member of a feminist reading group in Taipei, for example, there was a strong consensus that pure relationships constitute liberation for women (1992).

A common observation of women entrepreneurs and professional women is that they are liberated in the workplace, but suffer in their relationships with men. As one interior decorator said to me, "I don't see myself as a woman at work. I see myself as a professional." When I asked her when she sees herself as a woman, she said, "When I break up with a man. Then I turn into a crying woman." In a deci-sion that clearly underlines the transition to pure relations in Taipei, she broke up with her potential fiancé because she found out he was having sex with men on the side. She confronted him with that knowledge, and helped him accept his homosexuality. He has since adopted a gay identity and is now involved in a relationship with another man. She married a Belgian man she met at a concert and moved to Brussels. Her anguish at discovering her boyfriend's sexuality and the strong way she handled the situation changed both their lives. This chapter is about such fateful moments that transform relationships and shape identities.

Philosopher Charles Taylor sees "allegiance to the epiphanic act" as part of the Western "postromantic" age (1989: 422). Themes of rupture, epiphany, and decision are central to existential philosophy. The theme of the epiphany, however, is not found only in the West. It is also part of the discursive practice of many Taiwanese people, including many of the women in this study. Ong Siok-ting (Chapter 5), for example, experienced her epiphany upon seeing poverty in Thailand. True to her Buddhist ideology, she expresses herself as being like Prince Siddharta who realized the emptiness of life upon seeing poverty, sickness, old age, and death. Taiwanese people often describe these epiphanic moments in the Buddhist terminology of enlightenment (Mandarin *kaiwu*, Taiwanese *khui-go*). On a more mundane level, they may simply "open up their thinking" (Mandarin *xiang de kai*, Taiwanese *siu-e-khui*). Ya-hung's story illustrates how women can be inspired to make radical changes in their lives after sudden epiphany makes them realize their own subordination in a male-dominated society.

Epiphanies are often painful. As Sartre said, "It is in anguish that man [sic] gets the consciousness of his freedom" (1956 [1943]: 65). These fateful moments can lead to new decisions, reskilling, and empowerment, yet can also lead people to seek recourse to tradition (Giddens 1991: 142). That recourse to tradition is evident in Ma Ya-hung's narrative. A painful divorce seems to have actually strengthened her attachment to family values, as can be seen in her will to reunite her natal family. Her change in identity from wife and thau-ke-niu to divorcée and entrepreneur led her to emphasize other forms of goodness in her life. With a reputation tainted by gossip, Ya-hung makes even more explicit references to her moral framework than most Taiwanese women in her everyday presentation of self. Charitable works have thus become an integral part of her self-identity.

The ability to step out of unhappy marital relations is a basic form of empowerment at the level of interpersonal relations. Women, however, need adequate sources of social and financial capital if they are to divorce their husbands in such circumstances. Ya-hung was able to amass both kinds of capital, and become one of Taipei's most successful café owners. She had sufficient social capital because of close ties to her natal family, and adequate financial capital because she had the foresight to register property in her name while still married. Many Taiwanese women are now able to opt out of marriage if they ever feel the need. Yet an even stronger form of empowerment for women is the power to decide not to marry in the first place. The next chapter thus discusses entrepreneurship and the construction of lesbian identity in Taiwan.

NOTES

1. Note how she attributes evil to the ethnic other. The attention to ethnic identity in her narrative is very common, as will be seen in the life histories yet to come.

2. A year later, he was managing the coffee shop in Shanghai. She was training a select group of employees with the idea of sending them to open coffee shops in other Chinese cities.

3. She used the Chinese Buddhist term *jingjie* here: state of mind, way of perceiving life, *Lebenswelt*.

Chapter Eight

A Lesbian Bar

I first encountered lesbian entrepreneurs while conducting a pilot study for this project in Tainan and Kaohsiung in 1998 (Simon 1998a, 2001, forthcoming). Although I interviewed more than one lesbian entrepreneur in Taipei, only one woman chose to be represented as such in this book. I thus start this chapter with a brief summary of a life history that I have already published in Chinese. This life narrative, although situated in Kaohsiung rather than Taipei, provides insights into an earlier stage of LesbiGay consciousness in Taiwan and is a good background to the main narrative of this chapter. It is also interesting in itself as the story of a traditional thau-ke-niu who changed her life after contact with the lesbian community. The main narrative in this chapter, however, brings us back to Taipei with the story of "Sharon," a dynamic thirty-eight-year-old entrepreneur and prominent lesbian activist.[1] These women's stories reveal much about entrepreneurship, power, and individual agency.

NG BI-CHHUN'S STORY:
A BOSS-WIFE COMES OUT

Ng Bi-chhun's story is especially revealing as the case of a woman who, like many other women in this book, started her career by working for her husband's company. By the time I met her, however, she had already divorced and transformed herself into an outspoken lesbian entrepreneur. In her late forties, she introduced herself to me in self-deprecating humor as a member of the "Olay" tribe (*Oulei zu*). Olay, she explained, was first the brand name of a skin cream used by middle-aged women to prevent wrinkles. But in LesbiGay slang, it also refers to the initials "O. L." for "old lesbian."

Bi-chhun began our conversation by saying that she was raised in a farming family as one of six children. As is typical of the "coming-out" narrative, she stated that she has known since middle school that she is attracted to women. At that time, she was very close to another female student and they became physically involved. Her parents, however, discovered them in bed together and forbade her to see the other student again. Furthermore, they tried to change her behavior by finding a man and forcing her to marry him, even though she had only ever seen him once before their wedding day. In the 1970s, the practice of arranging marriages between individuals who had never met was already being replaced with formal courting and even love marriages. Bi-chhun's experience was even more atypical since they did it consciously to "cure" her of homosexuality. Back then, she emphasized, there was little room for resistance. Little information was available about homosexuality, and she did not even know that lesbian desire could be the center of a lifestyle.

After her marriage, Bi-chhun worked in her husband's company, a small factory that manufactured electronic parts. She pointed out bitterly that she worked hard, but never received any wages:

> If I had worked as an accountant in another factory, I would have received a salary. And if my husband had needed to hire an accountant on the labor market, he would have paid her a salary. But in Taiwan, a woman will work for free in her husband's company and in the end the money is all his. The bank account, the house, everything, is in his name. You can use them, but you have no way to really own them yourself.

For years, Bi-chhun lived a life like most other thau-ke-niu, and even had two children with her husband. In the late 1980s and early 1990s, however, she started to become aware of homosexuality through discussions in the media. Consciousness raising and political pressure groups were established throughout the island, including the first lesbian group "Between Us" (*Women zhi jian*), founded in 1990. As soon as she learned about that group's existence, she started participating in its activities and learning more about lesbian lifestyles. With the new information she gained, she realized in 1997 that she no longer wanted to endure the loneliness of a lesbian in a heterosexual relationship. She asked for a divorce.

Disempowered by patriarchal ideologies that mark homosexuality as deviant and shameful, she demanded no financial support or property at the time of divorce and left a once prosperous lifestyle with no more than an automobile and her own clothing. Legal custody of the children went to their father and they continued to live with him, according to Taiwanese norms in divorce. Bi-chhun, however, continued to share the children's expenses and visited them several times a week. She was unaware of any laws regulating the division of property at divorce:

> In Taiwan, everything is regulated by the people involved. I claimed nothing at my divorce. The most important thing was my independence. The best thing to do is never marry at all. When I set off on my own path, I didn't get support from anyone.

Bi-chhun said that she had fantasized about being her own boss for years. It was only after the divorce, however, that she was able to finally open up a noodle stand with capital borrowed from her parents, relatives, and a few close friends. The noodle stand, she stressed, is important to her emotionally as well as financially, as it gives her the basis of a new livelihood. Still, the most important aspect is the income. "What can you do after fifty?" she asked with a rhetorical flourish. "Life is only comfortable after fifty if you have money in your pocket." When I met Bi-chhun, her noodle stand was prospering. She had hired some women to work for her, and rarely went to work herself, except occasionally to manage finances and pay her workers. She said that it was the business that gave her the funds and free time needed to participate in lesbian activities and socialize with other women.

At the same time, her ex-husband's business failed and he had to declare bankruptcy. Bi-chhun expressed a sense of *Schadenfreude* about her husband's failure, saying it proves the importance of her former role in the company. She said, "I always told him what to do. When he didn't listen to me, he lost money. When he listened to me, he earned money. Now that I am gone, he has gone bankrupt. He really needed me for the business to succeed."

Growing up before democratization made it easier to get diverse sources of information, Bi-chhun learned about alternatives to heterosexual relations relatively late in life. By contrast, her son in college has learned about homosexuality at a young age and has been one of her strongest moral supporters. She summed up her own life course rather bitterly:

> It's not easy to suddenly follow your own path when you're already middle-aged. I have to think about all of the people in my life, my family, my friends. I have no personal space in Kaohsiung, and one really needs a place to develop one's own personal space. The best thing is to move to a new city, like Taipei, when one is still young. It's easier to be gay in Taipei, in a new place with new friends.

Indeed, it is in cosmopolitan Taipei where the LesbiGay community is best developed. Sharon's story illustrates well the development of new lesbian identities in Taipei, and the role that entrepreneurs have played in the construction of that new global lifestyle.

SHARON: THE HUMBLE
BEGINNINGS OF A LESBIAN ENTREPRENEUR

Sharon is one of the best-known figures in Taipei's gay and lesbian community, and a self-identified "T." Although the categories are fluid and some women do not make the distinction, Taiwanese lesbians usually make a social distinction between masculine "T's" (short for "tomboy") and feminine "*po*'s" (a Chinese word for "woman"). These categories are only superficially similar to the "butch" and "femme" lesbians of North America (Chao 1999, Cheng 1997). In imitation of stereotypical male behavior, "T" lesbians often smoke and drink profusely, and take pride in their sexual conquests. They sport short hair, and often wear dark suits and ties. Many of them even strap down their breasts to complete the masculine look. "Po" lesbians, on the other hand, adopt ideal-type female comportment. They have long hair, wear cosmetics, and dress in feminine dresses or skirts. More open to bisexuality, some "po" lesbians eventually end up married to men.

I have known Sharon since I arrived in Taiwan in 1996, and was a frequent customer in her first LesbiGay bar, Locomotion. New to the gay community myself and rather timid about the possibilities that it presented, I quickly felt at ease in her small pub located in a second-floor residential apartment. The quiet, smokeless atmosphere and large selection of nonalcoholic drinks—which I would later learn were concessions to complaining neighbors—appealed to me more than the larger disco pubs. In addition, I was often the only customer, a situation that allowed us to build up a friendship. Although I spent my first three years in Taiwan in the south of the island, I visited her every time I was in Taipei. After I moved to Taipei, I sometimes joined her and her American lover for dinner in Thai restaurants, where we competed with one another to see who could eat the spiciest foods.

Like many Taiwanese entrepreneurs, Sharon constructs her life history in reference to humble origins. She was born to a Native Taiwanese farming family in Hualien County, the seventh of eight children. She describes her father, unsuccessful at both farming and small business, as "worthless." She has always been closer to her mother, who supported her family financially by selling food from mobile stalls on the streets of Hualien City. Most of all, Sharon's childhood memories are those of poverty:

> We were one of the most pitiful families in our village. Neither of my parents had any education, and my older brothers had all left home. We all lived together. I always wanted to be free, but I had no way to be free. Seven of us—my father, mother, my younger brother, older sisters, and I—all slept in the same bed. There were seven people in one bed, and that only because my elder brothers left Hualien. I only wanted to grow up quickly, in order to be free.

As a teenager, she finally got the freedom she desired by testing into junior college in Taipei, where she was to study actuary science. Because she continually stressed the theme of freedom, I asked her what kind of freedom she desired:

> It's because my mother was always nagging. I had my own ideas, but I didn't really know what freedom meant. I just wanted to get out of there as quickly as possible, so I moved to Taipei. I soon discovered that my new environment was just another kind of difficulty, another kind of pitiful existence. In fact, there was some pleasure at coming home to laugh and relax with my family. But Taipei was a different kind of pain. My mother was no longer there to protect me. At home she would cook for me, but

in Taipei there was nobody to feed me. I always had to be careful to please my landlord, and I didn't get along with my classmates. When people say that life is joyful, I
say that is because they have never understood pain and bitterness.

Her biggest difficulties at the time were financial. Since the remittances she received from her mother were not enough to support a student life in Taipei, she
moved from one part-time job to another. Already adopting a "T" identity at the
age of eighteen, she suffered the job discrimination often reported by masculine
lesbians (Simon 1998a: 77), who cannot fit into the work environments where
male bosses prefer to hire beautiful and feminine young women. She slipped into
entrepreneurial activity simply because she needed money:

> I was working in a cram school. My job was to write the sample questions on prac-
> tice tests. I used my brother's name to open a post office box and register a business.
> Then I put advertisements in the newspaper, and sold the practice tests that I brought
> home from work. I don't remember the exact price, but I sold the same practice tests
> at half the price asked by my boss.

Since she and her American partner have long discussed the relative benefits of
entrepreneurship versus career planning in formal employment, Sharon added,
"You Americans don't understand why people go into business. In fact, a lot of it
is because of poverty. You need to get by, so you think of ways to earn money."
Sharon said that she learned many of those facts about entrepreneurship and human life from her first girlfriend.

LEARNING FROM OTHER WOMEN: SHARON'S FIRST LESBIAN RELATIONSHIP

In Sharon's words, her first lesbian lover was a "foreigner," an overseas Chinese
woman living in Hong Kong. Sharon was only nineteen years old at the time and
her lover was forty. Her lover, she explains, grew up in a poor family like her own;
and also had ambitions that took her far away from her family. She was a dynamic
women entrepreneur in her own right:

> She was an overseas Chinese in Thailand. She married and had three children, yet she
> always wanted a divorce. Because her family was poor, she went to Hong Kong think-
> ing that the city would be like Heaven. She was twenty years old when she went. She
> had a plan, to be successful by the age of thirty. She wanted to earn as much money
> as possible, and then get a divorce.

> She was older than me. She understood things better than me, and taught me not to
> overvalue emotional relationships. Of course, she wasn't just playing with me, but she
> also didn't want me to disturb her life. She had three children. She lived in Hong

Kong, but frequently came to Taiwan and had an apartment in Kaohsiung. She had three children. She said she hoped that I could be her lover in this corner of the world. It was very painful for me.

Pointing out how that woman taught her the value of money, Sharon said:

When I was young, I thought she was very impressive. But by the age of twenty-two, I no longer thought so, because she wanted to borrow money from me. Since I loved her a lot, I wanted to help her. But she asked for NT$300,000 and there was no way I could get so much money. By the time I was twenty-seven, I had earned enough money to help her out. By then, she said, "That's already past."

Sharon reflects, moreover, on that lover's lifestyle in much the way that Ma Ya-hung in the previous chapter remembers her husband:

I don't think she is very successful. I think her life is just chaos, that she is very lonely. She has a lot of girlfriends. Now, I don't think that raising three children and putting them through school is all that difficult. But her life was full of gambling, karaoke, scotch, and lots of women. She loved to drink alcohol. I remember the last time I saw her. She already had three houses. But I didn't think she was successful.

"What is success?" I asked. Sharon said:

Basically, success is having a full life, a happy one, and self-confidence. You should have a beautiful house, but not too many friends. You should have high standards. That is the kind of success I have. I am not lonely. She may be twenty years older than I am, but I think her life is a failure.

In the eight years they were together, however, Sharon worked hard to earn the money she wanted, and learned the survival skills that would soon turn into entrepreneurial flair.

JOB DISCRIMINATION AND FAILED LOVE

At the age of twenty-two, Sharon graduated from junior college. She went to Tamkang University to study international trade, but quit after one semester when she perceived the discrimination that she would later suffer on the job market. Women in Taiwan are frequently selected for positions as receptionists, secretaries, and even as accountants on the basis of personal appearance. In the corporate environment, such pink-collar workers are expected to dress beautifully, wear cosmetics, and serve coffee or tea to clients and business partners in an elegant, feminine manner. At the time Sharon entered the job market, moreover, women were still expected to leave their jobs when they became pregnant, and there was neither the opportunity nor the expectation for women to advance in careers over a life course. Sharon, however, refused to shed her "T" identity and adopt the feminine "po" demeanor that would allow her to pass as heterosexual:

> Even when I was looking for a part-time job, nobody wanted me because they thought I was too ugly. Women that graduate in international trade become secretaries. Companies want a beautiful woman to translate English and type. But the bosses didn't want me. When I looked for a job, those bosses would say, "Why don't you do sales?" Apparently, my face is only beautiful enough to do sales. That was a real attack on my self-confidence.

Once Sharon realized she would face job discrimination in a career as a foreign-language secretary, she quit school and started to work in sales. Her strong personality, however, made it difficult for her to fit into hierarchical corporate environments. She was fired after working a mere three months at her first job:

> It came as a big shock. When he asked me if I had any suggestions about the business, I gave him a lot of advice. He just responded politely that it would be better if I didn't have any suggestions. But I still had lots of suggestions, and nobody wanted to listen to me. Of course, I couldn't accept being fired, so I fired my boss. I changed jobs.

Sharon quickly learned to defend herself and negotiate strongly in the job market, changing jobs often as a strategy for gaining regular increases in salary:

> Let's say your salary was originally NT$20,000 a month. You would tell the next boss that you were earning NT$30,000. Then he would ask if you can accept NT$27,000. I was pretty tricky. But that is because I have been hurt so much by society. Whenever I talk to other people, I always protect myself first.

With what she describes as her strong personality, she continued to hustle her way into ever higher-paying jobs, changing firms every few months for two years. She even forged a university diploma to get a job in one larger, prestigious firm. Each job, however, ended like the first, as her outspoken manners often caused friction with her bosses:

> Once again, I got a job at a major trading company. My salary was always increasing. But I realized that it just wouldn't work out. That's the way Taiwanese society works. Finally one of my foreign girlfriends said, "With your personality, you should start your own business." I always said directly what I thought, and that's not how Taiwanese society works. I always made my bosses uncomfortable. So that is when I started to dream about going into business for myself.

At the age of twenty-four, she finally rented a storefront in the night market near National Taiwan University and opened up a teahouse specializing in "bubble tea." That business dream lasted a mere six months, largely, she said, due to her own immaturity:

[In the night market] you have to open very late in order to succeed. But after 10 P.M., friends would invite me to go to the pubs. I would just close up and go. After a while, my mother came to help me, but she wanted me to stay with her to work at night. She wanted me to stay and work, but I just wanted to play. I hadn't grown up yet. Then, since there was just one older woman in the shop, the young customers [students] stopped coming. It was like a culture: only a few *obaasan* ("old women") went there, and no young people.

Six months later, she went out of business. More tragically yet, an important relationship failed. The German woman she had been dating suddenly decided to leave the lesbian lifestyle and marry a man. "I decided not to fall in love again," said Sharon, "and I went back to Hualien."

FROM DISCRIMINATION TO
EMPOWERMENT: SHARON COMES BACK

Sharon faced even more job discrimination in conservative Hualien. She got her first job as an assistant manager in a large grocery store. The problem, she said, was that lesbian friends often came from Taipei to visit her. At first, she had fun entertaining Taipei friends and local coworkers together, but that lifestyle eventually caused trouble. "One of my friends told my boss that I am lesbian," she said. "He got angry and fired me. I was fired because I was a lesbian."

She then found a job in management for a large chain of convenience stores headquartered in Tainan. After training in Tainan for a year, she was sent back to Hualien as manager to help develop the market there. Eventually, however, she hit the glass ceiling that women often face in corporate environments. She said, "A lot of the managers were women, and we got along well. But in Hualien, all of the assistant managers were men. They didn't like having a woman as a boss. I couldn't tolerate their attitudes, so I left."

Sharon returned to Taipei and went back into business. This time, she went into the travel agent business. She described her strategy for getting into that field, saying:

At first I was in sales. . . . I only wanted to be a boss. I didn't know why it is better to be a boss. I hadn't even made the calculations. I was getting about NT$70,000 a month: NT$40,000 in basic salary and NT$30,000 in commissions. I learned the trade very quickly. But after three months, I got fired.

This time she got fired in a dispute with her boss over unemployment insurance payments. She just moved on to another travel agency, with even greater ambition of becoming her own boss. After three months of organizing tour groups, she devised a strategy for setting up her own travel agency in the informal sector:

I had my own office, but I didn't have a travel-agent license. What do you do in a case like that? You look for a part-time job in a travel agency. When you issue a ticket yourself, you have to borrow the invoice from your boss. I had my own office with a desk, everything but a legal business. All the clients assume it is your business. When you purchase an airplane ticket, you go to sales and not directly to the boss, right? But actually, many of the sales people are working for themselves. They just don't have enough capital to open up a formal business. Two years later, that travel agency went out of business, so I bought it.

She bought the travel agency as a joint venture with the eight other women working in the original company. She took charge of publicity, she said, going out herself to set up name card or poster displays. "I was busy day and night," she said. She worked as a travel agent for six years. After several years in the travel agency, she became dissatisfied with the amount of business she was getting in comparison to her partners. That is when she opened up her first LesbiGay pub, Locomotion.

With its brass and wood décor, Locomotion had less the atmosphere of a pub than of a coffee shop. It was located in a second-floor residential apartment in a narrow lane off Hsin-yi Road. She did not play loud music, in order to avoid offending her neighbors, and could not open too late at night:

> But it was okay, because I lived at Locomotion. That way I didn't have to pay rent. I still worked in the travel agency by day. I paid NT$23,000 for rent, and I had a place to sleep. And I was grossing about NT$70,000 from that. I earned another NT$70,000 from the travel agency. I always had enough money.

Sharon started to get more involved with the growing gay and lesbian movement in Taipei. She participated in the lesbian group "Between Us," and volunteered as a disc jockey on a gay and lesbian radio program. Unlike some lesbians, she has always tried to reach out to the male gay community as well. Her attempts toward gender inclusiveness in the lesbian and gay community, however, contributed to the difficulties she had in running Locomotion. To begin with, her only two employees were gay men:

> I wanted to open a lesbian bar. But I wanted to let men come in, too. But when women came in and saw the men working at the bar, they would get angry and leave. They didn't like me. They said I had opened a gay bar. I thought it should be a Lesbi-Gay bar. What happened is that lesbians said I ran a gay bar, and gays said I ran a lesbian bar. I was caught in the middle.

Her clientele ended up being composed mostly of young gay men. On weekend evenings, groups of men would meet there, have a drink, and then proceed to the more lively disco pubs. After three years of building up Locomotion, and retiring from the travel agency, she was forced to move:

> I was under a lot of pressure. My neighbors protested. They said that my store attracted a lot of gay men, and they were all sissies. They said that they made too much noise by coming and going through the front gate outside. And they gathered in the

lane in front of the apartment block. When my lease expired, the landlord decided not to renew it.

She found a new location near National Taiwan University, not far from where she had unsuccessfully started up a teahouse more than a decade previously. She bought a pub on the second floor of a building on a commercial street, and changed it into the lesbian bar Jailhouse. She immediately expanded into the third floor, where she opened up Borderland Restaurant. Jailhouse is a purely lesbian bar, with only female employees and a majority female clientele. Borderland, designed for a gay, lesbian, and straight clientele, attracts a large number of students. Sharon and an American lover moved into the fourth floor above the restaurant. She described how she utilized the social network of her gay and lesbian activism to build up those two new businesses:

> I just had a pub. I didn't have a restaurant, but I thought it would be better to open up two businesses. I also thought I had adequate resources, since I had name lists from those gay groups. I decided to use that to do business. When I opened up my two shops, I sent out my name cards to let gays and lesbians know about me. I set up a new environment, where they could come and eat.

She now relishes the freedom that comes with running her own business. When I ask what she gains from entrepreneurship, Sharon said:

> Freedom. And money. I am responsible for all the decision making. I can't get fired for no reason. I have to think out everything for myself. That is great, because I can try out many different things. If you go to work and have a boss, you can't do that. It doesn't matter if it is right or wrong, you always have to listen to the boss.

Sexual orientation is the main component of Sharon's public identity, and she takes pride in being a masculine "T." A strong personality herself, she has little patience for either women or gays who make even the smallest compromises with a patriarchal system. Once when I walked into Sharon's restaurant, I noticed a Chinese translation of de Beauvoir's *Second Sex* on her bookshelf. When I pointed it out, she dismissed it outright: "I don't understand those heterosexual feminists. If you are going to be feminist, you should do it completely. Only lesbians are real feminists."

DISCUSSION

For women, lesbian relationships can indeed be used as strategies to subvert patriarchy (Rich 1983, Wittig 1992 [1980]) or to escape some of its more oppressive dimensions. Some feminists even argue that heterosexuality as an institution supports patriarchal power and subordinates women and that lesbianism is a strategy of resistance. Adrienne Rich, for example, wrote, "Lesbian existence comprises both the breaking of a taboo and the rejection of a compulsory way of life. . . . We may first begin to perceive it as a form of nay-saying to patriarchy, an act of resistance" (1983: 192). As a public spokesperson of the gay and lesbian rights movement, Sharon boldly encourages both lesbians and gays to resist social pressure and affirm their own individual sexual identities.

For many gays and lesbians, however, discrimination remains the main problem, and many people are understandably reluctant to accept public gay identities by "coming out." Discrimination against gays and lesbians exists in Taiwan, even as it takes on different forms than in North America. Unlike in the United States, antigay violence is extremely rare, and there have never been laws forbidding homosexual behavior in Taiwan. Nonetheless, other subtle forms of social pressure and discrimination exist. For gay men, there is strong social pressure to marry and provide their families with descendants. All gay men know well the symbolic violence they suffer through the Confucian edict that "There are three kinds of unfilial behavior. The most serious is the failure to provide descendants." Gays and lesbians face discrimination in the workplace, and thus fear coming out in public.

Sharon is an exception in this regard. She is not the only lesbian woman whose story is part of this book. One other woman asked that I not mention her lesbian relationship of more than ten years, as it is not part of her public identity. Other lesbian entrepreneurs whom I interviewed in southern Taiwan, including Bichhun, had more difficulties in affirming a lesbian lifestyle. Whereas Sharon has never even considered marriage to a man, other lesbian women report family pressure to marry and the difficulties involved in getting out of unhappy marriages.

The family is one of the most challenging social fields in which gay and lesbian individuals either hide or affirm their homosexual identities. Once again, Sharon is lucky to have the emotional support of her parents, who know about and accept her lesbian identity. Sharon frequently shares her coming-out experience with other gays and lesbians, and encourages more reluctant individuals, including her American girlfriend who has not yet told her parents, to bravely face family pressure. Her poor family background, however, may explain the relative ease she has had in gaining the acceptance of her family. Sharon herself said of her mother:

> She has to accept it [my homosexual lifestyle] because she is poor. I am not going to get an inheritance. If I were, I wouldn't want to make trouble. But my mother doesn't give me money. I give her money, so she has to accept it. Besides, it is impossible to really communicate with those old country women. I just told her. She couldn't do anything about it, so she finally just accepted it. It is because she is poor. I am realistic enough to know that.

Family landed property may give women's brothers an additional material incentive to push unmarried women out of the family. In spite of laws that require equal inheritance, most Taiwanese families still follow the traditional custom of distributing landed property to sons in the form of inheritances at the death of the parents, and movable property to daughters in the form of dowries at the time of their marriages. Women from propertied families thus feel pressure to "marry out" (*jia chuqu*), take their dowries, and relinquish claims on what is perceived as the rightful property of their brothers. I know of one illustrative case in Kaohsiung in which the parents constructed a house in Thailand for their openly gay son. Since he was a man, they perceived it as natural that their family property would gradually be placed under his ownership. When their lesbian daughter asked for an apartment in Kaohsiung, however, they told her she should get married and live with her husband in spite of the fact that they knew of her sexual preference. Since Sharon does not come from a propertied family, she does not face the problem of competing for family property with brothers anxious to see her marry out of the family. On the contrary, the more flexible family arrangements of the rural poor meant that her mother was even able to leave her husband in Hualien at one time in order to come work in Sharon's Taipei teahouse.

Nor did Sharon mention the cultural pressure to marry that some lesbians report is reinforced through practices of ancestor worship. Men are worshiped in their lineages even if they remain single and childless for life. Women, however, are expected to marry and are not perceived to be permanent parts of their natal families. Since it is considered inauspicious to keep spirit tablets of unmarried women on ancestral altars, such women are often worshiped in other places, like in the kitchen where they are appeased with anonymous hungry ghosts. This then operates as a form of symbolic violence that strongly enforces norms of kinship and marriage. Men and women on the margins of the family system must thus find ways to negotiate their way around these practices. One lesbian I interviewed in southern Taiwan, for example, reported that her mother accepts her decision to avoid heterosexual marriage and live with a female partner for life. Her mother, however, encouraged her to enter a vegetarian hall so that someone would take care of her spirit tablet after death. As of 2002, she still had no intention of actually following that advice.

The workplace is another social field where lesbians and gays face discrimination. Once again, lesbians face considerably more discrimination than gay men, since the main problem is discrimination against visible gender radicals rather than against sexual behavior in itself. That dynamic is visible in the differential experiences of "T" and "po" lesbians in the job market. The feminine "po" lesbians, with their cosmetics and flowery dresses, adapt well to the social requirements of the corporate environment. "T" lesbians, however, are perceived as overly masculine and "ugly," which makes it difficult for them to find and keep pink-collar jobs. "T" lesbians are more successful in blue-collar jobs such as factory work or truck driving. Some working-class "T's," in fact, have played key roles in the Taiwanese labor movement. In Taipei, some have organized a working-class lesbian group called "Queer and Class."

In contrast to lesbians, gay men tend not to divide into visibly different genders. Many identify as tops or bottoms, referred to as "ones" and "zeros" in Taiwanese gay slang, but there are no visible markers of these identities. Some young gays are highly effeminate, but those traits are usually forcibly removed, permanently in most cases, during the obligatory military training. Once again, the discrimination is against gender performance rather than sexual behavior. Masculine gay men report active and unproblematic sexual lives throughout military service, and many discover their sexual orientation as soldiers. Although the Taiwanese military does not prohibit gay men from serving, more effeminate men of any sexual orientation still suffer greatly from harassment on the part of their colleagues. The result is that most gay men learn to "pass" in their early twenties and face less discrimination in the workplace than lesbians. Only those who continue to act in an effeminate manner are discriminated against in public spheres.

One important type of workplace where men in general fare better than women is the family firm. Gay men can, and do, inherit family firms from their fathers. One gay man I interviewed in Kaohsiung runs his family's catering service and lives upstairs from the store with his lover, whom he hired as an employee. Using the excuse that business keeps him too busy to get married, his lifestyle and dedication to his father's firm are actually perceived as a form of filial piety. Since his brothers have children anyway, his family has given him no pressure to marry (Simon 2001: 78). Since women do not normally inherit family businesses from their parents, unless they have no brothers, lesbians usually do not have such options. When they go into business, they can count on little family support and must do so on their own.

One response to the reality of discrimination has been the emergence of lesbian and gay entrepreneurship, an experience parallel to that of North America (cf. Edwards and Stocker 1993). Since the 1970s, gay bars and saunas have provided the beginnings of a gay community (Lai 2000: 147). By 2001, other gay-friendly businesses including coffee shops, restaurants, bookstores, gift stores, and clothing boutiques had opened across Taiwan. In Taipei, gay and lesbian entrepreneurs have joined together to form a "rainbow community." Gay and lesbian entrepreneurs advertise collectively on a "rainbow map" distributed to customers in gay-friendly establishments. Sharon has been one of the leading figures in that community, and her business establishments have given lesbians more lifestyle space.

Through the efforts of these entrepreneurs and other activists, homosexual identity has become increasingly visible in urban Taiwan, and has so far met with less conservative backlash than in North America. In 2001, the Taipei city government officially sponsored a gay and lesbian festival for the second time, and published a handbook for the public on gay and lesbian issues. Taiwanese politicians, from Taiwanese president Chen Shui-bian of the Democratic Progressive Party to Taipei mayor Ma Ying-jeou of the Kuomintang, compete with one another to show their support for gay and lesbian human rights.

By mid 2001, when I left Taiwan to take an academic job in Canada, prospects for gay marriage seemed good. On June 26, the Ministry of Justice submitted a draft of the Basic Law on the Guarantee of Human Rights to the Legislative Yuan for approval. On the recommendation of Minister of Justice Chen Ding-nan,

Clause 6 states, "The government shall protect the rights of homosexuals, and homosexuals shall be allowed, in accordance with the law, to establish families and adopt children." If the basic law passes as written, Taiwan will surpass most countries, including the United States, in its legal protection of gay and lesbian rights.[2] Lesbian entrepreneurs like Sharon have been integral agents in the political and social struggles that made such advancements possible. The increased agency they have gained through entrepreneurship has helped them form a social movement and press for political change that would have been unimaginable only a generation ago.

NOTES

1. In accordance with her stated preference, I use for her the pseudonym "Sharon," which is also the nickname she uses in the gay and lesbian community. It is common practice for Taiwanese gays and lesbians to use pseudonyms in LesbiGay social contexts in order to protect their anonymity.

2. A year later, the bill had still not yet come up for discussion in the legislature.

Chapter Nine

An Eel Exporter

Chhoa Hiong-gun, a forty-six-year-old eel exporter, is one of the first women entrepreneurs I encountered in Taiwan. In fact, I have known about her entrepreneurial activities since 1997, when I was writing my Ph.D. dissertation in Tainan and living with her nephew, then a student at National Cheng Kung University. At the time, I was already interested in female entrepreneurship, and conducting a pilot study through interviews in Tainan and Kaohsiung. "You should meet my aunt," suggested my roommate. "She is incredible. She drinks and smokes just like a man. And she has never married." He whispered, "She might be a lesbian."[1] He and I have often discussed her business. Unmarried and childless at age forty-six, Hiong-gun has long hoped to cultivate her sister's son to take over her business. He, on the other hand, plans to pursue graduate school in the United States and dreams of an eventual career in Silicon Valley.

In the technological era of the early twenty-first century, it is understandable why he would not wish to take over his aunt's business, which is more closely tied to Taiwan's past than to its promises of a high-tech future. Eels are one of the oldest products fished out of the waters of the Taiwan Straits, and members of the trade are as dependent on the natural supply as were their ancestors in the past. Baby eels are found in the coastal waters between Taiwan and China, and then transferred into eel farms where they grow to maturity. After they reach an age of about ten months, they are either slaughtered and sold domestically or sold live to Japan. Although surely not one of the most appealing careers of the new century, the eel business has been central to Hiong-gun's life.

"WE TAIWANESE": ETHNIC
DIMENSIONS OF IDENTITY

Hiong-gun was born in rural Taichung County in 1954 to a family of the local Taiwanese elite during the Japanese occupation. Her father was a graduate of Waseda

University, and married a graduate of the Tainan Junior College of Home Economics, a school founded in Taiwan during the Japanese occupation. Her mother was a housewife and focused her energy on her children's education. After the end of Japanese occupation, however, the family fell on hard times in a period when Mandarin-speaking Mainlanders took over many of the jobs previously held by the indigenous elite:

> Before, our family was doing quite well. But for a period of time, we became really poor. I remember that when I was a child, sometimes we didn't even have enough to eat. We were really poor. For a long time, my father didn't have any work. He was the child of a wealthy family, and such children often end up failing in business themselves. For about ten years, he worked in a pharmaceutical company, making cough syrup and cold medication. Then he retired.

Hiong-gun still remembers her parents speaking Japanese at home, and draws attention to "prohibition" of that language under KMT rule[2]:

> When we were children, my parents would sometimes speak Japanese to each other. But the only time they ever used Japanese was when they were fighting. Back then, they were not permitted to teach us Japanese.

Hiong-gun has strong praise for the Japanese administration of Taiwan:

> I don't know if you have heard it our not, but many of us real Taiwanese people[3] say that the Japanese were better than the Kuomintang that later came to Taiwan. Many people say we would be better off under Japanese administration. I don't know if you have heard that. They [Native Taiwanese] can't accept Mainlanders, but they can accept Japanese. Most elderly people think that way. Moreover, education during the Japanese period was very effective. In the Japanese period, family education was good, and social rules were strict. For example, they were very strict with thieves, and they enforced the law strictly. So, public security was very good. I remember that we never locked our doors or windows when I was young. We never feared thieves, as there simply were none! Now Taiwan is no longer like that.[4]

Hiong-gun's affinity with Japan has been reinforced by her career over the past twenty years. She says, "I really like Japan. I think that Taiwan can learn from them in every aspect. I hope that we can learn from countries more advanced than our own." Her own business has been one way in which she has done that.

EELS IN A CHANGING POLITICAL ECONOMY

Hiong-gun sells live eels to Japan, and draws attention to differences in consumer preference between Japan and Taiwan. She is proud to specialize in a product derived from Japanese imperial tradition:

> Eating eels is a Japanese custom. Back in the imperial days, only the emperor's family ate eels. Japanese people would go out to sea and fish for eels to serve the emperor,

but it was a dangerous job. Many people died while at sea fishing for eels. Since eels were so difficult to find and the fishing so dangerous, they were considered valuable and only suitable for royalty. But now that there is sufficient capital, it is possible to raise eels here. After we raise them, we package them and ship them to Japan.

When I asked her if she sells any eels domestically, she insisted that Taiwanese people know little about the delicacy. Although Taiwanese people do eat Japanese eel with rice in both Japanese and Taiwanese restaurants, she still contrasted the Taiwanese, who "only know how to make soup from eel meat," with the Japanese, who have "made barbequed eel over rice into a common food."

Like Taiwanese entrepreneurs in other occupations, however, Hiong-gun is threatened by competition from China. Unlike the case of labor-intensive industries moving to China, however, the eel industry has been threatened mainly by loss of natural supply. She had to adapt to changing conditions:

> Before I had two plants, but I closed one of them because everyone moved production to China. For a while, we Taiwanese couldn't catch any eels. As you know, eels live along the Taiwan Straits. Since the coastlines of Guangdong and Fujian are longer than those of Taiwan, they could catch over ten times more eels than we could. Now, about five years ago, the eel population moved closer to China. . . . Where we could once fish 100 tons, they dwindled down to only 10 tons. So where there were once 100 companies raising eels, they dwindled down to only 10.

It was only through maintaining high quality that she and some of her competitors could continue to stay in business:

> We Taiwanese had to concentrate on the highest grade of produce. Since China didn't have enough experience, the eels they produced were not so good. Yet since we Taiwanese had so few eels, eel became a valuable and expensive commodity. The only way we could survive was to follow the road of high-quality produce. Also, in order to send live eels to Japan, we Taiwanese have a geographical advantage over China. We have a lot of flights to Japan, far more than China. Also, they are a large continental country. When they ship eels on such a long trip to the airport, a lot of eels die in transit. When they ship 100 kilos, half die on the way. Because of that, their eels don't have much economic value when they arrive in Japan.

Firms in the labor-intensive field of eel processing, however, have suffered more as the result of Chinese competition:

> In terms of live eels, Taiwan is in a better position than China. But we were beaten to death in terms of processed eels. We Taiwanese once had twenty-four processing plants, but all of them have closed down. All of them took their capital and invested it in China, opening up new factories. About five to six years ago, from 1991 to 1998, Taiwan's entire eel industry was washed clean. Back then, more than 500 companies were catching eels. Now there are only ten companies in all of Taiwan.

Hiong-gun has no intention of investing in China:

> China is not a safe country, and it is especially dangerous for women. Also, I have no
> confidence in China economically. A lot of Taiwanese people have invested in China,
> but very few of them have actually earned a profit there.

In terms of live eels, Hiong-gun insists that Taiwan can still compete with
China, due to China's lack of "social capital," a term which she uses in reference to
business skills. Experience with China has given her pride in Taiwan and reinforced her strong sense of national identity:

> China still can't compete with us in terms of social capital. In terms of good products
> of high quality, the market is still ours. In terms of perspectives on international
> trade, we are much better than they are. For example, we are much quicker in our
> business transactions. If the customer wants the goods immediately, we can ship them
> in three days. From China, they need a week.

Hiong-gun attributed part of that social advantage to Taiwan's long history of
interaction with Japan:

> Taiwan already learned a lot of techniques from Japan during the occupation period.
> We pure Taiwanese people have a close relationship to Japanese people. Maybe it is
> because of their perspectives or education, but they have had a strong influence on us
> Taiwanese, on the real Taiwanese.

A GENDERED DIVISION OF LABOR

As Hiong-gun tells her story, it is clear that she is breaking a previously gendered
division of labor in the eel industry:

> All the others are men, since this is a male-dominated market. I am the only woman
> in the industry. The most important reason for that is that the eel industry is not desk
> work. It's not paperwork; it is completely on-site work. When the eels come into the
> plant, you have to go in person to see if the eels are good enough to export. This is
> the kind of work that men usually like, and it is more suitable for them.

Yet Hiong-gun modestly describes her entry into the field as merely the natural
progression from earlier employment. After graduating from high school, she took
her first job as the only woman employee in a Japanese-owned fish cannery operating in Alaska. For three months, she worked on a boat with native Alaskans canning salmon caviar. She was then sent to the company's head office in Tokyo for a
further three months of training. Returning to Taiwan after six months abroad, she

rejected the usual women's career trajectory in her company of secretarial and accounting work by moving into the eel processing plant as quickly as possible:

At first, I was just an employee. When I was an employee, I also did on-site work. That's usually the kind of work that women don't like. It's too tiring! That company had already started up in the 1960s. I entered the company when I was twenty-one. When I first started, my job was to prepare and type documents. I did all of the export documentation, draft negotiations, starting from the most basic things. Then, I thought that I needed to do on-site work if I wanted to have a career in the business. That would be the only way to get professional knowledge. So I moved into the processing plant. At first, they weren't willing to let a woman do that, because it involves evening work. The eels arrive at night. You can't do it in the daytime, when the sun is strong, since that will kill off all the eels. So you do it at night when there is no sun. So, three times a week, I drove to the plant at night. Most women wouldn't dare to do that. I don't know why, but I only wanted to learn the business and the only way to do that was to go on-site at night. I started doing administration when I started doing that on-site work.

Hiong-gun's abilities were only recognized after years of hard work and struggle, a time lag she attributes to gender discrimination:

I have been into eels for more than twenty years. Since I've never done anything else, it's the only thing I know how to do. Normally, the eel industry is one place where women have very little space to develop. My clients, moreover, are Japanese, and women suffer a lot of discrimination in Japan. It is said that when a woman has 100 percent ability, she still gets graded at 70 percent. Women are not really respected and their abilities are not fully recognized.

Eventually, however, Hiong-gun was boss:

My company was formerly run by a Japanese conglomerate. They ran the company in Taiwan to purchase live eels. But in the 1990s, the number of eels caught was reduced so much that they were no longer profitable and closed down. After they closed down, I bought the company.

Experience on-site eventually made it possible for her to overcome most of the gender discrimination she subsequently encountered as a woman supplier in an overwhelmingly male business. She emphasizes that she overcame those obstacles by producing a brand recognized for high quality:

My idea is that if I sell a quality product, customers will come looking for me. If my product is not good, I have to go looking for customers. My quality is by far the best in the industry. My company's mark is sold directly on the Japanese market, and my eels are evaluated there as the highest grade of quality. The proof is that our mark is the most expensive one in Japan. I think that quality is the reason that I have been able to survive in this business.

The key to selling good eels, she said, is skillful selection of high-quality eels as they come into the processing plant at night.

> At night, the eels are shipped to the plant by truck. I have to look at all of them, and grade them according to quality. One kilo has three, four, or five eels. We release them all into the water tank, and I select them, dividing them by size. The bad ones get selected out. Some are ill, or the colors are not good. I either return them to the supplier or sell them on the domestic market. In fact, our second-rate products all get sold domestically at very low prices. The truly good products get exported.

The most important thing is to find healthy eels. Proud of her work, she draws attention to the fact that she has learned from experience how to evaluate the health of an eel. She can observe the health of the eels by their coloration and by the energy levels they exhibit as they enter the water. A live eel, she stresses, will fetch more than ten times the price of a dead eel upon arrival in the Japanese market. Identifying which eels are healthy and which are too sick to survive the transit to Japan, "is our technique":

> We have to think of ways to keep them alive. In order that they don't die while wrapped up and in transit, we have to give them oxygen, and use the right amount of ice. We have to judge the amount of ice to be used according to the weather. If it is hot, we use more ice; and if it is cold, we use less ice. I have learned to judge that by my own feeling. It's not as if there is some precise standard of adding so many ice cubes when the temperature is at some particular degree. The whole process is based entirely upon personal experience. That way, the eels won't be dead when they arrive in Japan. You have to judge for yourself if the eels are good or not. You should try it for yourself; it is different from other occupations. This is not at all like machines or computers, where everything is automatic. In this business, everything is done by hand.

TAKING OVER THE COMPANY: PRODUCING QUALITY FROM THE HEART

Hiong-gun is understandably proud of the way she took over the company in seemingly impossible circumstances. The Japanese company she worked for was part of a major conglomerate that invested in construction, steel, and other products. When the baby eel population moved towards China, their Taiwanese eel operations became less profitable and they decided to close down. They sold her the processing center at what she called a "fire sale" price and then left the business entirely in her hands. She then faced her first business challenge: suppliers unwilling to sell her eels for fear she would be unable to pay them:

> When I first took over the company, everybody said that the company was already defunct. Nobody dared supply me with goods. They spread rumors about me, saying that I didn't have enough capital and that I wouldn't be able to pay for the eels.

She attributed many of the problems to gender discrimination:

> That was the biggest setback I ever encountered. Since I was a woman, everyone in the industry hoped that I would be unable to survive. All the others were men. So they would spread harmful rumors, such as saying I didn't have the money to pay for eels. I wasn't raising eels on my own; I was just buying and selling. I needed a supply, someone to sell me eels, in order that I could sell the eels to Japan. That was the greatest pressure I ever had to endure, since so many people spread malicious rumors.

She explains how she overcame those early problems with reference to Chinese practices of cultivating one's own "heart." A good heart, says Hiong-gun, is the key to successful business practices:

> It doesn't matter if you are Taiwanese or Japanese, when you do business, the most important thing is your own heart. No matter how well you speak, it is the heart that is important. You have to be honest with people. And when you are honest, the things you produce will also be good. It all depends on your heart.

The moral character of the heart, she said, is what permits her to produce eels of higher quality than any of her competitors:

> In order to produce good quality, one needs to have internal quality oneself. One also needs to work hard and be different from other people. The products need to be different from other people's products. If the products are the same, the competition will all be based on price. But if your product is of a very high quality, the price will also be different from that of other people. That is competition based on quality. Since I am exporting to Japan, I compete on the basis of quality. The Japanese market is willing to pay a high price for good quality. Of course, maintaining a consistent level of quality is very difficult. When those eels go out with my trademark on the package, people see it and say, "That brand is excellent!" That way, people will naturally come to me.

The moral qualities that allow her to consistently score so highly on quality extend well into her relations with suppliers, customers, and workers. As she revealed later in the interview, she even projects a moral dimension onto her relationship with the eels themselves.

BUILDING RELATIONSHIPS WITH SUPPLIERS

Building up a relationship with her supplier was the most challenging part of going into business. The practice in the industry, she said, is for the suppliers to provide eels on one day, and to receive payment several days later—a practice that entails a great deal of trust. When she first took over the business, people feared they would have trouble getting paid in time. I asked her how she overcame that problem:

Only people who trust me will supply me with goods. Of course I must pay them in a timely way. Most people take three days; I'll do it in one. I always do things even better than people imagine. But to be honest, by paying up-front, I didn't have to make promises. And I tell you, when people trust me, I won't abandon them. Still, at the beginning nobody dared to sell to me. Only one person sold to me.

Her relationship with that person has become one of mutual trust and benefit. She explained the relationship as a matter of reciprocity in personal relations:

Since then, I have always done business with him. When he is in trouble, I help him. I do that in order to repay him for his goodness. He has been good to me, and I return it. That way, it becomes a virtuous cycle. In the past, he was just a small middleman. Maybe he just hadn't heard the rumors about me, or maybe he really trusted me; to this day I don't know for sure. But he was the only person who wasn't afraid to do business with me. He sold me his goods, and I paid him the next day. He thought, "Hey! That's pretty good," and continued to sell to me. As a result, he is the only supplier I deal with to this day. In the end, when other people want to sell to me, I don't buy from them. I only buy from him.

Using Buddhist epistemology, she drew attention to a cause-and-effect relationship between his goodness to her and his later success. In this line of reasoning, which is quite common in Taiwan, his goodness towards her has produced more than a kind response from her and a stable business relationship. It has also brought him positive karma and contributed to his prosperity in the present lifetime:

As a result, he has become Taiwan's largest eel broker. He started out as a small broker, expanded into raising eels, and is now Taiwan's largest broker. I was his window. After that, he continued on his own. He is Taiwan's most famous broker, and is well known in Japan as well.

Much of his success is attributable to the same kind of self-cultivation to which Hiong-gun aspires: "The most important thing is that his individual personality is very strict. He is very strict, and works very hard. He is always looking for the best quality. It is a kind of cause-and-effect relationship."

According to Hiong-gun, this kind of self-cultivation requires constant self-analysis:

Of course, we have to analyze ourselves. At the time, I asked myself, why don't people supply me with goods? Why did people distrust me for such a long time? I was always analyzing myself. Is it because I was bad to people at some time? Was it something I did when I was young? Maybe I wasn't good enough to people; maybe the way people mistreated me was the way I mistreated people in the past. During that time, I was constantly analyzing myself. Had I committed some error? Had I done something bad? Why did nobody help me in my time of greatest difficulty?

Only by working on her own heart did she find a relationship of trust and mutuality with another person and achieve success in the eel industry. She attributes her reputation for quality partly to the steady relationship that developed with her supplier:

> My company is the most stable in the industry because I sell directly to the markets. How can I consistently provide such high quality, but at the same price as the others? It's because I am stable. The most important thing is to consistently provide goods, and to buy consistently from the same supplier. That way, the eel raisers don't have to worry about not finding a market. Since they know they can sell, they can concentrate on raising quality eels. Since they know they can depend on me, it becomes a virtuous cycle.

BUILDING RELATIONS WITH WORKERS

Hiong-gun stresses the good relations she has with her workers, noting that she cares for their needs:

> I owed a lot of money. After I took over the company, I had 200 employees. The Japanese didn't care if we disbanded or not. It was entirely my responsibility. I mortgaged my own house, I put all of my property up for collateral with the bank, and took out loans to pay their salaries. At the time, I carried a debt of NT$10,500,000. I was so worried about just making the interest payments. And I couldn't let anyone know, or else they would refuse to sell me goods.

No one in her family was in a position to help her out. Her parents were too poor, she had no brothers, and, she pointed out, her five younger sisters had already married into other families. In addition, as the unmarried elder daughter with no brothers, she needed to provide for her mother. There was no way she could realistically back out of the project:

> I had nobody to help me. With no assistance, that was the most bitter time of my life. Yet at least it was only financial bitterness. I kept thinking that I should change careers. But there was no way I could do that. Every month, I had to pay NT$300,000 in interest payments. It's impossible to find a job that pays a salary high enough to cover that. The only thing I could do was struggle through. For two years I persevered through bitterness. But in two years, I had come through it. We slowly started to make money. Every day, I worked in the office, and every night I went to the processing plant.

In the restructuring of the company that followed, she sold off the roasted-eel processing plant and focused on live-eel processing, a company with twenty employees. In accordance with the Labor Standards Law, she had to compensate each of the 180 laid-off workers with a severance pay equal to one month's salary for every year of work. Yet such radical restructuring was necessary in order to ensure the survival of the company as a whole. Hiong-gun emphasized that she has maintained good relations with the workers in the live-eel processing plant, especially those whose loyalty helped her through the hard times shortly after taking over the firm:

> They [the workers] have been with me a long time. The oldest is the plant manager, who has been with this company for twenty years. We were colleagues for twenty years. He is already seventy years old, and has done this job ever since he finished military duty. I am happy to have those employees. In the beginning, they helped me a lot, and to this day not one has left. I told them that I was encountering difficulties. I told them that the company would soon go bankrupt and they should leave if they find better jobs. They were very clear about the company's condition, but not a single person left. So that became my responsibility. I needed to work hard, and get more orders. So I told them, "Don't think of me as a boss. I'm just the one who takes the orders and makes money from the Japanese. After that, I distribute wages to you. If you don't do well, there is nothing I can do. We won't be able to sell our goods, the Japanese won't give us money, and we won't have any orders. You won't be able to keep on working." We have that kind of relationship.

Part of the reason for this kind of labor relationship was that she was younger than her employees:

> I told them not to treat me as a boss, since they were all older than I. We want to have a feeling of running the company together. If we have more orders, their wages are higher, and I also give them annual bonuses. The more they work, the more I pay them.

Gender, too, influenced her relationship with the workers:

> Male bosses are better in this occupation. They can drink together, and talk dirty. They [the workers] are always together. You know workers. They like to drink together and talk dirty talk, so a male boss can get closer to them. But I can't do it. For everything, I talk to the plant manager and he talks to the workers. Actually, I get along with them, but there is still some distance. Nonetheless, the fact that they are willing to stay with me for so long shows that they think I am more stable than the other companies. I don't work for a while, and then suddenly say, "Let's all go drinking together!" My personal character is very stable. I am also more far-sighted. And I don't negotiate with them to press their wages down.

She points out that she can afford to pay higher wages because of her single marital status. Without the expenses of children and a family, she can afford to give her workers higher salaries rather than push them to the lowest possible limit with the goal of maximizing her own personal profit. Her primary values, she said, include taking care of people outside of, as well as within, her own family, and that makes her different from other people. She also maintains a Buddhist ethic of living for the present moment:

> I think it's because I am single and have fewer responsibilities that I don't need to earn so much money. Of course, I have saved some money, but I don't think it is necessary

to stress money so much. Money can be earned anytime. The important thing is to have enough money for your old age. But even then, it doesn't matter if you have an extra million dollars or not. Even if I have an extra million dollars, what use is it if I suddenly kick the bucket? It will just go to someone else. So I figure it is better to use my money to make the people in my life happier. Live for the present! Nobody knows what will happen tomorrow, so for the moment I treat my employees better and give them better pay. Maybe other bosses can't be that way, but the workers are dependent on me so I want to make them feel happier than other people.... I don't think money is so important. But your work should make you happy, and the employees should be happy. It is happiness that counts most.

DOING BUSINESS IN A MALE WORLD

Her female gender, however, necessitated learning how to meet those goals in ways that differ from male business practices. Networks of business relations in Taiwan are often solidified through male rituals of "flower drinking" that emphasize feasting, drinking, and womanizing. Hiong-gun does not engage in such practices:

> Some of the men in this industry drink alcohol with Japanese customers. But they say one thing and do another. That works in the short term, and they get a lot of orders. But eventually problems arise. I am different. I don't speak much, but I show people what I can do. One thing is sure: my quality is very good, even better than you imagine it can be.

That attitude has allowed her to cultivate a reputation of quality among Japanese clients. Exhibiting her skills in the eel processing center, rather than merely dealing with clients in her office or through entertainment, is her way of proving to industry peers that she is an insider. It is common understanding of techniques, rather than other forms of bonding, that solidifies their business relations:

> Some Japanese bosses really want to do business. They don't come to Taiwan to play, and they are very respectful of women. When I show them the way I work, they know that I am an insider. They give me all of their orders as a result, because they know that I am really doing business. I'm not just playing at doing business. But I don't get orders from bosses who just come to Taiwan to play, since I don't entertain them or take them out to play.

Through what she considers to be more professional business practices, she has built up a network of clients in Tokyo, Nagoya, Osaka, Fukuoka, and other Japanese cities. She emphasizes that she sells directly to market sellers, rather than going through middlemen who often demand entertainment or negotiate harshly for lower prices that she can scarcely offer without sacrificing quality. Comparing herself to the other male bosses in the industry, she said that she maintains high quality and cultivates her customer relations by getting personally involved in production and grading:

Most Taiwanese bosses don't go to their plants. They just stay in their offices, talk on the telephone, take orders, and order their plant-operations people to take care of on-site processing. But I insist on going to the plant to see to it myself. If there is a problem, if the Japanese complain, I know where the problem is and I can improve. If you don't do that, and the Japanese complain, you won't have any idea what they are talking about and you can't improve.

Taking care of customer relations is perhaps the most important part of her job:

When people complain to you, you must know wholeheartedly that they mean it. You should not doubt them and argue with them. I don't argue with them. I figure it must be my own problem. I record everything they tell me, and I investigate the reasons myself. Since I don't want to make the same mistake twice, my company is always improving.

Even when customers make financial claims to resolve their problems, she tries to find a solution that contributes to their ongoing business relationship. Once again, she contrasted her own style to those of others:

When the Japanese call to complain about the goods, most bosses argue with them. But when they claim damages, I pay up. I think of that as my tuition fee for the lesson I have learned. I'll pay, but I certainly won't permit myself to make the same mistake again. By doing business with my customers like that, we develop a long-term relationship of mutual trust. And since the Japanese see me working so hard on their business, we almost never have to pay any kind of compensation. I have very good relations with the Japanese. I don't think it helps at all to argue with them.

Her business creed, she says, is "neither friends nor enemies are eternal." Always able to protect herself, she decides what to do according to the people involved, and manages to solve problems peacefully:

If the customer really is just talking nonsense, you can decide not to do business with him. But you don't want to have conflicts. I say, "neither friends nor enemies are eternal." Maybe someday you will need his help, so you don't want to argue too much. Even if you are on good terms, you can have problems if there is a conflict of interest. There are no eternal friends. And even if you are on bad terms, he will come to you when he needs your help. Now if you have fought and argued to a serious degree, those circumstances can make him feel very awkward. My principle is that I would rather be peaceful and suffer a small loss. If people aren't good to me, I go ahead and suffer that small loss. I would rather others let me down than let other people down. That way, when we meet again, they are the embarrassed ones, not me. I am very peaceful. That is the way to work with the Japanese.

As a shrewd businesswoman, however, she does know how to turn those circumstances to her own advantage:

Arguing is meaningless. Even if I lose some money, it's not as if there won't be opportunities to earn it back. When I pay someone's claim, I'm thinking, "OK, I'll pay one million Japanese yen. But in the next one or two weeks, I'll earn it back from you anyway. It's all the same to me!"

Curious about the strategies that have made her such a successful business-woman, I asked her how she earns the money back. She explained:

As for earning it back, you need the goods and I provide the best quality. Of course you will buy from me when you need them. And when you buy from me, you won't care at all if you pay an extra five or ten yen—because you need those goods. Now, if you argue with the customer and ruin the relationship, he won't come back. And you'll miss out on the chance to get revenge. He's not your enemy; it is just a profit relationship. It's just a money problem; and any problem that can be resolved with money is not a real problem. Money is temporary. Most likely, if you lose a million yen now you can earn back two million yen in the future. So, don't ruin your customer relations. First, it shows a lack of class. Second, it gives you the chance to keep making money from him.

Harmony, says Hiong-gun, is the heart of business strategy when dealing with Japanese. In her experience, however, Taiwanese men are poor at doing business harmoniously due to their masculine work culture. Women, she insisted, are more skilled than men at maintaining harmonious relations with customers and suppliers.

GENDERED CULTURES AT WORK

The military ethic that "might makes right" expresses itself through the behavior of some of her Taiwanese suppliers. Violence, in fact, is often a means of resolving business conflicts:

In doing business with the Japanese, harmony is the essence. But men are not like that. They curse each other and mess things up, even getting into physical fights. A lot of people are like that. They throw things and get in fights. I've seen it all, even in my own plant. The eel industry is basically a gangster industry. Sometimes the eel dealers come and they're all covered with tattoos. Sometimes the eels are not in good condition, or are even sick, but he [the consigned driver] still wants you to take them. He'll just take off his shirt and show off all those tattoos. But here's the way I think: If you were a real gangster, you wouldn't be in this business. This kind of sales is just buying and selling. Each time, you earn NT$10,000 to NT$20,000. Real gangsters earn a lot more money from things like arson. So you are just trying to frighten me. I always explain things clearly to them. I explain that I can't take the eels because they are sick. Since I am more professional, I can convince him. If I sell those sick eels to Japan, I may even be able to pass them through the buyer. But when they turn around to sell the eels to others, there will be problems. So I can't take sick eels. I would rather let you down in Taiwan than let the buyer down in Japan.

Nonetheless, she explains that she tries to empathize with her supplier and find a way to solve the problem together, a strategy she considers to be feminine:

> I always ask how much money he will lose. I'm willing to take some of the loss, even though I don't have to. I tell him, "Even if you are a gangster, we have to be reasonable. Don't tell me that black is white." He'll listen to me and afterwards become my friend. I have a lot of tattooed friends [gangsters]. I can do that because I avoid conflict. Gentleness works better than anger. In this industry, other people are always getting into fights. Maybe that's just the way that men give vent to their frustrations. They like to have conflicts with one another, and they like to fight. But there is no reason for that. Even gangsters have their proper way.[5]

In her relations with suppliers, workers, and customers, Hiong-gun tries to maintain harmonious long-term relationships. She views this as part of her own moral training, yet also sees it as something easier for her to accomplish than it is for the men in her field. Men, it seems, are more likely to waste money on drinking or womanizing with customers and workers. They are also more likely to get into violent conflicts with suppliers. Interestingly as well, her practices of empathy and benevolence even extend beyond the human realm.

HIONG-GUN'S MORAL RELATIONSHIP WITH EELS

Strange as it may seem to outsiders, Hiong-gun has come to love eels and is proud of the affinity she has developed with the animals. When I expressed some squeamishness about the snakelike animals, she held up a dead eel for me to inspect:

> The first time that I saw so many eels in that tank, I thought they all looked like snakes. It gave me goose bumps all over. I was terrified! But now I think eels are really cute. I can't say that I haven't ever been bitten. But when eels bite a person, it is usually because they are sick or have something wrong with them. Besides, their mouths are very small. Since men's hands are big, when they bite a man, they can't even grab the flesh. But I was bitten once, and the teeth cut very deeply into my hand. But I've been working with eels for so long and I've only been bitten once or twice. Eels are really gentle animals.

Hiong-gun feels such a strong affinity with eels that she refuses to eat eel meat herself. Driving me to her processing plant in her Mercedes-Benz one evening, she said, "I can't eat eel meat. I depend on them for my very existence. In effect, they sacrifice their lives for me. So it would be wrong for me to eat them."

The fact that her occupation involves the eventual killing of living animals is indeed one of the most disturbing elements of her occupation for many Taiwanese people. Ong Siok-ting (Chapter 5), for example, has encouraged her to abandon the business, as it will generate negative karma for her in the future. Hiong-gun has thought through those problems herself, however, and has come up with what she says is an adequate solution. She erected a spirit tablet to dead eels in a Taipei County temple, and the monks pray for their spirits twice a month during ceremonies for the dead. That reverence towards eels and the affinity she feels for them are the products of her own process of self-cultivation, and she sees these as part of the moral universe that explains her success in business. Her enthusiastic attitude towards work is contagious:

> Every day when I go to work, I think of the feeling I had the first time I worked with eels, the first day of work. That way I won't lose my enthusiasm. Once you lose that enthusiasm for work, you will no longer do it well. That is my way of thinking. I don't think of what else I could do to have a better life or something; I just work hard to be the most outstanding in my field and I do it well. The most important thing is never to forget that original feeling of the heart. You should be the very best at your work, or not do it at all. That's why my brand of eels is number one in Japan.

Hiong-gun reports that work provides her with a strong sense of meaning, and provides her with happiness:

> I am very happy with my work. I think of it as a kind of entertainment. You have to enjoy your work if you want to do it for a long time and if you want to do it well. The first thing is to enjoy it. That way, you will have a sense of enthusiasm, do well in the job, and gain a sense of success.

FATAL ATTRACTIONS:
MARRIAGE, ROMANCE, AND DESTINY

In explaining her own success, however, Hiong-gun looks beyond these workplace considerations and attributes it also to the fact that she never married:

> If I had a family, I might not be able to work so well. After all, a person's time and energy are limited. I think that if a woman stays at home, that is her job. It's her job to raise children, manage a household, and cook well. They [married women] and I don't use our skills in the same place, that's all. Maybe if they came to do my work, they would also do a good job. Many talented people are buried inside their families.

In fact, she draws parallels between herself and housewives, saying that she learned her work ethic from her mother:

> My mother is a very talented woman, with a sharp brain and an ability to eat bitterness. At home, she gave us children a very strict education. My own personality is very much like my mother's. Everything she did was strictly in order and went according to a plan. If she said she would do something, she would definitely get it done. For example, if she said she was going to the Matsu Temple, nobody could stop her, even if it was raining

or a typhoon was coming. And when she had an appointment with someone, she always went. From a young age, we learned to carry through with our promises.

In terms of personality and moral training, Hiong-gun has followed her mother's example. She says that her single marital status is involuntary, yet entails moral responsibilities just like married life:

If I were a housewife, I think I would be quite good at it. As I should! But I have never had the opportunity. Living by myself, I think that those household tasks are meaningless. If you are single, you have to perform well at work and maintain yourself. Otherwise, you will become a social problem. Sometimes I think I don't want to work. I could find a husband and let somebody else take care of me. I've thought that way, but you can't just order everything you want like you would an item from a catalog. That's impossible. You can't say you want a baby and then suddenly get a baby. That's a very difficult thing to arrange. It is much easier to succeed at work. If I have a plan and work hard at it, I can get a lot of orders. But a baby or a husband, that's not something you can get by working hard. I think it is a very difficult thing. But, I work hard and I take good care of myself. My thinking is always correct, yet I never abandon that thought. I always have the hope that I can find it.

Hiong-gun related the problems that single women face in Taiwan's masculine culture:

Sometimes I meet someone I like, or I run into someone who might make a good partner, but I think it is meaningless to dwell on that issue. Of course I have met some men, but most of them are already married. That is impossible! That would be a very painful affair. Before you love a person, you should analyze his personal life. Even if you love such a person [married], it is impossible. That is really painful. I think that love is a very painful affair. Sometimes you love a man, but he doesn't love you. That hurts. You are always thinking of how much you love him, but you don't dare to express it. And then if he isn't interested in you at all, you think that there must be something wrong with you. Maybe I'm not beautiful enough, or worthless—anyway, it makes me feel like there is something wrong with me. So, I figure I don't want to take it so seriously. If one has it, one has it. If one doesn't have it, one simply doesn't have it.

Hiong-gun has been empowered enough by her business endeavors to see through the ideology of romantic love and marriage:

Not every one has to walk down that road. There are many roads, and all roads lead to Rome. Some people take the road to marriage. Some walk another road. But in the end, every individual is alone. Even if you have a family, in the end you are still alone. When you really suffer, or when you are sick, nobody can help you. And when it is time to leave this world, you are still alone. When it is time to return to dust, even if you have children and a happy marriage, you are still alone. Human life is by nature solitary.

Whereas many Taiwanese people see marriage as a cure for loneliness, she finds companionship elsewhere in her life:

> Solitude is not the same as loneliness. Some people are surrounded by others, but they still feel very lonely. But even though I am often alone, I don't feel lonely at all. I am very happy just to be myself. I have my sister, my nephew, and I talk to them every day on the telephone. That makes me happy. And at work, my clients are very good to me. I feel that my existence has value. My life on this earth isn't just eating, drinking, and sleeping. I still have the strength to make a contribution, and society hasn't abandoned me either. Even though I don't have children, a husband, or a cozy family life, I still give a lot to the people in my life. That makes me feel very happy.

Taiwanese women often feel pressure from their parents and other family members to marry. Hiong-gun also felt such pressure when she was young, as her mother hoped she would marry. Nonetheless, she said, "I told my mother, five of her six daughters fulfilled her wishes. If only one has not fulfilled those wishes, her overall grade is still not bad."

Hiong-gun says she has just not met an appropriate man. She contrasts her life philosophy to that of some Japanese women who, she claims, reject men and marriage entirely as part of a feminist ideology. Instead, she explained her single status as merely the result of *en-hun*, or destiny, in a folk understanding of Buddhist concepts:

> In Japan, a lot of women don't want to marry. I'm not like that. I think it is best to just follow destiny and not make demands from life. Once I read in the newspaper, "When destiny arrives, there is no escape; when destiny departs, there is no means of keeping it." That's just the way it is. It's not like I can like somebody and then get him. In my work, if I work hard, the Japanese will like my goods and I'll get orders as a result. But men, even if I really like a man and I work hard, sending him flowers and things, but his heart is not moved, well, then, all of my efforts are in vain. All it can do is increase my feelings of unworthiness. We should just follow our destinies. I understand well that truth.

What has concerned her more than love and romance with a man, however, is motherhood. Concerns about not becoming a mother were even harder to overcome than loneliness without a husband:

> For a while, I really wanted a child. I wanted to adopt a child. I found it very frightening to think that if something were to happen to me, if I were suddenly to disappear, there would be nobody behind me. I felt so empty without descendants. I don't know how you men think, but I find that very empty. For a while, I wanted to adopt a child, but I never had the chance. Then my mother said to me, even if I have a child, it doesn't necessarily belong to me. A child also has its own life and can't always be with me. And if it does always stay with me, then it really has a problem. A child should grow up and become independent. If it doesn't leave, that means it has no independent personality. It has to go out and create a world of its own. When that happens, even after you have raised it to adulthood, you will still be alone, like my

mother. After my father passed away, she was still alone. Even though I talk to my mother on the telephone every day, and even though she lives with my sister and her family, in the end she is still alone.

She explained her life-world in Buddhist terms of impermanence, saying:

When I think about human life, I realize that the human realm is just temporary. There will still be a day when you leave this place. Even if you have a house, parents, brothers and sisters, a husband and children; in the end everything is temporary. Nothing is forever. Since it is impossible to possess those things forever, I figure one should not desire so much. I won't say, "I have to have a house or I want to be beautiful." There is no need for that, since everything is impermanent. Destiny is temporary.

Comparing her fate to the experiences of married women she knows, Hionggun even describes herself as relatively fortunate:

Don't think that getting married means your husband will always be with you. Maybe after several years of marriage, he will fall in love with another woman. I comfort myself with that thought. I think if I find a good husband, he could change his mind in a few years anyway. If he falls in loves with someone else and then leaves you, you will suffer a lot. Therefore, I think it is better to be alone. Still, if life were a test, I would give myself 80 percent. The missing 20 percent is from my lack of a family.

She explained her lack of a family through a Buddhist cosmology of karma and the forces of time of birth that she believes shape personality:

Since I am a Cancer, I enjoy a warm home life. I would be willing to stay at home and cook, but maybe I did something in a past life. Maybe I did a very bad thing in a past life. That would explain why I have never been able to find [the family] that I have always wanted.

In order to accept that fate, she focuses her energy on work and her relationship with her mother. She explains her resigned attitude in terms of the worship she does before an image of Kuanyin in her home:

The best I can do is perform well at work. And then, find ways to be happy in my personal life and live well with my mother. My most intimate relationship is with my mother. Every day I pray to Kuanyin for my mother's health and success in my job. If I had a husband and children, I would have to ask that bodhisattva to take care of so many people. But this way is easy, just my mother and me. Before I reached the age of thirty, I anxiously wanted to get married. But now I am happy to be single.

Considering how widespread the ideology of romance is, it was not easy for her to find peace with herself:

All of my classmates married; I was the only one who didn't. For a while, I couldn't deal with that. But gradually I realized that isn't something that I can obtain if only I work hard at it. After I got my thinking straightened out, I didn't have a problem with it anymore.

Hiong-gun has found it difficult to accept her single marital status in a society that highly values marriage and family. These difficulties show the strong force of cultural expectations on individuals, as even individuals who do not conform to social norms still tend to define themselves in relationship to them. Her single marital status, moreover, has caused her problems and conflicts in her work as well.

AN UNMARRIED WOMAN AT WORK: PROBLEMS AND CONFLICTS

As a woman, Hiong-gun found it difficult to be accepted in the eel industry from the very beginning:

> Since all the other people in this business are men, they were very bothered that a woman was doing it. At first, they hoped I would retire from the business entirely. . . . I have never gone to their meetings, their industrial association, whatever. I didn't want to appear in their presence . . . I didn't want to irritate them. Only in the past five years have they started to respect me. They have even started coming to me for advice, because my company has become so big in the past twenty years.

The biggest problem she faces as a woman, however, is sexual harassment from her clients. She has learned to deal with that by carefully selecting her customers, and refusing to deal with customers who have harassed her verbally. She also protects herself by lying about her marital status:

> Some of my customers ask if I am married. I almost always tell them I am married. I know it can be disadvantageous if they ask me that. They think they can bully unmarried women. So if I don't know them very well, I tell them I am married in order to protect myself.

The main problem is a male culture in which it is acceptable for men to treat women as sex objects:

> If a customer occasionally says I am beautiful, I like it. But if he keeps saying that every half hour, it's disgusting! I hate it! I have learned that I have to be careful. . . . I don't like it when customers treat me like a woman. I like it when they treat me like a man. Treat me like a man and we can all relax. Treat me like a woman and my burden is very heavy. . . . Except for physical strength, I can do anything a man can do.

Nonetheless, her gender prevents her from socializing with her customers in ways that men would. Businessmen in Taiwan often entertain customers with elaborate banquets, drinking, singing in karaoke parlors, and even collective visits to strip joints, massage parlors, and prostitutes. For self-protection, she only invites male customers to dinner and turns down all invitations to drink alcohol, dance, or otherwise enjoy Taipei's nightlife with male clients. Yet even simple dinner invitations have caused her trouble:

> About twenty years ago, when I first started doing business with Japan, I sometimes had problems when I took a cab. Some of the old Mainlanders have especially bad impressions of Japanese. So when I took a cab with Japanese customers, those old Mainlanders would refuse to give me back change. They would say, "It's easy for you women of that kind [implying prostitutes] to earn Japanese money." They didn't respect me. They thought I was some kind of bar girl. When I was young I always had that problem.

BACK TO ETHNIC RELATIONS:
TENSIONS BETWEEN MAINLANDERS
AND NATIVE TAIWANESE

Just thinking about those negative experiences aroused anger in her towards Mainlanders:

> Twenty years ago, Taiwan was a really backwards place. Those old mainland soldiers came from abroad, and they had a really bad image of Japanese. They were always bringing up the Nanjing massacre. In the beginning we also rejected those Mainlanders. I have never had a good image of Mainlanders.

She referred to the ethnic division of labor that redistributed elite positions to Mainlanders and confined Native Taiwanese to small-scale business:

> You probably think that the KMT arrival contributed something to Taiwan. In fact, I don't think they helped at all. I have an opinion about that. The ones who really worked diligently were we Taiwanese people. It was always we, the Taiwanese people, who did manual labor, plowed the fields, worked in factories, and planted vegetables and rice. The Mainlanders were all doing paperwork and government work. They could earn money very easily. But we had to earn our money one drop of sweat at a time, one drop of sweat for one NT dollar. Actually, we Taiwanese were quite pitiful. Real Taiwanese people, especially the middle-aged generation, have worked really hard. They ate bitterness and endured hard labor. We were happy if we could just earn a meager subsistence. For just a small income, we would work really hard, never daring to let go. Even now, when life is so good, we never forget that bitterness and we keep working hard. Why can we Taiwanese people be like that? Because we remember bitterness and don't dare to return to those days. But those second-generation Mainlanders get money from their parents and have never tasted bitterness themselves. They just take that money and then they fail. But we real Taiwanese people, we are a cordial, hardworking, and diligent race. That's the way we are.

DISCUSSION

Hiong-gun's personal narrative illustrates well most of the key elements of identity formation in Taiwan. I have heard her narrative not only through one interview, but also as she retells her stories to other women in social contexts. I have
also observed her daily life at work and at home. Her life history reveals a woman
very different from those described by Susan Greenhalgh in an earlier generation.
"With few alternative sources of social identity," wrote Greenhalgh, "women's fates
were tied to their families of marriage, giving them few options but to play by
those families' rules" (1994: 759). In contrast, Hiong-gun's identity is a complex
whole shaped by occupation, gender, marital status, ethnicity, religious beliefs,
and even personal identification with her astrological sign, Cancer.

Gender is an important dimension of her identity, as can be seen throughout
her narrative. To a certain extent, her female gender limits her activities in the eel
industry work culture. Labor relations, for example, must be carefully arranged
through a male plant manager who plays the male role of drinking and talking
dirty with employees. Her relations with customers are also influenced by her inability to enter into a male business culture. In order to avoid sexual harassment,
she must choose her customers carefully, which has surely limited her profits to
some extent. She cannot enter into the male-oriented world of flower drinking,
where many business deals are concluded. Women are largely excluded from this
business culture where men consume the company of women. I have not met even
a single woman entrepreneur who drinks with men in such places; and many have
said that the custom limits their ability to compete in business with male entrepreneurs. Experience teaches these women that a truly "free market" is only an
ideology, unattainable in a world of social structures and cultural ideologies that
restrict women.

Gender ideologies are part of Hiong-gun's daily existence. Even close family
members find it strange that she is a single woman entrepreneur at her age. Her
nephew's comment that she might be lesbian, a member of a group perceived to
be aberrant, is a classical way of casting doubt on successful women as if they lack
a normal life. Hiong-gun claims, however, that her gender has actually helped her
succeed and become one of Taiwan's leading eel exporters. When she talks about
the moral characteristics that lead to success, she argues that women are better at
cultivating their hearts and maintaining long-term relationships with suppliers
and customers. They are also better than men at business practices based on harmony and compromise. Men, she says, are more prone to resort to violence when
problems and conflicts arise, whereas she can appear to put the customer first in
all situations and then earn any short-term loss back in subsequent transactions.
Her unmarried status, moreover, helped her overcome some of the limitations
faced by most women. Without childcare or elder responsibilities, she was able to
work in the company at night when married women might be expected to stay
home with their families.

Hiong-gun's marital status is also an important part of her identity, especially as she often has to explain her single status in social life. Unmarried lifestyles are rare for women in Taiwan, and the percentage of never-married women in her generation is only approximately 3 percent. In 1990, of Taiwanese women aged 45 to 49, 3.1 percent had never married, 90.2 percent were married or cohabiting, 3.1 percent were divorced, and 3.6 percent were widowed (Census Office of the Executive Yuan 1992: 176). Knowing well that she is different from most women, she has developed a personal narrative to explain her relationship to the family system. Although it would be tempting to draw a parallel between single women entrepreneurs and marriage-resistance movements in Chinese history (Sankar 1984, Siu 1990, Topley 1975), Hiong-gun describes herself as neither a feminist engaged in political struggle nor as a gender radical seeking to subvert social norms. Most importantly, she differs from participants of marriage-resistance movements because she has no opportunity to join a community of like-minded women where identity is solidified through collective rituals and practices. Instead, she must justify her single marital status to others, which she does through a narrative of fate and destiny.

Hiong-gun takes a self-reflexive attitude towards her personal identity and refers to a number of cultural themes. Those cultural themes are diverse, including even the Western astrological tradition, but draw above all upon folk Buddhist conceptions of a self as an entity that survives multiple reincarnations, meeting other individuals in a destiny (*en-hun*) strongly influenced by one's past deeds and actions. Hiong-gun thus faces both work and personal life with the same attitude: bravely trying to accept what fate brings her, seeking to create good karma for future prosperity, and above all working on her own heart. "Heart" in Chinese epistemology is the most important tool through which individuals deal with the external world. Buddhist practices refer to cultivating the heart; Taoists "cleanse" the hearts of wandering ghosts during the seventh lunar month. In this case, cultivating the heart articulates with Charles Taylor's concept of modern identity aiming towards a moral good and is the lens through which she frames her workplace identity (1989). Yet Hiong-gun does not perceive all people as equally good. Most importantly, she identifies goodness and the value of hard work only with her own particular ethnic group.

In the conversations that Hiong-gun maintains in the course of social interaction, she makes frequent references to ethnicity and Taiwan's changing political economy. Hiong-gun is a so-called Native Taiwanese, which she refers to as "real Taiwanese" or simply "we Taiwanese." Since her family has lived through the Japanese occupation of Taiwan and she herself does business with Japan, her identity is oriented towards a Japanese image of Taiwanese modernity. In her narratives, Hiong-gun often stresses affinities between "real Taiwanese" and Japanese people that she sees in such things as a strong work ethic, attention to quality, and harmonious business practices. Hiong-gun, who was born nearly a decade after the end of Japanese rule, claims to remember how safe Taiwan was during the

Japanese occupation and even states boldly that Taiwan was better off under Japanese than KMT rule. Clearly, she has appropriated the discourses of older people as her own memories and they have become a part of her ethnic identity. She contrasts Minnan-speaking Native Taiwanese frequently with Mainlanders, whom she describes as culturally backward and lazy, yet as powerful agents of Taiwanese oppression. At the international level, she also draws a strong distinction between the modernity of Taiwan and the backwardness of China, a discursive practice that strengthens her distinctly Taiwanese identity. The ethnic aspects of her identity are so strong that she brought them up at both the beginning and the end of her formal interview; and she discusses them whenever possible in other social contexts. These ethnic identities, which have long been part of Taiwanese life (Gates 1987, Mendel 1970), are important to the lives of most men and women in contemporary Taiwan.

NOTES

1. I have no evidence that she is lesbian. I once brought up the subject of homosexuality with her, which she dismissed as "disgusting." This comment, which could be interpreted as a slur, is one way in which strong women are often perceived as somehow different than other women or aberrant.

2. In the first four decades of KMT rule, schoolchildren were fined for speaking Japanese, Taiwanese, Hakka, or aboriginal languages in school. Memories of this practice later contributed to resentment against the KMT and the emergence of a linguistic Taiwanese nationalism.

3. By "real" Taiwanese, she means Native Taiwanese as opposed to Mainlanders.

4. This commonly told tale is much like Chinese stories about not locking doors in the good old Maoist days (Mark Selden, personal communication). In Taiwan, it is common for older people to embellish the benefits of Japanese colonialism as a means of criticizing the KMT.

5. This is a reference to the Chinese philosopher Chuang-tze. Taiwanese people often quote Chinese philosophers, usually without knowing the source, through proverbs that they learn in school.

This woman sells noodles on the street, but closes down twice a year to go abroad and teach I-Kuan-Tao faith.

A Western-style bakery in Taipei

An eel exporter and her male workers

Former Miss China Wang Li-ling has become an animal-rights activist and runs a non-profit animal shelter.

A proud mother assisting at the opening of a new lesbian bar.

Selling aboriginal crafts in Taipei

This woman entrepreneur has donated generously to monasteries in Tibet. *Photo courtesy of Ong Tiok-sing.*

The anthropologist and a group of women entrepreneurs enjoy dinner in a woman-owned Burmese restaurant.

Chapter Ten

A Nonprofit Dog Shelter

I noticed Wang Li-ling, a former beauty queen turned animal-rights activist, shortly after moving into my Taipei neighborhood in Neihu. Coming home on a motorcycle late at night, I often saw an elegantly dressed older woman feeding stray dogs from the back of a van in a park near my home. When a neighbor told me that she was the founder of Taiwan's Help-Save-a-Pet Fund (HSAPF), I searched for her on the World Wide Web (www.hsapf.org.tw), called her office, and asked if I could interview her as the only nonprofit entrepreneur in my study. She generously invited me to her home in a heavily guarded planned community nearby, and permitted me to take down her life history. She also supplied me with a wealth of articles written about her life history, which have been published in environmental journals, entrepreneurship magazines, and other venues.

The literature distributed by the HSAPF is lightly sprinkled with Buddhist terminology, as well as the concepts of the self to which Taiwanese people make frequent reference. The motto of the organization is "through human self-reflection, to truly establish a harmonious and peaceful Pure Land on Earth for all creatures." In the fall 1999 issue of their publication "You, Me and It," for example, the Taiwanese opera star Randy Yang describes his "sweet and sour, hot and bitter life with six dogs" he adopted from the streets. Yang, described as a gentle Aquarius with blood type O, outlines in detail the personalities of all six dogs. In each case, he explains his relationship to them in terms of "destiny" (*en-hun*). His relationship with Kiong-kiong, for example, seems to have been destined. One summer, a religious master predicted that Randy Yang would soon encounter a disaster involving loss of blood. Shortly thereafter, he adopted Kiong-kiong, a large dog that had been abandoned at the door of a pet shop. The dog bit Randy every time he was washed, even to the point of cutting the skin and drawing blood. One day, after being scolded for urinating in Randy's studio, the dog disappeared and was never seen again. Randy concluded that the dog had appeared only to create the blood-loss disaster, and then disappeared as soon as his duties had been fulfilled.

121

Randy was thus saved from what could have been, for example, a fatal traffic accident.

Similar interpretations of destiny are not uncommon in the narratives of Taiwanese people. As Li-ling said during her interview, "Chinese people talk about destiny. Our meeting today is destiny. If a dog lives in your house and acts as your child today, it is because you have a destined relationship." This and other Buddhist concepts permeate both her personal life story and the history of her foundation. Yet she shows as well how those fated relations are embedded in the political economy of Taiwan.

CANINE PERSPECTIVES
ON THE TAIWAN MIRACLE

Li-ling explained her project, which is surely a fundamental project in the existentialist sense:

> The reason I set up this foundation was to teach Taiwanese people, Chinese people, how to protect animals. I have been taking care of animals outside for about twenty years. When I was young, there were dogs in Taiwan, but there were no stray dogs.

She attributed changing human-dog relationships, not unlike changing relationships between classes or genders, to shifts in the Taiwanese political economy and the development of capitalism on the island. Dogs were no longer just farm animals to "guard the door," but had become commodities in themselves. Women entrepreneurs played an important role in this process:

> When Taiwan was an agricultural society, people raised dogs, and all of the neighbors and friends knew which dog belonged to whom. When dogs barked, people thought they were noisy, but nobody thought of killing dogs because of that. But, around 1977, it was the Chinese Year of the Dog. A lot of business people got the idea of advertising "dogs bring prosperity" and selling dogs. They started smuggling dogs in from the mainland and other places and raising dogs here. They let them have a lot of babies, and then started selling them. Business was terrific! Since everyone wanted to get rich and needed good luck, everyone wanted to raise dogs. A lot of housewives, who needed money but were staying at home with nothing else to do, went into raising dogs as a side business. They started raising dogs at home and opening up small stores like "Mama's Dog Store." It seemed as if everyone was raising dogs. But just one or two years later, stray dogs started appearing on the streets. Why? Raising a dog isn't easy. Dogs need to eat, they get sick, and they have to be kept clean, but not everyone has so much time.

The problem was surely compounded by the rapid growth of an urban middle class at the time, a new class with strong desires to express its new status with symbolic commodities of distinction (cf. Bourdieu 1984). Purchasing and displaying expensive dog breeds were ways to express entrance into bourgeois society:

People bought dogs because they wanted to earn money, and they thought dogs would bring them good luck. Some of them thought they should buy pure-breed dogs that cost more than NT$20,000. Then, they could show off a beautiful and expensive dog to their friends. Some children wanted dogs, and their parents bought dogs for them as toys. They just didn't have the heart to raise dogs. They didn't have an emotional relationship (Mandarin *ganqing*) with their dogs.

Dogs, however, as living creatures that get sick and age, quickly outgrow their usefulness as symbolic capital and become a burden:

> Once they are old, their hearing disappears, they can't see well, and they get sick. It's embarrassing to have people see that. Since they are burdens, people just throw the dogs out on the street. Many people buy dogs for their children during the summer or winter vacation. But when school starts, they don't have time to take care of the dogs. Their mothers don't have time to take care of dogs either. So there are more and more stray dogs.

People often use Buddhist ideology to justify their abandonment of dogs to the streets, seeing it as analogous to the practice of purchasing caged birds, fish, or turtles and then releasing them in front of a Buddhist temple. That practice, originally meant as an expression of sympathy for animals, has long been a commercial practice in front of temples as a means of purchasing good karma:

> Some people are good-hearted. They say they release their dogs. Chinese people say "releasing living things" (Mandarin *fangsheng*). They may buy a bird or a turtle and then go somewhere to release them. Anyway, people think in their hearts, "It doesn't matter if I release that dog outside. Since I didn't kill him, it's not a sin. He can live if I set him free." So lots of people set their dogs free.

This practice, however, quickly contributed to the environmental damage caused by rapid industrialization and urbanization in Taiwan, especially since dogs reproduce quickly. Citing research "done in England," Li-ling argued that one female dog, released in the streets, could potentially produce up to 67,000 descendants in a period of six years. Once government authorities noticed that stray dogs were becoming a problem, municipal and county governments hired dogcatchers and built facilities to destroy the animals. The methods used to kill dogs, as documented by the HSAPF and other animal-rights NGOs, were often unusually cruel. In Tainan, for example, dog-catching units have been accused by activists of burying dogs alive, throwing them into pits with other hungry dogs, either to be attacked and eaten by the living or suffocated amidst the cadavers of the dead.

FROM BEAUTY QUEEN TO "DOG MAMA"

Aware of this cruelty, Li-ling found it necessary to emerge from obscurity and into the media limelight as a social activist. She first gained media attention when she organized a protest march of activists—with their dogs—to the steps of the Taipei city hall. She established the HSAPF in 1988, one year after martial law was lifted and it was possible to found private NGOs. She became one of Taiwan's most outspoken international animal-rights activists, speaking out against global practices ranging from Spanish bullfighting to Taiwanese dog-meat restaurants. Her most intensive work has been in the promotion of stray-dog sterilization and a dog-adoption program run out of her own shelter. None of this, however, started suddenly:

> At first, I went out to rescue dogs all by myself. After I rescued a dog, I would take it to the veterinarian. The doctor would wash it, vaccinate it, and sterilize it. Then, I would ask the veterinarian to give the dog to somebody who wanted to adopt a pet. I bought lots of canned dog food, and gave it to him. In twenty years, I gave away a lot of dogs. Up until the two hundredth dog, I kept count. After that, I lost count. But I thought, Taiwan has so many dogs that I can't rescue them all on my own. I gathered together several friends, and we set up the Help-Save-a-Pet Fund.

Lobbying for animal rights in a new democracy not yet accustomed to activism was one of her greatest challenges. In an event that reveals her ability to mobilize social capital from both Taiwan and abroad, she pressured the Taipei municipal government to change its practices in the treatment of stray dogs:

> I was very radical at the beginning. When I saw the city's dog pound, I held a press conference and told the press to observe how cruel the government is. It was quite unbelievable! I also sent out press releases to the foreign media, asking them to support us and to say that Taiwan should not be that way. I worked really hard. About eight years ago, so two administrations ago, I even sued the Taipei mayor. I took him to court, saying that his methods of catching dogs were too cruel. After I worked so hard on it, the government knew better. And what made me happiest of all is that a lot of people came to support me.

BECOMING MISS CHINA

The narrative of how a former beauty queen became "Dog Mama" has captivated the Taiwanese public, and become a part of Li-ling's well-rehearsed public identity. In both published and private narratives, she makes frequent references to her family background and the "social graces" she learned from her mother. That home education, she explains, is the inspiration for her attention to beauty as well as for her "independent personality" (K.-T. Chang 1997: 209):

> My paternal grandfather was born in Suzhou. He was a *jinshi* [Confucian scholar-official] back in the Qing Dynasty, and very successful in the government. Then he bought a lace factory in Shanghai. Back then, all of the gentry studied traditional things like Chinese medicine and Chinese philosophy, but he also knew Western ideas. That's why he encouraged his children to be independent and to pursue careers of their own.

My parents met in Shanghai, and they had a "free romance" back when few people married due to free romance. My family didn't suffer the bitter lives of refugees. China at the time was all chaos and war, but my grandfather's factory was in the International Concession. My family lived in that district with foreigners, and we learned from them. You know what they used to say about the Chinese people, that they are not unified, that they are like a plate of shifting sand, very selfish. But my family wasn't like that. We were always concerned with society.

She explained as well how her family moved to Taiwan in 1948. At a time when the KMT was replacing the Japanese-speaking cadres of Taiwan with Mandarin-speaking cadres from China, and shortly after many of the Taiwanese elite had been decimated in the 2:28 Massacre of 1947, there were ample employment opportunities for immigrants from the mainland. Her family was among the new immigrants in search of a new life:

I came to Taiwan at the age of five. When I came, China was not yet communist. My father came to Taiwan to work for the Land Bank. My father was only twenty-five years old and living in China at the time. The government told him that Taiwan needed a lot of young people to go over to work and asked if he was willing to go. My father agreed, and took the whole family to Taiwan. When we arrived in Taiwan, it was still peaceful. It was still possible to go back and forth.

Li-ling described her childhood in the 1950s, a time when Taiwan was already rapidly absorbing American influences. Elvis Presley was king, called "Cat King" (*Maowang*) in Taiwan. Young women dreamed of glamorous occupations, such as flight attendant, that could take them to the promised land of America:

There were five girls and two boys in our family. I was the second oldest sister. When I was young, I was very beautiful, and wanted to be a movie star. But my parents objected. Back then, you know, movie stars were considered to be a kind of entertainer, and that was considered to be very low-class. I liked art and music. I liked traditional Chinese painting. I also liked music. My mother—that was the time of the "Cat King" and Rock Hudson—always played music at home when I was in middle school. We also had a piano and I took piano lessons. It was a very literary environment.

Her mother encouraged her to get involved in the Miss China beauty contest:

The Miss China contest wasn't just some roadside beauty contest. My mother wouldn't let me do that. It was government-sponsored. It was a kind of people-to-people diplomacy, and would give me the chance to learn a lot. That's why my mother encouraged me to do that. That's why she taught me how to do make-up, and how to wear a *qipao*. She taught me the social graces that made it possible for me to win. There are many beautiful girls in the world. And the other contestants were people like stewardesses, all very beautiful. But it is the social grace I learned from my mother that made me win. Social grace is very important.

ACTING MISS CHINA:
REPRESENTING "TAIWAN" TO THE WORLD

Having won the national contest, Li-ling toured America as Miss China in 1961:

In 1961, I won first place in Taiwan, and then went to Miami to participate in the Miss Universe contest. In the Miss Universe contest, I got sixth place. I was extremely happy during that time, since I got to do people-to-people diplomacy. In the Taiwan of thirty years ago, nobody abroad knew about us. Very few people had heard of Taiwan. Some people had heard of Formosa, but Formosa was very small and nobody knew where it was. We had a responsibility. I went to the beauty contest to introduce Taiwan to the world. Before then, only the Taiwanese government officials went abroad. I was the first Taiwanese woman to go out and promote Taiwan as ambassador to the world.

Li-ling spoke with pride of the powerful places she could visit as Miss China and representative of the ROC:

I was in America for more than two months. I went everywhere. Wherever I went, they gave me the key to the city. It was always the mayor, in Houston, in Washington, who gave me the ceremonial key to the city. They always came out to the airport to meet me. Before, Miss China was very important. Now there are too many beauty contests, so it no longer has the same meaning. But back then, it was important since you were a representative of the government. I went to visit the United Nations. Taiwan was a member of the United Nations at the time, and we still had an ambassador to the UN. I went to our embassy. All of the American officials knew about me, and invited me to dinner. It was as if they considered me to be a representative of Taiwan.

While in America, Li-ling nearly had a chance to fulfill her dream of acting in films, and even auditioned in Hollywood. In an expression of the Chinese chauvinism that still exists in Taiwan (M.-K. Chang 1988), however, she was angered when asked to play the role of a Thai woman, an incident she described to the Taiwanese public as "an attitude of disrespect" (H.-F. Tai 1994: 129). Instead, she returned to Taiwan and got married.

VIRTUOUS WIFE AND GOOD MOTHER

Pointing out the photo of a uniformed man standing next to Chiang Kai-shek, Li-ling told me about her powerful family of marriage:

My father-in-law is Chou Chih-rou. He was the provincial governor. Before that he was the commander-in-chief of the Chinese—the Taiwanese [sic]—Air Force on the mainland. He's the one who built it up. He attended the Cairo Conference. During the Second World War, he was in charge of the forces in the Pacific. He has a certificate that he received from the military at that time. When MacArthur and those people came, he became good friends with them. After they came to Taiwan, he brought the Air Force from the mainland to Taiwan. He was very important to Chiang Kai-shek. Afterwards, he was the provincial governor. Back then, the provincial governor had a lot of power, not like today.[1] During one big typhoon, he even went without sleep for seventy-two hours because they had so many emergency meetings. He worked very hard because he loved Taiwan very much.

The marriage of Miss China to the son of a leading politician was no easy matter, and even attracted the attention of General Chiang Kai-shek himself:

> Because I married the son of the provincial governor, our marriage was a very sensational event for Taiwanese society. A Miss China marrying the son of a leading cadre—it was big news. Our Chiang Kai-shek asked me if we could marry outside of Taiwan. Back then, Taiwan was still under martial law, so we couldn't have such a festive event. He wanted us to get married in Penghu.[2] I told him that my mother shouldn't ride on a ship to go over, so we ended up getting married in Kaohsiung. I didn't invite my friends. It was just a very simple tea party. After marriage, I didn't want the kind of public life where I would be recognized wherever I go. For a while I didn't go out. I only came back into public life to help animals.

As for her husband, she said:

> He was in business. He could have done many things. He could have worked in the government, since the sons of many officials in Taiwan do well in government careers. But my father-in-law wouldn't let him do that. He said, "You can't do that. Since I do government work, I won't let my son do that."

Cautious of a culture of *guanxi* ("relationships") (Yang 1994), which could get a high-ranking cadre's son promoted faster than he merited, his father also kept him out of the military. The most attractive option was thus business, importing wool from Australia. Even then, he never accepted government contracts and conducted business exclusively through a network of partners he had built up while in school at Berkeley. Li-ling stayed home as a "virtuous wife and good mother."

During her twenty years as an "ordinary housewife," Li-ling focused her attention primarily on her daughter's education. She emphasized the values that she has instilled in her only child, Emily, who now holds a Ph.D. in political science from Cambridge University:

> I used to take Emily to visit homes for the elderly, and to orphanages to play with the children there. I wanted her to understand what suffering is like, to understand those children who have no mothers and fathers. In my life philosophy, I have always empathized with weaker groups in society.

Empathy with weaker groups in society extended even to the smallest of animals. She reminisced about her experiences teaching Emily about kindness to animals:

> When Emily was a child, our domestic help would buy those "Roach Motels" and put them in the kitchen. I went into the kitchen and saw those cockroaches with their feet stuck to the ground in there, with no way of moving. I called Emily over, and we took the cockroaches outside. One by one, we released their little legs with tooth-picks and let them go. Today that's like our inside joke—people would say we were crazy! Why did we do that? Because I thought the way they die is extremely cruel. They starve to death.

Similarly, she and Emily sometimes freed rats from the traps set up in restaurants, taking them to parks so they would be spared the common fate of being scalded to death with boiling water. To this day, Emily is one of her mother's most faithful volunteers, even acting as the HSAPF's "foreign affairs minister" by networking with foreign animal-rights groups. Li-ling's husband has also been very supportive:

> I'm very lucky, since my entire family supports me, especially my husband, that is to say my own family. My husband has loved animals since he was a child. When he was a child on the mainland, he raised a dog that had been given to him by Madame Chiang Kai-shek. He raised that dog until he went to America at the age of eighteen to study economics at Berkeley.

STANDING UP FOR ANIMALS

By 1988, when Emily was already studying for her B.A. in political science at the University of Michigan, Li-ling decided to devote herself full-time to animals by founding the HSAPF. Media descriptions at the beginning depicted Li-ling and her husband sleeping with adopted stray dogs in their Japanese-era home in downtown Taipei. The daily practice of caring for animals has remained central to her life, and her house is filled with cats and dogs in need of personal care. The musty odors of animals permeate the stately elegance of her villa, reminding visitors that this is no ordinary home. And even while entertaining guests, Li-ling is acutely aware of every feline cry at the door, rushing to open the door and feed hungry cats as they arrive for their daily meals.

Li-ling opened her first dog shelter in Tamsui. By 1997 it had already become overcrowded and too noisy for the neighbors, and they were forced by circumstances to move to Kung-liao in Taipei County. Running a shelter required that Li-ling raise money from sources beyond her family and circle of acquaintances:

> When the media began reporting about my work, people started sending their dogs over for adoption. At one time, I had eighty dogs at home. Without money, I couldn't do much more. So I started raising funds from people. And the number of dogs kept increasing. If we wanted to do more, we had to do more fund-raising. That was very

difficult. Now, I have more than 500 dogs at Kung-liao. Taipei also has some helpers who raise stray dogs and we help them. They are all volunteers. We needed to raise the money to feed so many dogs, clean up after them, let them see the veterinarian, etc. That all takes money.

Much of her work has been political as well, lobbying politicians at all levels of government to stop euthanasia of stray animals and implement sterilization programs instead. The HSAPF was one of the main forces behind the dog-tag programs—later replaced by laws requiring pets to have microchip implants—that make it possible to identify the owners and return stray pets to them. Even more impressive yet, since it involved wide-scale cultural change, Li-ling's anti-dog-meat campaigns successfully altered winter eating habits in urban Taiwan. Whereas dog meat was once widely perceived as an effective antidote against the cold, it is now widely seen as an inhumane practice and has been made illegal throughout Taiwan.

At the beginning of Chen Shui-bian's presidential term, Li-ling looked to the new administration for progress in animal rights:

> I hope that we can let him know that being good to the people means being concerned about living things. He might think that some person suffers because of poverty and take care of him. Or he may support a hospital to make the sick more comfortable. That shows that he is a benevolent person. But why doesn't he empathize with other living beings? Because dogs are like people. They love their masters, and would even die for them. So I think that the best president is one that takes care of all animals. I hope that I can influence him on behalf of dogs.

That kind of influence requires a great deal of social capital, and in the past Li-ling has proved adept at mobilizing it to her cause. The new administration, however, has new priorities.

ETHNIC IDENTITY
IN A CHANGING TAIWAN

In an era of increasing Taiwanese nationalism—expressed not least in the election of the Democratic Progressive Party's (DPP) Chen Shui-bian as president—Li-ling's mainland heritage and family connections close to the Kuomintang and Chiang Kai-shek no longer provide the same social capital as before. In contrast to the empowerment that Native Taiwanese like Chhoa Hiong-gun (Chapter 9) feel in this era, the mainland elite has experienced a relative decrease in power. Families like her own, seen by Taiwanese nationalists as carpetbaggers at best and colonialists at worst, are losing status to a new "native" Taiwanese elite:

> We didn't have a lot of power like Lien Chan,[3] but my father-in-law and husband were still very successful. If one has a lot of power and then loses it, it can be very painful.

As the Chinese proverb says, "Smoke dissipates into the clouds," but we didn't have that problem. If one has something meaningful to do in one's own life, one can avoid that problem. In our case, it is our work with living beings.

In order to do that work effectively, however, she must continue to accumulate and manipulate social capital as efficiently as possible in a changing Taiwan. Like Mainlander politicians James Soong and Ma Ying-jeou, therefore, she has learned to emphasize her new Taiwan identity to the greatest extent possible. The issue weighs heavily on her mind:

> When I came to Taiwan as a child, I got along very well with Taiwanese friends. Since I went to school in Kaohsiung, all of my good friends in grade school and middle school were Taiwanese. They didn't know that I was a Mainlander. I spoke Taiwanese. In fact, I even know a lot of very old expressions that a lot of Taiwanese people don't necessarily know nowadays.

Although ethnic conflict between Native Taiwanese and Mainlanders has long been observed by anthropologists (Gates 1987) and political scientists (Corcuff 2000, Mendel 1970), it was only with the shift in political winds under Native Taiwanese presidents Lee Teng-hui and Chen Shui-bian that Mainlanders became disadvantaged in ethnic discourses. From Li-ling's perspective:

> Back then, there was no idea of provincial identity at all. When I introduced myself in the United States, my first sentence was always "I am Taiwanese." I don't really understand why things [ethnic relations] have become like this. In America, I had to do public-relations work, since many of those overseas Chinese were not from Taiwan. Many came from the mainland, from Korea, from other places. But in their hearts, they all knew Taiwan. They liked Taiwan better than the mainland, because they didn't like communism. They thus took Taiwan very seriously.

Relatively disempowered in the ethnic politics of Taiwanese life, she has sought to construct a nonethnic identity that is at once globally environmental and locally Buddhist.

CASHING IN ON THE
GLOBAL IMAGINATION

Li-ling makes reference to an imaginary global ecoscape, where the earth is under siege by a greedy humanity and needs to be rescued through local action everywhere:

> We don't like it when any animal, any living being, loses a life. We have no right to take away their lives.[4] We live on this earth and have long lives, so why can't they? We

also don't want to pollute their environment. Air pollution, nuclear waste, those are all types of pollution.[5] We can do much more environmental protection, but we don't do it. Everywhere in the world is the same.

Drawing on a common theme of the Taiwanese environmental movement (Weller 1999), she stressed the fact that the earth must be preserved for future generations:

In order to have a better life, we develop science and we do research to make life happier and more convenient. For now, we all eat well, but several centuries from now, our descendants won't have anyplace to go. I think that this is the selfish side of humanity, and it is very unfair.

In her final solution for the stray animal problem she calls for a program of eugenics to solve the problem of animal overpopulation:

I think it is much better to control their reproduction, by sterilizing them and not letting them give birth. It's not just dogs. There are also cats, rats, and other animals that people think are disgusting. We shouldn't let them reproduce. Why do we let them continue to give birth, and then kill, kill, kill? We should not continue like that!

Skilled at taking a global approach to local problems, Li-ling often places Taiwanese animal-rights problems within an international context and compares the situations in different countries:

It is not just our society that is cruel to animals; the world is like that. I have heard that the bullfighting in Spain is very cruel, especially the way they kill the bulls. They call bullfighters "heroes," but they aren't really heroes, since all they do is kill one bull after another. What meaning does that have? But that is culture, the culture of their country. They need to earn foreign currency, and since lots of tourists come to see bullfighting, they earn a lot of money.

For Li-ling, cooperation with international NGOs is an important part of her mission. It is part of her job to cooperate publicly with global NGOs. In 1992, for example, the HSAPF because affiliated with the British Royal Society for the Prevention of Cruelty to Animals. It has also joined the International Association Against Painful Experiments on Animals, and lobbied internationally against painful animal experiments. Identification with these foreign NGOs has endowed Li-ling and her HSAPF with social capital.

BUDDHISM AS SOCIAL CAPITAL

Her most visible form of symbolic capital, however, is the use of Buddhist themes, which permeate her organizational literature and public narratives:

> When I was young, I was not a Buddhist. I was Christian because my mother taught classes in a Christian church in Shanghai. After my mother came to Taiwan, she rarely went to church, but she hung a Jesus figure on the wall and we prayed to it every night. So, twenty-five years ago, I was not Buddhist. . . . Afterwards, I asked Jesus if I could become Buddhist, since my mother-in-law is Buddhist. Every day, she recites sutras in front of a Buddha figure. We Christians don't burn incense, but my mother-in-law wanted to worship our ancestors every day. My daughter also had to burn incense. If I said I didn't want to burn incense, the older people would say I was very disobedient.

Nonetheless, she apparently feels a need to justify conversion, at least to me as a Westerner whom she perceived as potentially Christian:

> I still respect Jesus, and believe in him. I believe that the god of all religions—regardless if it is Buddhism, Christianity, Catholicism, Islam, even I-Kuan-Tao—is in Heaven. He can see everything we do. In fact, every religion is good. Each religion teaches us to do good deeds, to help others, to not be too selfish. So I told Jesus, it isn't because I don't believe in him, but I want to convert to Buddhism. After I became Buddhist, I started to learn many of the ideas that the masters talk about.

After conversion to institutional Buddhism, Li-ling started attending Buddhist classes and learning about Buddhist epistemology. As an animal lover, she picked up immediately on the theme of benevolence towards all living things. One of the main doctrines of Buddhism is that one should not kill living things, since all are equal. She said, "I learned about the six paths of reincarnation. The bodhisattva Kuanyin said that all living beings are equal." She came to save all living things, including cats, dogs, and all animals.

Li-ling's belief in reincarnation is reflected in her discourses about animals. Like Chhoa Hiong-gun, who sponsors Buddhist ceremonies for the souls of the eels she sells to Japan, Li-ling draws attention to even the lowliest animals:

> I'm not afraid of rats, because I realize that rats have their own life-worlds (*jingjie*). A rat doesn't come into this world to live because he wants to. He himself doesn't know why he is here, right? But after he comes, he has infectious diseases and he eats people's food. So people kill rats. If I told people that we should protect rats, everyone would scold me. But I've seen the rat's world. Rats have fathers, mothers, and children. Rat mothers are very good to their children. They feed their children, and they go out in search of food for their young. Once I even saw a rat . . . his friend, well, I don't know what relationship they had, but he died. I saw a dead rat, and I saw the hole where they lived. After a while, the other rats came out of the hole and they took

the dead rat back into the hole with them. Rats take care of their dead, because they are intelligent. They have a heart. I think the world is like that.

After conversion, Li-ling has been adept at learning Buddhism and using it to further her project of saving animals:

> Buddhism also says "everything is emptiness." But I am an ordinary person. I can't be like a Buddhist master, shave my head, and sit there without doing anything. I am only capable of sitting at home and reciting sutras, but I think it is far better to stand up and rescue living beings. I want to influence many other people. I hope that all the people around me will be influenced by me.

Li-ling has skillfully used Buddhist teachings to convert people to the animal-rights movement. In interviews with the media and in her own writings (Wang 1997: 211), she stresses that animals have souls. In the Buddhist *Golden Lotus* magazine, she argued that since dogs have souls, people should not eat dog meat (Jinse Lianhua 1994). She also argued that abandoning dogs creates bad karma. The media constantly borrows Buddhist terminology in saying that she has a "fated relationship" (*en-hun*) with dogs (e.g., Shih 1995). Li-ling, moreover, calls on Buddhist ideology to defend herself against public criticism of her activities.

Li-ling has cultivated relationships with well-known Buddhist leaders, including Master Shengyan of Dharma Drum, a Taiwanese Buddhist organization with a wide following both domestically and abroad:

> People don't understand what I am doing because they don't understand Buddhism. Buddhism says that people and animals are equal. Maybe in a past life, you were a dog. Or in a future life, you will be reborn as a dog. It is a question of reincarnation. Once I spoke to Master Shengyan about that. People say that a dog comes into the world because he did bad things in a past life. He is born as a dog to receive bitterness. People say you shouldn't save dogs because they are born as animals to receive punishment from Heaven. I asked Master Shengyan about that. He said that their idea is incorrect. Besides, if I were helping old or handicapped people, who are also receiving punishment for past deeds, people would jump in to help. I can do the same for animals. I think that when a dog encounters the person who wants to save him, he has served out his sentence. I asked Master Shengyan about that, and he said that I am right.

FACING THE PUBLIC

Li-ling nonetheless has had a difficult time facing the Taiwanese public. She has to feed the dogs in the middle of the night, for example, because she has been scolded, even beaten with brooms, by people who say she is attracting stray dogs to their neighborhoods and thus polluting the environment. She has also been troubled by "rumors" about her (Wang 1997: 213), and public critics who say she has become an animal-rights spokesperson only because she seeks to increase her own fame (Chiu 1996: 14). She says, "Only my family understands me."

Li-ling's husband has been supportive and cooperative all along, perhaps because she has created her project within the ideology and language of his family's religion. When I first saw that soft-spoken man, in fact, I mistook him for her driver. Semiretired, he now drives her through Taipei as she makes nightly rounds to feed homeless stray dogs. Buddhism has made it possible for her to channel the resources of her husband and her family to her project. It has gained her widespread social support from public figures such as Randy Yang, as well as donations and volunteer time from a broad Taiwanese public. She has influenced Taiwanese society, not in the least by changing the former habit of eating dog meat. As a whole, Li-ling is satisfied with the work she has accomplished:

> I've been working hard at this for more than ten years, but there are still many dogs on the streets. But when I think about it, I realize that if I had not done that work, if I had just lived my own life, then Taipei, and all of Taiwan, would have many more stray dogs today.

DISCUSSION

Religion is one of the main sources of social identity for women in Taiwan. In my conversations with women entrepreneurs, I found religion in its various manifestations to be an important part of their personal narratives and social lives. At the most basic level, most Taiwanese women use religious metaphors of fate and destiny to explain their life situations, just as Chhoa Hiong-gun did in the previous chapter. Some women, moreover, are intensely involved in organized religion. The owner of an exercise-equipment shop whom I encountered during survey research, for example, is a member of the Presbyterian Church and uses her shop as the base for a Christian crusade to end prostitution.[6] A noodle-shop owner closes her shop for a period of two months every year so that she can go to places as far away as Malaysia and the Dominican Republic to proselytize her syncretic religion of I-Kuan-Tao. Ong Siok-ting (Chapter 5) actively promotes Tibetan Buddhism in Taiwan. Religion constitutes an important part of these women's self-identities and lifestyles. Buddhism, which claims 40 percent of all Taiwanese religious believers (Laliberté 1998: 44) is probably the most influential. Wang Li-ling's story is interesting as a clear example of how religion can be harnessed as social capital. Due to her family and ethnic background, it is especially important for her in contemporary Taiwan.

Marxist and feminist observers have generally viewed religion as a people's opiate that disguises the real nature of hegemonic power relations. Simone de Beauvoir (1989 [1952]), for example, saw religion in women's lives as a form of existentialist "bad faith." If women lack love, she argued, they turn to mystic religion, which in turn prevents them from embarking on transcendent projects of their own. Marxist approaches have similarly interpreted religion—including Chinese ideas of fate—as an ideology that keeps peasants, workers, and other oppressed groups in their places (e.g., Hinton 1966). Anthropologist Stevan Harrell (1987) found the only unequivocal examples of true fatalism in Taiwan to be in the domain of relations between the sexes. In those cases, belief in fate tended to keep women in unhappy relationships, resigned to the finality of "marry a rooster, follow a rooster; marry a dog, follow a dog." Feminist scholars in Taiwan [e.g., M.-T. Hsu (1998)] have similarly argued that women are oppressed by such ideologies.

Although it is certainly true that religion can be used as a tool of hegemony, Wang Li-ling's story shows well that religion is not necessarily a form of oppression. Even in gender relations, women can transform religious ideologies into strategic tools of empowerment. Wang Li-ling's experience provides one good example of how women can use religion as social capital while constructing public identities. Like many Taiwanese women, she eventually chose to convert to the religion of her husband's family. She was, however, able to use that religion to her advantage as she embarked on a fundamental project of her own.

As a well-known animal-rights activist, Wang Li-ling has critics within Taiwan. Café owner Ma Ya-hung (Chapter 7), for example, once voiced strong criticism of Li-ling as the two of us stood in attendance at Chen Shui-bian's victory celebration in 2000. Having experienced an unhappy marriage and also being fond of stray dogs, Ya-hung offered a cynical guess about the former beauty queen's psychological motivations: "She has had an unhappy marriage, and her husband doesn't love her. So she puts all of her energies into loving dogs." The fact that Li-ling's husband drives her around Taipei nearly every night, however, suggests strongly that Ya-hung's interpretation is mistaken. At a personal level, adept use of religious ideology has permitted her to attract her husband and many others to her fundamental project.

Buddhist religious values have also played an important role in Li-ling's construction of a public identity. Buddhist virtues of compassion and equality between living creatures have helped her accumulate the social capital needed to start and run her dog shelter. In addition, however, Buddhism also places a certain emphasis on individual autonomy and human identity. These ideological themes, argues Taiwanese anthropologist Lu Hwei-Syin (1998: 549), have permitted Buddhist women to transcend the traditional gender identities that once restricted Chinese women to the home. That dynamic may also be working in Wang Li-ling's life. In her own narrative, however, she perceives herself restricted less by her gender identity than by her ethnicity.

With the political changes that have happened in the past decade, Li-ling's background from a prestigious Shanghai family with close KMT connections is no longer as valuable as it once was. She has lost power at the same time that the rise of the DPP has empowered Native Taiwanese like Chhoa Hiong-gun. Li-ling uses two discursive techniques to defend her power in such a context. First, she tries to embrace a "New Taiwanese" identity in public. It is interesting to note how she now emphasizes the Taiwanese dimensions of her identity—very important as social capital at the turn of the twenty-first century—rather than an ROC identity, which was the only possible public identity for an elite Mainlander in 1961. She remembered beginning every public lecture as Miss China by saying she represented Taiwan, a discourse impossible when the KMT was the only representative of China recognized by the United Nations, the United States, and most states. In a slip of tongue, she even mistakenly referred to her prominent father-in-law as commander-in-chief of the Taiwanese air forces on the mainland in 1945— although Taiwan was part of Japan at the time and neither he nor his troops could have ever even visited the island. The tensions that arise from this narrative, not unlike Chhoa Hiong-gun's false memories of the Japanese period, show how even personal memory and identity are contingent upon changing political and economic contexts. In this case, it reveals a loss of power.

Li-ling's story reveals many of the tensions and contradictions that arise in the construction of social identity. People construct these identities, and express them as public narratives, in ways that permit them to amass and utilize the most social capital possible. Women have long been disadvantaged by Confucian ideologies that would limit women to the domestic sphere, and Buddhism has been one way in which women renegotiate those. In this case, gender has been less limiting than ethnicity. Li-ling has attempted to overcome ethnic tensions by instead publicly identifying with universal Buddhist values and the global animal-rights movement. Her strategy of avoiding ethnic tensions and instead constructing identities on the margins of the global and the local is not uncommon among women entrepreneurs in Taipei. The next chapter looks at two other examples.

NOTES

1. During Lee Teng-hui's presidency, Taiwan began the process of "freezing" the provincial government, seen as redundant after the ROC gave up its pretensions of wanting to take back mainland China.

2. There were in fact large weddings during the period of martial law. According to long-standing rumors, the wedding was kept low-key because the marriage itself took place in scandalous circumstances. In order to avoid ethical problems of putting informants under undue duress, I did not pursue the issue.

3. Vice president under Lee Teng-hui and KMT candidate for president in 2000.

4. She is a vegetarian.

5. The construction of a nuclear power plant at Kung-liao, location of her dog shelter, was one of the most controversial social issues in Taiwan during 2000–2001.

6. Unfortunately, she was not interested in doing a life-history interview.

Chapter Eleven

A Global Café

Ng Bi-chu runs Kandahar Café, a coffee shop in a narrow alley near Taiwan Normal University. Her coffee shop does more than provide coffee and conversation, however. Like its namesake, a stop on the Silk Road, it is a center for cultural exchange. The walls are draped with exotic textiles from India and the Middle East, and she occasionally exhibits works from local artists. On weekend evenings, there are musical and dance performances of great variety: folk dances from Bali, folk guitar adaptations of aboriginal songs, even occasional performances by some of the aboriginal pop singers now popular in Taiwan. Bi-chu explicitly claims that she is not an entrepreneur. "I think that my experience is a little different from other people," she says. "I think I am just living my own life. I'm not a big boss." It is her nonconformist and noncapitalist work ethic, she said, that distinguishes her from other Taiwanese bosses:

In Taiwan, I have seen many people who work very industriously. First they open up one store, and then they work to open up branch stores. Most people, after they find pleasure in earning money, work very industriously. They get up very early, and go home very late. But I seem to be very different from them. I am very lazy. Like this café, I don't start work until 6 P.M., and then we are open until 2 A.M. Other people are open on Sunday, but I take every Sunday off. Now, with this café, I am still relatively industrious and hardworking. Before, when I opened a shop, I only opened four or five days a week. I would work for eight hours a day, sometimes six hours. So I think that my experience is a little different from other people.

Like many Taipei entrepreneurs, all of whom have lived through a historically unprecedented period of economic growth, Bi-chu tells a rags-to-riches story of a humble country person who grew up to find happiness in the city. Bi-chu's initial experiences in the city were not positive. She was unsuccessful in school, and equally unable to adapt to the pressures of daily work. Surely exaggerating, she said that she changed her job more than ten times a year in the beginning, taking various positions in places such as trade offices and accounting firms or in large corporate offices. Her narrative makes it clear that she was alienated from her jobs, very much in the Marxian sense. She attributed her inability to conform to a corporate environment to her own "individual character" (Taiwanese *ko-seng*, Mandarin *gexing*):

> That kind of life made me feel very nervous. And, it was so corporatized. Every day you have to do whatever your boss wants. Many times I told my boss that I wanted to leave and study. I said, "Sorry, I won't work here any longer." When I left a place, they would often call me on the telephone and ask me to return. But I didn't do well at school and I wasn't able to accept a corporate environment either. I think I failed to adapt because of my own individual character. I think that many people can do it, moving up in a corporation one step at a time, and they do it very well. But back then, if I wasn't happy, I would just quit work and look for another job. I did sales, insurance—insurance is no fun at all—and worked in department stores, but I thought that all of those jobs were no fun.

Yet Bi-chu had many friends who were going into business on their own, opening up art galleries, coffee shops, or clothing boutiques, and she would often "help out" in their stores. "Perhaps I was influenced by them," she said. It was just a matter of time before she decided to go into business for herself. Her first business venture was a clothing boutique, which she bought from a woman who had decided to sell off after getting pregnant. She sought out another woman as her first business partner:

> I wanted to open a store, but I didn't have any money, so it would be better if I looked for a partner. I had a friend who had come up to Taipei to open a teahouse. We looked all over Taipei in search of a place to open our shop. Since we didn't have a lot of capital, it was really difficult to find an appropriate place. At first, we couldn't find a place in Taipei, so we looked in Taoyuan, but still couldn't find a place. We even tried Taichung and Chiayi; then we came back up to Taipei again. We finally went through a friend. She sold clothes that she dyed by hand herself. She was twenty-seven years old, and had graduated from a university design department. Her business was very good and we all wore her clothes. We went to see her and told her we wanted to open a shop. She told us, "Hey, I know a place. The boss got pregnant, and had to close up shop. Go take a look!" So, I went over with my friend. That was on Tunhwa South Road in East Taipei. Originally, we had wanted to open a coffee shop or teahouse. We had never even considered selling clothes. But I thought we should give it a try. After all, we had been searching for more than a year.

She was able to start her business with the help of her parents:

> We didn't invest much. She invested NT$200,000, and I invested NT$300,000. I got NT$200,000 from a revolving credit society, and the remaining money as a loan from my parents. At first, my parents strongly opposed the idea, because they thought I shouldn't take the risk. My father suggested I become a teacher. With his support, I could go back to the countryside and become a substitute teacher or something with no problem. And

then in the summer, I could have a vacation. So, why would I want to open a store? He was also afraid that I would lose a lot of money. But he also saw that in the past, I was always changing jobs, and in the past year hardly had any employment at all. I was always just talking about looking for a storefront. So he decided to help me out.

Even then, she stressed, she was not a capitalist entrepreneur:

> My main motivation was never to become a boss. I just thought our clothes were not ordinary clothes, and we were very interested in fashion. We thought we could be models and wear pretty clothes. In fact, you could say that we were the second phase of design. We would try on the clothes, add something here or there, and then make alterations. People liked the concept. In the daytime, since a lot of our friends were in art or whatever, we would bring in designers for shows and events. Those days were a lot of fun, but we weren't very good at selling clothes, to the point where the store could really take off. We didn't earn a whole lot of money.

Like many entrepreneurs, the first store was just the beginning of a career in business. Before long, she had difficulty getting along with her partner, and decided to leave:

> Sometimes when there were no customers there, we would get into arguments over small affairs because she had her ideas, and I had mine. She was very strong in the artistic angle. It wasn't just a matter of selling clothes. We both had our own ideas of what we should do, how we should express ourselves. If she set up a display, I would tear it down the next day and put up my own. The next day, she would do the same. We were like that every day, changing back and forth. Our customers thought it was very interesting, but later we thought the store was really too small. The two of us had no way to manage that store together.

Bi-chu joined another joint venture with six investors in a combination coffee shop/clothing boutique, but then also left that job when the partners could not reach agreement on management style. "There were too many partners there," she said, "with too many ideas. So I went on strike and refused to go there." Finally, she left that store, and opened up her own boutique, what she calls a "gypsy" shop where she sold a variety of items including furniture, cloth, and clothing. At that time, she was already relishing the autonomy that entrepreneurship provided, especially in contrast to the conformist environment of the workplace. She contrasted her own individual style to that of her neighbors, stressing the imagined global aspects of her identity that made her stand out from the others:

> I am a Minnan person, but the neighbors thought that my way of seeing things was different. They would ask me where I am from. They didn't think I was Taiwanese. I said, "I'm not foreign. I'm from here." But they thought I was Japanese, or Southeast Asian, or whatever, because I didn't dress like other people. I did a lot of creative things, and I was always wearing unusual clothes. I lived in East Taipei. I would first take a taxi and then walk through the vegetable market. People always stared at me. My neighbors

thought I was acting weird. They thought that was very bad. Apparently, my customs were different. But I thought, those are other people, and I only wanted to be myself. But I never thought that it was bad. It was just what I wanted to do.

The gypsy store gave Bi-chu international experience, as she often went to Indonesia and other Southeast Asian countries on buying trips. Traveling alone in countries she had never visited, she would find suppliers and even carry back the goods without help:

I went to Jakarta, and I used a method. Even though I didn't know anyone there, I had money. I just paid someone to be my driver and my tour guide. I asked him where I could buy cloth. He drove me around in a taxi. He also wanted to earn commissions, but he took me to stores I didn't like, and they didn't sell what I wanted. So I would say "I'll come back next time," and buy nothing. But on the street, I would see a market and ask, "What is that market?" He would tell me and I would remember. Then, the second day, I didn't use him. I used my own method.

The design of that store attracted the attention of many people:

Back then, there was a group of twenty or thirty people—apparently Americans—and each one of them had a name card. I wasn't quite sure what they were doing on that street. I went over and asked what they were doing. They were doing some kind of market research on that old street, doing interviews and stuff. All of them came into my shop, and they took pictures. My English wasn't so good, maybe I didn't understand, but they also wanted to know how could there suddenly be a shop like mine. It was a completely different world from the rest of the quarter.

Her store also attracted the attention of foreign students studying Chinese in Taipei, and she started making foreign friends for the first time in her life. She remembered that first experience with internationalism with ambiguity:

I met people from many different countries and we talked. No matter if they were Jordanians, Arabians, Irish, Swedish, or whatever, they could all speak to me in Chinese since they were all studying Chinese. I could learn to understand them and make friends, but later I realized that it is hard to avoid some distance. Their social backgrounds and cultures were all different from mine. As for the locals, I made lots of friends here, especially female friends. I also expressed myself to them quite generously. Since we all had the same culture, we could be real friends.

At that point, her life changed dramatically. She fell in love with one of her male customers. Her health was deteriorating, and the city offered to buy her store so they could use the land for road construction. With the encouragement of her lover, she "rested for one and a half years."

He also ran a business, but I didn't know much about him because we only met once or twice a week. I like to have my own space and don't like to be together every day.

He also said that he was busy with work, and I always believed him. Why did I believe him? Was I so innocent? So stupid? I think that I am very naïve in many circumstances. I don't really doubt other people very much. I think that if a person can be with me and be my friend, then I will trust him completely. When I had doubts, I asked him. And when he explained, I believed him.

Her romantic dreams of marriage, however, fell apart when she discovered that her lover was already married to someone else:

At Christmas, I waited for him three days and three nights; then one of his secretaries told me he was married. . . . I couldn't believe in love anymore, I was really confused and upset. But he hoped that we could be together, because he thought that I gave him a different kind of life space. He thought that if he could be with me it would complete his life. He was doing construction engineering. He apparently liked my lifestyle very much. He worked very hard on those psychological difficulties. Even his wife and brother said he wanted to stay with me for a lifetime. He also said that, but he didn't want a divorce. Anyway, as my health got better I realized that there is no reason to continue like that. There was no hope, because he wasn't able to solve his problems.

With the end of that relationship, she went back into business for herself:

All of my friends thought I should open a store again. They said I shouldn't just wait and hope, allowing myself to live so miserably. I needed some economic activity. I needed to survive. I needed to be busy again and stand up on my own. I decided to leave and open a store again.

She once again immersed herself in her own projects. With capital from her family and a revolving credit society, she opened up a clothing boutique by herself:

Because in Taiwan, anyone can design clothes. All you have to do is draw up a sketch, use a different kind of cloth, change something here or there, then you can be a clothing designer. Because Taiwan is the kind of place where, if you think you can do something, if you can find subcontractors, and if you have a small amount of money, all you need is a place to sell your product and you can live on that.

She tried to focus on the upper range of the market, selling clothing that she designed herself. She set up a modeling runway in the store, with the idea that women could express their fantasies of being fashion models, and provided every detail from hair styling to leather accessories. The store was unsuccessful, and she became frustrated when customers did not accept her concept so readily. Many women, she said, were willing to try on clothes in the store or even buy single pieces, but rarely dared to wear the unusual items in public. Bi-chu was even more frustrated with the customers she described as *obaasan* ("old women"), saying, "Those customers would want to bargain with me over the price. In the vegetable market, maybe people are like that with customers. But I am not so easy; there is no way I can accept that. I don't want to live like that."

KANDAHAR CAFÉ:
CREATING A NEW GLOBAL LIFESTYLE

Frustrated with the clothing business, Bi-chu stopped selling clothing, and redecorated the store as a pub:

I spent NT$1,100,000. I got it from a revolving credit society and my boyfriend. He was interested in that kind of concept. He put in about one-third and I came up with the rest. I don't know why I can always solve money problems. I have never known. There is the revolving credit society. But in addition, I borrowed money from friends. I don't know why those people are willing to loan money. Maybe they also like the concept, but it is certainly not a good investment.

As Bi-chu relates the story of that enterprise, she relishes in the details of its decoration and management style. Creating her own space, it seems, has always been a meaningful part of her life. She even describes it as a way of finishing a personal project begun in a previous life:

Anyway, I just changed it into a pub. My design space was very special. I now have many customers who miss that place very much. Actually, many people miss my old stores, because each one had a different style. I like to design. From that first clothing store to this one, each shop has a different design. In that place, I used a lot of crafts. I planned and made them myself. I needed lots of mosaics in those days. In one evening, I could do a lot, and then put them on the walls. At that place, the design was very exotic, for example, things that looked Indian, Nepalese, Turkish, or maybe that had a Mediterranean look, Spanish. I designed them myself. I did it with my own hands. I don't know how I did it. Sometimes when I was painting those things, I would think that maybe I was a painter in my past life.

A spiritual affinity with the Silk Road, with Afghanistan, began to arise out of her work, even though she had never been to that part of the world:

Ever since that first clothing shop, I had always chosen the name "Socrates." But then we became a pub. Not long after I had opened the café, some friends came in. They were foreigners, and they had just come back from Kandahar. It is a place name in Afghanistan. That place . . . why did I name my shop after that place? At first, I chose that name because some of my cloth was imported from there. Afghanistan was a center of trade and a stop on the Silk Road. There were many nationalities there, and its society was very pluralistic. But their ethnic character was very fierce. I had seen the name of that place in my high-school history books, and looked it up on the map. I translated it into Chinese phonetically. That was my idea about naming my café. But I had never been to that place. I had no idea about what that place is like. Therefore, when those people came, they were very surprised. They had just come from there and they thought my café was a strange place, so they came in. It happened that I was wearing a sari. They thought that maybe I was from there, or that I had been there. They really thought that. They were surprised that I had never been there, and that I had never even seen pictures of that place. Later, they showed me materials from that place, and showed me that it is just like my pub. I can't explain how it happened that way. Maybe the best explanation is that I have been there, maybe in a past life or something. I can't explain things like that.

Bi-chu's pub, especially after she started offering dance performances, started to gain fame in Taipei. It was featured in the *China Post*, and began to attract tourists as well as local customers. On weekends, hotels or tour operators even began bringing in groups of tourists for drinks and dance performances. The management style was very similar to that of her current shop:

> That shop became a center for music and dance, world music. Because my boyfriend was always collecting material on that, I had a lot of world music and folk music. I listened to that, and then I dressed up and danced, like belly dancing. I think that's a lot of fun. I often had activities. People forced me to do that, but back then I didn't have any employees, and I didn't open until nighttime. My performances were very simple, and my mixed drinks were also very simple. Most people just drank beer, Taiwan Beer from the bottle. I didn't want to wash a lot of beer glasses. I originally wanted to do food, but there was no one to help me prepare it. And I didn't want to do things with oil and smoke. But next door, there was a noodle shop, so I told people to go next door, eat, and then come back. My way of opening a café was very simple. I always put my energy into dance, and decorated the café in very different ways [from other coffee shops]. With different kinds of cloth, I thought that was very interesting. But then the pressure on me got greater and greater. I had to be responsible for music, cloth, my dance, lights, music, and I relied only on myself.

With this café, Bi-chu incorporated the international into her own identity. She identified with imagined versions of Central Asia, imagining those places to be free of the corporatization and social conformity that she found repugnant. She even claimed to have been from Kandahar in a past life, and was remarkably successful at using this "global identity" as social capital. To this day, identification with others gives her the freedom to express herself by wearing saris and walking around Taipei barefoot. The global nature of her coffee shop also attracts a certain regular clientele, people of similar natures seeking to escape from corporate Taipei for an evening or longer, and provides her with a fairly generous income stream. Yet unlike many other Taiwanese people who, having received years of KMT education, identify modernity with the United States, she resists Americanization. She takes pride in the fact that few American customers frequented her shop:

> It's interesting that very few Americans went there. There were almost no Americans. I wondered why that was. In fact, there are a lot of Americans in Taiwan, especially at Taiwan Normal University, but they very rarely came to my shop, only one or two. There were relatively more French people, or others, from England, Africa. . . .

On the rare occasions when Americans appear in her personal narrative, it is as powerful individuals whose power makes them intimidating. She described one individual in particular:

Once, there was once an American woman who looked just like Marilyn Monroe. She had a bodyguard. I don't know what she came to Taiwan to sell, or why they brought her to my café. When they brought her over, I didn't think it was very appropriate. In my café, I often go barefoot; and I like to sit on the floor. I thought, it is so strange, people like that shouldn't appear in my space, but they kept coming. And they wanted me to perform. They wanted some kind of atmosphere. So the pressure on me was very great. I couldn't accept that. I told the *China Post* not to promote any more of my activities. I can't operate like that. So they didn't mention my café name or phone number or whatever anymore.

Gradually, the tourist business drifted elsewhere and Bi-chu's café developed a more intimate atmosphere, a place to explore Persian folk dances or Flamenco with a group of regular customers who became like friends. Soon, however, that café was forced to close. The neighbors upstairs complained about the noise, and began calling the police regularly to come and request that they stop the musical performances. Eventually, the neighbors sued her and forced her to close down on the grounds that she was operating a business without a license. She identified with that place so much that it was one of the most disappointing moments in her life:

> It seemed as though everyone had been having such a good time there. Everyone seemed like a big family. They told me their hopes, what they wanted. So when I closed down, it was the end of those emotions. So back then, my emotions also seemed to come to an end. My health was very bad. My mental state, my body, everything. I just relaxed, taking off one year. I left behind everything. I went to the place where I now live. It's in the mountains. I wondered why my café had become such a big problem. Was it because of my personality, or was it just that my fate is like that? Because I always just wanted to be myself. I never paid attention to society, or what people thought of me.

FROM THE MIDDLE EAST TO FORMOSA: BI-CHU'S RETURN TO LOCAL IDENTITY

Bi-chu's entrepreneurial dream destroyed, she swore never to go into business again. Yet, attempts to secure a job working for others consistently ended in failure, due to her own strong character and nonconformist attitudes. She described, for example, an experience working as a waitress in a restaurant:

> It was a very high-class place. I had to dress the way they wanted me to: white blouse, black skirt, high-heeled shoes, and the shoes had to be black! I did very well, and they also liked me a lot. The hours were short, and the pay was high, but I had to act in the way they demanded. There were managers, and they thought that they should control everything. I had to be so formal. There were rules about how to treat customers, how to open up a bottle of wine, whatever. When I ran my own shop, I would just pour the wine quite naturally, but at that place I had to pour it in a certain way, and with ice cubes, a wine towel, the special equipment. How crazy! I'm not like that, but I played the role quite well.

In the end, it was her own success at playing the role that led to her failure:

> Eventually, I had many special customers. People would ask when I was there, and only want to go when I was there. I would introduce wine to them since they wanted to understand wine. But since many people only wanted to be served by me, the management started to get strange ideas about me. Some of my old customers would come in, and I would sit down to talk to them while I opened up their wine bottles. Then, my boss would get upset. He would say, "This isn't a wine shop (*chiu-diam*).[1] Why do they always come looking for you?"

Bi-chu resented being treated as a "waitress." Growing excited even as she related the story, she used the English word to emphasize her dislike for the title:

> Customers would come looking for me, and he would get unhappy. He said that I had turned his place into a chiu-diam. I said, "I don't have that kind of ability. How could I turn it into a chiu-diam?" The way I dressed, the way things looked, how could he say his restaurant had become a chiu-diam? And what he paid me, how could it be a chiu-diam? I was just helping him do business. We were always having arguments. He said I wasn't a good and obedient waitress. But I told him that I originally wasn't just a *waitress*. How could he expect me to be a *waitress*? If you want a waitress, don't look to me. I am not obedient. That's not the way it works. What kind of a waitress can raise your profits from NT$400,000 to NT$800,000? I worked so hard, but I couldn't deal with him. I didn't want to change my lifestyle. I helped him manage the place, and he paid me, and it had to be on my terms. I couldn't take it and I quit.

At that time, she met another man. Due to her previous failed relationships, she only reluctantly got involved with him:

> That was when I got to know my current boyfriend, who is from the Rukai tribe.[2] He is a musician, and he helped me a lot. I didn't want to fall in love. I just saw him as a normal friend. I hadn't thought of love, and didn't want to enter into any kind of romantic relationship. I was not at all interested in it. I just thought about my past and wondered how my luck could be so bad. Since I had experienced too much, I could no longer believe in that kind of [romantic] discourse. Anyway, he stood beside me and encouraged me.

He, along with many of her other friends, encouraged Bi-chu to go back into business for herself. Accepting that only reluctantly as her *mia*, or "fate," she reopened a pub, which she also called Kandahar Café. It was, however, somewhat different from the previous incarnation. A sudden transformation from a very global to a very local identity, the opening of the new pub was, as she describes it, a homecoming:

> When I had performances, I returned to some rather indigenous Taiwanese things. In that earlier pub I had been doing world music, folk music, Indian music, Indonesian

music . . . international music. Now, when we came back here, and since my partner was aboriginal, I came back to Taiwan. Taiwan was originally an aboriginal place. Also, back in that earlier café, even though I didn't know my current boyfriend, I had some aboriginal friends. They did artistic performances. I already understood a little. But after I opened this café, I learned a lot from him and got to meet even more people. Some of my Taipei friends even needed me to do some social-movement or artistic activities. They would come to my café. And there were some Hakka events. So, I just designed it in that direction. I came back. Because back then, I was always fantasizing about things I didn't understand . . . something Turkish, or Indian, Middle Eastern, whatever. But this has to do with my own roots. So, I came back to Taiwan and began organizing aboriginal concerts. Or Hakka concerts.

DISCUSSION

The material gained from one three-hour interview with Bi-chu, not to mention a year of social interaction with her and her aboriginal boyfriend, is rich and provocative. Many themes emerge in her narrative: rural-urban migration, alienation from wage labor, family dynamics, disappointment with the ideology of romantic love, and national and ethnic identity are but a few. There is no doubt that entrepreneurship has empowered Bi-chu. In terms of relations with men, her experience reveals the promise of agency to be gained by entrepreneurship. On the one hand, entrepreneurship gave her the economic foundation she needed to reject the man who wanted to keep her as a mistress, and to escape psychological dependency on him. Economic autonomy also allowed her to enjoy the relationship with an aboriginal lover, yet refuse to marry him. She has chosen a lifestyle of creativity and nonconformist experimentation. Entrepreneurship has allowed her to experiment in relationships with men as well as with other aspects of life.

Entrepreneurship has also given Bi-chu control of her own work environment. She has been empowered in terms of capital investment, labor allocation, design, artistic content, and performance. From the very first business she opened, she has used entrepreneurship to avoid the "corporate" environment she finds stifling, to create her own lifestyle, and to construct a personal identity. Interestingly, she herself finds the greatest pleasure in empowerment at the level of personal identity. Her constant attempts to forge a new and unique identity for herself reveal an awareness of the dangers implicit in social identities gained through relationships with men. She takes pride in her ability to do things on her own, whether that be finding her way through the streets of Jakarta, moving furniture, painting, or learning to belly dance.

For Bi-chu, entrepreneurship is not merely a way of making money. It is a total lifestyle, and a means of self-realization. In each business she has owned, she has expressed herself through interior design in a way she finds meaningful: a "gypsy" store, a clothing store with a runway for make-believe fashion models, and a pub called Kandahar Café. In the first incarnation of that store, she played with Middle Eastern themes, identifying with Afghanistan and even evoking the possibility that she may have lived there in a past life. The freedom she sought in that theme had nothing to do with the lived realities of women in Afghanistan, but that is not the point. What is important is that identification with the foreign permits her to play with the gendered expectations of her own environment and becomes a tool of agency in her hands.

Bi-chu's nonconformist attitude towards life is embodied as well in the way she adorns her body. She takes great pride in dressing differently than other Taiwanese women, appearing in her own narratives and in real life dressed in a sari or belly-dancer's outfit, and more often than not, barefoot. This most basic level of empowerment may seem trivial to some, but it fills her life with meaning, becoming a life project in much the sense meant by Sartre. She would experience far less power at this level if she worked in a corporation, and she is well aware of that fact. It is for that reason that she contrasts her own lifestyle so clearly with those people who go to work every day. Her life is a basic form of resistance against a society that would imprint itself on every detail of her environment and her own body. Her attitudes towards America, moreover, indicate a resistance against an American-centered vision of modernity and globalization.

Bi-chu also uses entrepreneurship to forge an ethnic identity very different from the more common division between Native Taiwanese and Mainlanders. For years, she embraced instead an individual identity based on an imagined Afghanistan. That belief in reincarnation allowed her to transcend nationality by declaring it temporary and ephemeral. It is clearly a rejection of the sinicization attempts of the KMT educational system. By the end of the narrative, as Taiwan began a collective search for a new non-Chinese identity, she had abandoned that strategy and began to identify strongly with Taiwan. In a more universal approach to Taiwan, however, she refused to accept the Native Taiwanese ethnic nationalism seen in some factions of the DPP and in many Native Taiwanese individuals like Chhoa Hiong-gun. Instead, she embraced an identity with Formosa and its Austronesian heritage.

Kandahar Café has become more than the stage on which Bi-chu enacts her own identity, however. Through the performances she sponsors, she also provides room for musicians and music fans to work through those questions of identity on their own. She has been so successful in promoting aboriginal culture and attracting aboriginal customers that her café is even identified by aboriginal activists as a gathering place for aboriginal people (Shanhai Wenhua Zazhi 1999). Like Taiwan, she lives on the margins between the global and the local. Entrepreneurship has given her the creative space to forge that new identity.

NOTES

1. This is a reference to the "flower-drinking" establishments where men go to drink in the company of women.

2. Rukai is an indigenous tribe from mountainous areas of Pingtung, Taitung, and Kaohsiung Counties.

Chapter Twelve

A Fashion Designer

Sophie Hong's workshop in the shaded alleys behind Taipei's mosque is a carefully crafted atmosphere. Large open windows reveal the brick walls and trees outside. Inside are intricately crafted pieces of furniture, almost baroque with their decorations carved in metal. The walls are adorned with silk clothing, designed in styles to recall *qipao* and Sun Yat-sen uniforms. The walls are painted a velvet-like red; and modern paintings hang above the clothing exhibits. Near the door are racks of postcards for sale; among them are portraits of Sophie herself.

The most distinctive characteristic of Sophie Hong's clothing is her creative use of texture and color. She specializes in lacquered silk, a technique that dates back to the Ming Dynasty. The texture varies greatly from piece to piece. Some are smooth and sensual like oiled skin. Other pieces are stiff like rough paper or even denim. And others have both the texture and appearance of snakeskin. All of her clothes are in somber colors of black, brown, deep red, and pine green. For both men and women, the clothes are loose-fitting and elegantly layered. They are designed to cover up the skin, self-consciously, like the Confucian scholars of previous centuries. In addition to fashion design for retail sales, Sophie Hong has also done costumes in traditional Chinese style, including uniforms for the National Palace Museum and for lay disciples of Fokuangshan, a popular Buddhist center in Taiwan. She has also designed costumes for a Taiwanese production of *Madame Butterfly*.

Looking around her studio on my first visit, I said, "It's like a museum." In a characteristic mixture of Chinese and French, she replied:

This place, *n'est pas seulement pour acheter les vêtements*.[1] People come in to enjoy this space. It is very small, but it has its own atmosphere. In the past, I had another studio on Chunghsiao East Road. It was twice the size of this studio. It was an exhibition space. I let young designers exhibit there, and I also sold my own products. That is what I hope to do here. People can come here and have meetings, a lot of workers (*gongren*) together. I always keep the hope that someday this will become a museum of design.

At forty-four, Sophie is herself a work of art; her clothing, hairstyle, and the first wrinkles appearing on her face come together in a harmony that makes her one of the most elegant women I have met in Taipei. Her playful approach to life, revealed in her clothing and furniture design, as well as in her personal appearance, shows up again in the way she crafts personal identity. I asked her how she identifies herself ethnically.

"A Hsin-chu person," she said. "I am from Hsin-chu, Taiwan, but my paternal ancestors probably came over from Fujian. I am a Hsin-chu person, from Hsin-chu City."

Sophie's life narrative reaches back into early childhood, and even the life histories of her parents, to trace a development from her past to the future. Her father was a pharmacist, trained in the Health Department during the Japanese occupation. That family background in itself has probably shaped her national identity, as Japanese-trained medical professionals in Taiwan have long been at the forefront of a new Taiwanese identity (Chen 1998, Lo and Robertson 2002). Yet with characteristic humor, Sophie emphasized more the influence it has had on her choice of occupation:

> I wanted to be a doctor. But in a way, I'm doing the same thing because I have to use scissors to cut cloth. Both occupations are the same because they require the use of a knife. I wanted to be a doctor and save people. But I also liked artistic creation. By doing clothing design, I can take care of both at the same time.

Her family background had long exposed her to both business and artistic careers:

> I had an uncle. He was a retired teacher and went into business breeding dogs. My other uncle, my cousins, they are all in business and have their own factories. A few [of my relatives] were in the arts. My older sister is a painter. She lives in Brazil.

Yet she claimed it was above all her illustrious neighbor, Lee Yuan-tze's father,[2] who influenced her the most:

> He was a Hsin-chu person. I am also a Hsin-chu person. When I was small, he lived next to the Hsin-chu Movie Theatre. I didn't know him, but his father was a painter. I used to walk by there, and I would stop to watch him paint. It was a lot of fun. Then starting in grade school, my school sent me to participate in every painting contest. So from a very young age, I had those kinds of opportunities.

Childhood experiences, as well, explain why she chose a career in clothing design:

> I have liked to wear pretty clothes ever since I was a small child. My sisters were ten and twelve years older than I was. They liked to dress me up like a doll. My mother would have clothes tailored for me, and take me outside for others to see. So I was used to that from childhood. Later on, I realized that art and clothes are closely related, so I mixed them together.

Sophie began her career by studying fashion design at Taipei's Shih Chien University College of Design, known as Taiwan's best design school. After graduation, she continued her studies in New York, Tokyo, and Paris, including two years of internships with Christian Dior and Chanel. She has done exhibits in Taiwan, Japan, France, Italy, Germany, and the United States; and her creations have even been collected by the Parisian *Musée de la Mode et du Costume*. Her design goes beyond clothing to furniture and includes exhibits such as the 1985 "Art Body Design" and the 1991 "Moving Images of Clothes and Metal." The "Sophie Hong World Network" includes her workshop in Taipei, an office in Paris, and affiliated boutiques on three continents. In both artistic media and national space, Sophie is a border-crossing itinerant. "I think it is important to keep moving forward towards my goal," she said. "It's not just in Taiwan, but goes beyond that. I think that's very important." The global potential of this rising designer can be seen in the fact that she has frequent shows in Paris and New York as well as in Taipei and Hong Kong.

SOPHIE'S PRESENT AS A FUNDAMENTAL PROJECT OF GLOBALITY

Sophie's career has been very much a "fundamental project" in the sense meant by Sartre. As a Francophone by choice, she even used those words in the language of Sartre to describe a project of education and foreign work experience. She said, "After I finished school, I have never stopped doing clothing design. I just keep going towards the goal ahead of me. I think that is very good. I haven't just been in Taiwan, but have climbed out of that. I think that's very important."

The defining experience of her early career was the two years she spent in France:

> It let me learn how people live there. Since Taiwan is a beautiful island where all seasons are spring, there is no particular winter, spring, or fall season. So I had to learn to understand how climate influences clothing. The biggest difference is climate. Taiwan doesn't have such cold weather. I could only understand that by really living there for some time. It was important for me to learn how to design clothes for a cold winter climate. Of course, I also studied a lot of other professional knowledge. That time was very important to me.

By emphasizing climatic rather than cultural differences, Sophie presents herself as a global person capable of living anywhere. Living in Paris gave her the chance to become part of a global network of fashion designers. Her internships there, she said,

> gave me the confidence to do things differently than other people. Also, it is important to strengthen one's personal networks. That is more important than anything else. In setting up personal relations, I had to realize that my works are a different thing over there. I was really brave to go there and exhibit.

She emphasized that she is part of the global fashion scene. Designers in Paris, she says, are "very good friends" and "I became a part of that." In the process of working with those people, she said:

> I have become a global person. I am not a person who has just gone over from Taiwan to travel and then come back. That's not the way it is. When I am in New York or wherever, I often think that I am just one of the local people. It is very easy for me to get accustomed to a new environment. Language is very important.

Sophie embodies a cosmopolitan spirit in which ascriptive identities of nationality and ethnicity play lesser roles than individual abilities to adapt to new circumstances and enjoy the diversity of human experience. Anyone, it seems, can become a global person and adjust to life in any city:

> The Taiwanese environment might be different from that of other countries. Let's take architecture, for example. At the beginning, newcomers to Taiwan might think that the architecture is just chaos. But eventually, they will begin to realize that it also has its beautiful places. Gradually, they will begin to like it here. Since every place has its own special character, you have to find a way to like it. Only then can one become capable of settling down there. But a lot of people aren't like that. They should improve their own attitudes, and then they can live more comfortably here.

Sophie herself appreciates most in Taiwan its free-wheeling business atmosphere: "Taiwan is a gentle, yet lively place. You can do anything you want in Taiwan, since it is so free. That is Taiwan's most valuable asset. Everyone can be a boss! As long as you are brave enough to do it, you can start up on your own."

For Sophie's career choice, a lifestyle as boss has meant living in Taipei, but frequently exhibiting her designs abroad and trying to reform the institutions of fashion marketing in Taiwan. In terms of production, she does things no differently than other companies in an economy of satellite subcontractors that make Taiwan an island of bosses (Shieh 1992):

> I have about a dozen full-time employees. But in Taiwan, satellite subcontractors are very important. Our former vice president Hsieh Tung-min talked about "living rooms as factories" [cf. Hsiung 1996, Ka 1993]. So, a lot of people have been trained in textile production. Those skilled people who worked in textile factories when they were young now need some work to do at home.[3] That's all here in our domestic economic institutions. High-quality production isn't something that comes from mass production. The workers need experience and technical expertise to do that. And they have it. A lot of famous foreign name brands make their clothing in Taiwan.

In terms of marketing, Sophie started out in business like most other Taiwanese clothing designers:

> I didn't decide to go into business. I just did it naturally. Twenty years ago, it was very easy to start a business, just like it is for young people today. With just a little bit of

money, they can work together with classmates, make some clothes, and then sell them on consignment. They can start a business that way. I also started that way. I got my initial capital from my father and from revolving credit associations. I made clothes and sold them in department stores. I made a lot of money that way until I could open my own store. In the past few years, I have been focusing my attention on the international market.

Sophie emphasized that the most important step was leaving the department store consignment system, which strikes her as onerous:

> In a department store, I have to follow along with a lot of special activities, like discounts. If my sales are low, they'll ask me to take down my stand. And the saleswomen are hard to manage. Doing business like that raises overhead. Overseas, they use a buyer system. The buyer takes the risk. If I am a good buyer, I can see the trends. I buy and then I sell, so I can make a profit. I think the whole system should be like overseas. I do a show; the buyer sees it and places orders for the season. Then, I can plan everything in advance—production, buying cloth—and then sell according to a plan. I prefer to do things that way.

After having attained a degree of success on the global market, she has been able to leave the department store networks used by other Taiwanese designers and produce in the way she desires. She maintains her own store in Taipei, has sales offices abroad, and does business through buyers she meets at international fashion shows. She describes it as an ambitious capitalist project:

> I am absolutely commercial! Of course I do business because I want to earn a profit. At the same time, I insist on very high quality. I want my clothing design to have a distinct style. And in the end I want a high profit. I plan out all of my work with that goal in mind. That is my fundamental project.

FAMILY RELATIONS

Sophie's fast-moving career has given her a different relationship to her family from that of many other Taiwanese women. Unmarried, she draws attention first to her natal family:

> In fact, my father doesn't even understand well what I do. He just knows that I make clothes. Every time I see him, he tells me to take good care of my employees. He says that making clothes also means taking care of people. He doesn't know that I have been so successful abroad, or that I am famous. He doesn't know that I have continued to design clothes in France. I have been doing it so fast. I just keep working no matter what, and then I see my family when I am in Taipei.

Sophie also identifies with her brothers and sisters, even though their relations are sometimes strained. Notably, she is not the only member of her family involved in clothing manufacturing:

I have four brothers and two sisters. All families had a lot of children back then. I was the youngest girl, and the fifth child. Two of my brothers are also in the textile business, but we don't get along so well. Still, I wish them well and we help each other out when needed.

Like Chhoa Hiong-gun (Chapter 9), Sophie has decided not to marry and finds that a single lifestyle is suitable for a woman entrepreneur:

If you want to make a career, you have to spend a lot of time on your business. It is important to work hard on that. I have already found a good partner, and we help each other out. That is already very good. I think we can live well like that.

Yet, unlike many other women, she reports that she has never felt pressure from her parents to marry:

My father has never asked me if I intend to marry, at least not until now. And my mother passed away a long time ago. In the past, I had boyfriends and she never liked any of them. So, they have never asked me to marry. They worry about my elder brother not having children, but they don't worry about me not getting married. They think I can take care of myself quite well.[4]

SOPHIE'S FUTURE:
TAKING TAIWAN TO THE WORLD

Sophie's single marital status has given her the freedom to construct a strong identity outside of marital relations, yet she has done more than just work on her own career. Her fashion design is a way of reflecting on questions of identity. Sophie has a strong sense of Taiwanese consciousness, embraces a Taiwanese identity, and seeks to make Taiwan known to the world. As for her future career development, she hopes for increased support from the Taiwanese government:

In order for very famous name brands to sell all over the world, they need a strong economic base. I don't have that. That is what I lack the most. It would be good for me if the government were to support me by sending me abroad to do exhibitions. I think I am a special case, because Taiwan has never had a brand name like Sophie Hong before.

Arguing that she would not be the only beneficiary of state support, she said:

"Sophie Hong comes from Taiwan and is a leader of the Taiwanese textile industry." At first glance, it seems as if only I would benefit from that. But it would be a good opportunity to promote the entire Taiwanese fashion industry. Taiwan is now very strong in computers and electronic goods, but the government has done very little to promote other industries. Someone should work on that problem. I have always thought of fashion as a kind of soft people-to-people diplomacy. When I have a fashion debut, it gives foreign guests a chance to see that Taiwan produces good things.

Even without government support, Sophie has worked hard to make that idea a reality. In the past two years, she has become increasingly well known throughout the world, leaving Taiwan nearly every month to display her products at international fashion shows:

> My ideal is to let everyone get to know Taiwan. I promote Taiwan with my clothes. I sell my clothes in nearly every country of the world except Africa. When we did a men's fashion show in Paris, they hung up a great big Taiwanese flag with all twenty other participating countries.[5] I think that is a very great thing.

Fashion shows, it seems, are an effective way of promoting Taiwan in people-to-people diplomacy. She said, "They hang up the Taiwanese national flag along with the Chinese communist flag. When I go to those shows, nobody objects when I hang up the Taiwanese national flag." Sophie's identity thus fluctuates between her membership in a global industry and her proud national citizenship in Taiwan.

In order to illustrate to me her international success, Sophie showed me a photo album filled with articles about her that have appeared in a number of magazines including *Elle*, *Marie Claire*, and even *Playboy*. She pulled several articles with titles such as "La tradition Taïwanaise," "Taiwanaise Sophie Hong," and "Twenty Years of Taiwanese Design." She pointed out one article in Japanese with the headline, "She is not just a fashion designer; she is an artist." Knowing that she identifies as Taiwanese more than Chinese, I read out loud one headline, "Chic, c'est Chinois." She sighed sadly and said, "There's nothing I can do about that."

DISCUSSION

Sophie Hong is a clear example of a Taiwanese woman who has been empowered by entrepreneurship. With an ambitious career and a strong will to avoid marriage, she is very different from the Taiwanese women in Susan Greenhalgh's essay, where "women's fates were tied to their families of marriage" (1994: 759). Women such as Sophie are crafters of their own identities, and an autonomous career is often part of that identity. Having chosen an international career in fashion design, Sophie has become a "cosmopolitan" person (Giddens 1991: 190) at home in many contexts. She stresses that she is part of the world of those global fashion designers, and that she feels at home in all major fashion cities of the world. She thus uses her work project to claim citizenship in a global civil society. Entrepreneurship, a successful global career—as well as a single lifestyle—have empowered her to focus on identity by occupation and by nationality rather than on the social and cultural restraints of gender.[6]

Sophie resembles most other Taiwanese people in that national identity is a major question in her life, yet she thinks about the problem in a different way from most. As could be seen in previous narratives, Taiwanese people are often concerned with the domestic division between Native Taiwanese and Mainlander identities. Of all the people I interviewed, Chhoa Hiong-gun is the staunchest ethnic nationalist, and her ideas are not uncommon. She emphasizes constantly her Native Taiwanese identity and what she perceives as the moral supremacy of Native Taiwanese over Mainlanders. Coffee-shop owner Ma Ya-hung (Chapter 7) has a strongly contrasting perspective on ethnic relations. She proudly asserts a "Shanghai" identity and even blames her husband's infidelity on contact with Native Taiwanese businessmen who took him flower drinking. Both of them base their ethnic identity on affiliation with a postwar ethnic group in Taiwan.

Once they enter the public sphere, these ethnic identities can be even more difficult for women entrepreneurs to manage and negotiate than gender identities. Mainlanders have had an especially difficult time with the erosion of Mainlander power and slow rise of a Native Taiwanese middle class in the past two decades. Some of the women in this book have thus tried to construct new forms of social identity. Mainlander Wang Li-ling (Chapter 10), for example, downplays her Mainlander identity and refers instead to the universal humanity of Buddhism. Yet even Native Taiwanese people often tire of ethnic conflicts and seek social harmony, since they have to do business with people of all ethnic backgrounds. Native Taiwanese Ng Bi-chu (Chapter 11) rejected Chinese social identities altogether, first identifying with an imagined foreign past life and then identifying with rural Taiwan primarily through aboriginal music. Such individuals are beginning to look beyond the old Native Taiwanese versus Mainlander bifurcation that has characterized social resistance, election campaigns, and private conversations since 1947.

National identity is nonetheless an important part of Sophie's identity, strikingly visible when she asserts a Taiwanese identity in international forums such as fashion shows. Sophie, however, refuses the older ethnic identities so hotly contested in Taiwan. Resisting that discourse, she initially refused to answer whether she was a Mainlander or a Native Taiwanese. Instead, she identified herself very locally as a "Hsin-chu person," identifying herself by place rather than ethnicity.

Place is very important to Sophie, as she holds a different identity contrast in mind. Accustomed to carrying a "Republic of China" passport and explaining her origins in global contexts, she focuses instead on her identity as *Taiwanese* rather than *Chinese*, meaning a citizen of Taiwan rather than a citizen of the People's Republic of China. That is why she refers to the ROC national flag as the "Taiwanese" flag, and is proud when the international press refers to her as part of Taiwanese tradition. She is disappointed only when the press refers to her as Chinese, a national identity she limits to citizens of the People's Republic of China.

Sophie's national identity is a new identity in Taiwan, because it is based on civic rather than ethnic nationalism. As documented and analyzed by Taiwanese sociologist Horng-luen Wang (2000), this new Taiwanese nationalism is a result of globalization and transnationalism, as international Taiwanese individuals seek the same kind of social recognition enjoyed by citizens of other nation-states.

With increasing globalization and the suppression of Taiwanese state activities in the international arena by China, this kind of identity is likely to become more common. On the domestic front in Taiwan, that may lead to eventual reconciliation between Native Taiwanese and Mainlanders. At the same time, however, other forms of identity are becoming more contentious. Chief among those identities are those of aboriginal people.

NOTES

1. This place is not just for buying clothes.

2. Lee Yuan-tze is Taiwan's only Nobel Prize–winning scientist and the president of Academia Sinica. Due to his political activities, he is known by virtually all Taiwanese people (see Chapter 1).

3. This refers to the young unmarried women workers who worked in the textile and other labor-intensive factories in the 1960s to 1970s. After marriage and childbirth, many of them started working in smaller subcontracting firms instead (Hsiung 1996).

4. These are common patterns. Sons are pressured to marry in order to ensure continuity of the family line. Daughters are encouraged to marry in order that another family will "take care" of them.

5. She is referring to the flag of the Republic of China, which to her is "Taiwanese."

6. Kondo (1997) argues that Japanese designers are marginalized in the global fashion industry. I think, however, that designers such as Yohji Yamamoto and Comme des Garçons have already proved themselves. Sophie Hong shows that Taiwanese designers have the ability to compete in a global market as well, albeit on a smaller scale. For more on transnational identity, see also Ong (1999).

Chapter Thirteen

A Breakfast Café

Shortly after I moved to Taipei in 1999, I became a regular weekend customer at the Sunrise Café, a breakfast restaurant in the upscale Eastern District of the city. The unique juxtaposition of Coca-Cola advertisements, large framed photos of aboriginal people on Orchid Island, and a large wooden canoe hanging from the wall initially drew my attention to the place. The menu was also attractive: scrambled eggs and bagels, pancakes smothered with maple syrup, and even a Tex-Mex breakfast burrito offered me a taste of home whenever the craving hit. And, perhaps useful to my study, the owner was a cheerful aboriginal woman from Orchid Island named Margang. I was so intrigued by the mixture of the global and the very local that I returned again and again, making it a favorite gathering place to meet friends. Margang's life history turned out to be equally intriguing, partly because she could give me another perspective on the ethnic division of labor that I had been learning about from other women entrepreneurs.

A BRIEF INTRODUCTION TO
TAIWANESE INDIGENOUS PEOPLES

In addition to Chinese ethnic groups, Taiwan also has a population of around 400,000 Austronesians whose ancestors were present on the island for thousands of years before Chinese colonialism. These indigenous Formosan ethnic groups include at least the officially recognized Tayal, Saisiat, Amis, Bunun, Tsou, Rukai, Puyuma, Paiwan, Ta'u,[1] and Sao tribes, although other groups are still seeking state recognition (see Allio 1998 and Stainton 1999 for research in English on Taiwanese indigenous movement). Members of these tribes live primarily on the east coast of Taiwan and in the central mountain regions. In addition, the *pingpu zu* (plains tribes) of the west coast have long intermarried with Chinese people and become assimilated into Chinese society. A large percentage of the "Han Chinese" in Taiwan thus consists of what would be considered *mestizos* in North America. Margang's home community of 3,000 Ta'u people on Orchid Island, sixty-two kilometers off the southeast coast of Taiwan, has been one of the most marginalized aboriginal communities in Taiwan (Arrigo 2002). During the Japanese period, when it was first administered as part of Taiwan, the Japanese intentionally kept the island in isolation as an anthropological museum. The Ta'u were thus largely undisturbed until control of their island passed to the ROC in 1945. Even then, the Taiwanese military kept the island off-limits to visitors from Taiwan until 1967 when tourism was first permitted.

In 1982, the Taiwan Power Company, without the consent of local people, began shipping nuclear waste from mainland Taiwan to Orchid Island. In the period from 1982 to 1996, when Ta'u protests finally stopped the shipment of nuclear waste, over 100,000 barrels of radioactive waste were buried on their island. Ta'u activists claim that the storage facility leaks radioactive materials into the soil, and that contaminated earth and water have been dumped into the sea, to be consumed by fish and then later by Ta'u people during the flying fish season every summer. Although the Taiwan Power Company and the Taiwanese government deny a connection, more than fifty children have been born on Orchid Island with birth defects, and cancer touches nearly every family on the island. Especially since tourism has not yet taken off on Orchid Island, it has remained an economic backwater in Taiwan. It is no surprise, therefore, that many young people migrate to Taiwan in search of work. Margang is part of a generation of Orchid Island people who have sought better lives in mainland Taiwan.

CHILDHOOD MEMORIES:
SITUATING AN IDENTITY OFFSHORE

Margang began her life narrative with childhood memories of Orchid Island:

> I lived on Orchid Island. I was like all the other kids. After school, we went to catch frogs, and we went swimming. We stole things from other people, like fruit. There was nothing special. Playing was playing. Swimming was swimming. Nothing special. We weren't like Taiwanese children, who play electronic games and watch television. Since we didn't have a television when I was young, we naturally went out and played outside, like going to the seaside and climbing in the mountains.

Margang finds in childhood experience the roots of what would later become her entrepreneurial drive:

> In one way I was different from the others. Ever since I was a little girl, I have liked to go out and earn money. From the time I was twelve years old, I helped people do laundry. I took in laundry and earned NT$200 a month. That made me very happy. I

would use that NT$200 to buy things for my mother, those people in my own family. That was one of my life habits when I was young.

When I asked if she had been influenced by other entrepreneurial relatives, she said at first that none of them had yet opened businesses. However:

recently some of them have. They have opened up general stores on Orchid Island. And my maternal cousin has opened up the representative office of a women's organization. Other than them, none of my friends or relatives are special.

Margang described the work lives of men and women in her home community:

Men go out and catch fish. Women wait at home and help their husbands when they come back from sea. They cook, wash clothes, those things. Women never went with the men to sea to catch flying fish. Never. Women stay at home and plant crops.

A Ta'u man may have described childhood as a process of learning how to fish, go out to sea, and catch flying fish. As a woman, however, Margang was restricted by tribal taboos from participating in such activities:

Sometimes father and mother farm together. Children don't have anything to do at home, so they go with their parents. But they don't help out by pulling weeds or something. They just play nearby. That's the way it was. When I was little, I lived with my grandmother (*a-ma*). I liked to go up to the mountain with my grandmother, so I was rarely with my mother. We had many children, and our ages were all close together, like maybe two years apart only. But my mother didn't take care of the relatively older ones. She only took care of one or two little ones. Once we were old enough to walk, she gave us to my *a-Kong* and *a-ma* to raise.

Margang credits her grandparents with teaching her a work ethic:

Back then, people of Orchid Island were very traditional. My grandparents had a very traditional thought. They thought that one day they would marry me out, so they couldn't have people think I was lazy, the kind of person who gets up only when the sun rises. So, they would wake me up at four o'clock in the morning saying "Get up, little ghost. Go get water." I would go down to the seashore and get water to bring in for cooking and other things. When I lived with my grandparents, I got up very early. I got up around four o'clock to go to the seashore. That is the kind of work I did.

When I expressed surprise that she was collecting water from the shore, she explained that she gathered freshwater from a well near the shore and saltwater from the ocean:

When Yamei people cook, they use half saltwater and half freshwater. That way you don't need to use salt. Of course, we don't directly use seawater. We mix them. Even when my grandparents cooked white rice, they would add a little bit of seawater. It was salty. That is because we were poor and didn't always have food to eat. But if you added a bit of salty water, the rice would taste better. That rice was given to us by World Vision. We couldn't grow rice on Orchid Island. In the past, we couldn't afford rice. We ate yams and potatoes.

THE LURE OF MONEY: FINDING
A PLACE IN THE CAPITALIST ECONOMY

As soon as she reached the age of fifteen, Margang moved to Taiwan in order to look for a better livelihood: "I went to Taichung because my older brother and sister were there. I had lots of relatives and friends there. That made it easier to find work. We could work together and take care of each other." She finished junior high school in Taichung. Along with many other aboriginal people, she subsequently found work in the subcontracting workshops of Taichung County that made sports shoes for the international market.[2] In very much of a Marxist trope, she described the alienation she felt in her job:

I worked in a factory making shoes. But that kind of work doesn't do much for the brain. It is always repeating the same movements. Stupid! I made shoes for two years. Then I did automobiles. But I didn't think it was very meaningful to always do the same work. And I was young. I didn't think that was enough because I liked studying English ever since junior high school. My classmates always teased me and said I should marry a foreigner or something. Everyone found that interesting. I liked music and dance. And I liked to improve my English. When we worked, sometimes we didn't eat lunch. We went to the dormitory and listened to music instead. I liked that. Then, when I was eighteen or nineteen years old, I thought that that life was not enough. I decided to see what I could do in Taipei.

As "fate" would have it, Margang found an American friend who helped her move to Taipei. She met him through a charitable foundation for aboriginal children with cancer, at a time when her own cousin was fighting off the disease:

I had an American friend. He owned a chain of language schools. At that time, his school was very famous and had lots of money. So, he helped a lot of aboriginal children. Some of his teachers donated all of their salaries to aboriginal children with cancer. My cousin was one of those children, and she went up to Taipei for treatment. She was only one year younger than me. I went with her to Taipei, stayed with her, and then met that American. I always thought I didn't want to work in a factory because it is so boring. So, I telephoned him and said I wanted to move to Taipei and study English. He was very kind, and said I could live with him. He said he had a lot of empty rooms. He wasn't married and he didn't have any children. Since he was so warmhearted, I was very happy. I couldn't concentrate on my work anymore. I was only thinking about going to Taipei and studying English.

Determined to move to Taipei, Margang studied for the high school entrance exams after work hours and finally took the test. Although she was confident that she had performed well, she never received the test results. Finally, at the age of twenty, she quit her job and moved to Taipei anyway:

> I told the *laobanniang* that I was only going to work until the end of the month and then quit, since I had taken the test for high school but had never received the test results. I always suspected that she had stolen the test results. Because when I had told her I wanted to take the test for high school and go to school, she had said "that won't do." She didn't permit me to do that because I always worked so fast that I could do the work of more than one person and save her money. She didn't want me to leave and go to evening school classes. Finally, I just took my NT$6,000 and went to Taipei.

She moved in with the forty-year-old American man. With his help, she was able to pass the exam and attend high school, supporting herself with only part-time jobs:

> In the first week, I didn't find work. I lived in that American's house. He helped me a lot. In that time, I thought that without money, there was no way I could go to high school. I was happy to just learn some English. In that week, I didn't have work, so I just stayed at his place and learned English. Sometimes, I went outside and looked for work. But in the end, one of my former workmates was very kind to me. She introduced me to a job in a *buxiban* ("cram school"). So I had even more contact with English. Sometimes that American would give me pocket money. But I was embarrassed. So at that time, I was very frugal. That was when I was at my thinnest. I wasn't fat like now! I weighed only forty-eight kilograms because I only ate lunch. I didn't have enough money to eat breakfast. I could eat for only NT$20.

Margang refused her American friend's offer to pay for part of her high school tuition:

> He said that didn't matter; he would pay for half of my tuition. Even though I agreed to live with him, I insisted on earning the money for my tuition. He was already very generous to let me live there without asking for any rent. So I could relax, earn my tuition, and then I successfully finished high school.

While living with him, Margang improved her English and learned how to cook American food. She finished high school at the age of twenty-two, and then started working in the restaurant business. Using the common Taiwanese trope of labor as "helping out," she described how she eventually went into the restaurant business through part-time jobs during high school:

> I started out by helping other people in their restaurants, which I started when I was twenty. When I was twenty-two, I already knew that I wanted to open my own restaurant. So I helped out other people for five years. I studied everything that I would need to know and wrote it down, things like menus and stuff.

By that time, Margang had lost her American patron, as well:

> He was also pitiable. At first, the other boss was in the military and left the American in charge of everything. But after the other boss finished military service, he got married. He and his wife saw that the company was doing so well that they thought of a way to get it completely into their own hands. They took the American to court and sued him in a process that took ten years. He had written all of the textbooks used in that *buxiban*. He not only lost the case; he lost everything. He also spent a lot of money on legal fees. He never managed to set up a new career, and was so sad that he left Taiwan. He went to the mainland [China]. Ever since then, he has been in the mainland. But he is still very concerned about us. Every time there is a holiday, or when he has some extra money, he sends a present over to us for Christmas or something. It is a good thing I knew him, as that made it possible for me to be here today. I am here today because of the way he helped me.

PROBLEMS OF STARTING OUT IN BUSINESS

Margang's first restaurant was a joint partnership with two Taiwanese. As the first person in her family to go into business, she had to face a long learning curve of experience. The first problem was with her partners:

> We three people opened a restaurant together. One of them didn't like to speak very much, and he had had a job delivering bread. I always thought he was a good person, but I didn't know he liked to gamble and drink alcohol. The other problem was his friend. She hadn't invested a single cent.

Like many Taiwanese entrepreneurs, Margang used the concept of destiny (*yuanfen*) to explain how she ended up in her first business. Not at all an easy destiny, it taught her her first lessons in the difficulties of raising capital:

> I didn't have money either at the age of twenty-five when I opened the restaurant, because I had had no time for psychological preparation. I didn't think that person would ask me to join them. That is destiny (*yuanfen*). He said, "Do you want to open a restaurant with me?" I said, "OK, but I don't have money." What could I do? Each person needed to invest NT$300,000 to open up a restaurant. I borrowed NT$100,000 [for the first part of my investment] from my older sister. But it still wasn't enough because that guy was weird. When you invest, you should put in all of the money you said you would. But he didn't do it. I kept asking him about money. And then, he said that his mother hadn't sent the money over yet, because he also came from an outer island. He was from Penghu Island.

> There were a lot of things that we couldn't do because we only had that NT$100,000. How could we buy the things we needed for a restaurant? Right? I used all of my money to buy tables, chairs, an oven, gas stove, etc., and then we had no money. Every

day, when I saw that not even one person came in to eat our things, I got even more nervous. He was working outside, but I didn't have any wages. I couldn't take wages, since we didn't have any customers. And we had to pay the rent every month.

Her initial investment of NT$100,000 was quickly spent buying equipment for the restaurant. When her partner finally came up with the initial NT$200,000 of his contribution, she used that for cash flow, rent, and food purchases, yet still did not have enough to draw a salary. Fortunately, however, she was able to get by personally by drawing on her resources in the urban aboriginal community. Friends in church helped her meet personal expenses as she worked in the restaurant without pay:

I knew people in church. They trusted me a lot. They said, "It doesn't matter. You can pay us when you have money. Take it first, and pay it back when you get money." They were like that. So, I kept taking money from them. Fortunately, I could eat here without paying money. So, I didn't have pocket money or wages, but at least I could eat. At that time, I was like that.

Unlike many Taiwanese entrepreneurs, who grow up in families where they can learn by observing others, Margang had to learn through trial and error. Her partner, whom she felt had contributed much less to the restaurant than herself, gave her additional pressure:

What I hated about him, whatever happened, every day he would come and ask how many customers we had. I thought that was such a bother, because I was already upset that there were no customers there. I asked my younger brother and nieces to help me distribute flyers on the street. I had a special. Now we have those specials for NT$200. Back then I sold them for only NT$50. I was losing money on it. But people thought it was too cheap and thus wouldn't taste good. They didn't dare come in. So I distributed flyers. Then, maybe in a day we would have ten customers. But the price was too low, and there was no way I could cover my basic expenses.

As often happens in small-business partnerships, the relationship between Margang and her partner deteriorated due to different ideas on how to run the business:

He suggested we do a Chinese buffet instead of Western food. But I had studied Western cuisine and didn't know how to do Chinese food. Of course I could do simple things. But there was no way I could cook so much Chinese food for a buffet. He had such simple ideas. So, I hated him. Every time he came at noon and he would say things like "The workers from Fridays [the American chain T.G.I.F.] need lunch boxes to eat. We can make lunch boxes for them." He knew those people because he also delivered bread to their restaurant. But I said that our stove wasn't big enough to take on such large quantities. I said I am happy when I get customers to come in and eat my Western food. I insisted on doing what I wanted to do.

As a Ta'u woman, Chinese food was almost as foreign to her as Western food, and would have entailed an investment in learning a new way of cooking. Sticking with Western food was thus for her the most rational decision. Eventually, however, the partnership ended due to that disagreement:

> He came back the next day. He was angry. He said, "Margang, if I ask you to leave, would you leave and never come back to this restaurant?" I said, "Yes, I would leave." Then he said, "If I am the one who leaves, would you reimburse my money?" I said I would. I didn't think about whether we were doing good business or not. I just thought that if I were here, I would be able to do it gradually. I would be able to reimburse him over time. But it was very strange. He said that wasn't good enough. He wanted me to borrow NT$200,000 from my family and pay him immediately.

Unlike Taiwanese entrepreneurs, who often can borrow such large amounts of money from relatives, find friends to act as investors, or turn to revolving credit societies organized by people in their social circles, for Margang that demand created a major hurdle:

> Who could I turn to? My brother has no money, since he has to raise four children. There is no way he could give me NT$200,000 to reimburse him. My elder sister gave me some money, since she only has one child. I talked to them about it. My brother-in-law was reluctant, since it takes aboriginal people a very long time to earn money and save up NT$200,000. I told him not to worry. I told him that I would return the money to him. After I approached them for the money about seven or eight times, he finally agreed. But it was hard for them since they gave me all their money. I returned the money as quickly as I could. It wasn't like they came here and did business with me or anything.

ON HER OWN: LEARNING THE ROPES

Finally, Margang was on her own, free to run her restaurant as she liked. She still, however, had many lessons to learn. Many of the skills she had to learn were social. Urban Taiwan can be a rough and threatening place. From childhood, Taiwanese people are taught to fear strangers, and to guard strict boundaries around the in-group of their families and close friends to protect themselves. The fear of outsiders is evident in the fact that most windows and doors on homes and businesses are covered with iron bars. Entrepreneurs must remain especially vigilant to protect themselves from shoplifters, tax investigators, officials enforcing zoning or fire regulations, and other threats. Having grown up in such a *habitus*, Taiwanese people are often wary of strangers and defend themselves by developing a tough, mean exterior. Margang, however, had learned none of that on Orchid Island and thus had trouble with gangsters:

> Back then, electronic gambling machines were very popular. Every day, five or six gangsters would show up at my restaurant. They said they wanted to install gambling machines in my restaurant. My landlord didn't want it. I didn't want it either. But they forced me. They said that "if you don't let us install them, we won't let you do business

here anymore." What could I do? None of my relatives helped out. And I didn't have enough money to hire people and pay wages. I was always alone in the restaurant. When I saw that gangsters were coming, I just locked the door and hid underneath a table. I was afraid to get up. I was afraid to answer the telephone. I was always trembling in fear. I thought that there was no way that one young woman could deal with that kind of people. There was no way I could win over them or get along with them. But with experience, I learned how to deal with such situations. I couldn't depend on others, since nobody would come to help me. When things like that happened, I had to learn how to communicate with them and even become friends with them.

Eventually she learned from some young men how best to deal with gangsters:

I even sat down with them. I said, "You guys are handsome. Surely you can find better jobs. You don't have to make money from those electronic gambling machines." I said, "There are a lot of good jobs waiting for you. Why do you do that kind of illegal thing? Don't you know that the people who fear you are going through a lot of pain?" I told them directly, because I know that some people don't refuse them. Some people don't know how to say no. Then they are forced to install those gambling games, and they are angry about it. But they don't dare do anything, since they are afraid that people will come beat them up or burn down their stores. That is the way it is. So I asked them how to react when somebody comes in and wants me to install gambling games. They said, just tell them that the boss isn't in. I learned a lot of things from them. Then, when other people came in, I would just say, "Sorry, the owner is not here. I am not allowed to decide." Then, I was like that and they would leave. But then they would come back and ask when the owner would come in. I said he just comes in at the busy times, takes care of money, and leaves immediately. There was nothing they could do, so they would just leave.

The business climate got better after Chen Shui-bian was elected mayor, she said. His administration forbade the use of electronic gambling games and enforced laws against the gangsters that had previously intimidated entrepreneurs all over Taipei. With the rule of law more solidly in place, at least in her relatively upscale neighborhood, Margang was able to concentrate more on actually promoting her own restaurant. It was then that she was best able to employ the social capital of English skills and American cooking that she had previously learned from her American patron:

When Chen Shui-bian became mayor, my business started to turn a profit. I had a customer, a foreign customer from the *China Post.* Before, I had been reluctant to face him. But then I knew that I had to face my own business. I had to find a way to make my business succeed. That foreigner lived in the neighborhood. One day when he was walking by, I spoke to him. Since I knew he was a journalist from the *China Post,* I invited him to come in for a cup of coffee and a piece of apple pie. He came in, and we chatted for a while. Even though my English was poor, he still understood. And I also understood his English. He said he would help me by writing about me in the *China Post.* So, in two months time, after working alone for so long, my business became good.

That restaurant review, she said, helped her to establish a regular clientele base among Taipei's expatriate community:

> He wrote a column about me. I was really excited about that day. He said it would come out on Thursday. On Wednesday, I was so excited I couldn't sleep. I got up at 6 A.M. I get to work at 7 A.M., but I got up at 6 A.M. to go buy a newspaper on the way to work. I thought it would be just a very small article. I didn't think that an entire half-page would be dedicated to writing about my restaurant. I was really happy. In the past, I had never had many customers. On Thursday, I still didn't have many customers, since everyone has to work on that day. But the third day was a Saturday and people had the day off. Even before I had opened up, there were already foreigners waiting at the door for me to come in. I was so happy! That was the first time since I opened up that there were a lot of people in my restaurant. Every table in the restaurant was filled. I was so happy, and very thankful to that person. After that, whenever he came to my restaurant, I never accepted his money for coffee. I always gave it to him for free. It was because of him that I was able to make this business work.

Margang's Sunrise Café thus became an expatriate hangout, as well as a place where Taiwanese people could meet foreigners and sample American food. One of my Taiwanese friends enjoyed sitting in that café and pointing out what he called "flowers stuck in cow shit"—older Western men in relationships with young Taiwanese women or men. Margang herself took pleasure in the restaurant as a meeting place between Ta'u and Western culture, and thus decorated her restaurant with photos and material culture from Orchid Island. Her Ta'u friends, however, understood little of what she was doing:

> A lot of my friends thought I was opening up a Chinese-style *Mei-er-mei* ("breakfast franchise") with sandwiches and hamburgers. When I told them I was doing Western food, they immediately thought of a steakhouse. But I said all of that was wrong. It's not Mei-er-mei. It's also not a steakhouse. It is just the small things that Americans eat at home. They would just say, "Oh." They would be curious about what that meant. But Orchid Island is so far away. They don't have many opportunities to come over and see for themselves.

Even her aboriginal friends who lived and worked in Taipei were unlikely to eat in her restaurant frequently. The daily special, at NT$200 with coffee, was already four times more expensive than breakfast at Mei-er-mei or other breakfast places. She thus referred to their decision not to come sympathetically:

> Some of them still came. But they can't come frequently. For them, this is expensive. It is not like the buffets outside where you can eat all you want for NT$100. All of our dishes cost more than $100. Since our costs are high, we can't price things so cheaply. So, maybe they come only once a month. They are good friends, but they can't come all the time.

Even her parents know little about her business endeavors:

> My parents don't get proud because I have a restaurant. Some of their friends praise me, saying I have done well by opening a restaurant. They might feel good, but not particularly, because I don't earn a whole lot of money. In fact, the profit is just something that I earn really slowly, drop by drop, and there isn't much money there.

NEW PRIORITIES: A MOMENT OF DECISION

Shortly after Margang's restaurant started to turn a profit, her life changed in other important ways. First, she got married. Her husband, a Ta'u man who works in carpentry and interior installation in Taipei, was from her home community:

> We were classmates in primary school. I knew him for more than ten years before we got married, but I had never thought of marrying him. In fact, I didn't even like him at first. He was from a very large family with lots of brothers. On Orchid Island, that makes them a big family and they were very proud. But once I went back and he invited me to eat in their home. I just laughed and accepted as if it were just a joke. Then I went, and I left my address. He wrote to me. I figured he was just an old classmate and wrote back. At first we wrote letters two to three times a month. Then it became every day. Then we got married.

A second change occurred when her father became fatally ill with cancer. She described how that changed her priorities regarding work, career, and family. At first, she was content working on Taiwan and sending back remittances to her family:

> I thought, my life was so poor when I was young. Even though I open up a store in Taipei, my family in Orchid Island doesn't eat well. Sometimes I would send them things to eat, and if I had extra money, I would send them money. Later on, they were living better because I was sending money back.

Soon, however, that was no longer enough:

> After the second year, my father got cancer. I gave them a lot of money. Orchid Island is like that. If you manage to save up a little bit of money, something happens in your family. So, I asked my father to move up [to Taipei]. My father wasn't feeling well. Every time he went to the bathroom, his stool was black. So I asked him to come up and see a doctor. The doctor wasn't very good. He was always just writing down his own things. It is just like you interviewing me right now. You are always writing down things, and you aren't really listening to what I am saying. So, the doctor would say, "That doesn't matter. It will go away." He would prescribe some medicine and send him home. My Dad also thought it was nothing. It would go away by itself. He went back to Orchid Island.

She admitted at this point her frustration with taking care of aging parents un-accustomed to urban ways, especially with the cultural dissonance they experienced arriving in Taipei from Orchid Island:

> I found it very difficult when they were here. We lived in an apartment here. When they went outside, they wouldn't look to see if there were cars on the road [while crossing the street]. And when they came home, they couldn't open the door to the apartment. I thought it was a big responsibility.

The fact that she was her own boss, she emphasized, was the only thing that made it possible for her to take care of her parents adequately:

> Thank goodness, I was my own boss. If I were working for someone else, I couldn't take off time every day to go open the door for my parents or take them around from place to place. I said that I could take care of them for a week. But I couldn't do it for a long time. I would hardly get started working, when I would have to worry if they got lost or if they got hit by a car or something. So, I couldn't take care of them. When my father saw the doctor and went back, I thought it was a minor problem.

Her father would have gone back to die, she said, if she had trusted the doctor. Instead, she compared experiences with friends and then challenged her doctor:

> A week later, my dad said his stools were still black. One of my friends said that could be serious. He said that his father also had black stools, and then it turned out to be stomach cancer. When he said his father had been diagnosed with cancer, I became very nervous. Even though the doctor had not even mentioned it, I called my father a week later and asked him to come back for another examination. I told the doctor. I really wanted to argue with him, because I had already told him a lot of things but he was always busy writing his own things and hadn't listened to what we had to say. Then, I said my father's stool was black. He said I hadn't mentioned that before. I said I had but he wasn't listening. So he did the tests. Then a week later the results came out that it really was stomach cancer. I cried and cried and cried. A lot of things happened after I started this restaurant, but the most painful of all is having a member of your family get seriously ill.

She contrasted that pain to what then seemed like minor disagreements with her former business partner:

> When I started this business, there was a lot of pain, but none of it was as painful as that. When I started out, that man [her former partner] would get angry and then he would destroy things in the restaurant. But when my father got sick, I thought, "How can that happen to us? I can do my business so well, but how can that happen to us?" So I always cried. Then my father had surgery and stayed in the hospital. It took half a year. I was always visiting him in the hospital. For half a year, I spent all of our family's money on my father.

She also changed her life for him:

> When my father was sick, I wanted to fulfill his wish and have a child. So I got pregnant and bore a child. Three months later, my father left us. But at least he saw the child. He said, "Don't scold him too much" and "Educate him well." Then he passed away. To educate our son, my husband speaks Ta'u to him at home. I speak Chinese to him and sometimes English.

Her dedication to family, she said, was made possible only through her business. She pointed out that the greatest form of empowerment she got from entrepreneurship was the ability to take care of her family financially. Her father, indeed, got much better care in Taipei than he would have received with the care available in the one medical clinic on Orchid Island:

> Thank goodness I had this store, since it made it possible for me to meet the economic needs of my family. I was happy that my regular customers always remembered to come see me. So, I could keep doing business. In July, it will be exactly six years that I have done this. It has been a long time. But now my priority is family.

FROM ELDER SISTER
TO MOTHER AND WIFE

Margang described the many ways in which she has been empowered by entrepreneurship:

> First, I get to meet different kinds of friends. Then, my life is relatively flexible. It is not like working for other people and having a boss tell what you can do and where you can go. Like if you wanted to go to the hospital to see your father, you would have to think about all of that. But if you are the boss, you have other people to help you out. You just don't have to worry about that kind of problem.

She enjoys as well a larger income and the spending power it gives her:

> I couldn't afford an apartment before. Now I have money. I can afford to rent a place. And then, some things that I couldn't afford before, like listening to CDs, or seeing home videos, I can afford all of that. But [if you work for others] you get only meager wages.

She also pointed out the importance of what she has learned from her customers, particularly regular customers who become like friends. More specifically, constant contact with Chinese customers taught her to play the stock market like other Taiwanese investors, using strategies similar to those described in Hertz's (1998) ethnography of the Shanghai stock market:

> You can also learn a lot of information about a lot of things. Like before, I didn't know how to play the stock market. But after listening to my friends [here], I know how to play the stock market. I know how to play mutual funds. So it has become that the

money that you didn't even have access to before, becomes money that you can invest in other things. And that allows you to earn even more money. It becomes like that. It is more relaxed.

What she found most difficult was negotiating a pattern of labor relations that she found acceptable: "The only time I find business a little bit bothersome is when I have to distribute wages. But if your business is good, it doesn't matter." Owning her own business, however, gave her the organizational power to hire the workers of her choice. She decided to hire only young women from Orchid Island, whom she refers to in fictive kinship terminology as younger sisters, saying that she can now help others like she had been aided when she first arrived in Taiwan:

> My younger sisters also do very well. We are all from Orchid Island. With noon and evening shifts, we have a total of eight people. So every month, I have a heavy burden of paying a lot of wages. Yet because I started out doing all of the most basic work, I know what my employees are going through. I don't give them too much pressure.

Not unlike many other entrepreneurs in Taiwan, she discussed labor relations through the metaphor of firm as extended family. She insisted, however, that her company is unique in that aspect and that she prefers that kind of labor relationship because she is aboriginal rather than Taiwanese. Using English words for emphasis, she said:

> We don't make a distinction between owner and employees. We are all like a big "*family*" [English]. We all eat together. If you want to eat something, you just go ahead and cook it. You can do what you want. They are very free. As long as it is not our busy time, you can go out and do what you need to do. It is mutual. Because they take care of things when I have to go out to take care of other matters. They say, "Go! It doesn't matter!" Yet, they also need time to take care of personal affairs. We can use the manner of friends to take care of one another. Those are some lifestyle things that are different from other people.

Her husband, however, does not approve of that relatively generous form of labor relations, and points out that she loses money by allowing her employees to eat as they like or leave the restaurant on paid company time to run personal errands. Summarizing her husband's criticisms, she said, "He thinks that kind of system is stupid. He thinks we don't earn enough money. So he tells me what I should do."

In general, however, she depicted her husband as encouraging and helpful in her entrepreneurial endeavors:

> In fact, the one who has helped me the most is my husband. He is always encouraging me from behind. Even when my business was no good, he didn't give me a lot of pressure because our life was bad, or anything like that. He said, "Go do what you want." And he went outside to work and help at earning money. He said, "I can help

you make up for the things you need in life." That's the way he is. Of course, if he thinks I am not doing things right, he will tell me. This restaurant isn't just me alone. My husband is always behind me, helping me.

She thus insisted that the restaurant is a joint project between her and her husband:

Everyone thinks this restaurant is mine and has nothing to do with my husband. But in fact, it is also his. We don't distinguish between my things and his things. Nobody ever sees him working in here. It is only me. I go out and talk to the customers. So customers all think that this is my restaurant and not my husband's.

When I asked what specific contributions he has made to the restaurant, she pointed to the photos of Orchid Island and the boat on the wall:

He put up all of these decorations. He has helped me with everything, except for capital. He has never invested a single dime here. But we can't work together. He has his job and I have mine. We can't work together because our personalities are too different. I like to do things quickly, and he is too slow. I would get upset if customers were waiting and he were in the kitchen cooking in his slow way. I would always be yelling at him. He never gets angry, but I do. So it is better that we don't work together.

That independent attitude explains why Margang is known, especially among Taipei's aboriginal community, as a strong and ambitious woman entrepreneur. When I asked her what suggestions she would give to other women going into business, she said:

You have to insist on attaining your own goals. You have to think it through. If you think you can do something, then you absolutely have to do that. If you insist on doing things your own way, you will surely succeed. Because every time I do something, I first set a goal of what I want and when I want to get it. That is the way to get what you want. When some people open a store, they think, "I'll just open for three months and then see. If business is bad, I'll think of something else." But I am not like that. I think that every time a person thinks like that, their store is destined to go out of business in three months. There is no way they can succeed. You have to tell yourself that you are going to succeed no matter what.

DISCUSSION

Taiwanese aboriginal people began migrating to cities in search of work during the rapid industrialization of the 1960s to early 1980s. Until Taiwanese industrialists started importing foreign workers from other Southeast Asian countries in the 1990s, aboriginal people did much of the dangerous work in construction and heavy manufacturing. Their already marginal position in the economy was further weakened in the 1990s when manufacturers moved industrial production en masse to China, leading to even higher unemployment for Taiwanese indigenous workers. Whereas the better-educated Chinese have made a relatively successful transition to technological and service sectors, indigenous communities have been left behind. The indigenous unemployment rate of 25 percent in early 2001, for example, exceeded the general unemployment rate of 4 percent. In all indices of social and economic development, indigenous people lag behind the Chinese majority (Executive Yuan Council of Aboriginal Affairs 1999). Individuals like Margang have done well in difficult circumstances.

At the most basic level, Margang has been able to achieve a much higher standard of living than most aboriginal people. As a Ta'u woman, she said, she is expected to support her biological parents in old age. Margang found a great sense of satisfaction in being able to fulfill those cultural expectations, and to do so much better financially than most people on Orchid Island. As she pointed out by telling me about her father's cancer treatment in such detail, entrepreneurship allowed her to contribute to the needs of her natal family in a way that she found fulfilling. Margang thus stands as a good example for other urban aboriginal people, and has even been portrayed as such in a guide to aboriginal entrepreneurs published by the Executive Yuan Council of Aboriginal Affairs (Shanhai Wenhua Zazhi 1999).

Margang has also been empowered by entrepreneurship in other ways. In terms of personal identity, she was able to create a space for herself where she can affirm her aboriginal identity. She affirms her Ta'u identity in the workplace by decorating her restaurant with Ta'u art, including a replica of a fishing boat, and with photos of Orchid Island. She often explains to visitors how Ta'u women farm and Ta'u men hunt for flying fish during the migration of the fish past Orchid Island every summer. This work activity is inevitably mentioned as a unique Ta'u characteristic in museum exhibits, documentaries, and publications of Taiwanese indigenous peoples. Margang affirms a Ta'u identity by incorporating the same themes into her own store décor and her personal narratives.

Since she serves a primarily expatriate clientele, Margang says she enjoys the opportunity for cultural exchange between Ta'u and Western cultures. English has been one of her main personal interests since middle school, and opening up a Western restaurant made that foreign world an intimate part of her own life. The narratives that she shares with those customers, as well as anthropologists, help build an aboriginal identity. In her narratives, for example, she contrasts her experience growing up in the natural environment of Orchid Island to those of "Taiwanese" children who grow up in the city.

As her story about the gangsters illustrates, she perceives aboriginal people as morally superior to Native Taiwanese people. This is a common discursive practice among Taiwanese aboriginal people. Aboriginal people often claim that they are trusting and "naïve," making them easy targets for swindlers and con artists. The moral dimensions of this discourse are further made apparent in their epithet for Native Taiwanese. They call them *bai-lang*, derived from the Taiwanese *phai-*

lang for "bad people." This discourse of moral supremacy is a "weapon of the weak" (Scott 1985) or form of "hidden transcript" (Scott 1990). It is part of the discursive strategies through which urban aborigines like Margang understand their social position and shape their own identities.

Margang is also empowered to the extent that she can control labor relations in her own business. Aware of the unemployment problems faced by aboriginal people in Taiwan, Margang has a policy of hiring only workers from Orchid Island and treats them as members of her extended family. She could surely adopt such a strategy because she already had a strong sense of identity as a Ta'u person.

Yet when I asked Margang if she thought entrepreneurship was a good strategy for Orchid Island people as a whole, she had strong reservations:

> Maybe, but I think that only a few people would earn money from it. . . . Orchid Island people are relatively naïve. So, doing business on Orchid Island is inconvenient. Maybe doing business on Orchid Island right now would not be very good, unless it became a tourist destination so that we could earn money from outside of Orchid Island. That would be the only way to help Orchid Island people. But if we did it among our own people, the money would just circulate more. There would not be more money. And the money would go only to those people who do business. Those who didn't do business would stay poor. That is the way things are now. Those who are capable of doing business are in business. Those who are not capable are still not doing it. Unless it becomes a tourist destination. Because they have not yet made it into a national park, so there is nothing that can be done. There is not much new that we can offer to other [Ta'u] people.

She insisted that entrepreneurship would be profitable for Orchid Island only under the condition that it became a tourist destination capable of earning money from Taiwanese and foreign visitors. Laughing off the idea of running a restaurant on Orchid Island with its population of 3,000 Ta'u people, she said, "We are divided into six villages. Maybe only the people from your own village will go to your place. There is no way I would think of driving to another village to eat a meal. Impossible! That's enough! Thank you!"

NOTES

1. Margang is from the Ta'u tribe of Orchid Island. During the Japanese occupation, Japanese anthropologists referred to them as the "Yamei" tribe. The name has remained in popular usage in Taiwan, and is also used by Margang herself. T'au, which means "human being" in their language, is now the official name of the tribe. Margang, the pseudonym used in this chapter, means "sunrise" in the Ta'u language and is used as a female name.

2. These networks of small shoe producers have been studied by anthropologist Ian Skoggard (1996).

Chapter Fourteen

An Aboriginal Crafts Dealer

As I showed in the previous chapter, one of the major problems of structural inequality in Taiwan is that between people of Chinese descent and the island's indigenous inhabitants. Restaurant owner Margang was able to empower both herself and her fellow aboriginal "sisters" through entrepreneurship, but had little to say about economic development for aboriginal communities in general. Thirty-eight-year-old Yuma Nogan, who organizes craft production and sells the products abroad, is more outspoken about such issues. Yuma has participated in the indigenous peoples' movement in Taiwan, and has even visited Central America as part of a delegation of Taiwanese aboriginals. As I show below, she has dedicated a portion of her work to economic development projects in the Tayal community. Her story thus says even more about how entrepreneurship can have a positive impact on society as a whole. To better understand her story, however, it is necessary to first put the Tayal tribe into historical and cultural perspective.[1]

THE TAYAL TRIBE:
HISTORICAL AND CULTURAL BACKGROUND

The Tayal tribe, with a population of 61,597, is Taiwan's second-largest indigenous group. Dispersed throughout the mountainous regions of Taipei, Taoyuan, Hsinchu, Miaoli, Taichung, Nantou, and Hualien Counties, they have the largest geographical range. Due to their uncompromising resistance to Han Taiwanese and Japanese violations of their property rights in past centuries, as well as a strong warrior tradition of head-hunting and tribal warfare (Mowna 1998: 211), they have earned the reputation of being "fierce barbarians" (*xiongfan*). Their facial tattoos, which both men and women traditionally received after successfully attaining maturity, were also perceived as a sign of fierceness by Han Taiwanese colonialists, because criminals in Ch'ing Dynasty in China were sometimes branded on the face. These practices were eliminated during the Japanese occupation of Taiwan.

The Tayal tribe was the last tribe to be brought under Japanese domination. By the 1920s, the Japanese had already built police stations, schools, and health clinics in most aboriginal villages. Japanese administrators, police officers, military officials, business people, and teachers worked all over the island alongside educated Taiwanese, Koreans, and Okinawans. Strict legal enforcement, however, meant the abandonment of many valued cultural practices such as facial tattooing. Aboriginal tribes were also forcefully settled, which often involved the forced migration of entire communities to new settlements. Resistance against the Japanese grew among the Tayal, who perceived the Japanese occupation to be a violation of *gaya*, their communal moral order (Bawan 2002).

In what is known as the Wushe incident, a group of over 300 Tayal warriors attacked Japanese officials and their families who had gathered at a sports event in Wushe (now Nantou County) on October 27, 1930, killing 130 men and women. It took Japanese forces two months, and the deaths of 216 aboriginal people, to quell the subsequent uprisings. In an event that still remains a central part of Tayal collective memory today, the Japanese brought in Amis aboriginal militia to behead 101 Tayals and return them to the Japanese for bounty payments. Tayal people still discuss this incident as evidence of Tayal resistance against injustice and an Amis tendency to collaborate with outside oppressors.

Before their integration into the successive Japanese and Chinese (ROC) states, the Tayal lived in close-knit communities regulated by strong religious beliefs. They believed that all of nature belonged to the omnipresent spirit *rutux*. The universe was structured according to a moral order called *gaya* or *gaga*. Any violations of the moral order gaya were perceived to be polluting and to bring misfortune upon the entire community. Individuals who violated gaya, for example, would fail to catch wild boars while hunting, would fall easily on dangerous mountain slopes, and would be bitten more easily by mosquitoes. Major violations of gaya, including the breaking of sexual taboos, required certain rituals to restore order (Mowna 1998: 59).

In practice, rules of gaya strongly reinforced patriarchal power. In the event that a man and woman were discovered to have engaged in premarital sexual relations, for example, the family of the woman would reclaim its honor by attacking the man's property, either destroying his house or killing his domestic animals. The man's family would then be required to provide animals as sacrificial offerings, and the woman's family would perform a ritual to remove moral impurity from the community. Adultery, as well, was perceived to be a violation of gaya (Mowna 1998: 59).

All men and women were expected to marry at an appropriate age. Those individuals who did not marry were perceived as incompetent, as men who cannot hunt well or as women who cannot weave and perform household chores. For both men and women, prolonged celibacy brought shame on their families and ridicule to individuals. Women who did not marry were called *putot*, a pejorative term referring to incompetence. Monogamy and marital fidelity were strictly enforced by rules of gaya, and divorce was rare until the 1960s. The cultural ideal was that both men and women would have only one sexual partner in a lifetime (Mowna 1998: 68).

Like Han Chinese, but unlike the neighboring matrilineal Amis tribe, Tayal kinship is patrilineal. Residence patterns, however, differed from those of the Han. Whereas Han families preferred extended families with sons and their families living together if possible, the Tayal lived mainly in nuclear or stem families. After marriage, most couples lived neolocally or, depending on which was more convenient, with the parents of either the husband or the wife. Although not entirely unknown, Chinese-style living arrangements were extremely rare, as it was considered improper for a man to live in the same house as his sisters-in-law (Mowna 1998: 72).

Marriage involved a ritual transfer of the woman from her father's family to her husband's family, and was referred to as *mebali koyox*, or "buying a wife." Traditionally, parents arranged the marriages of their children. The young man was then required to perform a duty of corvée labor for the family of the woman, in order to prove his trustworthiness and competence at work and hunting. Once the husband was deemed acceptable, his family would "purchase" the woman with a large bride-price. Since the wedding itself was considered to be a major community event, the husband's family was required to slaughter a large number of pigs and chickens for the wedding feast. Many of those wedding customs persist to this day, the ritual slaughter of pigs being considered especially important.

Japanese anthropologists studying the Tayal from 1909 to 1915 praised the Tayal for their system of gaya encouraging strict monogamy, abstention from premarital sex, and fidelity after marriage. They maintained, however, that the ideology actually trapped women in unhappy marriages and contributed to domestic violence. Kojima's 1915 ethnography, *Studies of Aboriginal Customary Laws*, contended that:

> In actual fact, husband and wife are in a command and obey relationship. The husband protects and guards his wife, she obeys him, thus maintaining order in the family. The husband has the right to punish his wife, should she disobey him, in the form of reprimand, beating and confinement (Kojima 1996 [1915]: 181–182, cited in Huang 2002).

Feminist anthropologist Huang Shu-ling has corroborated this observation in interviews with Tayal *yagi*, or older women (Huang 2002). All available evidence suggests that the Tayal have been historically as strongly patriarchal as the Han, and that women of both cultures were similarly disempowered. The Tayal bride-price pattern, however, may have been even more oppressive to women, as brides do not retain control of the money themselves as in the dominant Chinese dowry pattern.

After more than 100 years of colonial rule by outsiders, the Tayal have assimilated to a large extent within a Chinese-dominated society. Yuma, like many aboriginal individuals, however, still uses knowledge of historical customs as reference points in the construction of personal identity. In prefacing her own life history, for example, she describes how Tayal marriage practices have changed over time:

We have a monogamous system. We no longer have arranged marriages like before. We Tayal people are relatively free; we have so-called free love. In earlier days, like when my older sisters were young [the 1970s], there would be arranged marriages, but they didn't like it. They would have secret relations and then those relationships would succeed [result in marriage].

Rather than adopting the critical stance of Japanese colonial or contemporary Han feminist anthropologists toward gaya, however, she takes a strong pride in this moral code:

> In comparison [to the Han], Tayal people respect a principle of one wife and one husband. That is to say, if I marry you, I want to marry you forever. There is no question of divorce! But now that some people have started going outside [into Han society], there have been some divorces.

She acknowledges, however, that like the Han, the Tayal have a tendency to "value men and treat women lightly." She compared Tayal customs to those of other aboriginal groups, including the Amis tribe, which is known for its matrilocal system: "The Amis value women and treat men lightly because they are a matrilineal society. The Paiwan aren't like that. To them, the eldest child is the heir, regardless if it is a boy or a girl."

ROOMS OF HER OWN:
YUMA GOES INTO BUSINESS

Yuma grew up in the impoverished Hsiu-lin Township of Hualien County on Taiwan's east coast, site of some rather controversial conflicts between cement companies and aboriginal landowners (Simon 2002). Her parents were both teachers. Her mother had three children, but died when Yuma was only five years old. Yuma's father remarried and eventually had a total of twelve children. Yuma, encouraged to go into a medical profession, specialized in radiology and took her first job in a military hospital. From the very beginning of her career, when she was an intern in the military hospital and also worked part-time doing sales in a night market, she felt alienated from work as a radiologist. She described her first job in terms of alienation caused by her "individual character":

> I figured there was no room for advancement in that hospital, and there was no way I could accept some of the surprising ways they did things. I thought the whole system was unreasonable. The problem was our commanding officer. There was a lot of talk about medical ethics, but I never saw any of that in the hospital. That was because of the commanding officer! I had to obey his every command. I guess that obedience is part of military life, but there is no way I could accept that. Since my individual character could not accept that kind of obedience, I simply decided to leave.

Like Chhoa Hiong-gun (Chapter 9), who started out her career by traveling abroad, Yuma left Taiwan and spent six months traveling alone in Thailand:

> I spent a little money to travel alone. When I came back, I decided that I would rather go into business. I had already worked part-time at a night-market stand and realized that I preferred that. Since that made me feel happier, I opened up a stand at the Shih-lin night market [in Taipei]. I knew that crafts were cheaper abroad [in Thailand]. But those things had to be imported and I was the "*carrier*" [English]. It was very difficult. Every time, I brought back a lot of things. In order to save money, I had to think of a way to do it without going over the airline's weight limit and then I would take everything on the airplane. That's the way I did it. And I developed gradually from there.

Her immediate problem was conflict with her father who, in accordance with patriarchal norms, expected obedience from his children. He opposed her decision to abandon radiology:

> At that time, my father could not forgive me. He said, "How can you do that after I spent so much money for you to study radiology? And then you don't do it! You go open up a night-market stand!" He couldn't forgive me for that, and we had our conflicts. But I figured that my own interests were more important, and there was no way I could stand that [hospital] work environment.

Showing strong individualistic traits she associates with aboriginality, she simply disobeyed her father, did as she wished, and patiently gave him the time he needed to get accustomed to the idea. She needed to prove to him, moreover, that entrepreneurship could be even more profitable than nursing:

> I started out with a night-market stand. Then I established a small company and started trading. Then I realized that selling things in the night market was too slow. You have to watch the weather. When the weather was bad I had to stay at home, but at home I had no income. At first I wasn't even thinking about the work. I just thought I would make as much money as I could and then play with it or go abroad and travel. But then my ambitions started to grow. I realized that I could earn money that way. I started to ask myself how I could earn even more money.

The first thing she learned was that she had to leave the night market if she wanted to make a better income and have more capital to reinvest and expand:

> I realized that I would need a permanent shop. If I had a storefront rather than just a movable stand, I could tell the clients where to find me if they needed me. At the night market, customers can't even find the sellers again if they have a problem with the goods they buy. Once I opened up a store, my business got much better than it had been, because my customers knew how to find me. Then I realized that I could make even more money if I sold in greater quantities, like in wholesale. But if I do it myself, there is a limit to what I can carry. So I read some books on the import/export business and I opened up a company. Then I started doing imports and exports. I started with small orders and then gradually expanded. People are ambitious!

She soon expanded well beyond her original store. In stark contrast to Sophie Hong (Chapter 12), who prefers the autonomy of her own store, Yuma found it advantageous to work with department stores:

I started selling outside of Taipei. My only outlets at the time were in department stores. I discovered that department stores were a good place to be, since they didn't demand a deposit on the rent and I didn't have to spend money on interior design. That was all paid for by the department store. They just drew a commission. They kept a certain percentage for themselves and gave a certain percentage to me. I had to provide the workers, so I found women employees to help me out. Department stores are good. The business is not so difficult, since they do the selling for you. The profits are not as high as you get by selling independently, but still they are higher than just doing wholesale. First, I worked through one department store, and then I added one after another.

Yuma compared the advantages of doing commission sales in department-store sales versus the wholesale business:

In wholesale, sometimes people don't want what I buy. But in a department store, I can mark down the prices of things from my warehouse that people don't want. It's not that the quality is bad. Sometimes I would display things in one place and nobody would buy them. Then I would display them someplace else, and they would sell well, because different people like to buy different things. One person will hate a thing, and the next person will love it. You have to find a way to get things to the people that like them, and that is very difficult. Our record was selling in over fifty stores.

Yuma soon had agents all over Taiwan, each in charge of sales in a stipulated number of department stores. When the economy was strong and sales were good, she profited from the sale of her gift items. When the Asian crisis hit in 1996, however, and was followed by a drop in the stock market and consumer confidence, her problems began:

Business just fell off. When the stock market was high, people would buy our products when they had money and use them to decorate their homes or give to other people as presents. But because our products are not necessities, they bought less of them when the economy went bad. I stood through that for two years and then realized I couldn't hold on any longer. I had to close down all of those department store displays. I went back to having only one store.

Closing down, however, was a major challenge because it involved a nationwide network of sales agents also suffering from the economic downturn:

I had big problems when I closed down, since a lot of people didn't pay me my money when it was time to settle accounts. I had agents in all four directions! My biggest agent in the south suddenly took off, with both goods and money. I lost a lot of money with him. Now if people see that one person is no good, they will just follow along with him. All of a sudden, I couldn't collect money, and I didn't have my goods anymore either. That was the lowest point. So I just closed down everything, and started again in this small store.

The Formosan aboriginal handicrafts, now the items most prominently displayed in her store, represented only a minor sideline at first:

> I had been doing that all along. My main product lines were crafts from foreign aboriginal peoples. I was just "playing" with Taiwanese aboriginality. By playing, I mean that it was just my own collection. If someone wanted something and they offered me a high enough price for it, then I would sell it. But they were expensive.

Market forces, however, had long forced her to take Taiwanese aboriginal crafts out of her department store stands:

> Once in a department store, the manager said he had something he wanted to talk to me about. I said, "OK, speak!" He said, "You have this place. It is in the corner of our store. And you are exhibiting aboriginal things. But they don't sell well. Don't you think that is a waste of space?" He thought like that since they calculate how much they sell in each square foot. If I am using ten square feet of space, then I have to provide ten square feet of sales. But I was only giving him eight square feet of sales, since my two square feet of aboriginal things weren't selling well. They figure you shouldn't exhibit things that don't sell. From their perspective, there was nothing wrong with that logic. After all, they were collecting a commission instead of rent. They earn less money when my business is poor.

Yuma explained the problem of selling aboriginal crafts in the mainstream Han Taiwanese market. She claimed that many people dismiss her goods as products of *hoan-a*, a Taiwanese word for "barbarian":

> First, aboriginal things were not very fashionable. Second, Han people would say, "That person is selling hoan-a things. She must be hoan-a." That word is very impolite. It means that a person is very barbarian. They are prejudiced against us; sometimes they wouldn't even look at our products. As if that isn't enough, sometimes they would even curse at us.

To illustrate the problem of racism, she related the story of a conflict her younger sister once had while selling crafts from a stand in the train station:

> At that time, the supervisor called to tell me that my sister had slapped a customer, and that the customer was reporting it to the station manager. I found that strange and went over to take care of things. My sister said that the customer had dropped and broken something. Since that item had been placed so high, she knew he had dropped it, otherwise it wouldn't have fallen to the floor, but the customer denied it. My sister was already angry, and then the customer said, "You hoan-a are so unreasonable. That is the way hoan-a are." My sister was so angry, she slapped him across the face.
>
> Since the station manager doubted my sister, I went and asked the client if he had indeed said that. He said, "Hoan-a are hoan-a. That's the way they are." I said, "OK!

First, you have to pay for the good. Second, my sister is not apologizing." I explained to the station manager that it was the customer who had attacked first with his impolite language and that furthermore he touched her goods and broke them. I said, "He is the one who is in the wrong. Things don't just jump to the ground themselves if they haven't been touched." In the end, I said, "It doesn't matter if he broke our thing and doesn't pay. But I want him to apologize to my sister."

I said there was no way we were going to apologize to him. I was so angry! When he said we were being unreasonable, I told the station manager to make his own judgment. The customer said, "Your employee is so unreasonable. Now I know it is because the boss is so unreasonable that she has become like that." He just swore at us and left. I ignored him. Once the customer left, the station manager was nice and apologized. He said he never thought that people were like that to aboriginal people.

Yuma explained the incident to him by drawing historical parallels to the Wushe incident and other cases of indigenous resistance. She said, "You see, we weren't to blame! We only killed people to defend ourselves. They all think that indigenous people are murderous, but none of it was without reason."[2]

Yuma described to me other negative stereotypes held by Han Taiwanese about aboriginal people. Han Taiwanese, for example, often refer to aborigines as prone to drunkenness, crime, and violence. Yuma, however, drew my attention to the daily television reports of crime—which tend to dominate the electronic media—and contrasted that to aboriginal life:

Look how many Han criminals there are! Are there more Han or more aboriginal criminals? Every time there is a murder or arson or bank robbery, it is a Han Taiwanese. Tell me the truth: Do any of those cases involve aborigines? When we aborigines drink alcohol, the worst we do is get in fights among ourselves in our own villages, or pass out and fall asleep at home. There is no way that aborigines would ever go outside and kill somebody. So the way that Han people judge us is completely wrong.

These stereotypes, which one often hears from Han entrepreneurs who hire aboriginal employees, are the basis for discrimination in the workplace. Yuma thus mentions that entrepreneurship gives her individual freedom from discrimination. Like Chhoa Hiong-gun, she draws attention to the freedom to choose the people she does business with:

Of course prejudice does influence my business to some extent, but I have already been working at this for over ten years. When you accept me, I continue to do business with you. If you don't accept me, then I just don't do business with you. I can choose! At the very least, I have my dignity. When I first started out, people would say, "How can that be a mountain person?"[3] But if they wanted to buy those things, they had no choice but to come to me, and if they wanted to come to me, they had to respect me. Sometimes customers would say, "Your hoan-a things are too expensive!" I would just say, "If you are not happy, you can go elsewhere. I don't mind. But I do ask for you to speak more respectfully." I would say, "We are people, too."

It would be much harder for her to speak so forthrightly if her commodity were her own labor power in a workplace controlled largely by Han Taiwanese people. As mentioned previously, indigenous people tend to have lower average incomes and higher unemployment rates than Han Taiwanese, a social phenomenon indigenous activists usually attribute to institutional racism. Many Han Taiwanese bosses justify repressive labor practices with a discourse of Han industriousness versus aboriginal laziness. Yuma, by contrast, emphasizes differences in work ethics that make aboriginal individuals more "passive":

> When they are looking for work, aboriginals are less ambitious than Han people. I think I should admit that. When Han people know that there is a job opening, they will go and compete for it, but it seems as if we aborigines can't go and compete. An aborigine won't ask how much he will get paid for his labor power. He won't insist on getting a certain salary before he will work. As a result, he is more passive. He won't go look for a certain work environment on his own.

SHARING HER ROOM: ENTREPRENEURSHIP AND INTERPERSONAL RELATIONS

As for her own personal life, she says she has a "pretty good boyfriend," whom she has known for sixteen years. She met him shortly after he moved to Taiwan from Hong Kong:

> Now he is my business partner. But when he first came to Taiwan, he was the main chef—*chairman* [using English for emphasis]—in a restaurant. He didn't have to work. He just told other people to work, but he judged if the dish was tasty enough or not. He was in charge of the kitchen, and represented the boss.

Shortly after they met, however, he came to work in her company, a change which she said was done for *her* convenience:

> Since my business was so busy, I asked him to come and help out. I asked him how much money he was making in the restaurant. I told him that I would give him the same salary if he came to help me. In the end, I was even able to give him more, so he just threw himself into the work completely.

The partnership was successful, she said, because of the way they were able to divide up responsibilities and powers equally:

> He has his way of doing things, and I have mine. So I do my thing and he does his. In the end, we get everything done through our two ways of doing things. For example, he is responsible for dealing with certain countries and I am responsible for others. Then I don't need to go to the countries he takes care of, and we travel to different

places. I am responsible for dealing with Southeast Asia, India, Nepal, Tibet, and Taiwan. He is responsible for mainland China and Hong Kong. We both have training in import/export. We also do exports. He is responsible for exporting to the mainland. I am responsible for exports to my countries.

Yuma explained the export side of her business:

I do business with Vietnam, for example. When I go there, I don't just import their products. I also export my things. Sometimes we don't even use cash. We would barter my things for their things. But now it is not so easy to do that. Now their economy is bad and they don't import as much from here, so most of our exports are to the mainland. The mainland buys machinery and machine tools from Taiwan. Vietnam and other Southeast Asian countries buy textiles from us. I just sold some to Papua New Guinea.

The fact that she and her boyfriend also live together as life partners, however, caused her conflict with her father. Her father, of course, still lives in the Tayal rural community and has to face the strong social pressures of conforming to gaya. Eventually, however, he was able to accept her lifestyle as part of modern Taiwan:

At first, my father couldn't accept it. Our relatives said it was an . . . unnatural relationship. They said that you should not live with a guy if you aren't married. My father said that the main reason I should get married is because my grandmother—my mother's mother—was getting old. He said she would be very sad if she never got to see me get married. But you can't use the feelings of the older generation to judge the behavior of this generation.

Like several other Han women entrepreneurs I encountered, she resisted patriarchal norms by refusing to get married and have children:

I don't think it is necessary to get married. What if you get married and then later get divorced? Isn't that a bad thing? I figure if I get married today, I will marry only once. There is no way I would get a divorce. That is my choice. But I don't dare to do that. I am afraid that we would end up getting divorced within a year. So I have remained like that [unmarried] to the present day.

The main reason for not marrying, however, is she feels that cohabitation gives her more dignity in the relationship. Having seen the outcomes in patriarchal marriages, she fears that, once married, she would be expected to be subordinate to her husband:

This way I am less limited. I don't want anyone to tell me what to do. So, we are like that. He is free, and I am free too. I don't control him and he doesn't control me. It is natural like that. If he were to fall in love with another woman, then let him love her. I wouldn't mind. But if we were married and he loved another woman I would find it very painful. To me, it is not important if I am married or not. What is important is whether I am happy or not. This way, I have a greater feeling of self-respect.

Although neither she nor her partner wishes to have children, they have donated money to orphanages: "We have adopted children in Thailand, Nepal, and Hong Kong. We send them money and we visit them sometimes."

In this sense, entrepreneurship empowers her to effectively resist patriarchal pressure to marry and allows her to claim greater control over her own affective and reproductive life:

> But of course, not marrying does not mean that I am promiscuous. It means that I am in control of my own behavior and I don't control that of others. I just think I have to respect myself. I think that people should live for themselves and not for other people. I just "*do myself*" [English]. I don't care what other people say. I ignore them when they say, "Look, she is so old and she isn't married." It isn't as if nobody wants me. It is the way I want it to be!

MAKING ROOMS FOR OTHERS: YUMA AS BOSS

Coming from a family with no entrepreneurial background, Yuma had few people to turn to for help. Experience and the professional help of an accountant, however, taught her how to organize her business and manage finances in order to maximize profits:

> I have three companies, and I keep them all distinct. There are the Taiwanese aboriginal handicrafts. One company is in charge of that. There are the imports and exports. One company is in charge of that. We have another company that is in charge of distribution. We keep all three company accounts separate. Even though all three companies are all mine, the accounts can't be mixed together. In the beginning, we mixed the accounts together, and as a result we lost money. I don't know why we lost money, but we hired an accountant who told us that. In the end, we had to separate the accounts. In the beginning, it was the aboriginal stuff that made us lose a lot of money, since the rest of the business was subsidizing that.

Yuma and her boyfriend did the import/export business, she alone worked with the aboriginal handicrafts, and they distributed the goods via a third corporation with commission agents contracted to do department-store sales and return to her a percentage of the profits. Separating into different legal corporations in that way permitted her to keep track more easily of the expenses and profits of the import/export company and keep those profits safe from both the riskier distribution business and the less profitable sale of aboriginal crafts.

As for formal paid employees, she has only one permanent worker, another aboriginal woman who helped her keep the store open in Taipei and contributes to production of some goods for sale. Beyond the apparent simplicity of labor organization in her own firm, however, is an entire network of producers all over Taiwan and Southeast Asia. Her company directs flows of capital between those independent organizations, bringing income from relatively wealthy consumers in Taiwan to craftspeople in poorer communities. Not least, her work has been important to Taiwanese aboriginal communities both by providing income and by valorizing their culture.[4]

YUMA AS AGENT OF CAPITALISM

It was only through repeated contact with Yuma that I noticed the power she yields at the structural level. In addition to her work in Taipei and travels abroad for her export/import business, she dedicates several days a week to travel to Tayal communities in Hualien, Taipei, and Hsin-chu Counties of Taiwan. None of the communities is easy to reach, and some of them are high up in the mountains. She has helped in the organization of several women's weaving cooperatives and tries to help them find a market. She has, for example, taken orders for bags that Academia Sinica and other academic organizations distribute to conference attendees. The weaving cooperatives supply the cloth; she and another Tayal woman sew them into bags in her Taipei storefront. Because she already has an adequate income from the import/export business, she can continue to do such work in spite of its low profits.

> If I only did Taiwanese aboriginal handicrafts, I would not be able to sit in here so comfortably today. That business is very difficult, because the profit is low, and Taiwanese aboriginal crafts don't sell well. The overhead costs are very high. Since they are luxury goods, I do what I can do. As long as it doesn't interfere with my ability to survive, I do it. Otherwise, I would give it up, since I have done nothing but lose money on aboriginal crafts so far.

Trade in aboriginal handicrafts has been difficult for Yuma in terms of both supplies and markets. Although weaving cooperatives have been established and there are many individual artisans, their work ethic is still not the same as that of the Han Taiwanese in Taiwan, who have been incorporated into the capitalist world system for a longer period of time. Aboriginal artisans and weavers tend to produce more when they need money, and schedule production around other events in their lives. For that reason, Yuma often finishes products such as cloth bags herself, rather than trying to organize just-in-time production in the villages. She has learned from experience that the aboriginal workers may not finish such products on the time schedule needed by the final customers in Taipei.

In terms of marketing, Yuma also faces a great deal of risk, as the demand for aboriginal crafts in Taiwan is limited. I have accompanied her to sell crafts at aboriginal social events, including an ancestor worship festival in Hsiu-lin Township and the opening of the Taiwan Prehistory Museum in Taitung. In Hsiu-lin Township, she and her father set up a large display of aboriginal handicrafts and tried all day to sell them under the hot sun. Aboriginal people themselves, however, rarely see a need to buy such products as mobile phone cases embroidered with aboriginal symbols, which are more expensive than factory-made products. And the hoped-for tourists never arrived. Considering that she only sold a few small items, she spent more money driving from Taipei to Hualien than she earned in profits.

Because of the limited demand, Yuma insists that producers bear much of the risk. She sells the crafts on commission, rather than purchasing them with cash up front from the producers:

> A lot of my things come from aboriginal villages. But you can't first give them cash up front. It would be hard for me to give them cash, because the turnover is slow. That is really difficult, so I have learned to control the business strictly. That is to say that I buy relatively little. Before, I bought [their crafts] without limitation. But the Taiwanese aboriginal things are really dependent on my import/export business. I now use 10 percent [of my capital] to do aboriginal crafts. If I did more than that, my company would not survive. In the end, I decided to invest only 10 percent in that. If I lose it all, then I will "*finish*" [English]. If I don't lose it all, then I can continue to do it.

Yuma emphasizes that her sale of aboriginal crafts is unprofitable, and that she can only continue to do it because she earns an adequate profit from her import/export work. Unlike Southeast Asian handicrafts, moreover, there is almost no international market for Taiwanese aboriginal handicrafts. Due to higher wages in Taiwan, they are uncompetitive with similar products from Thailand and Indonesia. Her only international market for Taiwanese aboriginal handicrafts is Japan, where a specific niche market still exists for Taiwanese ethnological artifacts fifty-five years after the end of Japanese colonialism.

Yuma herself emphasizes largely the individual benefits that she gains from the business:

> I think it would be just dog farts (*goupi*, "nonsense") if you said that I was doing this to help my community do something. I am not so concerned about that meaning of it [her work]. The most important thing is to live well. When I live well, I am happy, and it is only when I am happy that I can do something that really helps my community. It would simply not be true to say that helping the community was the significance of my work. Why? I wouldn't be able to live so happily because I don't have that much extra energy. What I mean by living happily is that I have my self-respect and I have enough to feed and clothe myself. Whenever I can, I do what I can to help the people of the community. I think that is the most important thing. I won't say that helping the people of my community is the only meaningful thing. If I help them, but I am not happy, how can that be a good thing? I think the most meaningful thing is to give myself a lot of space, and to enable myself to live without asking help from others. Only then is it important to help other people. The most important thing is to make myself happy and satisfied.

She has gained far more than a higher income from entrepreneurship:

> I never pressure myself. Since I have already been educated, I don't think of money as so important. In the past, I thought that money was the most important thing. Then,

when people didn't return my money, I truly suffered. But when I thought about it, I stopped thinking of money as so important. Self-respect is the most important thing.

DISCUSSION

From her own perspective, Yuma has enriched herself both economically and emotionally from entrepreneurship. Opening her own business has permitted her to further develop the personality traits of strength, independence, and individualism, characteristics that are common to successful entrepreneurs as well as highly valued in Tayal culture (Hsu 1991). It allows her to avoid the pressures of having a boss and the discrimination that aboriginal people often suffer in the workplace. It has permitted her to merely live with her boyfriend, rather than marrying him and bearing children, in strict defiance of both Tayal and Han Taiwanese social norms; but it has also enabled her to contribute to her community in a way that demonstrates her personal competence. She is thus highly respected in the aboriginal community. Most of all, entrepreneurship has empowered Yuma to claim dignity as an aboriginal person, and to demand respect from those who wish to do business with her. It has allowed her to take control of her life, and affirm a positive aboriginal identity in ways that would have been difficult in many workplaces. She sums it up by saying she gains a good life and self-respect from business, and downplays the idea that she is a benefactor in any way.

That, however, is the promise of capitalism. Each individual, by actively pursuing his or her own self-interest, also provides for the common good. Even in the simplest case of women selling breakfast food on the street, they provide a needed service to commuters only because they want the extra revenue that business provides. Yuma makes a respectable income from most of her work, especially the import/export company through which she brings crafts to Taiwan from Thailand and her Hong Kong partner sells Taiwanese machine tools to China. Since she makes a good profit from those activities, she is also able to contribute to the Tayal community by providing a limited market for their crafts.

In the long run, that activity is likely to be her biggest contribution to the development of her community. In spite of the limitations and relative unprofitability of aboriginal handicrafts, Yuma's involvement in the trade does bring a modest income stream that would otherwise not exist to artisans and their remote mountain communities. By providing a market for aboriginal crafts, moreover, she is helping to maintain and valorize indigenous material culture. In this way, she instills among aboriginal people a pride in their heritage. In a political-economic context that otherwise encourages assimilation, such contributions need to be recognized.[5] This particular part of her business deviates from the behavior of the capitalist *homo economicus* who lives only for increasing profits.

Some romantics may mourn the loss of traditional culture that such capitalism supposedly entails for aboriginal communities, but much of that has already been lost through decades of both Japanese and Chinese colonialism and industrial development. The Tayal have little chance of returning to their old ways of hunting, gathering, and slash-and-burn cultivation, especially since their former hunting territories are now protected national parklands. And as integrated into Taiwanese consumer society as they are, few Tayal individuals would probably want to. Small-scale capitalist enterprises, like those that Yuma encourages, can give people more control of their own lives than the working-class occupations that aboriginal people usually hold. A business-friendly institutional environment makes that possible.

The idea that capitalism is liberating is not merely a reflection of the free-market ideology of our time. Marx and Lenin both argued that capitalism is a progressive force, although they added the caveat that it would eventually bring about its own destruction. It is fair to conclude that capitalism provides the promise of empowerment to entrepreneurs of most genders and ethnic groups. The fact that it actually delivers on those promises is made evident in the stories of women entrepreneurs who gain empowerment in spheres of life from the most intimate to the most public. Some observers such as sociologist Bryan Turner (1996: 157–58) thus argue that capitalism liberates women and breaks down the walls of patriarchy.

There is, however, a darker side of capitalism, as individuals enter the market from different starting points. Capitalism may free some individuals from prior social restraints, but it can also reproduce and even strengthen structural inequalities that are already present. In the 1970s, for example, patriarchy was strengthened when young unmarried women workers were expected to work long hours in multinational corporations and return their wages to their fathers. As the Taiwanese economy grew and wages rose, however, that phenomena disappeared from the Taiwanese economic landscape. By the beginning of the twenty-first century, the most glaring example of capitalism's dark side in Taiwan is the booming sex industry. Although it has empowered certain individuals, including women, it has also reproduced both gender and ethnic inequalities in yet another context. That is the subject of the following chapter.

NOTES

1. Like the Ta'u of Orchid Island, the naming of this tribe is a subject of controversy. Most anthropological accounts, from the Japanese period to the present, refer to them as the Atayal. Tayal is closer to their native pronunciation, however, and is the preferred spelling used by the Presbyterian Church. There is also controversy within the community at Hsiu-lin Township over the question of whether the people there are a branch of the Tayal or constitute a separate Truku tribe. Yuma Nogan, the subject of this chapter, comes from Hsiu-lin and self-identifies as Tayal. I follow her usage in this book.

2. This story is only one example of the discrimination that Yuma and other aboriginal people face in Taiwan, as well as of how it influences their identity formation. For Yuma, historical reference to the Wushe incident is a strong act of resistance. I have also observed the same discursive practice in another context when a Tayal land-rights ac-

tivist asked an Asia Cement spokesman during a protest if he intended to provoke another Wushe incident.

3. Another common word for aboriginal people, but without the strong negative connotations of hoan-a, is *soa-te-lang* for "mountain people."

4. I know this from discussion with aboriginal activists all over Taiwan. She is known for both her craft sales and her participation in the aboriginal movement.

5. I came to appreciate this myself only when I visited one such community in July 2002. The older women take great pride in their weaving and are thankful to Yuma for providing them with a market, however limited.

Chapter Fifteen

Women in a Flower-Drinking World

Flower drinking is a set of cultural practices in which men in groups of two or more visit commercial establishments that offer varieties of erotic entertainment. These sex clubs assume the public identity of barbershops, cafés, teahouses, hotels, bars, dance halls, KTV salons, saunas, massage parlors, or "grandpa shops." To those who know how to read the signs, they are clearly visible in such forms as a gaudy barbershop with smoky windows open twenty-four hours a day or a small house in an alley with a red lantern lit at night. The clientele in such places is almost exclusively male and the services are exclusively provided by women, except in the very small worlds of gigolo and transvestite services. Services provided by the hostesses include drinking, conversation, playing fist games, singing, dancing, and various forms of physical contact.

The extent of the sex industry in Taiwan is remarkable. With a total market value of two trillion NT dollars and employment of 700,000 people, it was Taiwan's largest service industry in 1991 (Huang 2001: 3). Since sex is not among the services offered by most of these clubs, it would be a simplification to describe them as brothels or mere fronts for prostitution. Some clubs, however, provide space for sexual transactions, and in many places it is possible for customers and hostesses to arrange sexual transactions outside the clubs. These clubs are similar to the hostess clubs in Japan studied by the American anthropologist Anne Allison (1994), and they constitute one of Taiwan's sex cultures.

The existence of the flower-drinking culture is an undercurrent throughout this book, precisely because it constitutes the backdrop of many women's lives. Some women have worked in the sex industry, and some have lost their husbands to it. Many more define their own virtuousness in contrast to it or in feigned ignorance of it. Yet in no way does work in the various sex trades carry the same social stigma that prostitution does in the West (see Wolf 1972: 205–214).

Since business transactions are often conducted in the male-oriented context of flower drinking, women entrepreneurs in male-dominated industries have to find ways of dealing with it. Some hire male relatives or employees to go flower drinking as needed for sales, procurement of supplies, and labor negotiations. Others deal only with clients who do not insist on flower drinking. The vast majority chooses to do business in industries where the practice is unnecessary, such as cafés and retail boutiques. All agree that it is impossible for women to engage in flower drinking as customers. The flower-drinking culture thus affects far more women than merely the individuals directly involved as workers. One of its effects is that it makes it difficult for women to enter occupations where flower drinking is part of the business culture.

Although it can involve sexual contact, flower drinking is not like Western prostitution, which is oriented towards the sexual needs of individual men. It is primarily, although not exclusively, a group activity. Many men have their first contact with flower drinking by going with older male relatives or classmates in high school, or in groups of soldiers while in military service. In that respect it functions as a rite of passage toward masculinity (Wang 1998). In a wide variety of professions, including manufacturing, construction, the Mafia, the media, and even government procurement, flower drinking provides a necessary context for exchanging resources and building networks. Feminist sociologist Huang Shuling argues that male emotional repression makes it necessary for men to use women as bridges to connect socially. For wives, however, this particular kind of male bonding can lead dangerously to the destruction of marriage, family, and emotional security, whether or not it leads to long-term sexual relationships with other women (Huang 2001).

Since soldiers and workers also engage in flower drinking, it is clearly more than a business practice. For men, it is a public display of masculinity and an opportunity for male bonding. Flower drinking involves highly coded behavior with precise drinking rituals and unspoken rules of conduct. Alcohol, for example, is never taken alone, but must be imbibed as part of a toast between at least two individuals. For inevitable moments of individual thirst, nonalcoholic beverages such as tea and soft drinks are also served. Such drinks do not require a group toast. Men exhibit their masculinity by flirting with the women and fondling their breasts, a ritual that transforms women's secondary sexual features into symbols of a man's virility. To complete their tasks of boosting individual masculine identities, the women hostesses pretend to welcome the flirtation and to find the men attractive. Like marriage, where men are said to "take" wives, flower drinking thus affirms masculinity through the consumption of women. Men do not necessarily enjoy it. Some feel forced into it by pressure from work superiors, and even gay men must conform to the heterosexual flirting rituals (Huang 2001: 11).

It would be a mistake, moreover, to assume that the individual women involved are powerless. The sex industry is not merely a case of women as victims of male power. Women can use the industry to assert their own agency. They can enter and leave the industry at will, and have a great deal of choice in selecting clients. The bosses, moreover, are not always men. Two of the women I interviewed have been involved in the industry, one in the local market and one in a global market exporting Taiwanese aboriginal women to hostess clubs in Japan. Conversations with these women reveal much about the paradox of women and structural power.

A TAIPEI BRIDGE TEAHOUSE

I visited the Taipei Bridge Teahouse twice: once with a group of businessmen and once with a group of acquaintances whom I knew enjoyed flower drinking. The teahouse was in the alleys of Taipei's historical Tatung District. Just across the bridge from Sanchung in Taipei County, it drew its clients largely from the workers and petty capitalists of that proletarian district. The facilities were minimal: small rooms with folding tables and chairs for beer and tea drinking, and naked light bulbs hanging from the ceiling. A busy kitchen kept hostesses and customers supplied with Taiwanese dishes and snacks. Since the women were mostly aging matrons at the end of their careers, or women whose figures were wider than generally considered desirable, this establishment was at the low-price and low-prestige end of the spectrum. Whereas elaborately decorated KTV parlors with young, slim women can demand upwards of NT$20,000 a visit, this place cost only NT$2,000 a person for three hours of drinking and fondling, including unlimited alcoholic drinks for male customers and female hostesses.

Both visits revealed to me the drinking rituals of masculine bonding, as well as the general operation of the teahouse. Women drifted in and out of the room, drinking and chatting with the men and getting to know their personal tastes. When a woman found a man she felt comfortable with and who liked her as well, she would spend more time with him and encourage him to drink. In order to slow down their own drunkenness caused by drinking with so many men each evening, the hostesses mixed their own beer with generous portions of water. The main event was conversation and drinking rituals between men, although all the men flirted with women, holding them on their laps, exchanging massages with them, and fondling their breasts.

Frankly, I found the rituals to be somewhat distressing as violations of my own feminist-inspired ethics. Fortunately, the three-hour time limit was strictly enforced both times, after which we were politely escorted to the door and warmly invited to return another night. Two women, however, left the possibility of future contacts open by exchanging mobile phone numbers; and they did actually call me later. I also got to meet the owner, Ong Siu-kim, a Native Taiwanese woman of forty years. On the second visit, she agreed to meet me for a life-history interview the following morning at eleven o'clock.

When I arrived that morning after an hour-long motorcycle drive across Taipei, the air was full of incense. I noticed that she had just left fresh offerings on the altar to Tho Te Kong (the earth god) just inside the doorway. Empty alcohol bottles, evidence of last night's business, were stacked up underneath the altar: Taiwanese beer, Taiwanese-produced sake, Kinmen *ko-liang-chiu.* The small rooms, filled with male customers at night, were all empty. Since I had made an appointment, and even then had arrived late due to heavier than usual traffic, I walked back into the kitchen in search of Siu-kim. She was standing on a stool, rummaging through a plastic bag of ritual paper money.

"You're so early," she said. "I just got here. I haven't even had time to *pai-pai* ('worship and burn incense') yet."

She led me down the narrow hall to a small room up front. It was only a small table with two stools, which made me realize for the first time that some customers come alone to drink and talk to the women. Some men apparently become addicted to flower drinking and return for more personal reasons. Siu-kim invited me to sit down and disappeared for a moment, reappearing a few minutes later with saucers piled with pistachios and watermelon seeds. "Would you like some coffee?" she asked. "No thanks," I said. "Water is fine." But she left again, returning with a small teapot. She took two small glass cups down from the plastic holder nailed to the plywood room divider, and poured two glasses of tea. "Wait here," she said and left. I sat alone in the dimly lit room for about twenty minutes. The room was bathed in a dim pink light, hardly enough to read by. A metal fan roared above. Summer would arrive soon, I noted, and the place was apparently not equipped with air-conditioning. I listened to the sounds of the women arriving for work, and an elderly man entering and taking a place in the room beside me.

One of the "sisters" (*sio-chia*) whom I had already met the previous night walked in and sat down. I began to wonder if Siu-kim remembered that I was here for an interview or if she thought I was the first customer of the day. The woman picked up a handful of watermelon seeds, and ate them one by one, discarding them in an ashtray. I began the conversation, saying, "It must be a hard job, to work here." She looked at me in a perplexed manner. Picking up on a common complaint of service workers, I continued, "You always have to smile and look happy, even if you are in a bad mood."

"It's not so bad," she said. "The first time I meet someone, I have a hard time talking to him. I don't know what to say. But then I get to know his individual character. We try to match up customers to the appropriate girl according to their personalities."

Siu-kim returned as suddenly as she had left. She sat down and extended her hands out for me to see. "Look at these rough hands," she said. "These are the hands of a person who has led a bitter life. My hands are not beautiful." Short fingers, rough skin, her hands indeed looked more like those of a farmer than of a city girl. "Can you tell how many children I have given birth to?" she asked, trying to elicit a guess. "No," I said. "Four," she said. "I can't tell," I said. "You seem so young."

After chatting for a few minutes, I gave her a consent form explaining my project and said that I was doing a study of women entrepreneurs in all different occupations. "And I'll represent this occupation?" she asked. "Yes," I said. She laughed, happily or nervously, I wasn't sure which. She requested that I take notes rather than tape record the conversation, which seemed reasonable considering the semilegal nature of her business. All varieties of the sex industry are closely regulated, with different licenses and tax scales imposed according to the category under which the businesses register. They most frequently register as "snack shops" or teahouses, in spite of the fact that they serve alcohol, in order to avoid being taxed at the higher rates levied on pubs. Some do not register at all.

Warming up to my foreign and academic identity, Siu-kim said, "I have a friend who went to England to go to school. She said that my life is so bitter that one could write a book about it." When I told her that was my intention—albeit in English and using a pseudonym for the interviewees—she began to tell me her story:

> I was born in Ilan. It was only after I came to Taipei that I worked in a dance hall. We were a poor family and lived in the mountains. We were seven children, and I was the second oldest. When I graduated from grade school, I came to Taipei. I came with a friend. She wasn't a relative, just another girl I knew. We came to Taipei together and worked in a factory making paper boxes. We earned NT$1,000 a month. I still remember. We paid NT$25 for the bus ticket from Toucheng to Taipei back then. But of course we couldn't go home very often because we were busy working.

Soon, however, disaster struck her family:

> When I was fifteen, my mother died. I returned to Ilan to take care of my younger brothers and sisters. I had to feed the ducks and the chickens. I still remember taking my younger sisters out with me into the fields to plant ginger. One was five years old, the other seven. My younger brothers went to school. In my family, both boys and girls got the same education, but the girls weren't old enough to go to school yet. Since my father needed my help, I stayed on the mountain for a year. Then I went to a nearby town. I worked in a textile factory there, making clothes, for five years. I was there from the age of sixteen to twenty-one.

Like most young women factory workers at the time, she left the factory at marriage and started working at home:

> I worked there until I got married. After I got married, I became a housewife. But I didn't stop working. I did subcontracting at home. I think I was very good. I was very industrious. In fact, I am still very good. I would be a woman worker now if I had the chance, but I don't have the chance anymore. All of those jobs have moved to China.

When I asked about her husband, she described him as violent and oppressive:

> He was the oldest son. And like me, he had no mother. His mother had already passed away. He was a farmer, so he just planted fields. We were married for fourteen years. But my husband loved alcohol, and he also loved to beat me. We had four children.

Eventually, she could no longer tolerate the violence and pain of marriage. At the age of thirty-three, she left her children and moved to Taipei:

I thought I was very pitiful, being beaten all the time. So finally, I came to Taipei. In Ilan, I had been earning NT$40,000 a month. That was a lot of money at the time, especially in Ilan. But in Taipei, it was difficult to earn so much money, and the cost of living was much higher than in Ilan.

Initially, she had high hopes for Taipei:

> At first, I planned to open a café. I went to work in a café, wanting to learn about the business. A woman ran the café. She said she would teach me, and then help me open my own shop. But I was cheated. I just washed dishes from morning to night for NT$30,000 a month, NT$1,000 a day.

Siu-kim's husband, however, soon caught up with her. She explained the situation, saying, "My husband came and pleaded with me to return. He brought the children and asked me to come home for their sake. I went back. I still hadn't thought things through. It was only after my divorce that I returned to Taipei for good." The children remained with their father.

It was then that she entered the sex industry:

> I found work in a dance hall. When I first started working in the dance hall, my body was still covered with injuries from being beaten by my husband. Around my waist, I had been beaten black and blue, and I had to wear a medicinal band. I had to work really hard at the job, since I had to pay my husband for childcare. The "Mamas" ahead of me all spoiled me.

Her sister, also in Taipei, then helped her find a job in a teahouse like the one she would later own:

> Then, at the Chinese New Year, we had a fifteen-day vacation. I went with my younger sister to the teahouse where she was working. It was like here. I quit my job at the dance hall and stayed there for two years. In that kind of place, there isn't much pressure.

In 1999, Siu-kim decided to open up her own teahouse and rented her current location with her own savings and an interest-free loan from her younger sister:

> Opening this shop was very difficult. When I first rented this place, it was in really bad physical condition. Even the water pipes had to be repaired, but I fixed it up all by myself. I've been running it for seven months. It's hard to manage the place, especially since the women love to gossip. Worst of all are all the fines we have to pay. I'm here every day from 11 A.M. to 12:30 A.M. Then I go home to sleep. I wake up and go to market. Then at noon, I open shop. We get customers from the moment we open the door. I like to dance, but now I don't have the time to go dancing.

Nonetheless, her project gave her a new life outside of marriage:

> I'm doing really well with this, much better than when I was married. I don't know why I stayed with my husband for so long. I should have divorced him much earlier,

when I was young. I wasn't able to think it through. As soon as I realized what was happening, I got a divorce. The last time he beat me, I spent three days in the hospital.

"What does your father think about you starting this business?" I asked.

"My father doesn't know what I do," she said. "If he did, he would beat me to death. I told him I opened a KTV parlor. Anyway, he knows that my sister is also very bitter, so he doesn't have any say in the matter."[1]

I asked her what difficulties she faces in running the business. The sums of money she mentioned reveal the profits that can be earned in their business.

I manage it not badly, and business is all right. What gets me is that the police come in and raid occasionally, and then we have to pay fines. Recently, I was fined NT$400,000. I don't mind the fines of NT$60,000 to NT$70,000. That is nothing. But NT$400,000 is too much. I feel so helpless.

"How often do the police come?" I asked. Matter-of-factly, she responded.

"Irregularly. But we aren't doing anything illegal. Think of it as a café. People just come here to drink. I am tired and would like to stop doing it. But so many women depend on me. I can't let them down."

She emphasized that much of the pleasure in the business comes from relationships with customers:

The customers are quite good. The big brothers (*toa-ko*, slang for gangsters) are very good to us. Of course, since we are dealing with alcohol, there are some problems. Some of them don't pay. Yet some of our clients are of a very high level. They own factories, and go abroad to do business. Some of them tell me, "Come along with me. Go to a foreign country and look around. I'll pay for the ticket." But I have never gone. I'm simply too busy here. I don't have much education, but a lot of high-class men chase after me.

"What advantages do you get from opening a business?" I asked. "What do you like about it?" Quite pragmatically, she said, "When I see a lot of cash, that makes me happy. My life is like that. I come to work. I make money. Every day is like that. I like seeing the money, thousands of dollars, coming in every day."

Yet this is not her only business venture:

I try other things, too. Once I invested NT$2,000,000 in a stone company.[2] It was a big brother who was doing that business in real stones, big stones. I invested in his business, but it didn't work. I lost all of my money. He didn't cheat me, but a lot of things happened. The economy took a downturn and there was a big typhoon. It's not his fault that it didn't work out.

Changing the topic back to her present occupation, I asked if many women open such businesses. She described it as a largely woman-dominated field:

From what I can see, most of the owners are women,[3] at least here around Taipei Bridge. Men are not appropriate for this field. Of course, there are some men who own shops like this. There are also some places where men serve female clients, like Fridays.[4] Those are mostly owned by men.

Still, she admitted she would like to get out of the business:

Actually, I would like to open a café. It's relatively simple, not like here. Here it is not so simple, since there is alcohol involved. And the women don't stay long. The mobility rate is so high that some just stay for a few days. So I always have to look for new women.

"How do you find the women?" I asked.

"They just come in looking for work," she said, "but then they leave really quickly. They think they can earn more money elsewhere."

The money in the field is so good, she said, that many women engage in the business at some time in her lives. Referring back to her student friend, she said, "Even my friend who goes to school in England comes back to Taiwan once a year and works in a dance hall for several months to earn money. Then she goes back to England. That's how she puts herself through school."

With that assertion of identity with an educated middle class, she indicated that we were finished and excused herself. "I have to go burn paper money," she said. "In this business, you have to pai-pai every day. That's the only way you can do good business." "Who do you pai-pai to?" I asked. "Kuan Kung and Tho Te Kong," she said, referring to the earth god. "In this business, everyone worships Tho Te Kong."

Viewed from Siu-kim's perspective, the sex industry can be empowering for women. Like other women entrepreneurs, opening a business has given her room to develop her own capacities, which she expresses through pride in having renovated the building herself. In terms of her personal relations, she experienced her moment of existential rupture as a battered wife lying in an Ilan hospital room, and realized that the sex industry gave her more control over her body than marriage ever had. Entrepreneurship has allowed her to craft her own life free of the pain and constraints of marriage. It also gave her organizational power over other women employees, although that power is undermined by high labor mobility in the industry.

Siu-kim is aware of the low-class position she occupies due to this form of entrepreneurship. In our interactions, therefore, she attempts to save face through reference to "high-class" men that pursue her and even a friend studying in England who works in the business during return trips to Taiwan. Her main regret, however, is not having entered the industry, but that she didn't begin earlier. It is precisely this kind of empowerment among hetaeras that Simone de Beauvoir found so paradoxical: "the geishas of Japan enjoyed far greater liberty than other women of their times" (de Beauvoir 1989 [1952]: 567). Although Taiwan is no longer under Japanese control, the life-worlds of Taiwanese hostesses are still not much different from those of contemporary Tokyo. The following story shows how intimately related those life-worlds can be.

EXPORTING ABORIGINAL TAIWAN:
THE GLOBAL SEX MARKET

I first met Yulan Watan in the home of Chou Ing-tai, a Mainlander who runs an un-registered childcare center in one of Taipei's many *juancun,* or residential villages for retired Mainlander soldiers and their dependents. Yulan, a single mother, had left her children with Ing-tai for years, and they remained friends long after the children were old enough to take care of themselves. I initially wanted to interview Yulan, a forty-seven-year-old Tayal woman, because of her current business: eldercare in her own home. On our first encounter, however, she suggested yet another story, that of her previous involvement in the international sex industry. In a low whisper, she said:

> When a landslide destroyed my family's home, I discovered that it is important to earn a lot of money. I did a lot of things to earn money, including working in the so-called entertainment business. I can't talk about that right now, since my son is in the next room, but if we meet for coffee another day I will tell you all about it.

Several weeks later, I visited Yulan in her home in the foothills south of Taipei, where she cares for a seventy-nine-year-old retired medical doctor in need of twenty-four-hour care after a stroke. She, her mother, the retired doctor, and I chatted in Japanese for a while—the only common language we all shared. Then, as her mother and the older man slept in their rooms all afternoon, she began to narrate her life history to me. A talkative woman with a detailed memory, the story eventually stretched out over three encounters and fifteen hours of conversation. From her, I learned much about the ethnic dimensions of the sex industry.

Representation of aboriginal women in the sex industry is far out of proportion with their presence in the Taiwanese population. Although aboriginal people constitute less than 4 percent of the total population, 19.4 percent of underage women arrested as prostitutes between 1987 and 1991 were aboriginal. Among Taiwan's ten officially recognized indigenous groups, the Tayal are the most involved in prostitution. In Taipei's Hua-hsi Street red-light district, for example, thirty-three out of eighty-six prostitutes in 1997 were aboriginal, and twenty-two of them were Tayal (Huang 2002). Yulan thus began her life narrative with an explanation of aboriginal participation in the business:

> People in construction and other businesses need to drink to do business. We call it "flower drinking." Most aboriginal women in the city end up working in those bars to support their families. When they are old they become "aunties" [the older women who cook and clean in such establishments]. Aboriginal people are really naïve. We don't believe that there are bad people in the world, and thus don't protect ourselves adequately. That is what I have learned in the past thirty years.

She herself has endured many bitter learning experiences. She started out with a description of the poverty in her childhood:

I grew up in an aboriginal village in Ilan County. The environment was not bad. We were six children: three boys and three girls. When I was in the fourth grade, I was the best in my class. My teacher told my parents to send me to school in Ilan City, so I would have a better chance to test into middle school. Although my parents were poor, they sent me to Ilan City for fifth and sixth grade. I lived with my uncle and worked part-time in an electronics factory. I then tested into middle school, one of only three aboriginal students accepted, and received a scholarship. Before the scholarship started, I got money from the church to buy books and supplies.

While in middle school, Yulan became aware of her family's poverty, which was suddenly visible to her in comparison to relatively wealthier classmates:

I always saved my pocket money [from the scholarship]. I didn't spend it on myself. My father always came asking for money and I would give it to him. My mother told me not to give it to him, but I decided I had to earn money to help my parents. My grandmother spoiled me, but there was never rice to eat. We had meat and fish whenever my father came back from hunting or fishing, but we never had rice to eat when he was not there. We only had rice porridge made with lots of water. Once when my grandmother offered me rice, I refused. I said it wasn't right to give it to me but not to my brothers and sisters. It was then that I decided to help my parents.

Whereas other girls in her village got married just out of primary school, Yulan was able to continue her education. While at school in Ilan, she discovered the sexual attention of men:

There were university students who came to our village as volunteers in "engineering teams." They went out to the countryside to clean up the roads. I hated it when those boys came. Some of them wanted to approach me, but I always refused them.

After finishing middle school, she wanted to attend military school. At her mother's insistence, however, she attended a Catholic nursing school in Ilan. She moved in with her aunt, who had married a Mainlander soldier and was living in a juancun. Her father wanted her to marry a young man of mixed Japanese and aboriginal heritage. She, however, fell in love with her neighbor, whom she referred to throughout the rest of her narrative as simply "the Hubei person." Marriage with him, however, was not destined:

My parents liked the Japanese guy. Some people from Zhejiang had told them that Hubei people are immoral. They said, "The nine-headed bird preys on Heaven; and the Hubeinese on Earth." My mother believed that and forbade me to see him. But he became my boyfriend, and we met in secret at my aunt's house. Nothing [sexual] happened, since we were so conservative back then.

When she finished nursing school at the age of nineteen, she finally gave in to her parents' strong objections and broke up with the Hubei person. Heartbroken by that turn of events, however, she decided to leave Ilan, since "I didn't want to marry early and I figured there would be no opportunities in the countryside for self-development." That decision led to one of the most traumatic experiences of her youth. She described a scenario eerily similar to stories of other young Tayal women being "sold" into prostitution at the time (Huang 2002):

> Obeying my mother, I went to the health clinic and did an interview. The director was a forty-year-old Amis man. He said he would take me to Taipei to work. My mother helped me pack my bags, but she didn't give me any money, not a single cent. While I was waiting for the bus, that Hubei person came looking for me, but I told him to go away. I took the bus to Ilan and then the clinic director took me to the train station.
>
> When we arrived in Taipei, there were so many lights. I had never been in the city before. We took a taxi to Chunghua Road near Wuchang Street. He took me to a second-floor hotel. That Amis man said, "We will sleep here." But since there was only one bed, I had a bad feeling. When he was in the shower, I ran away. I didn't know where to go. There were so many people on the street. I didn't know my way around the city, and I didn't have any money. Suddenly, the Hubei person showed up, and took me back home. I was so angry with my mother who sent me without knowing. I yelled at her and we got into an angry fight.

After passing the nursing license examination in Ilan, she moved to the Taipei district of Pei-tou, a neighborhood known for its hot springs, teahouses, brothels, and various forms of sex-industry establishments. Following her parents' instructions, she cut off all social contact with the Hubei person. She then met her first lover:

> My uncle had a friend from the cement factory in Nan-ao. One day, he showed up in my clinic and said he had injured his arm in a motorcycle accident. Actually, it was only scratched up; I later realized that he had done it on purpose. He took me out to the night market to eat, and then he kept telephoning me. He was very patient. I loved him a lot. We decided to get married and we lived together. Then I found another woman's letter in his bag. She was a Mainlander in Hualien. She said she was pregnant with his child. When I told him I was leaving, he took me to meet the other woman and introduced me to her as his fiancée. The other woman and I asked him to choose between us, but he didn't answer and I left. They both followed me and pleaded for forgiveness. The other woman later had a miscarriage; she and I became friends. But I want an honest marriage; one where we can communicate with all our hearts. So I left him.

Still hurting from that experience, she quit her job at the clinic, moved into the bus station dormitory with a Tayal woman friend who was working there, and started drifting from job to job. She worked briefly as a hospital nurse, a department-store clerk, a worker in a plastics factory, and as one of Taiwan's first insurance brokers. "But nobody ever wanted to buy insurance," she said. "They just wanted to talk to me about their love lives."

Yulan soon heard a rumor that her ex-lover from Nan-ao was living with a dance-hall girl. Jealous and angry, she decided to get a job in a dance hall herself just to spite him:

There were three aboriginal girls working at the bus station. One of them said, "My friend is a dance-hall girl and earns a lot of money." They decided to go with them. I did it to get revenge on my boyfriend. We all three went to the Singapore Dance Hall and applied for the job, but they only wanted me.

In what was surely a reference to my identity as a scholar, she added an aside and said, "The cultural level was very high. They [the male clients] were all college graduates. I hated those men, especially those with glasses. I don't think scholars should go to such places." Her tactic, she said with pride, did indeed have the intended effect on her ex-lover of eliciting his attention:

I worked there for two months; then I called him to tell him where I was working. He came to get me immediately and grabbed me by the throat. He said I am not allowed to leave with the customers. That's when I met my son's father. He was a big factory owner, but I refused all of his advances, since I knew that he had a family. He was impressed because I refused him, but I let him walk me to the corner. When he tried to kiss me, I bit him.

Her would-be suitor got her phone number from another of the girls, however, and started calling her at home. After a year, he proposed to her and promised to divorce his wife. Yulan said to me that she was still thinking of the Hubei person at the time. Nonetheless, when her ex-lover from Nan-ao continued to pursue her, she spitefully announced she was going to marry the factory owner:

After I said that lie, I had to marry him. I didn't really love him. He went out with men all the time and had a lot of girlfriends. Sometimes he would even leave for one or two months without coming home, and then we would fight. After he beat me the third time, I demanded a divorce. He wasn't evil. He knew that outside was just "play" and that I was his family, but I couldn't deal with it anymore.

At the divorce, she left the house with only her clothes and two young children: one aged five years and the other six months. I asked if she had claimed a divorce settlement. She said, "It is better to be happy and raise the children alone. I didn't want the pain of a difficult divorce." Using the Buddhist term "seeing through the world of dust" (*kanpo hongcheng*), which is not entirely dissimilar to Sartre's idea of rupture, she said, "You have to see through the illusions of the world. My attitude from then on was that I have to be free." Married at twenty-three and divorced at twenty-nine, she was ready for a new life.

AFTER THE RUPTURE:
A NEW LIFE BEGINS

At approximately the same time as her divorce, disaster also struck her home community. A typhoon and resulting landslide destroyed the entire village. In her words, "all that remained was the cross from the church." In order to make money for her children and parents, she left her two children with Chou Ing-tai and took a high-paying job that took her to dance halls as far away as Singapore and Hong Kong. Able to earn more money as a hostess abroad than in most jobs in Taiwan, she saved enough money to start her own "entertainment agency" at the age of thirty-five. Already able to speak Japanese, which had been the *lingua franca* in her aboriginal hometown, she sent her women to serve as hostesses in Tokyo. The fact that she and other young women from her village spoke Japanese gave them an edge in Tokyo:

> When I was working in Southeast Asia, I watched how those agents did it. Then I started my own company. I did the administrative work, like seeing that they get work permits and necessary documents. Then I would go [to Japan] once a month to make sure the women were doing well. Otherwise, I stayed here.

Yulan rented a large place in Taipei where she could train women to work as hostesses in Japan. Preferring to hire Japanese-speaking aboriginal women from her own village, she housed them in a dormitory. More ambitious than most agencies in the industry, her company included an office to receive Japanese brokers, a training area for new hostesses, and a dormitory.

Although the business was profitable for nearly a decade, Yulan had to branch out into other endeavors to make the money she wanted for her family. With a Hong Kong friend she had met while working as a hostess, she even got involved in a scheme to export used cars from Japan to South Africa. Eventually, however, her business deals soured. First, she lost money on the car export scheme. Second, under suspicion that the aboriginal women being sent to Japan might be involved in prostitution, the Japanese government began limiting the number of "performers" she could send.[5] With all of those problems, she closed her business and went back to nursing by doing eldercare in her home. "Although I failed," she said, "I have gained experience. I hope that my children can learn from that."

In spite of Yulan's eventual business failure, she was empowered in the same way as most entrepreneurs. She found the space to express her own identity in the workplace; which in this case meant training women to be hostesses in Japan. She was able to support herself and her family, even giving her father enough capital to invest in a pear farm. As a boss, she had some control over labor, even as she found the women to be difficult. "A lot of aboriginal women have worked as prostitutes," she said. "You can't boss them around." She herself saw all of those endeavors, however, as merely ways of earning money in a life with other priorities. She summarized her life to date, not in terms of career history, but rather in terms of destiny and her relations with men:

> Everyone has a fate. Life is like a road. Both of us are on the side of the road. You reach out towards the person on the other side of the road, and he reaches out towards you. We give, but the other person may not accept it. They give, and we may not even notice it, like me when I hurt that Hubei person. So it is better to be loved than to love,

even if the loved one is unaware of it. That is fate. Even the relationship between parents and children is like that. Parents take care of their children for as long as they can, but nobody knows how long they will live. It is just fate if parents die and their children end up in an orphanage. The important thing is to give as much as you can.

LEARNING FROM A LIFE:
HOW LIFE STORIES BECOME MORAL TALES

All individuals construct their identities through life narratives that aim towards the good as they perceive it. Unlike most women entrepreneurs in this study, Yu-lan constructs her life story as that of a woman who has learned about male infidelity and then decided to devote her life to giving to her parents and children rather than to men. She is the subject in this narrative, empowered by her business to be almost as transcendent as a man. Although her business failed in financial terms, she described it as a success in terms of personal development and consciousness. Interestingly, however, her story, once transformed into a moral tale by friend and confidant Chou Ing-tai, also objectifies her.

Ing-tai had two clients who sent hostesses to Japan, and thus acquired a good knowledge of the business. The other woman, whom she refers to as simply Ms. Chen, was Han Chinese. Without moral commentary on the nature of the industry, Chou Ing-tai explained how Ms. Chen had succeeded by using rational business practices and Yulan had failed because she let personal relations get in the way of profit. Referring to Yulan by her Han surname of Kao, she explained:

> As an aboriginal, Ms. Kao had more advantages than Ms. Chen in the beginning, because she already knew Japanese. But why was Ms. Chen more successful? Why did Ms. Kao fail in the same business? Ms. Kao failed because she employed only aboriginal women and they were all her relatives. Once they came to Taipei, she housed them and fed them for free. Ms. Chen, on the other hand, only fed her girls when they came in for training. That way her expenses were much lower. As for Ms. Kao, she fed and housed so many people twenty-four hours a day. Isn't that more expensive? And then, since they were all her aboriginal relatives, she gave them an equal share of her own profits. Ms. Chen just gave them the low wages they agreed on, making a clear distinction between wages and profits.

In addition to mixing up business with the need to take care of relatives, Yulan (Ms. Kao) lacked capitalist discipline, the this-worldly asceticism of the successful entrepreneur. Chou Ing-tai continued to compare the two women:

> Even Wang Yong-qing is not as generous as Ms. Kao.[6] When she had money, she would take our entire family to the Sogo Department Store in a car. We would help her buy a whole carload of presents for people. But then when she wasn't earning a profit, she didn't even have enough money to get a haircut. At the Mid-autumn Festival, I had to give her moon cakes and pomelos. Ms. Kao just lives from day to day. Ms. Chen lives by a plan.

Most of all, however, Ms. Kao's problems stemmed from overinvolvement with men, which is the lesson Chou Ing-tai wanted her own daughters to learn:

Ms. Chen is forty-five years old. She has never looked for a boyfriend. Never. Ms. Kao was much prettier than Ms. Chen, but she couldn't manage her emotional relationships properly. She depended on her "woman's capital" [physical beauty] to get a man. If that man fell on financially hard times, she didn't want anything to do with him anymore. After she had had several lovers, people knew she was that kind of person. She wasn't willing to help out. After a while, she began to age and she couldn't rely on women's capital anymore.

Chou Ing-tai said she draws a moral lesson from the contrasting experiences of Ms. Chen and Ms. Kao: Ms. Chen who never married versus Ms. Kao who has been with many men, Ms. Chen who succeeded in business versus Ms. Kao who eventually went bankrupt. The moral of the story, as she teaches her own daughters, is that:

It doesn't matter if you get married or not. It doesn't matter if you have children or not. Just look at the experience of Ms. Kao: the most important thing is that you can take care of yourself financially. If you are financially independent, it doesn't matter if your husband treats you poorly or if your children are unfilial. I always tell them that the most important thing in life is to be able to provide for yourself.

Chou Ing-tai, who has heard many bitter stories as a caretaker for the children of single mothers, has developed a cynical attitude toward men. She thus plans to send her daughter to architectural school in America so that she will have the foundation for a lucrative and autonomous career. What is important to her and many others is that women can use entrepreneurship to gain agency for themselves as individuals.

DISCUSSION

The paradox of the sex industry is that women can gain agency and power for themselves, but only to the extent that they gain control of the sexual objectification of themselves and other women. The most empowered women in the industry are those who themselves become "Mamas" or even bosses as they age. By running sexual enterprises, they can empower themselves and earn a generous income to use as they please. Many of them are even empowered more as sex workers than as battered housewives. In de Beauvoir's language, they thus become subjects almost like men. Because so many sex workers themselves emphasize the empowerment they gain from their work, some Taiwanese feminists have even publicly supported the right of women to work in the industry. The industry, however, is almost symbolic of the feminine condition in patriarchal systems, as it illustrates well the limits of female agency and women's enduring position of structural inequality.

Women's weak structural power is undermined by cultural practices and discourses that define masculinity, femininity, and the dynamics that bind them. As Turner argued, the struggle is no longer one of wresting economic power from family patriarchs, but of an ideological conflict between feminism and a misogynistic ideology of patrism (1996: 157–58). Patriarchy, or the control of women's (and younger men's) labor power by older men, has lost its grip in an era where women can empower themselves through participation in the capitalist market system. The main field of contention is now ideological, as men try to restrain or control women's behavior through patristic ideology.

One major field of contention is the hegemonic arena of a sex industry in which men are consuming subjects and women are objects to be consumed. This chapter thus examines the paradox of women who gain individual agency and power in the sex industries, loosely defined. The very ways in which these women gain power, however, reveal the weak structural power of women in society as a whole. When women become entrepreneurs in this business, they empower themselves by exploiting other women.

In the sex industry, women are disempowered when they accept the dominant ideology of patrism. Some hope to gain respect by marrying men from among their clients, but then some who succeed find themselves sitting at home while their husbands go out and "play" with younger women. Several of the women I interviewed (cf. Chapter 7), and not just Yulan, have suffered from the pain of this type of infidelity. These all-too-common personal strategies are rooted in part in the culture of flower drinking in which men must exhibit their masculinity through the consumption of women. They are a product of a culture that demands women tolerate their husbands' extramarital affairs while remaining loyal themselves.

As Siu-kim noted, there are also places where women go to be served by men; Taiwan does have male strippers and its "Fridays." The fact remains, however, that there are exponentially more hetaeras than there are Fridays and that men are socially sanctioned when they go flower drinking, whereas women are not. Some attribute the double standard to stronger male sexual desire. As Emma Goldman pointed out, however, that double standard expresses greater male power rather than greater male desire (Connell 1987: 113).

The life histories of these women reveal as well the inequality inherent in heterosexual marriage. While many women in the sex industry have sad stories of violent and oppressive marriages, the number of gigolos running away from abusive wives probably approaches zero. For such women, the industry is only empowering when compared to the alternative of marriage. Far too generous is the conclusion that "the only difference between women who sell themselves in prostitution and those who sell themselves in marriage is the price and the length of time the contract runs" (de Beauvoir 1989 [1952]: 555–56). Hetaeras and prostitutes actually have an easier time of picking, choosing, and leaving clients than do women trapped in abusive, but psychologically interdependent marriages. The two women in this chapter thus found the industry more empowering than staying in unhappy relationships with men.

More than any other occupation, the sex industry reveals the limitations of entrepreneurship as an empowerment strategy for women. Entrepreneurship does empower individual women, and at all levels of power. It does not, however, challenge the overall structure of a capitalist system that articulates with patriarchy in the consumption of women. The deepening of capitalism makes it more and more possible for women to launch their own businesses. It also entails the expansion of sex industries, and development of the culture of flower drinking into more and more intricate forms. Women's position of structural inequality thus goes beyond limitations on access to capital, property, and business skills. It is constrained by cultural norms of masculinity and femininity, which are not complementary opposites like yin and yang, but actually men and women embraced in unequal power structures. Liberal capitalist feminism, therefore, does not work. In order to liberate women from patriarchy, feminism must be radical, challenging the cultural practices that reproduce oppression.

NOTES

1. She is referring to the fact that her sister has also gone into the sex industry.

2. This was plausible in the bubble economy of the early 1990s, as capital was easily available from informal rotating credit associations.

3. Huang Shu-ling (personal communication, 2002) says that most of the owners are actually men. Only the smaller shops are likely to be owned by women.

4. This is a reference to the American chain restaurant T.G.I.F. (Thank God It's Friday). An unfounded rumor once circulated that waiters at T.G.I.F. were actually gigolos. Since then, popular slang has referred to gigolos as "Friday" boys.

5. According to Chou Ing-tai, they really were prostitutes.

6. Wang Yong-qing is CEO of Formosa Plastics and one of Taiwan's wealthiest men.

Chapter Sixteen

Concluding Notes

The narratives presented in this book provide a broad portrait of Taipei at the beginning of the twenty-first century. The citizens of Taipei now live in a world in which tradition has lost its grip, daily life is constituted in terms of contradictions between the local and the global, and individuals of all genders can choose from a broader menu of lifestyle options. If the feminist anthropological accounts of the 1970s and 1980s were accurate—and I believe they were—Taiwanese women of just a generation ago were tied to their families of marriage and depended primarily on emotional ties with their uterine families to gain power in that context (Wolf 1972).[1] Compared with that time, when unmarried women were competing to work in textile mills and married women were working in living room factories, women now have far more opportunities to become economic agents of their own. Taiwan's experience, which included universal education as well as economic growth, has permitted many women to empower themselves in ways previously unthinkable.

Some of the most affluent women entrepreneurs have launched regional and global careers, but even the smaller-scale entrepreneurs interviewed have lifestyles in the sense of "decisions taken and courses of action followed under conditions of severe material constraint" (Giddens 1991: 6). Problems of inequality and social exclusion still exist, but they have more chances to assert agency in their own lives. The rise of women entrepreneurs, in spite of the diversity and lack of equality among them, is one example of successful human capacity building in Taiwan. Taiwan has been largely successful at what Amartya Sen (1999) means by "development as freedom."

Self-reflexivity is a strong characteristic of the women I interviewed in Taipei, as well as among most Taiwanese individuals I have encountered in five years of research and residence in three Taiwanese cities. Taipei's entrepreneurial women—like members of local aboriginal communities, sexual minorities, or the entire Taiwanese public in the face of pressure from China—have learned to foreground identity concerns at a time of rapid change and social dislocation. Depending on individual circumstances, Taipei women may use entrepreneurship to craft and assert identities as professionals, as working mothers and wives, as lesbians, as divorcées, or as agents of social change. In doing so, they struggle for power at all levels of society, in a process of what Giddens (1991: 201) calls the emergence of life politics. Most of these women find that entrepreneurship is empowering, although not all of them put gender at the forefront of their narratives. The reason for that will be explored in this chapter.

These women's quest for individual identity and power is an integral part of Taiwan's history. Taiwan has developed at a rate with few historical precedents for most of the past half-century, and Taiwanese people of both sexes have struggled to find a place for themselves in that process of social change. The fact that Taiwanese women have "come a long way" is visible not only in life histories of selected women entrepreneurs, but also in social statistics based on the UNDP's Human Development Index and Gender Empowerment Measure. Many women have even learned to take gender empowerment for granted. Rapid development has created new identities. It has made it possible for both men and women to seek personal identities in new lifestyles, and that includes entrepreneurship as a choice of career. Women have thus benefited from development in absolute terms. Relative to men, however, the struggle for empowerment is still far from over.

Ortner's observation that women's agency differs fundamentally from men's agency, as it is inevitably bound in contradictions that undermine it (1996: 17), is applicable to contemporary Taiwan in the realms of culture, ideology, and discursive practice. Whereas men assume their subjectivity with relative ease, women must claim it with a chutzpah often perceived by others as brash assertiveness. In entrepreneurial families, men take over their parents' firms in apparently "natural" fashion, but women are expected to leave those families at marriage in order to work for their husbands as thau-ke-niu. When men go out and open up businesses, they are praised for their entrepreneurial abilities and skill at providing for their families. When women open up businesses outside of their homes, they are called "strong women," a term with connotations that they lack in other dimensions of life. When men become prominent bosses, they are perceived as rational profit-seeking human beings and even proud carriers of Chinese tradition. When women become prominent bosses, they are perceived as iconoclastic feminists influenced by Western ideas. Customers and other visitors rarely mistake male bosses for the help. They often overlook women bosses entirely and may even mistake hired teenage boys for bosses. Although women entrepreneurs are correct in perceiving that they have been economically empowered in the marketplace, they also realize that they face important ideological battles at home.

Women's structural power is not weakened only through limits on access to capital and property. If it were, the expansion of capitalism, women's credit programs, and legal reform would be sufficient preconditions for women's liberation. Women's structural power is undermined by cultural practices and discourses that define masculinity, femininity, and the dynamics that bind them. Turner thus argued that as capitalism has weakened the institutions that exploit women, the struggle has become an ideological conflict between feminism and patrism (1996: 157–58). Patrism, the ideological defense of male superiority, as opposed to patriarchy or the control of economic resources and labor by older patriarchs, is now the main problem for women. Women thus find that their main problems in life are no longer likely to be conflicts with controlling parents-in-law, but rather their relationships with their husbands. Domestic violence and flower-drinking customs are examples of problems that can arise in marriage. Important thinkers of the Taiwanese feminist movement, including the otherwise very different Hu Youhui (1995), with her call for neolocality, and Josephine Ho (1994), with her emphasis on sexual liberation for women, thus focus on the need for far-reaching changes in the institution of marriage.

Ever since de Beauvoir (1989 [1952]), many feminists have argued that the institution of marriage is oppressive to women. In religious ceremonies in the West, for example, men were long said to "take" a wife at marriage, whereas women are "given" in marriage to their husbands. Although significant progress has been made in both Asia and the West, women have generally played a subordinate role to their husbands within marriage and many still do. Traditions of hypergamy, gender discrimination in the workplace, and social prestige attached to the non-working wife have all combined to make women as a group economically inferior to men. A double standard prevails in sexual morality, moreover, with adultery more tolerated for men than for women (de Beauvoir 1989 [1952]).

These arguments, based on de Beauvoir's observations in France, resonate clearly with the lived experiences of many Taiwanese women, which may explain why *The Second Sex* and similar critiques of marriage have so strongly influenced the local feminist movement. Taiwanese women are said "to be given" (Taiwanese *ke-ho*, Mandarin *jia gei*) in marriage, and men "take" (Taiwanese *chhoa*, Mandarin *qu*) wives. Extramarital affairs, moreover, are widely tolerated for men, and naturalized as a "common weakness" of men. Many male entrepreneurs even view the presence of a mistress as a sign of social prestige. There is, however, a strong social stigma attached to married women who have affairs. That does not mean that women do not have affairs. Unlike men, however, their affairs are not tolerated socially or shown off as proof of economic power.

But there are important differences as well. Some of the women I interviewed even asserted that the Chinese family system is better to women than the Western system. Taiwanese women keep their own family names at marriage, which are in fact almost always the names of their fathers. Like other non-Western feminists (Bulbeck 1998: 212), they are often appalled at Western practices in which women adopt the names of their husbands. Women are also endowed with a dowry at marriage, and the money almost always stays in her control, becoming the foundation of her *sai-khia-chi* (Mandarin *sifangqian*), or private savings. Many women entrepreneurs get their start from these private savings. This dowry system, although imperfect, protects women to a certain extent by giving them property in their own names. In Taiwan, the practice of keeping separate property remains throughout marriage; joint checking accounts, for example, are rare. There is no reason to assume that Taiwanese women are more oppressed than Western women, but there is also no reason to deny that they are less empowered than men.

GLOBALIZATION AND EMPOWERMENT

Globalization has been important in the lives of Taipei women entrepreneurs, and is part of the backdrop to their search for identity. Arjun Appadurai looks at transnational identity and how globalization links individuals around the world through what he calls ethnoscapes, mediascapes, technoscapes, financescapes, and ideoscapes (1996: 33). The most international women in this book are directly connected to other parts of the world through financescapes, including Sophie Hong with her global network of fashion design, Fan Fut-moi with production in China and sales worldwide, and Chhoa Hiong-gun, who sells eels to Japan. Most of them are engaged in global ideoscapes, the ideologies of states and the counterideologies of social movements oriented to capturing power. Aboriginal people in Taiwan are the most obvious examples of involvement in this ideoscape, as they have appropriated for themselves the master narrative of colonized natives to struggle for their own rights and create a global aboriginal identity. The same can be said of the lesbian and gay entrepreneurs of Taiwan's major cities, who even adopt the rainbow flag, as well as Taiwanese women who accept and/or dispute global ideologies of feminism. In a world where women's rights are finally seen almost universally as human rights, women's claims to agency are part of the way in which they claim membership in a modern world.

Within the context of globalization, however, gender equality is frequently said to be a product of the West. In some contexts, such arguments are a blatant attempt to silence women. In their narratives of identity, women frequently engage in this debate. A small minority of them are so offended by the patrism of Taiwanese men that they seek out Western partners and attempt to emigrate from Taiwan. An interior designer I interviewed, for example, met a Belgian man at a concert and married him a few weeks later. Other individuals resist such discourses, as in the example of a woman manufacturer who told me, "I have never experienced gender discrimination in Taiwan. The only time I have ever experienced prejudice as a woman was when I went to Germany." She then related to me a story about a German customs officer who interrogated her husband about her personal identity. When she attempted to answer questions about herself, the officer told her to be quiet and let her husband speak for her. Women situate themselves vis-à-vis feminism and patriarchy, globalization and localization, and between modernity and tradition through the elaboration of life narratives.

Although personal narratives remain a prime material for identity construction, they are also perceived by their creators as maps toward human truths that can be shared with others. It is for that reason that aboriginal people share life experiences with racism in community publications, gays and lesbians relate coming-out stories in consciousness-raising sessions, and women entrepreneurs hold information seminars at FemBooks in Taipei. Women entrepreneurs are frequently consulted by other women, and thus have carefully constructed narratives that share truths of human existence on topics ranging from business tips to relations with men. Entrepreneurship itself is often a central part of their identities.

ENTREPRENEURSHIP AS IDENTITY

Life-history narratives usually involve elements of rupture or sudden change, and the life histories of entrepreneurs are no exception. The entrepreneurial model developed by Shapero and Sokol (1982) refers specifically to what they call the "entrepreneurial event." This type of life experience, although more elaborated in some life narratives than others, is a central part of the personal identity of entrepreneurs. Shapero and Sokol categorize three kinds of life path changes that intervene in the process of deciding to open a new business: (1) "negative displacements" such as migration, being fired, being insulted, angered, and bored with work (alienation), reaching middle age, or being divorced or widowed; (2) "between things" such as coming out of school, the army, or jail; and (3) "positive-pull" factors of influence from partners, mentors, investors, and customers.

It is possible to regroup the thirty life histories in this study into those three kinds of life path changes, although some individuals give multiple reasons for going into business. Ritual-goods seller Ong Siok-ting, Tayal exporter Yuma Nogan, and coffee-shop/bar/restaurant owners Ng Bi-chu, Sharon, and Margang, for example, all reported that they had felt alienated by their previous experiences in both white-collar and blue-collar occupations. Coffee-shop owner Ma Ya-hung and betel-nut seller Lim Koat-ho both went into business after their divorces, and one bakery owner set up a business in her father-in-law's house after a crisis in her marriage. Eight of the thirty women in this study can be classified as having become entrepreneurs due to negative displacements.

For women entrepreneurs, the category of "between things" needs refinement for the obvious reason that it does not include people at the conclusion of military duty. In this case, I include women who returned to Taiwan after studying abroad and "fell into" entrepreneurship, as well as domestic entrepreneurs who are trapped at home either because they need to combine work with childcare or because they are too old to reenter the workforce. The former category would include women who came back to Taiwan unsure of their career directions, including Nita Ing, who eventually took over her father's construction company and is now in charge of constructing Taiwan's high-speed railroad. The latter would include the beautician Tiu Bi-hoa, the soy-milk seller Tan So-hoa, and professional babysitter Chou Ing-tai. I would classify six out of the thirty women in this category.

Positive pulls were involved in the life histories of twenty out of the thirty women. In two cases, the women referred to both negative displacements and positive-pull factors in their narratives. Ong Siok-ting, for example, felt alienated in her earlier job of doing production work for her husband, but she was even more strongly pulled into entrepreneurship by the desire to help the poor and the help of a friend in the beginning. Ng Bi-chu, who felt alienated from her work and even went into business once as a reaction to a failed relationship, also experienced the pull factors of friends encouraging her to join in their partnerships. Sophie Hong and an interior designer also belong in this category, since they went abroad with the specific goal of pursuing further education in their chosen fields and returning to continue the same careers. All of the remaining women went into business either because, like Yuma Nogan, they perceived a market niche they could fill, or because they were encouraged to do so by friends and family members. Five women started out with their husbands as thau-ke-niu, but like jewelry exporter Fan Fut-moi, eventually became autonomous or semiautonomous women entrepreneurs in charge of their own enterprises. Other women who started out in business due to personal relations include one woman who took over her father's Japanese restaurant, another who took over her mother's wedding photo studio, and another who worked in her brother's furniture shop before opening her own. Many first went into business on the invitation of a friend to become a business partner.

These observations that female entrepreneurship is predominantly a result of positive pulls are further supported by the survey data. It should be remembered that 51.6 percent of the 122 women surveyed said that they went into business out of "personal interest." Only 23.8 percent said they went into business to supplement an inadequate family income or support themselves after divorce or death of a spouse. Even if we assume that some of the women who answered "husband's suggestion" or "other" could be categorized as negative-displacement or "between things" entrepreneurs, at least half of the women surveyed seem to have gone into business due to positive pulls of filling market niches, going into business with the encouragement of family and friends, or opening up lifestyle enterprises. The term "lifestyle enterprise" was even used by several women encountered throughout the study, who said that they went into business primarily for the social dimensions of creating space to encounter like-minded people.

The relative preponderance of positive-pull factors into entrepreneurship is the main difference between Taiwanese entrepreneurs and those elsewhere. Shapero and Sokol (1982), for example, found that negative displacement was the most common antecedent to opening new businesses. Similarly, Goffee et al., as cited in Dignard and Havet (1995), studied fifty women entrepreneurs in London and found that business creation was perceived by many as a last resort. In Taiwan, on the contrary, entrepreneurship is often viewed as the first choice. This is surely due to Taiwan's habitus as "Boss Island" (Shieh 1992), where it is commonplace and socially acceptable for people of both genders to launch their own business enterprises. There is no question that Taiwanese people in general place a high value on entrepreneurship and self-sufficiency. The women in this study share that common life-world.

In a historical context, however, this phenomenon can be perceived as a collective negative displacement. In a sense, all Native Taiwanese people are like ethnic entrepreneurs, who have learned to seek out market niches in small business because they have faced discrimination in society. In the early years of KMT rule, Mainlanders monopolized the choicest occupations of government work, teaching, and even post office jobs, keeping the Native Taiwanese confined to agriculture and the small-business sector (Gates 1987: 56). The fact that Native Taiwanese women are represented in my sample of women entrepreneurs in greater numbers than their percentage of the population is a reflection of this heritage. Studying entrepreneurship in Taiwan inevitably means studying Native Taiwanese people, and female entrepreneurship is just one more extension of that ethnic dynamic. As I show below, this ethnic identity is important.

As individuals, however, most women entrepreneurs perceive that entrepreneurship gives women more "free space" than they would otherwise have in society. The spatial metaphor, reminiscent of Virginia Woolf's *A Room of One's Own,* is very common in the discursive practices of women entrepreneurs, as I first discovered in my pilot study in southern Taiwan in 1998. In my survey of Taipei women entrepreneurs ($N = 122$), 62.3 percent strongly agreed with the statement "Entrepreneurship gives women more free space"; 15.6 percent agreed with the statement; 9.8 percent had no opinion; 7.4 percent disagreed; and 4.9 percent strongly disagreed. Women entrepreneurs thus gain a subjective sense of empowerment from their business endeavors. The value of that subjectivity should not be underestimated.

There is, however, extreme individual variation in how free space is used and in how much space individual women may claim. At one end of the spectrum are strongly individualistic women, such as coffee-shop owner Ng Bi-chu or lesbian-bar owner Sharon, who intentionally use entrepreneurship to create a space within which they establish new social identities and avoid the pressures of heterosexual marriage. By opening a bar that caters specifically to lesbians, Sharon has even opened up collective space for other women like herself. Some women, frequently coffee-shop owners, use entrepreneurship as a way of supporting themselves after a divorce or in preparation for a divorce. For women such as this, entrepreneurship is the freest social space of all, and an important arena for identity construction.

At the other end of the spectrum are the domestic entrepreneurs, women who run businesses out of their homes and combine self-employment with household tasks. On the one hand, these women can be said to bear a double burden of household labor and production for the market. On the other hand, they often prefer home-based entrepreneurship to formal employment outside the home, as it produces higher income than local minimum-wage jobs. It may also provide a bridge to other entrepreneurial activities at later moments in the life cycle. This dynamic is found among women entrepreneurs around the world (Tinker 1995: 32).

As a lifestyle choice, however limited, domestic entrepreneurship should not be perceived as merely another form of oppression among many. Even to those women who just take over the front room of their house for a restaurant or beauty shop, entrepreneurship gives them more social space than they would probably otherwise have. They physically possess a space identified as their own, they develop social identities that give them connections outside the family, and they bring an independent income into the family, which often gives them greater transactional power in dealing with both husbands and in-laws. One woman, for example, began to use the first floor of her mother-in-law's house as a bakery at a time when she was unhappy in her marriage. Her in-laws, members of one of Taiwan's older established clans, perceived divorce as a family shame and encouraged her to find more personal space within the family rather than leaving. The expanded space that was the product of her business enabled her to redefine the terms of the marriage rather than pursuing divorce. It is difficult to conclude that this was a case of prefeminist false consciousness, as she is immersed in feminist thought and has even become an important figure in the Taiwanese feminist movement. She claims that entrepreneurship has brought her happiness, liberty, and personal satisfaction.

In any case, the number of women who operate businesses out of their own homes should not be exaggerated. According to survey research ($N = 121$), only 19 percent of Taipei women entrepreneurs live in the same location as their place of business; 39 percent live in the same neighborhood; and 42 percent commute from outside the neighborhood. Even small restaurants or retail stands that look like domestic self-employment are in fact often using rented retail space. Taiwan is no longer a third-world country, and these women are not entering entrepreneurship as the only available alternative to poverty. In most cases, it is a lifestyle choice they have selected from among other possibilities. Most women entrepreneurs fit somewhere between these two extremes of women who use entrepreneurship to avoid or reject patriarchal marriage and those who use it as a form of domestic self-employment. The majority are married women, who rent or buy space away from home, and then run a business separate from the household as a career.

INDIVIDUAL VERSUS COLLECTIVE EMPOWERMENT

The main limitation of entrepreneurship as a development strategy is that business ownership is empowering primarily at the level of the individual. This problem is built into the very social values of liberal economics, which is based on a market economy of rational individuals pursuing their own self-interest. Some women denied that they were rational capitalists. Instead, they emphasized the social dimensions of their businesses, saying it gave them space to make social connections or explore their creative talents. The fact that several of them went into business to satisfy other needs is a powerful and appealing antidote to the neoliberal thought that profit maximization is the highest goal of life. In the final analysis, however, profits are vital. If they cannot earn enough to pay their rent, electricity, and other expenses including employees' wages and their own livelihoods, entrepreneurs have no choice but to eventually close up shop. All entrepreneurs in Taiwan know that fact of life and seek to earn money, even if each coffee-shop owner does not have the ambition to become a Taiwanese version of Starbucks. Itself a product of capitalist rationality, therefore, female entrepreneurship will do little to advance the empowerment of women as a collectivity unless concerted efforts are made toward that goal.

Just as Malcolm X encouraged African American entrepreneurship as a form of collective empowerment, there have been attempts to link business ownership to specific forms of collective identity in Taiwan. Gays and lesbians in Taipei, for example, have networked to create a "rainbow community" of shops, bars, restaurants, and other retail establishments (Simon 2002). One stream of thought in the Taiwanese aboriginal movement likewise sees entrepreneurship as a strategy by which aboriginal people can be more fully integrated into the national economy and take control of their own communities. Yet women as a group have not made similar attempts. Even feminist approaches to female empowerment are focused on the individual, and there is as yet no concept of gendered entrepreneurship equivalent to that of the ethnic entrepreneur. This has much to do with the question of collective identity.

At this point, a conceptual distinction has to be made between objective identity and group consciousness. Group identities, whether they are based on gender, ethnicity, nationality, or sexual orientation (see Simon 2002), have to be brought to the forefront of consciousness in order to be made into potent political tools. All identities are thus like class identity in Marxist thought, which has to be transformed from "class-in-itself" to "class-for-itself" in order to be an effective source of social change. Gender is clearly important to women's lives, since women frequently have very different life trajectories from men. But objective gender identity is different from gender consciousness. Taiwanese women in general, including those in this study, tend to be low in gender consciousness for reasons discussed below.

IDENTITY AND EMPOWERMENT

Survey research confirms the observation that gender is rarely perceived in Taiwan as a central axis of personal identity (see table 16.1). In a sociological survey directed by Wang Fu-chang (2000), 3,496 people were asked which two forms of identity are most important to them. The most common response was occupation, with 30.8 percent of respondents indicating that their work is important to their self-identity. The next common responses in descending order were educational level (25.8%), place of residence (19.4%), nationality (18.2%), and religious belief (16.3%). When cross-tabulated for gender, there are slight differences between men and women, although both men and women self-identify primarily according to work. In descending order, women think that the most important dimensions of personal identity are occupation (29.6%), educational level (29.1%), place of residence (21.9%), religion (18%), and nationality (15.6%). Men self-identify most by occupation (32.1%), education level (22.6%), nationality (20.8%), place of residence (16.9%), and religion (14.5%).

Table 16.1.   Main Axes of Identity in Taiwan by Gender: Percentage of People Who Said It Is Their Primary or Secondary Form of Identity

	Women	*Men*	*Average*
Occupation	29.6	32.1	30.8
Educational level	29.1	22.6	25.8
Place of residence	21.9	16.9	19.4
Religion	18.0	14.5	16.3
Nationality	15.6	20.8	18.2
Ethnic group	8.0	8.6	8.3
Class	7.8	11.1	9.4
Gender	5.5	4.9	5.1
Generation	5.5	5.7	5.6
Political party	3.4	6.3	4.8

Source: F.-C. Wang 2000 (Survey of Ethnic Relations).

Only 5.5 percent of women and 4.9 percent of men said that gender is either their primary or secondary dimension of personal identity. Women were far more likely to identify with occupation, educational level, place of residence, religion, or nationality. Likewise, in both surveys and life-history research, I rarely ran into self-identified feminists who explicitly placed gender at the forefront of their identities, even though unequal gender dynamics are important parts of nearly all the narratives. In the survey, moreover, the most common response to the open-ended question of what kind of entrepreneurship is most appropriate for women was to assert that "women can do anything men can do" or that "women should do whatever they want." Many women seemed surprised at my attempt to do a gendered analysis of entrepreneurship. Believing strongly in liberal ideology, most of them told me they think gender has little to do with business. Occupational identity as entrepreneur overshadows gender identity.

Gender consciousness is also muted because of the ways in which gender competes with other axes of identity. In terms of collective identities, some of the women I interviewed seemed to identify ethnicity as particularly salient. Eel exporter Chhoa Hiong-gun, for example, was an outspoken proponent of ethnic Taiwanese nationalism. She frequently contrasted her ethnic identity as Native Taiwanese to that of the Mainlanders who came to Taiwan after 1945. She stereotyped them as lazy and corrupt by nature, as well as guilty by association with the February 28 massacre. Mainlanders, such as dog-rights activist Wang Li-ling, showed by contrast a discomfort with the political rise of the Native Taiwanese. They often tried instead to affirm a new Taiwanese identity, and complained about growing ethnic tensions between the two groups. Other women entrepreneurs, disturbed by this ethnic bifurcation, have tried experimenting with alternative forms of ethnic identity or tried to cast it aside in favor of civic nationalism.

Aboriginal women were the most outspoken about ethnic identity, probably because they have suffered more ethnically based discrimination than other ethnic groups and have maintained an even stronger collective identity.[2] For them, the main ethnic contrast is between Han Taiwanese (including both Native Taiwanese and Mainlanders) and aboriginal people. Tayal people, however, also base their ethnic identities on not being Amis. Women of all ethnicities commonly drew my attention to questions of ethnic identity in both life histories and surveys. The relevant ethnic identities were all formed through collective and often violent historical experiences such as the 2:28 and the Wushe incidents.

Ethnicity was especially important during the historical moment within which I conducted my research. I began field research in 1999, when Lee Teng-hui, the first Native Taiwanese to be elected president of the ROC, was still in office. As my research progressed from 1999 through 2001, the opposition Democratic Progressive Party, which is dominated by Native Taiwanese, grew in strength and elected their candidate, Chen Shui-bian, to the presidency. Ethnic tensions were often tense during these times as Native Taiwanese grew in self-confidence and Mainlanders became identified as a reactionary opposition group. Ethnic relations were often highlighted in the media throughout this period, and the women I interviewed were simply reacting to the political changes of their time. They often wanted to discuss questions of ethnicity, a desire then reflected in their narratives. Even the women approached for survey research often brought up the topic separately, as when Hong Kong–born politician Ma Ying-jeou declared that all individuals who live in Taiwan and identify with Taiwan are "New Taiwanese," equal to any other citizens in the country. They simply wanted to know what a foreigner thought about these debates that are central to their lives.

There have been many attempts by politicians to mold new ethnic identities into political action, but such highly politicized attempts to create strong group consciousness have so far met with limited success. In fact, most people value social harmony to the extent that they resist attempts to politicize ethnicity, especially in Taipei where many ethnic groups live together in one city. In such contexts, ethnicity is relegated to private transcripts rather than public conflicts. Just as few people in the Survey of Ethnic Relations selected gender as primary or secondary dimensions of their identities, few said that ethnicity is more important than other forms of identity. Only 8.6 percent of men and 8 percent of women said that ethnicity is their primary or secondary identity.

The most important thing to learn from these various studies, however, is that identity is fractured. Allied as closely as they are to men of different ethnicities, classes, educational backgrounds, and occupations, women do not necessarily perceive gender as the most important dimension of identity, making it difficult for female entrepreneurship to become a source of collective empowerment as some proponents of microenterprise development projects would hope. If entrepreneurship is to become a tool of collective women's empowerment, it must be linked systematically to gender education and the feminist movement as a whole. Although feminist groups and even the Taipei Municipal Government have launched feminist initiatives in gender education, that will prove to be a difficult task precisely because identity is so fractured. As Simone de Beauvoir so insightfully pointed out, women are often more attached to men through other forms of identity than they are to other women through gender identity.

FEMINISM AND WOMEN'S EMANCIPATION IN TAIWAN

Taiwan is not the only place in which other loyalties of affiliation compete with gender identity, a situation that can easily become the Achille's heel of feminism. Many women perceive that sex/gender systems are not the main source of their oppression, and thus disagree with the feminist concept of universal patriarchy. The idea of a universal sisterhood, suffering from the same kind of gender-based oppression, is quite frequently contested by the non-Western, nonwhite women who are most aware of non-gender-based oppression. Audre Lorde (1984) and bell hooks (1982), to cite two notable examples, assert that white feminists in the United States have overlooked the importance of race-based oppression in the lives of African American women. Just as black women were once forced to sit on the back of the bus, they have also been forced to place racial oppression at the back of the feminist agenda. More relevant to Taiwanese women are the arguments of third-world women that first-world feminism overlooks the different interests of women located in different parts of the postcolonial global economy (Bulbeck 1998). As individuals assert themselves in structures of power, they face not only gender-based constraints, but also constraints based on race, class, and position in the global economy. In Taiwan as well, gender identity is often overshadowed by other concerns.

I entered the field in strong agreement with the feminist assumption that women, as well as male sexual minorities, are oppressed by patriarchy in all but a few small and marginal matrilineal societies. I assumed that women entrepreneurs would put gender at the forefront of their narratives and identify themselves as members of an oppressed gender. Yet frequently when I brought up the subject of feminism with women entrepreneurs and other women in Taiwan, they dismissed it as a Western discourse. Many of them argued that women in Taiwan are less oppressed than women in the West, most commonly using as evidence the fact that American women change their surnames at marriage, but Taiwanese women keep their own surnames. One woman even said that the United States is one of the most oppressive countries for women that she can think of, since that is the country where Christian terrorists bomb abortion clinics. These kinds of arguments are actually made quite frequently by non-Western women (Bulbeck 1998: 212), who in doing so forcefully and correctly resist the hegemonic discourse that modernity and women's rights are the exclusive property of the West.

My inability to find an interest in feminism among my interlocutors, however, is related to more than my own subject position as a white, foreign man. I understood that dynamic best through interaction with feminist scholars and activists. Like white, academic feminists in North America, Taiwanese feminists are often frustrated by the slowness of the movement to take root outside of the educated, urban,

Table 16.2.   Fragmented Identities in Taiwanese Feminist and Labor/Environmental Movements

	Feminist Movement (%)	Labor/Environmental Movement (%)
Members		
with postsecondary degrees	100.0	75.0
Upper- to middle-class members	61.6	20.0
Working-class members	2.6	18.5
Mainlanders	25.6	13.9

Source: Fan 2000.

middle class. Fan Yun, sociologist of Taiwanese social movements, did a demographic comparison of the feminist and labor/environmental movements in Taiwan (2000), with results that may explain why the former has been less successful than the latter two movements (see table 16.2). She found that 100 percent of the members in her sample of the feminist movement had college or graduate degrees, as compared to 75 percent of the labor and environmental groups; 61.6 percent of the feminists were identified as upper class or upper middle class; and only 2.6 percent as working class. In comparison, only 20 percent of the labor movement identified as upper middle to upper class and 18.5 percent as working class. In terms of ethnic background, Fan found that the feminist movement has been strongly influenced by Mainlander women. Mainlanders comprise 25.6 percent of the feminist movement, as compared to only 13.9 percent of the labor movement, and are thus represented in feminism out of proportion to their percentage in the general population.

The largely Native Taiwanese women entrepreneurs in my study, only 35.3 percent of whom have postsecondary education, thus have little in common with Taiwanese feminists. Most of them are also too busy to get involved in a social movement so remote from their own social circles. To a large degree, moreover, Taiwanese women have empowered themselves without direct participation in an organized feminist movement. At the same time, however, it is crucial to note that the leadership and lobbying efforts of the feminist movement have vastly improved the quality of life for women through legal reform. All Taiwanese women, even those who are unaware of it, have benefited from the hard work of the country's feminist organizations. As is widely acknowledged in the feminist movement, they will benefit even more after the movement finds ways to better address the specific needs of less-empowered ethnic groups and classes.

NEW CHALLENGES IN
THE TWENTY-FIRST CENTURY

When looking at Taiwan from the perspective of its female entrepreneurs, cracks appear on the edifice of patriarchy. Yet my research on female entrepreneurship does not lead me to entirely optimistic conclusions about the use of entrepreneurship as a universal development strategy. First, not all women are willing to or capable of embarking on entrepreneurship. In spite of the recent interest in microenterprise among development anthropologists, therefore, I think it is important to stress that entrepreneurship is not a universal panacea for poverty or for the oppression of women in patriarchal systems. Second, the fact that women entrepreneurs tend to be concentrated in low-capital, low-skill trades seems to indicate that there are still gender-based structural inequalities in the Taiwanese economy. It is somewhat discouraging to see that most woman entrepreneurs are concentrated in fields traditionally seen to be female fields of endeavor: food, clothes, and childcare. Women entrepreneurs themselves complain about gender-based discrimination in getting bank loans. Instead, most of them rely on high-interest revolving credit societies or loans from family and friends. Taiwanese women could probably benefit from a Grameen-style women's bank and business training for women interested in entrepreneurship. Women still suffer from the symbolic violence that men exercise against them in patristic ideologies, including a double standard of sexual conduct. Taiwanese women have come a long way, but still have a long road to travel before full gender equality will be reached.

Capitalist development has arguably shifted the gender-based balance of power. Since the family is no longer the main unit of production in society, and individuals of both genders can seek autonomy in the capitalist marketplace (Harrell 1997), women have greater potential than previously to strengthen their own material positions. As individual women do so, they also develop the ideological tools to justify and normalize their autonomous economic activities. Individual women can thus increase their power at the interpersonal and organizational levels, even though women as a group hold less power than men at the structural level. The struggle for power, however, is never-ending. As a group, men still possess greater structural power than women, and misogynistic ideologies are still strong. Patriarchy may be crumbling at the edges, but it is still far too early to declare its demise.

As Taiwan enters the twenty-first century, increased global integration will bring new challenges and opportunities to the women entrepreneurs of Taipei. Taiwan and China both entered the World Trade Organization (WTO) at the beginning of 2002, which will provide a framework for accelerated economic integration across the Taiwan Straits. Many Taiwanese women, as well as men, have come to see China as a promised land full of new business opportunities. Although the Taiwanese government would like to slow the movement of industrial production to China, the trend seems irreversible as long as China remains politically and economically stable and as long as such large wage disparities exist between the two countries. In such a context, more and more women will become like Fan Fut-moi, who became an autonomous entrepreneur as a jewelry exporter only after her husband shifted jewelry production to China and moved to Guangdong to supervise the new factory.

As manufacturing continues its exodus to China, moreover, factory employment will continue to drop in Taiwan. Unemployment has already begun such a rapid rise that the labor movement has called—so far with little effect—for restrictions on Taiwanese investment in China. If current trends continue, manufacturing will become even less viable as an employment option, and working-class Taiwanese people will have to find other ways to make a living. At the same time, however, there may be more service-sector and entrepreneurial opportunities. In the absence of strong welfare provisions, the number of women who open small enterprises or set up stalls in night markets and on street corners is surely going to increase.

At the same time, however, Taiwan's accession to the WTO will provide new challenges to women entrepreneurs. Already, private coffee-shop owners talk about the threat from Starbucks, which plans a massive invasion by opening up over 3,000 coffee shops on the island. The new competition was already putting downward pressure on prices during the time of my research. In 1999, it was rare to find a cup of Japanese-style siphon coffee in Taipei for less than NT$120. By 2001, it was available in many places for half that price. Unless they can continue to compete with higher-quality coffee and more comfortable drinking atmospheres, Taiwan's coffee-shop owners will find it hard to survive, and Taipei women entrepreneurs will lose one common path to empowerment.

There is still room for limited optimism, however, when one remembers that they already survived the introduction of Japanese coffee-shop chains in the 1980s and have continued to run successful small restaurants in spite of the omnipresence of McDonald's and Kentucky Fried Chicken. Like capitalism itself, globalization is full of contradictions. Just as they have learned the secrets of cooking delicious food through the contrasting flavors of sweet and sour, Taiwanese women may very well have the initiative to make good use of those contradictions. Human empowerment means grasping the best from every conjuncture of fate. I anticipate that Taiwanese women will continue to assert a place of their own no matter what destiny brings to their beautiful island of Formosa.

NOTES

1. This is not to say that Taiwanese women were entirely powerless in precapitalist eras. Historical research by, for example, Susan Mann (1997, 2001), Dorothy Ko (1994), and Patricia Ebrey (1993) all show the substantial autonomy held by women at various times in China, as well as ways in which Neoconfucianism challenged that. Thanks to Mark Seldon for pointing out the historical research.

2. In the Survey of Ethnic Relations, aboriginal respondents identified mostly with religion (47.6%), ethnicity (29.5%), and occupation (19.7%). Only 6.8 percent of Minnan, 13.5 percent of Hakka, and 5.4 percent of Mainlanders said that ethnicity is important to their identities. Aboriginal respondents are referring to the Christian religion, which has become a central part of aboriginal identity.

Appendix

Research Methodology

I have used two complementary research methodologies in this book. First, I designed a survey and administered it to women entrepreneurs selected through random sampling. Since no comprehensive directory of women entrepreneurs exists, many businesses are not registered, and many registered businesses do not register the name of the "real" owner, I could not take a random sample of women entrepreneurs themselves. Instead, I took a geographical sample of locations. Taipei is divided into twelve urban districts, which are further subdivided into wards and neighborhoods. The smallest unit is the neighborhood, which usually consists of a series of buildings on a Taipei street. I then visited the neighborhood in person, inquiring at each business enterprise if the boss is a man or woman. If the boss was a woman, I asked if she would fill out my survey. If there were no businesses in the neighborhood selected, which is a very rare occurrence in Taipei, I went to the nearest commercial street.

The main purpose of this method was not to gather a random sample for hypothesis testing, but rather to increase the diversity of women in my study. Because neighbors are more likely to be similar to one another than to individuals of other neighborhoods, I increased diversity in my study by interviewing fewer individuals in more neighborhoods rather than interviewing more people in fewer neighborhoods. I thus achieved my goal of gaining diverse ethnographic experience, and was also able to draw a gendered portrait of the Taipei small-business community. Survey research enabled me to place Taipei women entrepreneurs in their wider demographic context, gave me a wide understanding of different social milieu in Taipei, and permitted me to meet women interested in my research. It also helped me identify women-owned businesses for ethnographic research done through repeated patronage at their businesses.

My second research method consisted of in-depth unstructured interviews with thirty women entrepreneurs, as well as follow-up "participant research" in their lives. I met these women while doing survey research, as well as through a network of acquaintances. Except for basic demographic questions, the interviews were unstructured. They ranged in length from one to three hours, and allowed me to gather a wealth of material on women entrepreneurs' economic strategies, views towards their families, attitudes towards marriage and romance, and Taiwanese society. We met in places of their own choice, which meant either in their homes, workplaces, or the nearest Starbucks coffee shop. It should be emphasized that these formal interviews were only one part of the research process. In nearly all cases, and in all of the cases portrayed in this book, they were preceded or followed by further social interaction. With the exception of three women who asked that I use their real names, I use pseudonyms to protect the anonymity of the women in this book.

Life-history and participant-observation methods are both important to understand how individual, culture, and nation are integrated into personal life-worlds of women, as strategies of power are most clearly discernible in personal narratives, everyday "moments" (Okely 1996), or in "just talk" (Stewart 1996). Innovative anthropologists have thus developed methods of life-history research (e.g., Langness and Frank 1981, Watson and Watson-Franke 1985), which make it possible to discern the contours of power in the lives of ordinary men and women (Abu-Lughod 1993, Behar 1996, Mintz 1960, Rethmann 2000, Shostak 1983, Tsing 1993). The anthropological use of personal narrative has even led Appadurai to state that ethnography "must redefine itself as that practice of representation that illuminates the power of large-scale, imagined life possibilities over specific life trajectories (Appadurai 1996: 55).

From the moment I presented my research proposal to prospective participants to final presentation of the data, I have taken a reflexive approach to ethnography (Davies 1999). Most importantly, I have followed the critical insight of feminist research (Davies 1999, Roberts 1981) that research is a social relation and should be recognized as such. As Crick noted, "the ethnographic enterprise is not a matter of what one person does in a situation but how two sides of an encounter arrive at a delicate workable definition of their meeting" (1982: 25). My research is self-consciously a series of dialogues between myself and research participants, many of whom have embraced the project as an opportunity for reflection and creative self-expression. I thus position myself in the research, not as the privileged voice of science, but as a member of a cross-cultural and cross-gendered dialogue in progress. This reflexive ethnographic methodology has been necessary, in a form of critical realism, to heighten the objectivity of my study.

From the very beginning of our interactions, I presented the research to them as a collaborative project, in which we would construct together a piece of oral literature concerning their own life histories, growth experience, and perspectives on human life. Taiwanese women entrepreneurs often tell others their life stories and experiences of personal growth, primarily in the family realm, and how they overcame their difficulties through entrepreneurship. Since Taiwanese women are already accustomed to relating life stories, these life histories should be seen as an already existing genre of oral literature and not merely as a product of the research methodology.

Without exception, these interviews were pleasant for both interviewer and interviewee. Sometimes I found out only later, from mutual friends, that they had immensely enjoyed the research process. For some women, the interview was a chance to share their most intimate feelings and problems concerning both marriage and work. In those cases, they said they found my interviews useful to them personally, as I became what one woman called a "free psychotherapist." I was sometimes so touched by their stories that I would wake up in the night afterwards with tears streaming down my face, experiences that reveal how deeply anthropological field research can alter the researcher as well as the researched (Davies 1999: 24).

As an ethnographer, I was indeed a "vulnerable observer" (Behar 1996). In several cases, the interview was the beginning of a friendship, marked afterwards by repeated social interaction in other contexts. My research involved, as Oakley (1981) also experienced, the paradoxical combination of private friendship and public research. Oakley argued that women do more relation-based research, whereas men use cold, detached, objective interviews. I hope that this study reveals that feminist methodology based on reflexivity and self-conscious relations with research participants can be equally well done by both men and women.

Using this method, I successfully gathered a wealth of ethnographic data. I attribute that success to two main factors. First, the participants in the study were themselves motivated to do research. Some did it as a personal favor to me or to a mutual friend. Some did it through the desire to pursue friendship with me. And yet others did it out of genuine interest in the research. The life-history method was far more successful than the survey method because it gave greater control of the research process to the research participants themselves. Second, the participants were free to determine what was of interest to them under the general theme of "women entrepreneurs."

Translations and editing present problems of their own, as all students of life history are well aware. Yet I have left the dialogues as whole and complete as possible, while still maintaining readability, rather than merely using my own voice to interpret data and then selectively using quotes that support my own arguments. As a result, the interviews often flow into other topics and at times even turn a critical eye on the role of myself as anthropologist.

This process of collaborative research changed the nature of the ethnography I wrote. Whereas I had originally planned to write a narrowly focused monograph on gender and microenterprise development, I ended up writing about gender, power, and identity. As the project evolved, it became a series of dialogues with Taipei women's voices at the center, a joint project through which we self-consciously worked together towards a better understanding of Taiwanese society. This methodological approach and writing style should provide a more human perspective on political economy, focused as clearly as possible on the agents that make development possible. It is hoped that these methods have helped me avoid what Dorinne Kondo calls the "prison" of "assumptions in which aesthetics and politics, the personal and the political, woman and man, East and West form closed, mutually exclusive spaces where one term inevitably dominates the other" (1997: 49).

Glossary

TAIWANESE WORDS USED IN THE TEXT

Orthography adapted from Embree's (1984) *Dictionary of Southern Min.*
Tone markings have been omitted to facilitate typesetting.

a-ma 阿媽 grandmother

a-kong 阿公 grandfather

chabolang 查甫人 man

chhoa 娶 to take a wife

chhoa-bing 挫冰 shaved ice

chhi-a 青仔 fresh betel nut

chiu-diam 酒店 "alcohol store" (often implies the sex industry)

en-hun 緣分 fate, destiny

En-ping Bak Lo 延平北路 Taipei street name

hoan-a 番仔 "barbarian" (racial slur used for aboriginal people)

jim-mia 認命 to resign oneself to destiny

jin-seng 人生 human life

kang-chi 工錢 work money, wages

ke ke sui ke, ke kau sui kau 嫁雞隨雞，嫁狗隨狗 "marry a chicken, follow a
  chicken; marry a dog, follow a dog" (proverb)

ke-ho 嫁給 to marry (for women)

ko-liang-chiu 高粱酒 sorghum wine

ko-seng 個性 personality

Kuan Kung 關公 a god

mia 命 fate

obaasan 歐巴桑 old woman

pai-pai 拜拜 to worship, pray

pau-hiu-a 包葉仔 betel nut wrapped in leaves

phai-lang 壞人 "bad person" (epithet used by aboriginal people for Native Taiwanese)

sai-khia-chi 私房錢 private savings

sio-chia 小姐 "little sister," young woman

siong-ban 上班 to go to work

siu-e-khui 想得開 to realize

soa-te-lang 山地人 "mountain people" (said of aboriginal people)

tang-ki 童乩 medium possessed by spirit

te-diam-a 茶店仔 teahouse

thau-ke 頭家 boss

thau-ke-niu 頭家娘 boss-wife

Tho Te Kong 土地公 Earth God

toa-ko 大哥 "big brother" (gangster)

un-khi 運氣 luck

MANDARIN WORDS USED IN THE TEXT

buxiban 補習班 cram school

faxin 法心 "dharma heart," generosity

fangsheng 放生 to release living things

fengshui 風水 geomancy

fude 婦德 "women's virtue"

fugong 婦工 "women's labor"

furong 婦容 "women's expression"

fuyan 婦言 "women's speech"

ganqing 感情 feelings, emotions (between people, etc.)

gongren 工人 workers

goupi 狗屁 "dog farts," nonsense

guanxi 關係 relationships

I-Kuan-Tao (Yiguandao) 貫道 a religious sect

jia chuqu 嫁出去 to marry out (women)

jingjie 境界 life-world

jinshi 進士 scholar

jiyuan 機緣 fateful chance, opportunity

juancun 眷村 "dependents' village" (housing for retired Mainlander soldiers)

kaiwu 開悟 to see the truth (epiphany)

kanpo hongcheng 看破紅塵 "to see through this world of dust" (enlightenment)

Kuanyin (Guanyin) 觀音 a goddess

Maowang 貓王 "Cat King" (Elvis Presley)

lin 鄰 neighborhood

Mei-er-mei 美而美 a breakfast franchise (hamburgers)

nüqiangren 女強人 "strong woman" (said of women bosses, etc.)

Oulei zu 歐蕾族 "Olay tribe" (older lesbians)

pingpu zu 平埔族 plains tribes

po 婆 feminine lesbians

qipao 旗袍 a traditional dress for women

sancong side 三從四德 three obediences and four virtues

shaobing 燒餅 a breakfast pastry

shehui 社會 society

shengfan 生番 "raw barbarians" (unassimilated aborigines)

shoufan 熟番 "cooked barbarians" (assimilated aborigines)

Women zhi jian 我們之間 "Between Us" (a lesbian group)

xiongfan 兇番 "fierce barbarians" (formerly said of Tayal people)

yinyuan 因緣 relationship of cause and effect

youtiao 油條 a breakfast pastry

yuanfen 緣分 fate, destiny

Interviews

1. Tibetan Art/Ritual Goods Dealer, Native Taiwanese, Married, 45, 26 October 1999.
2. Coffee Shop Owner, Native Taiwanese, Single, 37, 29 October 1999.
3. Electronic Goods Manufacturer, Native Taiwanese, Married, 55, 14 December 1999.
4. Coffee Shop Owner, Mainlander, Divorced, 52, 29 December 1999.
5. Beauty Salon Operator, Native Taiwanese, Married, 49, 4 January 2000.
6. Restaurant (Western Food), Ta'u Aborigine, Married, 30, 11 January 2000.
7. Night Market Restaurant (Japanese), Native Taiwanese, Married, 67, 23 March 2000.
8. Furniture Shop, Native Taiwanese, Single, 38, 28 March 2000.
9. Art Gallery, Native Taiwanese, Married, 34, 1 April 2000.
10. Interior Design, Native Taiwanese, Single, 37, 7 April 2000.
11. Jewelry Export, Hakka, Married, 46, 11 April 2000.
12. Garment Manufacturing and Trade, Native Taiwanese, Married, 52, 14 April 2000.
13. Sex Industry (Teahouse), Native Taiwanese, Divorced, 40, 17 April 2000.
14. Non-profit Dog Shelter, Mainlander, Married, 57, 18 April 2000.
15. Fashion Designer, Native Taiwanese, Single, 44, 6 May 2000.
16. Lesbian Bar Owner, Native Taiwanese, in Lesbian Relationship, 37, 18 June 2000.
17. Gift Shop Owner, Mainlander, Single, 33, 11 July 2000.
18. Eel exporter, Native Taiwanese, Single, 46, 18 August 2000.
19. Restaurant (Japanese), Native Taiwanese, Married, 43, 18 August 2000.
20. Import/Export, Tayal Aborigine, Single, 38, 22 August 2000.
21. Childcare, Mainlander, Married, 50, 29 August 2000.
22. Computer Parts Manufacturing, Married, 45, 4 September 2000.

23. Florist, Native Taiwanese, Single, 30, 4 September 2000.

24. Construction, Mainlander, Divorced, 45, 5 September 2000.

25. Record Company, Immigrant from Singapore, Married, 36, 15 September 2000.

26. Photography Studio, Native Taiwanese/Japanese, Married, 44, 20 September 2000.

27. Soymilk Peddler, Native Taiwanese, Married, 55, 14 October 2000.

28. Elder Care, Tayal Aborigine, Divorced, 47, 14 October 2000.

29. Betel Nut Stand, Native Taiwanese, Divorced, 52, 30 November 2000.

30. Bakery, Native Taiwanese, Married, 42, 13 December 2000.

Bibliography

Abu-Lughod, Lila. 1993. *Writing Women's Worlds: Bedouin Stories*. Berkeley: University of California Press.

Academia Sinica Institute of Sociology. 1992. *EAMC Project Coding Scheme and Frequency Distributions*. Taipei: Academia Sinica Institute of Sociology.

Allio, Fiorella. 1998. "The Austronesian Peoples of Taiwan: Building a Political Platform for Themselves." *China Perspectives*, no. 18 (July/August): 52-60.

Allison, Anne. 1994. *Nightwork: Sexuality, Pleasure, and Corporate Masculinity in a Tokyo Hostess Club*. Chicago: University of Chicago Press.

Appadurai, Arjun. 1996. *Modernity at Large: Cultural Dimensions of Globalization*. Minneapolis: University of Minnesota Press.

Arrigo, Linda Gail. 1980. "The Industrial Work Force of Young Women in Taiwan." *Bulletin of Concerned Asian Scholars* 12, no. 2 (April-June): 25-38.

———. 2002. "A Minority Within a Minority." *Cultural Survival Quarterly* 26, no. 2 (summer): 56-61.

Baraka, Jessica. 1999. "The Gap Remains: Gender and Earnings in Taiwan." Working Paper of the Princeton Research Program in Development Studies.

Bawan, Danaha 沈明仁. 2002. "Wushe Shijian de Lishi Hejie: Cong Gaya de Guandian Du Zuqun Hejie"霧社事件的歷史和解: 從 gaya 的觀點讀族群和解. Pp. 253-269 in *Cong Hejie dao Zizhi: Taiwan Yuanzhu Minzu Lishi Chongjian* 從和解到自治: 臺灣原住民族歷史重建, edited by Shih Cheng-feng 施正峰, Hsu Shi-chieh 許世楷 and Busing Dali 布興 大立. Taipei: Qianwei.

Behar, Ruth. 1996. *The Vulnerable Observer: Anthropology That Breaks Your Heart*. Boston: Beacon Press.

Bonacich, Edna. 1973. "A Theory of Middleman Minorities." *American Sociological Review* 38, no. 5 (October): 583-594.

Bosco, Joseph. 1995. "Better the Head of a Chicken Than the Tail of an Ox: On Cultural Explanations for the Development of Family Factories in Taiwan." Taiwan Studies Workshop, Fairbank Center Working Papers, Number 12.

Bourdieu, Pierre. 1984. *Distinction: A Social Critique of the Judgement of Taste* (translated by Richard Nice). Cambridge: Harvard University Press.

Brinton, Mary C. (ed.). 2001. *Women's Working Lives in East Asia*. Stanford, Calif.: Stanford University Press.

Brook, Timothy, and Hy V. Luong (ed.). 1997 *Culture and Economy: The Shaping of Capitalism in Eastern Asia*. Ann Arbor: University of Michigan Press.

Bulbeck, Chilla. 1998. *Re-orienting Western Feminisms: Women's Diversity in a Postcolonial World*. Cambridge: Cambridge University Press.

Census Office of the Executive Yuan. 1992. *General Report: The 1990 Census of Population and Housing*. Taipei: Census Office of the Executive Yuan.

Central News Agency. 2001. "ROC's Divorce Rate Highest in Asia." Central News Agency, May 10 (www.taiwanheadlines.gov.tw/20010511/20010511s4 .html (accessed 23 September 2002).

Chang, Chin-fen, and Chin-chun Yi. 1999. "Before and After: The Impacts of Economic Restructuring on Women's Employment Chances in Taiwan." Working paper, Institute of Sociology, Academia Sinica, Taipei.

Chang, Kwang-tou 張光斗. 1997. *Yinwei you ni, wo huochu ziji* 因為有你，我活出自己. Taipei: Pingan Wenhua.

Chang, Mao-kuei 張茂桂. 1988. "Zhongguoren de Zhongzu Yishi" 中國人的種族意識. Pp. 249-264 in *Zhongguoren: Guannian yu Xingwei*. 中國人：觀念與行為, edited by Wen Chong-I 文崇一 and Michael Hsin-huang Hsiao 蕭新煌. Taipei: Juliu.

Chang, Tien-wan 張典婉. 1991. *Nüxing Chuangye* 女性創業. Taipei: Lianjing.

Chao, Y. Antonia. 1999. "Performing Like a P'o and Acting as a Big Sister: Reculturating into the Indigenous Lesbian Circle in Taiwan." Pp. 128-144 in *Sex, Sexuality, and the Anthropologist*, edited by Fran Markowitz and Michael Ashkenazi. Urbana: University of Illinois Press.

Chen, Yung-hsing. 1998. "The 2:28 Incident and the Taiwan Medical Profession." Pp. 113-134 in *An Introduction to 2:28 Tragedy in Taiwan for World Citizens*, edited by Tsung-yi Lin. Taipei: Taiwan Renaissance Foundation Press.

Cheng, Mei-li 鄭美里. 1997. *Nuerquan: Taiwan Nutongzhi de Xingbie, Jiating yu Quannei Shenghuo* 女兒圈：台灣女同志的性別、家庭與圈內生活. Taipei: Fembooks.

Chieh, Ma 潔瑪. 1993. *Xiandai Nüxing Chuangye Shichang*. 現代女性創業市場. Taipei: Hanyu Publishing Company.

Chinabiz. 2001. "Leading Cross Strait Economic Exchange Indicators." *Cross-Straits Economic Statistics Monthly* 101 (January 2001). (www.chinabiz.org .tw/maz/Eco-Month/home.htm) (accessed 23 September 2002).

Chiu, I-wei 邱怡薇. 1996. "Zunzhong Shengming: Sanfa Zhihui de Guang yu re" 尊重生命：散發智慧的光與熱. *Xiangyuan Toushi* 馨園透視 1, no. 2 (May): 12-15.

Chou, Chien-I 周倩漪. 1999. *Meimei Chuang Tianxia: Shi ge Renzhen Nüxing de Chuangye Gushi* 美眉闖天下：10個認真女性的創業故事. Taipei: Hongse.

Chung-hua Institute for Economic Research. 1989. *Conference Series No. 13: Conference on Confucianism and Economic Development in East Asia, May 29-31*. Taipei: Chung-hua Institute for Economic Research.

Connell, R. W. 1987. *Gender and Power: Society, the Person, and Sexual Politics*. Stanford, Calif.: Stanford University Press.

Corcuff, Stéphane. 2000. "Taiwan's Mainlanders: A Recent Category of Ethnicity." *China Perspectives*, no. 28 (March-April): 74-84.

Crick, Malcolm. 1982. "Anthropological Field Research, Meaning Creation, and Knowledge Construction." Pp.15-37 in *Semantic Anthropology*, edited by David Parkin. London: Academic Press.

Davies, Charlotte Aull. 1999. *Reflexive Ethnography: A Guide to Researching Selves and Others*. London: Routledge.

de Beauvoir, Simone. 1989 [1952]. *The Second Sex* (trans. H. M. Parshley). New York: Vintage Books.

de Certeau, Michel. 1984. *The Practice of Everyday Life* (trans. S. Rendall). Berkeley: University of California Press.

de Glopper, Donald. 1978. "Doing Business in Lukang." Pp. 291-320 in *Studies in Chinese Society*, edited by Arthur Wolf. Stanford, Calif.: Stanford University Press.

de Soto, Hernando. 1989. *The Other Path: The Invisible Revolution in the Third World*. New York: Harper and Row.

DGBAS (Directorate General of Budget, Accounting and Statistics). 2000. "Woguo Renlei Fazhan Zhishu Shibian Jieguo yu Guoji Bijiao" 我國人類發展指數試編結果與國際比較 · "(http://140.129.146.80/dgbas 03/bs2/89chy/Hdi.doc) (accessed 23 September 2002).

DGBAS. 2002. *Monthly Statistics of the Republic of China* 436 (May).

Diamond, Norma. 1979. "Women and Industry in Taiwan." *Modern China* 5, no. 3 (July): 317-40.

Dignard, Louise, and José Havet. 1995. *Women in Micro- and Small-Scale Enterprise Development*. Boulder, Colo.: Westview.

Dissanayake, Wimal (ed.). 1996. *Narratives of Agency: Self-Making in China, India, and Japan*. Minneapolis: University of Minnesota Press.

Ebrey, Patricia. 1993. *The Inner Quarters: Marriage and the Lives of Chinese Women in the Sung Period*. Berkeley: University of California Press.

Edwards, Loraine, and Midge Stocker (eds.). 1993. *The Woman-Centered Economy: Ideals, Reality, and the Space in Between*. Chicago: Third Side Press.

Embree, Bernard L. M. 1984. *A Dictionary of Southern Min*. Taipei: Taipei Language Institute.

Executive Yuan Council of Aboriginal Affairs. 1999. *Bashiba Nian Taiwan Yuanzhumin Jiuye Zhuangkuang Diaocha Baogao* 八十八年臺灣原住民就業狀況調查報告. Taipei: Executive Yuan Aboriginal Affairs Council.

Fan, Yun. 2000. *Activists in a Changing Political Environment: A Microfoundational Study of Social Movements in Taiwan's Democratic Transition, 1980s-1990s*. Ph.D. Dissertation, Department of Sociology, Yale University, New Haven, Connecticut.

Gallin, Bernard, and Rita Gallin. 1982. "Socioeconomic Life in Rural Taiwan: Twenty Years of Development and Change." *Modern China* 8, no. 2 (April): 205-246.

Gates, Hill. 1987. *Chinese Working-Class Lives: Getting by in Taiwan*. Ithaca, N.Y.: Cornell University Press.

———. 1989. "The Commoditization of Chinese Women." *Signs: Journal of Women in Culture and Society* 14, no. 4 (summer): 799-832.

———. 1996. "Owner, Worker, Mother, Wife: Taibei and Chengdu Family Businesswomen." Pp. 127-165 in *Putting Class in Its Place,* edited by Elizabeth Perry. Berkeley: Institute of East Asian Studies.

———. 1999. *Looking for Chengdu: A Woman's Adventures in China*. Ithaca, N.Y.: Cornell University Press.

Giddens, Anthony. 1991. *Modernity and Self-Identity: Self and Society in the Late Modern Age*. Stanford, Calif.: Stanford University Press.

———. 1992. *The Transformation of Intimacy: Sexuality, Love, and Eroticism in Modern Societies*. Stanford, Calif.: Stanford University Press.

Goffman, Erving. 1959. *The Presentation of Self in Everyday Life*. Garden City, N.J.: Doubleday.

Greenhalgh, Susan. 1985. "Sexual Stratification: The Other Side of 'Growth with Equity' in East Asia." *Population and Development Review* 11, no. 2 (June): 265-314.

———. 1988. "Families and Networks in Taiwan's Economic Development." Pp. 224-245 in *Contending Approaches to the Political Economy of Taiwan,* edited by Edward Winckler and Susan Greenhalgh. Armonk, N.Y.: M. E. Sharpe.

———. 1994. "De-Orientalizing the Chinese Family Firm." *American Ethnologist* 21, no. 4: 746-775.

Harrell, Stevan. 1985. "Why do the Chinese Work So Hard? Reflections on an Entrepreneurial Ethic." *Modern China* 11, no. 2 (April): 203-226.

———. 1987. "The Concept of Fate in Chinese Folk Ideology." *Modern China* 13, no. 1 (January): 90-109.

———. 1997. *Human Families*. Boulder, Colo.: Westview.

Hefner, Robert W. (ed.). 1998. *Market Cultures: Society and Morality in the New Asian Capitalisms*. Boulder, Colo.: Westview.

Hertz, Ellen. 1998. *The Trading Crowd: An Ethnography of the Shanghai Stock Market*. Cambridge: Cambridge University Press.

Hinton, William. 1966. *Fanshen*. New York: Vintage Press.

Ho, Josephine 何春蕤. 1994. *Butong Guo Nüren: Xingbie, Ziben yu Wenhua* 不同國女人：性別，資本與文化. Taipei: Independent Evening News Press.

hooks, bell. 1982. *Ain't I a Woman: Black Women and Feminism*. London: Pluto Press.

Hsieh, Chin-yu 謝瑾瑜. 1999. *Dangjia de Nüren: Ershiwu wei Nüxing Chuangye de Chenggong Jingdian* 當家的女人：二十五位女性創業的成功經典. Taipei: Chinese Women Entrepreneur Association.

Hsiung, Ping-chun. 1996. *Living Rooms as Factories: Class, Gender, and the Satellite Factory System in Taiwan*. Philadelphia: Temple University Press.

Hsu, Min-tao. 1998. "'Fitting In' to the 'No Return Trip': Women's Perceptions of Marriage and Family in Taiwan." *Proceedings of the National Science Council, ROC (C)* 8, no. 4: 527-538.

Hsu, Mu-tzu. 1991. *Culture, Self, and Adaptation: The Psychological Anthropology of Two Malayo-Polynesian Groups in Taiwan*. Taipei: Academia Sinica Institute of Ethnology.

Hu, You-hui 胡幼慧. 1995. *Sandai Tongtang: Misi yu Xianjing* 代同堂：迷思與陷阱. Taipei: Juliu Publishing.

Hu, You-hui 胡幼慧 and Chou Ya-rong 周雅容. 1997. *Popo Mama Jing: Tamen de Yuyan, Tamen de Quanyi* 婆婆媽媽經：她們的語言，她們的權益. Taipei: Dingyan Media.

Huang, Shu-ling. 2001. "Sex, Power, and Social Networking: Masculinity and Sex Industries in Taiwan." Paper presented at the Sixth Women in Asia Conference, Australian National University, Canberra, September 23-26.

———. 2002. "Ngasal" in the Blues: Marriage, Family, Prostitution, and Women of Atayal Aborigines, 1960-1998. Unpublished manuscript.

Jinse Lianhua 金色蓮花. 1994. "Wei Liulang Gou Zhao ge Jia: Fang Wang Liling" 為流浪狗找個家─訪汪麗玲．*Jinse Lianhua (Golden Lotus Magazine)* 金色蓮花 (October): 16-17.

Ka, Chih-Ming 柯志明. 1993. *Taiwan Dushi Xiaoxing Zhizaoye de Chuangye, Jingying yu Shengchan Zuzhi* 臺灣都市小型製造業的創業，經營與生產組織. Taipei: Academia Sinica Institute of Ethnology.

Kao, Cheng-shu 高承恕. 1999. *Toujianiang: Taiwan Zhongxiao Qiye "Toujianiang" de Jingji Huodong yu Shehui Yiyi* 頭家娘：臺灣中小企業「頭家娘」的經濟活動與社會意義. Taipei: Lianjing.

Kerr, George. 1965. *Formosa Betrayed*. Boston, Mass.: Houghton Mifflin.

Ko, Dorothy. 1994. *Teachers of the Inner Chambers: Women and Culture in Seventeenth Century China*. Stanford, Calif.: Stanford University Press.

Kondo, Dorinne. 1997. *About Face: Performing Race in Fashion and Theater.* London: Routledge.

Kung, Lydia. 1994 [1983]. *Factory Women in Taiwan.* New York: Columbia University Press.

Lai, Zhengzhe 賴正哲. 2000. "Zai Gongsi Shang Ban: Xin Gongyuan Zuowei Nan Tongzhi Yanchu Dijing zhi Yanjiu" 在公司上班: 新公園作爲男同志演出地景之研究. Pp. 131-186 in *Xing/bie Zhengzhi yu Zhuti Xinggou* 性/別政治與主體形構, edited by Josephine Ho 何春蕤. Taipei: Maitian Publishing.

Laliberté, André. 1998. "Tzu Chi and the Buddhist Revival in Taiwan: Rise of a New Conservatism?" *China Perspectives,* no. 19 (September-October): 44-50.

Langness, L. L. and Gelya Frank. 1981. *Lives: An Anthropological Approach to Biography.* Novato, Calif.: Chandler and Sharp.

Lee, Anru. 1997. "The Waning of a Hard Work Ethic: Moral Discourse in Taiwan's Recent Economic Restructuring," paper presented at the 96th Annual Meeting of the American Anthropological Association, Washington, D.C., November 19-23.

———. Forthcoming. "Between Filial Daughter and Loyal Sister: Global Economy and Family Politics in Taiwan." In *Women in the New Taiwan: Gender Roles and Gender Consciousness in a Changing Society,* edited by Anru Lee, Catherine Farris, and Murray A. Rubinstein. Armonk. N.Y.: M. E. Sharpe.

Lee, Tse-han, Ramon Myers, and Wei Wou. 1991. *A Tragic Beginning: The Taiwan Uprising of February 28, 1947.* Stanford, Calif.: Stanford University Press.

Lo, Ming-Cheng, and Jennifer Robertson. 2002. *Doctors Within Borders: Profession, Ethnicity, and Modernity in Colonial Taiwan.* Berkeley: University of California Press.

Lorde, Audre. 1984. *Sister Outsider.* New York: Crossing Press.

Lu, Hwei-Syin. 1998. "Gender and Buddhism in Contemporary Taiwan: A Case Study of Tzu Chi Foundation." *Proceedings of the National Science Council, ROC (C)* 8 (4): 539-550.

Lu, Annette Hsiu-lien. 呂秀蓮. 1990. *Xin Nüxingzhuyi* 新女性主義・ Taipei: Qianwei.

———. 1994. "Women's Liberation: The Taiwanese Experience." Pp. 289-304 in Murray Rubinstein, editor, *The Other Taiwan: 1945 to the Present.* Armonk, N.Y.: M. E. Sharpe.

Lu, Yu-hsia. 1998. "Women and Work in Taiwanese Family Business." Paper presented at the Conference on Social Stratification and Mobility: Newly Industrializing Economies Compared. Taipei, Taiwan, January 7-9.

———. 2001. "The 'Boss's Wife' and Taiwanese Small Family Business." Pp. 263-298 in *Women's Working Lives in East Asia,* edited by Mary C. Brinton. Stanford, Calif.: Stanford University Press.

Mann, Susan. 1997. *Precious Records: Women in China's Long Eighteenth Century*. Stanford, Calif.: Stanford University Press.

————. 2001. *Under Confucian Eyes: Writings on Gender in Chinese History*. Berkeley: University of California Press.

Marsh, Robert M. 1996. *The Great Transformation: Social Change in Taipei, Taiwan Since the 1960s*. Armonk, N.Y.: M. E. Sharpe.

Mendel, Douglas. 1970. *The Politics of Formosan Nationalism*. Berkeley: University of California Press.

Mintz, Sidney. 1960. *Worker in the Cane: A Puerto Rican Life History*. New Haven, Conn.: Yale University Press.

Mowna, Masaw 廖守臣. 1998. *Taiya Zu de Shehui Zuzhi* 泰雅族的社會組織. Hualien: Tzu Chi University Research Center on Aboriginal Health.

Murray, Stephen, and Keelung Hong. 1994. *Taiwanese Culture, Taiwanese Society: A Critical Review of Social Science Research Done on Taiwan*. Lanham, Md.: University Press of America.

Niehoff, Justin. 1987. "The Villager as Industrialist: Ideologies of Household Manufacturing in Rural Taiwan." *Modern China* 13, no. 3 (July): 278-309.

Oakley, Ann. 1981. "Interviewing Women: A Contradiction in Terms." Pp. 30-61 in *Doing Feminist Research*, edited by Helen Roberts. London: Routledge.

Okely, Judith. 1996. *Own or Other Culture*. London: Routledge.

Ong, Aihwa. 1999. *Flexible Citizenship: The Cultural Logics of Transnationality*. Durham: Duke University Press.

Ortner, Sherry (ed.). 1996. *Making Gender: The Politics and Erotics of Culture* Boston, Mass.: Beacon Press.

Oxfeld, Ellen. 1993. *Blood, Sweat, and Mahjong: Family and Enterprise in an Overseas Chinese Community*. Ithaca, N.Y.: Cornell University Press.

Phillips, Steven. 1999. "Between Assimilation and Independence: Taiwanese Political Aspirations under Nationalist Chinese Rule, 1945-1948." Pp. 275-319 in *Taiwan: A New History*, edited by Murray A. Rubinstein. Armonk, N.Y.: M. E. Sharpe.

Redding, S. Gordon. 1990. *The Spirit of Chinese Capitalism*. New York: Walter de Gruyter.

Rethmann, Petra. 2000. "A Hopeless Life? The Story of a Koriak Woman in the Russian Far East." *Anthropologica* 42, no. 1: 29-42.

Rich, Adrienne. 1983. "Compulsory Heterosexuality and Lesbian Existence." Pp. 177-205 in *Powers of Desire*, edited by Ann Snitow, Christine Stansell, and Sharon Thompson. New York: Monthly Review Press.

Roberts, Helen (ed.). 1981. *Doing Feminist Research*. London: Routledge.

Sankar, Andrea. 1984. "Spinster Sisterhoods. Jing Yih Sifu: Spinster-Domestic-Nun." Pp. 51-70 in *Lives: Chinese Working Women*, edited by Mary Sheridan and Janet Salaff. Bloomington: Indiana University Press.

Sartre, Jean-Paul. 1943. *L'être et le néant: Essai d'ontologie phénoménologique*. Paris: Gallimard.

————. 1956 [1943]. *Being and Nothingness: A Phenomenological Essay on Ontology,* translated by Hazel Barnes. New York: Washington Square Press.

————. 1963 [1952]. *Saint Genet: Actor and Martyr.* New York: G. Braziller.

Scott, James C. 1985. *Weapons of the Weak: Everyday Forms of Peasant Resistance.* New Haven, Conn.: Yale University Press.

————. 1990. *Domination and the Arts of Resistance: Hidden Transcripts.* New Haven, Conn.: Yale University Press.

Sen, Amartya. 1999. *Development as Freedom.* New York: Anchor Books.

Shanhai, Wenhua Zazhi. 1999. *Yuanzhumin Shenghuo Judian* 原住民生活據點. Taipei: Executive Yuan Council of Indigenous Peoples.

Shapero, Albert, and Lisa Sokol. 1982. "The Social Dimensions of Entrepreneurship." Pp. 72-90 in *Encyclopedia of Entrepreneurship,* edited by Karl Vesper, Donald Sexton, and Calvin A. Kent. Englewood, N.J.: Prentice-Hall.

Shengyan, Master. 1997. *Xin de Jingdian: Xinjing Xinshi* 心的經典：心經新釋. Taipei: Dharma Drum Culture.

Shih, Shu-I 施淑宜. 1995. "Yi Beimin Xin Jitui Cuozhe—Wang Liling" "以悲憫心擊退挫折—汪麗玲．" *Xingdong Daxue* 行動大學 (*Moving Education*) (January): 8-10.

Shieh, Gwo-shyong. 1992. *"Boss" Island: The Subcontracting Network and Micro-entrepreneurship in Taiwan's Development.* New York: Peter Lang.

Shostak, Marjorie. 1983. *Nisa: The Life and Words of a !Kung Woman.* New York: Vintage Books.

Silin, Robert. 1976. *Leadership and Values: The Organization of Large-Scale Taiwanese Enterprises.* Cambridge, Mass.: Harvard University Press.

Simon, Scott 史國良. 1994. *Economics of the Tao: Social and Economic Aspects of a Taoist Monastery.* M.A. Thesis. Montréal: McGill University, Department of Anthropology.

————. 1998a. "Zouchu Ziji de Lu: Taiwan Dushi de Nütongzhi Kongjian yu Chuangye" "走出自己的路：臺灣都市女同志與創業." *Xingbie yu Kongjian Yanjiushi Tongxun* 性別與空間研究室通訊, no. 5 (July): 73-82.

————. 1998b. *Not All in the Family: Class, Gender, and Nation in the Industrialization of Taiwan.* Ph.D. Dissertation. Montréal: McGill University, Department of Anthropology.

————. 2001. "Xingyishi, Wenhua, yu Zhengzhi Jingjixue: Minnan Tongzhimen de Jingyan" "性意識，文化，與政治經濟學：閩南「同志們」的經驗." Pp. 51-88 in *Tongzhi Yanjiu* 同志研究, edited by Josephine Ho 何春蕤. Taipei: Juliu.

————. 2002. "The Underside of a Miracle: Industrialization, Land, and Taiwan's Indigenous Peoples." *Cultural Survival Quarterly* 26, no. 2 (summer): 66-69.

————. Forthcoming. "From Hidden Kingdom to Rainbow Community: The Making of Gay and Lesbian Identity in Taiwan," in M. Moskowitz and A. Morris (eds.), *Taiwan: The Minor Arts of Daily Life*. Honolulu: University of Hawaii Press.

Siu, Helen. 1990. "Where Were the Women? Rethinking Marriage Resistance and Regional Culture in South China." *Late Imperial China* 11, no. 2 (December): 32-62.

Skoggard, Ian. 1996. *The Indigenous Dynamic in Taiwan's Postwar Development: The Religious and Historical Roots of Entrepreneurship*. Armonk, N.Y.: M. E. Sharpe.

Stainton, Michael. 1999. "Aboriginal Self-Government: Taiwan's Uncompleted Agenda." Pp. 419-435 in *Taiwan: A New History*, edited by Murray Rubinstein. Armonk, N.Y.: M. E. Sharpe.

Stewart, Kathleen. 1996. *A Space on the Side of the Road: Cultural Poetics in an "Other" America*. Princeton: Princeton University Press.

Stites, Richard. 1982. "Small-Scale Industry in Yingge, Taiwan." *Modern China* 8, no. 2 (April): 247-279.

————. 1985. "Industrial Work as an Entrepreneurial Strategy." *Modern China* 11, no. 2 (April): 227-246.

Suzuki, Daisetsu. 1960. *Manual of Zen Buddhism*. New York: Grove Press.

Tai, Hsiao-feng 戴小楓. 1994. "Cuican de Waibiao xia Yike zui Meili de Xin— Wang Liling" "璀璨的外表下一顆最美麗的心—汪麗玲‧" *Chenggong Zazhi* 成功雜誌 (*Success Magazine*, December): 128-130.

Tai, Po-fan 戴伯芬. 1994. "Shei Zuo Tanfan? Taiwan Tanfan de Lishi Xingguo" "誰做攤販？臺灣攤販的歷史形構." *Taiwan Shehuixue Yanjiu Jikan (Taiwan: A Radical Quarterly in the Social Sciences)* 臺灣社會研究季刊 17, no. 17 (July): 122-148.

Taipei City Government (臺北市政府). 2001. The Statistical Abstract of Taipei City (臺北市統計要覽). Taipei: Taipei City Government Department of Budget, Accounting and Statistics.

Taipei Times. 2001. "Vasectomies in Vogue for Taiwanese Businessmen." May 25.

Taylor, Charles. 1989. *Sources of the Self: The Making of the Modern Identity*. Cambridge: Harvard University Press.

Thornton, A. and H. S. Lin (eds.). 1994. *Social Change and the Family in Taiwan*. Chicago: University of Chicago Press.

Tinker, Irene (ed.). 1990. *Persistent Inequalities: Women and World Development*. Oxford: Oxford University Press.

————. 1995. "The Human Economy of Microentrepreneurs." Pp. 25-40 in *Women in Micro- and Small-Scale Enterprise Development*, edited by Louise Dignard and José Havet. Boulder, Colo.: Westview.

Topley, Margorie. 1975. "Marriage Resistance in Rural Kwangtung." Pp. 67-88 in *Women in Chinese Society,* edited by Margery Wolf and Roxane Witke. Stanford, Calif.: Stanford University Press.

Tsing, Anna Lowenhaupt. 1993. *In the Realm of the Diamond Queen: Marginality in an Out-of-the-way Place.* Princeton: Princeton University Press.

Turner, Bryan. 1996. *The Body and Society.* London: Sage Publications.

Wang, Fu-chang 王甫昌 (ed.). 2000. *Taiwan Zuqun Guanxi de Shehui Jichu Diaocha Jihua Zhixing Baogao* 台灣族群關係的社會基礎調查計畫執行報告．Taipei: Academia Sinica Institute of Sociology.

Wang, Hao-wei 王浩威. 1998. *Taiwan Chaburen* 台灣查甫人. Taipei: Lianhe Wenxue.

Wang, Horng-luen. 2000. "Rethinking the Global and the National: Reflections on National Imaginations in Taiwan." *Theory, Culture, & Society* 17 (4): 93-117.

Wang, Li-ling 汪麗玲. 1997. "Zunzhong Shengming" "尊重生命．" Pp. 208-217 in *Yinwei You Ni, Wo Huochu Ziji* 因為有你，我活出自己, edited by Chang Kuang-tou (張光斗). Taipei: Ping-an Wen-hua, pp. 208-217.

Watson, Lawrence, and Maria-Barbara Watson-Franke. 1985. *Interpreting Life Histories: An Anthropological Inquiry.* New Brunswick, N.J.: Rutgers University Press.

Weller, Robert. 1999. *Alternate Civilities: Democracy and Culture in China and Taiwan.* Boulder, Colo.: Westview.

Wittig, Monique. 1992 [1980]. "The Straight Mind." Pp. 21-32 in *The Straight Mind and Other Essays,* edited by Monique Wittig. Boston: Beacon Press.

Wolf, Margery. 1972. *Women and the Family in Rural Taiwan.* Stanford, Calif.: Stanford University Press.

Wou, Wei. 1992. *Capitalism: A Chinese Version.* Columbus: Ohio State University East Asian Studies Center.

Wu, Nai-teh. 1996a. "Class Identity Without Class Consciousness? Working-Class Orientations in Taiwan." Pp. 77-102 in *Putting Class in Its Place: Worker Identity in East Asia,* edited by Elizabeth Perry. Berkeley, Calif.: Institute of East Asian Studies.

————. 1996b. "Binglang he Tuoxie, Xizhuang ji Pixie: Taiwan Jieji Liudong de Zuqun Chayi ji Yuanyin." "檳榔和拖鞋，西裝及皮鞋：臺灣階級流動的族群差異及原因)." *Taiwan Shehuixue Yanjiu* 臺灣社會學研究 1 (December): 137-167.

Yang, Mayfair Mei-hui. 1994. *Gifts, Favors, and Banquets: The Art of Social Relationships in China.* Ithaca, N.Y.: Cornell University Press.

Yu, Wei-shin. 2001a. "Family Demands, Gender Attitudes, and Married Women's Labor Force Participation: Comparing Japan and Taiwan." Pp. 70-95 in *Women's Working Lives in East Asia,* edited by Mary C. Brinton. Stanford, Calif.: Stanford University Press.

———. 2001b. "Taking Informality into Account: Women's Work in the Formal and Informal Sectors in Taiwan." Pp. 233-262 in *Women's Working Lives in East Asia*, edited by Mary C. Brinton. Stanford, Calif.: Stanford University Press.

Index

About the Author

Scott Simon is assistant professor of sociology at the University of Ottawa, Canada. He has lived more than five years in Taiwan, where he has been affiliated with both the Institute of Sociology and the Institute of Ethnology at Academia Sinica. He has written articles in both English and Chinese on the social dimensions of Taiwan's development experience.